COPPER
CHORUS

Butte Bulletin, September 25, 1918

COPPER CHORUS

Mining, Politics, and the Montana Press, 1889–1959

Dennis L. Swibold

Montana Historical
Society Press
Helena, Montana

FRONT COVER PHOTOGRAPH: Editor Louis M. Thayer in *Helena Independent* office, Montana Historical Society Photograph Archives, Helena

COVER DESIGN BY Diane Gleba Hall, Helena

BOOK DESIGN AND COMPOSITION BY Arrow Graphics, Missoula
TYPESET IN Adobe Garamond Pro

PRINTED IN Canada by Friesens

Distributed by the Globe Pequot Press, 246 Goose Lane, Guilford, Connecticut 06437 (800) 243-0495

Montana Committee for the Humanities

This project is funded in part by a grant from the Montana Committee for the Humanities, an affiliate of the National Endowment for the Humanities, and the Charles Redd Center for Western Studies.

06 07 08 09 10 11 12 13 14 15   11 10 9 8 7 6 5 4 3 2 1

ISBN-13 (cloth) 978-0-9721522-8-0
ISBN-10 (cloth) 0-9721522-8-8
ISBN-13 (paper) 978-0-9759196-0-6
ISBN-10 (paper) 0-9759196-0-1

LIBRARY OF CONGRESS CATALOGING-IN-PUBLICATION DATA

Swibold, Dennis L.
    Copper chorus : mining, politics, and the Montana press, 1889–1959
/ Dennis L. Swibold.
    p. cm.
    Includes bibliographical references and index.
    ISBN-13: 978-0-9721522-8-0 (cloth)
    ISBN-10: 0-9721522-8-8 (cloth)
    ISBN-13: 978-0-9759196-0-6 (paper)
    ISBN-10: 0-9759196-0-1 (paper)
    1. Journalism—Montana—History—19th century. 2. Freedom of the press—
Montana—History—19th century. 3. Freedom of the press—Montana—History—
20th century. 4. Anaconda Copper Mining Company. I. Title.

PN4897.M893S95 2006
071'.8609034—dc22
                                                              2006000861

FOR JULIE AND COLTON

CONTENTS

ix   *List of Illustrations*
xiii   *Preface and Acknowledgments*

I   INTRODUCTION
       The Scribblers' Ball

19   1. Raising the *Standard*
        MARCUS DALY BUILDS A NEWSPAPER

39   2. Slinging Ink
        "COPPER EDITORS" IN THE CAPITAL FIGHT

63   3. The Longest Purse
        CORRUPTION AND COERCION OF THE FREE PRESS

93   4. Reform and the "Reptile Press"
        CORPORATE POWER AND A PROGRESSIVE BACKLASH

125 5. A "Community of Interests"
        COMPANY ALLIES IN THE DAILY PRESS

161 6. The Copper Press at War
        HYSTERIA ON THE HOME FRONT

195 7. The "Anvil Chorus"
        JOSEPH DIXON VERSUS THE COPPER PRESS

229 8. The Last Newspaper War
        ANOTHER CLARK CHALLENGES THE COMPANY

257 9. The Copper Curtain
        SILENCE AND SUPPRESSION

285 10. The Captive Press
        MOUNTING CRITICISM

313 11. Emancipation
        ANACONDA SHEDS ITS NEWSPAPERS

341   *Epilogue*
347   *Notes*
377   *Bibliography*
389   *Index*

LIST OF ILLUSTRATIONS

ii   "Poisoning the well" cartoon

xx   Butte, Montana, ca. 1910

2   Marcus Daly

3   Montana Hotel, Anaconda

4   Montana Hotel bar

5   Butte Labor Day parade illustration

7   "Standard" knight protecting "Miss Montana" illustration

8   William Randolph Hearst illustration

9   John H. Durston

12–13   Montana newsmen illustration

18   Newsmen printing the *East Helena Record*, 1899

20   James H. Mills and A. C. Schneider, ca. 1895

22   *Helena Herald* building, 1875

24   "Colonel" Sam Gordon, 1895

32   *Inter Mountain* and *Butte Miner* building, ca. 1886

36   *Anaconda Standard* office, ca. 1890s

38   Crowing rooster and "Helena's Victory" clip

40   William A. Clark's decorated carriage, 1894

42   *Anaconda Standard* production staff, 1893

43   Lee Mantle, 1895

44   Butte, circa 1895

52   "'Twas the Famous Handcar Limited" illustration

62   "Offended Montana Pronounces Sentence Upon the Man-Buyer" cartoon

63   William A. Clark, 1898

64   Oliver S. Warden

64   William Bole

66   John S. M. Neill

68   Fred Whiteside

70   "Left Shapeless in the Boodle Barrel's Pathway" cartoon

71   "Labor Breaks the Neck of the Beast Boodle" cartoon
73   *Anaconda Standard* artists
76   F. Augustus Heinze
77   "What Fusion Means in Butte" cartoon
81   "The Boss Boodler is Handy at It" cartoon
82   "Now and Then 'Kerosene' Catches a Lonesome Sucker" cartoon
83   "Fed in Montana, Milked in the East" cartoon
86   Marcus Daly and "Peacefully Comes Death" clip
92   "What the Domination of Heinze in Butte Would Mean" cartoon
94   Boston and Montana smelter, Great Falls, March 1903
95   Worker at Boston and Montana smelter, Great Falls
97   "Will Her Children Come to Her Rescue?" cartoon
100 Patrick A. O'Farrell
105 Butte *Reveille* extra and "F. A. Heinze Addresses an Audience of 10,000" clip
107 "The Master of the Hounds and His Pack" cartoon
109 "The Shadow Which Hangs Over Montana" cartoon
116 *Columbus News* office, ca. 1910
117 Miles Romney Sr., 1909
122 William K. Harber
124 Anaconda smelter, Anaconda, 1903
126 John D. Ryan, Cornelius F. Kelley, J. Bruce Kremer, and William A. Clark, ca. 1920
130 "They Heard the Whistles of Butte All Over the World on Resumption Day" illustration
132 Montana State Fair agricultural exhibit, September 1905
135 "Smoke Farmers" cartoon
136 Joseph M. Dixon, 1904
137 Arthur L. Stone
147 Destruction of the Butte Miners Union Hall, June 1914
152 Leon Shaw, 1907
160 "Listening to Miss Rankin" clip
172 Elm Orlu Mine, Butte
185 Montana Council of Defense members
186 George M. Bourquin
187 *Fergus County Argus* office, ca. 1915

190 William F. Dunne

194 "Nothing to Separate" cartoon

196 "Fake Patriotism" cartoon

198 "The Patriots Chorus" cartoon

199 Burton K. Wheeler, circa 1910s

205 "In the Coils of the Anaconda" cartoon

206 Miles Romney Sr.

207 Farm woman and child with wheat crop, Dawson County, 1911

208 Farmers outside Nonpartisan League office, Wibaux

218 "Will the Voter Kill the Goose that Lays the Golden Eggs?" cartoon

219 "Truth Told about Mine Taxation in Montana" clip

221 "Breaking the Camel's Back" cartoon

222 "Cheer Up! The Voters'l' Tear the Fence Down Nov 4" cartoon

225 John H. Durston

228 "Champion Liars Acknowledge a Superior" cartoon

233 Martin J. Hutchens

235 Tom Stout, 1906

240 "Varied Activities of the Anaconda Boss" cartoon

242 Wellington Rankin and Thomas J. Walsh, 1911

246 Dan Whetstone

256 *Butte Daily Post* newsboys

267 James E. Murray

275 Harry Billings

278 Emmett Burke and Ed Craney in radio station, ca. 1935

284 Anaconda Copper Mining Company logo

287 Open pit mining, Butte, ca. 1950s

312 "Many Flats and Sharps, But Much of One Tune" cartoon

314 Alex Warden

315 Philip Adler

316 Don Anderson

318 1953 Montana Power Company ad

331 Don Anderson, Betty Adler Schermer, and Lloyd Schermer

336 Montana Fish and Game live cage on the Clark Fork River, 1960

338 Lee Enterprises Montana newspapers map

340 Louis M. Thayer in *Helena Independent* office

344 *Shelby Promoter* newsboys, March 1966

PREFACE AND ACKNOWLEDGMENTS

IN JANUARY OF 1911, *Collier's*, the national weekly, launched a massive investigation of the American newspaper. For six months, reporter Will Irwin turned his beam on the practices of an institution that had largely escaped his fellow muckrakers' scrutiny. He marveled at the press's power to promote the public good and assured readers that most journalists were earnest searchers for truth. Yet he also told of editors and publishers who saw the news as little more than a commodity to be sensationalized, slanted, or suppressed to serve their political or financial aims. He exposed the cozy sociability and mutual investments of prominent publishers and industrialists. He detailed cases in which Big Business slanted or choked the news by the strategic placement and withholding of advertising. It was a subtle game, Irwin wrote, one that sometimes fleeced and endangered the public. It also sapped the spirit, independence, and credibility of honest journalists.[1]

A more pernicious influence, he warned, lay in industry's hidden ownership of newspapers. Certain of his suspicions but without the means to prove them, Irwin could name only the most blatant offenders. "[T]he process comes now and then to the surface—sometimes years after the fact," he wrote. "We know now, as we suspected then, that Senator [William A.] Clark secretly owned a string of newspapers, and that Marcus Daly subsidized another string, during the copper feud in Montana."[2]

Irwin's mistake was assuming that industrial ownership of Montana newspapers was a passing by-product of the state's scandalous "war of the copper kings." In fact, Daly's progeny—the Anaconda Copper Mining Company—would maintain its ownership and influence over the state's major newspapers for another forty-eight years. As Irwin suggested, the Anaconda Company was hardly the only industrial enterprise to own or control newspapers—railroads, banks, utilities, and other mining companies indulged themselves as well—but the length and notoriety of Anaconda's newspaper ownership trumped them all. Its origins lay in the company's enormous economic and political power in Montana. Born in the smell of sagebrush and dynamite along Silver Bow Creek, the Anaconda Company grew quickly to become a pillar of American industry at the start of the Electric Age and the world's largest nonferrous metals company for much of the twentieth century. Ruthless and pragmatic—with its interests in mining, smelting, energy, and timber—the company loomed over Montana's political and economic consciousness. Scholars seeking a greater case of corporate dominion over a sovereign state could point only to DuPont and Delaware.[3]

By the 1930s, Montana's reputation as an industrial colony was firmly in place. The image lingers in the state's historical memory, despite historians' efforts to show the complex ways in which Montanans embraced, rejected, minimized, or exaggerated the company's power to serve their own interests. Its durability remains a testament to the Anaconda Company's clout, which was real enough, and to the bitter opposition it inspired. Crucial to both perception and exercise of that power was Anaconda's ownership of Montana's principal newspapers.

In its froth and drama, the story of the "copper-collared press" is as colorful as any of the state's history. Montana's pioneer newspapers reveled in the rough and tumble of territorial politics and business. But as the stakes grew higher, they found their independence and scruples tested by competing industrialists who bought, bribed, or built newspapers to serve as weapons in their feuds. Some journalists sold their talents under duress, while others leaped at the chance to produce spectacular metropolitan-style dailies in markets that could hardly support them commercially. At great cost, some held tight to their independence and inspired a succession of fiery anti-company editors and politicians who kept the notoriety of Montana's copper press smoldering in the public's mind for generations.

Though the extent of the company's newspaper ownership remained officially secret until 1951, observant Montanans clearly saw Anaconda journalism for what it was. Still, many could marvel at the thunder of

Anaconda's early fighting editors, the skill of its writers, the sweep of their coverage, and the artistic talent, worldly features, and technological innovation that had once made these dailies famous throughout the Northwest. War and economic depression, however, took a toll, and by the 1930s the copper press had lost much of its fire. Constrained by the avoidance of controversy and hamstrung by their lack of credibility, Anaconda's dailies slipped into an ambivalent slumber arguably more dangerous in its consequences for democracy and free expression than their thunderous crusades had ever been. In the end, and in the words of one former Anaconda Company newsman, it was a "kept press—a prostitution of talent and integrity" that served neither readers' nor owners' interests. In the late 1950s—well into the age of modern public relations—company officials finally acknowledged what many Montanans and others had argued for years: the copper press was an embarrassment.

Anaconda journalism had serious consequences for Montana, though its record as an overt advocate for the company's conservative aims was decidedly mixed. The yawning editorial silence and news suppression of its final thirty years left the deeper marks by muffling political opposition, by diverting Montanans' attention from crucial state and local issues, by failing to provide a forum for public debate—and in doing so, feeding a debilitating sense that the state's problems were largely beyond its residents' control. Its impact on Montana journalism seems clear as well. Anaconda journalism stifled competition, muzzled reporters and editors, and delayed efforts toward enterprise and professionalism. In the end, it was bad for democracy, bad for journalism, and bad for the company itself. Its legacy resonates today in the concentration of ownership of Montana's daily newspapers. As massive corporate mergers reshape modern media, the journalistic ambivalence and timidity that marked the final years of Anaconda's distant, distracted ownership offer timely and pointed lessons.

So far, the story of Anaconda journalism has been told broadly, in passing, or episodically, its details scattered in unpublished theses and dissertations or in bound volumes of academic or professional journals. If nothing else, I hope to bring those efforts together in the larger context they deserve. For historical framework, I have leaned heavily on the writings of Jerry Calvert, David Emmons, Arnon Gutfeld, Jules Karlin, Michael Malone, Rex Myers, Richard Roeder, Richard Ruetten, and K. Ross Toole, who in turn drew heavily from Montana's newspapers. For history of the newspapers themselves, I am deeply grateful for the remarkable and largely unpublished scholarship of a corps of graduate students whose research provided invaluable stepping-stones through the story. My thanks to Robert Amick Jr., Marian H. Brod, Andrew C. Cogswell, Shirley J. De Forth, Forrest L. Foor, John P. Fought, Nancy Rice Fritz, Guy Ole Halverson, Lyle E. Harris, Charles S. Johnson, Christine L. Johnson, Mary Lou Koessler, Daniel J. LaGrande, William E. Larson, Susanne Lagoni MacDonald, John T. McNay, Barbara J. Mittal, Sheila Stearns, Ruth Towe, Ralph H. Wanamaker, Kurt Wetzel, and others, many of them Montanans or former journalists who revealed key aspects of the story despite the scarcity of documents detailing the company's newspaper ownership, most of which the company reportedly destroyed. I owe an equal debt to the *Montana Journalism Review,* founded by former University of Montana journalism deans Nathan Blumberg and Warren Brier, who encouraged their students' research and excerpted their work in the journal. *Montana The Magazine of Western History* provided critical elements of the story as well. New details concerning the end of Anaconda journalism were found in documents graciously provided by Lloyd Schermer, former chairman and CEO of Lee Enterprises, and in the Donald W. Anderson Papers in the University of Montana's K. Ross Toole Archives, which also offered the papers of former governor and newspaper publisher Joseph M. Dixon and those of U.S. senator James E. Murray, both influential critics of the copper press. Much of the story, however, emerged from the pages of newspapers themselves, and Montana is blessed with a rich newspaper morgue, carefully preserved in libraries throughout the state and especially in the Montana Historical Society Research Center in Helena.

I owe a great many personal debts as well. My heartfelt thanks to Dean Jerry Brown of the University of Montana School of Journalism for his support in time, money, and encouragement over the years of research and writing; to colleagues and friends Carol Van Valkenburg, Maurice Possley, Michael Downs, and Clemens Work for their advice, support, and humor and for reading portions of the manuscript; to historians Laurie Mercier and Brian Shovers, whose critical readings made the story stronger and more meaningful; to historians H. Duane Hampton, Harry Fritz, and the late Michael Malone for planting the seeds; to Charlene Porsild, Molly Kruckenberg, Rich Aarstad, and the patient reference librarians and archivists at the Montana Historical Society for numerous courtesies; to Ellen Crain and staff at the Butte–Silver Bow Public Archives; to Christopher G. Mullin and Donna McCrea and the Special Collections and Archives staffs at the University of Montana's Mike and Maureen Mansfield Library; to the staff of the Merrill G. Burlingame Special Collections at the Montana State University Libraries in Bozeman; to Jerry M. Hansen of the Marcus Daly Historical Society in Anaconda; to the helpful staffs of the Missoula and Billings public libraries; and to my sister Denise Swibold and former students Tyler Christensen and the late Katie Aschim for proofreading portions of the work in progress.

A special thanks goes to Clark Whitehorn, former director of the Montana Historical Society Press, for his guidance and early interest in the work; to his successor, Molly Holz, who saw the project through with skill and patience; and to Glenda Bradshaw, Tammy Ryan, and Clint Attebery for all their work. I'm grateful as well for the crucial support of the Montana Committee for the Humanities and the Charles Redd Center for Western Studies. Finally, I am grateful to the scores of Montana journalists, living and dead, who, despite the odds, have faithfully served and continue to serve the public's right to know. My deepest gratitude goes to the daughter of one of those journalists, my wife Julie, whose sharp eye, patience, and enduring love made this work possible.

COPPER
CHORUS

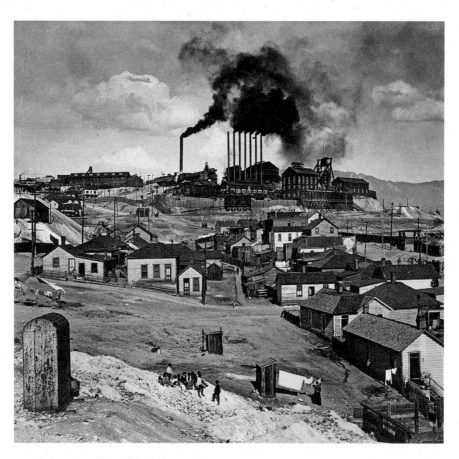

In 1899, members of the Montana State Press Association, en route to their annual meeting in Anaconda, traveled through Butte—one of the world's preeminent sources of copper at the onset of the Electric Age and the focus of a struggle for political dominance that came to be known as the "war of the copper kings." This photograph was taken about 1910.

N. A. FORSYTH, PHOTOGRAPHER, MONTANA HISTORICAL SOCIETY PHOTOGRAPH ARCHIVES, HELENA

The Scribblers' Ball

I T PROMISED TO BE A GLITTERING affair, a celebration worthy of a copper king. Across Montana in the early fall of 1899—only a decade since statehood and five years after the circus-like campaign that had made Helena the state's capital—dozens of newspapermen tossed aside their type sticks and inky aprons and boarded trains for the annual convention of the Montana State Press Association. For most, especially those who scraped meager livings from small rural weeklies, this would serve as the year's only vacation—five precious days to ogle the latest technology, commiserate with peers, sniff the political breezes, and engage in what one editor described as the usual fraternal "jollification." Mixing business with their drinks, some could glean crucial insights into keeping their papers solvent until the next election cycle or, failing that, find a buyer. Editions published at convention time might be thin on news, but as one wag at Butte's *Inter Mountain* explained, loyal readers deserved a rest from the "endless catastrophes that sizzle and seethe" through the "fissures" of an editor's brain. "To receive one issue of a great family newspaper that isn't trying to save the country must be a great relief to the average American newspaper reader who is brought in touch with a compelling crisis every 24 hours," he wrote. In other words, the news could wait.[1]

For many of the conventioneers, the journey ran through Butte, a bawdy, blasted, smoke-choked island of industrial enterprise, home of the "richest hill on earth" and the world's preeminent source of copper at the onset of the Electric Age. Veins of red ore coursed through dozens of Butte's mines, but the fattest lay beneath the claims of the mighty Amalgamated Copper Company, the latest incarnation of what Montanans then and later would always know better as the

Anaconda Company, whose story and that of its guiding genius, Marcus Daly, were as familiar to the traveling editors as their own. Reared in famine in Ireland's County Cavan, Daly escaped to the United States alone at the age of fifteen and worked as a messenger, stable boy, and dockhand before shipping to the California mining frontier by way of Panama. His miner's education began in Grass Valley, but his reputation for finding rich ores was made in Nevada's fabulous Comstock Lode and the silver mines of Utah. From there, Daly explored Montana's silver and copper lodes as a representative of a Utah firm but soon struck out on his own, buying Butte's Anaconda Mine and persuading a syndicate of California investors to back his play.

Marcus Daly bought Butte's Anaconda Mine in 1881 and, with the help of partners, parlayed it into one of the world's major mining companies. In his smelter city of Anaconda, Daly started a newspaper, the Anaconda Standard, *considered even by its rivals to be the equal of any "millionaire metropolitan sheet" in the country.*

Davis & Sanford Photographers, Montana Historical Society Photograph Archives, Helena

By 1899, eighteen years after its formation, Daly's venture reigned as one of the world's major mining companies. Butte, the throbbing heart of Daly's empire, reveled in its reputation as one of West's "wide-open" towns, as famous for sin as for riches. Some of the traveling scribes had arranged to spend an extra day there to help thousands of miners celebrate Labor Day amid the city's bars, theaters, and fleshpots. But on Tuesday, September 5, a large contingent of newspapermen, joined by the members of Butte's famed Boston and Montana Band, clambered onto Marcus Daly's little railroad with the grandiose name, the Butte, Anaconda and Pacific Railway, for the twenty-six-mile chug to Daly's "copperopolis," his smelter city of Anaconda, where Butte's rich rock gave up its red metal. Shortly before 2:00 PM, the train lurched past the

The 1899 Montana State Press Association convention met in the state's grandest accommodations, Marcus Daly's opulent Montana Hotel in Anaconda.
MONTANA HISTORICAL SOCIETY PHOTOGRAPH ARCHIVES, HELENA

smelter works along Warm Springs Creek and eased into the station. As the conventioneers spilled onto the platform, the musicians quickly assembled alongside a delegation of civic dignitaries and members of the Anaconda Typographical Union, who extended the city's gracious welcome. Thus received, the editors paired off in columns and, with pink convention ribbons fluttering from their lapels, marched behind the band to the steps of Standard Hall, just across the street from the state's finest accommodations, Marcus Daly's grand Montana Hotel.

Opened in 1889, the four-story brick building, trimmed for the occasion in patriotic bunting, boasted 185 rooms, an electric elevator, a chandeliered ballroom, and a kitchen from which black waiters wearing white gloves served strawberries in January and oysters in July. Its plush barroom, patterned after a New York canteen favored by Tammany Hall politicos, featured burnished brass, glowing mahogany, and, on the floor, a mosaic of exotic hardwoods portraying Marcus Daly's prize racehorse, Tammany, whose victory over the East's fastest champion a

Elegant and richly appointed, the Montana Hotel bar featured on the floor a mosaic of exotic hardwoods portraying Marcus Daly's prize racehorse, Tammany. Tradition held that anyone who stepped on the horse's likeness would have to buy the house a round.

THOMPSON PHOTO SHOP, PHOTOGRAPHER,
MONTANA HISTORICAL SOCIETY PHOTOGRAPH ARCHIVES, HELENA

few years earlier had given young Montana cause to crow. The newsmen must have marveled and stepped gingerly, for tradition held that anyone who stepped on the horse's likeness would have to buy the house a round.[2]

Daly's hotel was only one facet of his grand little city, a jewel of industry and culture set against peaks and forests. A stately new courthouse overlooked a communal green, a new library and town hall, an opera house, modern business blocks, and neat residential sections, all of which lay in the shadow of the Pintler Mountains and the prosperous smoke billowing from Daly's smelter. But of all the city's wonders, none impressed the arriving journalists more than Marcus Daly's daily newspaper, the *Anaconda Standard*. The thirty-four-page, three-section issue published that morning featured a display of technical and editorial artistry that no other Montana paper—and few in the

The morning paper of September 5, 1899, showcased the extraordinary talent of the Anaconda Standard*'s art department, leading off with an illustration of Butte's Labor Day parade.*

ANACONDA STANDARD, SEPTEMBER 5, 1899

West—could match. Beyond the usual excellence of its news report, Tuesday's *Standard* introduced the talents of its new illustration department, freshly stocked with artists lured westward with fat salaries and led by J. W. Trowbridge, late of the *New York Herald*. For readers used to long columns of text broken occasionally by small headlines

and an advertiser's rare woodcut, the effect must have been electrify-
ing. Tuesday's front page not only described Butte's Labor Day parade in detail, but Trowbridge's drawing of the event gave readers from
Hamilton to Havre and Denver to New York City a street-side view.

The issue would have been remarkable enough without its illustrations. Page after page of the paper's first two sections gave readers
comprehensive coverage of their world on the century's brink—from
the latest on the Dreyfus Affair and Boer War to the previous night's
fire behind Anaconda's All Nation's Saloon. Beyond the next-day stock
quotes, baseball scores, and prices of copper and other metals, the
Standard offered its subscribers a broad statewide report, produced by
talented correspondents in bureaus flung across Montana's map.

But now the artists made it all seem more tangible, and it was the
issue's dazzling third section that displayed their talents to full effect.
In an exquisite illustration sprawling across the section's front, a silver
knight, with the words "Standard" emblazoned on his shield, protected
a maiden, "Montana," amid a rugged allegorical landscape dominated
by symbols of the state's mining industry. Throughout the next ten
pages, in column after column of richly illustrated articles, *Standard*
editors celebrated the tenth year of statehood and the anniversary of
the paper's own birth and predicted a sparkling future for Montana
and those who told its story. In articles and drawings and poems, the
Standard celebrated the state's journalistic pioneers, past and present,
who toiled in the collaborative "up-building" of Montana, the profession's
noblest cause. Readers turning to the section's center spread found a double-
page layout on the convention, dotted with hand-sketched vignettes of the
state's leading editors and publishers.[3]

Such extravagance distinguished the *Standard* from any other newspaper in the state, and most in the Northwest, and for days afterward
compliments on the paper's statehood issue poured in from other editors, many of whom would remember it for years. Among Montana's
"quill drivers," there was no question of the *Standard*'s preeminence
among the state's newspapers, only amazement salted with envy at the
subsidies that maintained Daly's paper in a metropolitan style that revenues from circulation and advertising surely could not. In its birthday
wishes to the *Standard,* a rival daily, the Butte *Inter Mountain,* that

Celebrating the tenth year of statehood and the anniversary of the paper's own birth, the Anaconda Standard's *September 5, 1899, issue featured a silver knight, with the word "Standard" emblazoned on his shield, protecting a maiden "Montana" amid an allegorical landscape dominated by symbols of the state's mining industry.*

ANACONDA STANDARD, SEPTEMBER 5, 1899

city's only Republican sheet, joked that of the $16 million in copper and silver extracted from the famed Anaconda Mine in its first six years, half went to the construction of the Anaconda smelter—the rest to the *Standard*. "The only time the paper made a profit was when the business manager forgot to pay the staff," the paper quipped. Having avoided the usual "apprenticeship to poverty," Daly's paper had pressed its advantages to stand beside such papers "as the *New York Journal* and other millionaire metropolitan sheets."[4]

Few newspapermen would have missed the *Inter Mountain's* reference to William Randolph Hearst's *New York Journal,* the most exciting newspaper in America. Hearst's father, George, an early investor in Daly's Anaconda mining venture and others, had used his wealth to purchase both a U.S. Senate seat and the *San Francisco Examiner*. At his death, his fortune went to his wife, Phoebe, who spent some of it on such trifles as a new Greek Revival library for the town of Anaconda but mostly on the ambitions of her headstrong son, whose leap into New York journalism and true fame she financed by selling her company stock. It was no coincidence then that the *Standard*'s birthday edition carried William Randolph Hearst's portrait over a congratulatory letter in which the nation's first true media mogul paid the paper his regards. He studied the *Standard* regularly, he wrote, and found its "issues expensive and excellent beyond what one would naturally expect," good enough to be published in one of the nation's greater cities, yet "[t]here is no reason why the people of Montana, who are as intelligent and progressive as any in the Union, should not continue to have a newspaper as able and enterprising as any in the Union," he added.[5]

MR. HEARST SENDS BIRTHDAY GREETING.

The Anaconda Standard*'s birthday edition carried a congratulatory letter from newspaper mogul William Randolph Hearst, who found the* Anaconda Standard *"expensive and excellent beyond what one would naturally expect."*

Anaconda Standard, September 5, 1899

The *Standard* owed its existence to Daly's wealth, but John Hurst Durston made the paper excellent beyond its means. A tall, energetic man with a walrus mustache, a stormy temper, and graceful touch at the piano, Durston cut an imposing figure among the Northwest's early editors. A New Yorker with a degree from Yale and a doctorate in literature and linguistics from the University of Heidelberg, the former professor had made the *Syracuse Standard* a power in the Republican politics of upstate New York but left the paper when his backers, who also controlled the local water company, insisted that he drop his crusade for the municipal ownership of utilities. Durston traveled west, landing eventually in Montana, where he dabbled in mining and hobnobbed with leaders of the territory's earthy, energetic society, catching Marcus Daly's eye. After a storied courtship, Durston accepted Daly's offer to build a newspaper worthy of its mentor.[6]

Durston hired the talent, bought the presses, and suppressed his own Republicanism to support Daly's wing of Montana's Democratic Party. From the day of its launch on September 4, 1889, the *Anaconda Standard* was Montana's most vibrant daily newspaper. Though it was published in a city of fewer than four thousand souls, the bulk of the paper's readership came from Butte and beyond, and within three years of its debut the *Standard* boasted the state's highest circulation.

The Anaconda Standard *owed its existence to Marcus Daly's wealth, but editor John H. Durston made the paper excellent beyond its means. Here Durston posed (second from right) with other founding faculty of Syracuse University.*

Rival editors envied Durston's access to Daly's wallet. They also acknowledged the editor's talent. "Money alone . . . would not have brought the Standard to its present position of newspaper excellence had it not been supplemented by journalistic talent of the best type in all its departments," the Butte *Inter Mountain* confessed. It was Durston who led his young troops into the political battles and crusades that made the newspaper a force few could ignore. It was Durston who campaigned to end Butte's open roasting of ores, a practice that covered the city with a thick, deadly smoke each winter. When the great Pullman strike of 1894 shut down Montana's railroads for three weeks, it was Durston who persuaded crews of idled workers to man the handcars and pedal-powered velocipedes that relayed the *Standard* to readers in Missoula and Livingston. From there, riders on horseback rushed the news to tourists stranded in Yellowstone National Park. It was Durston who led Daly's spectacular if hapless fights to wrest the state capital from Helena and to deny Helena's champion—and Daly's bitter rival—William A. Clark, a seat in the U.S. Senate. When Populism swept the West in 1896, Durston's editorials boosted the messiah of "free silver," William Jennings Bryan, whose national presidential campaign Marcus Daly largely underwrote.[7]

Now, it was a gracious Durston who welcomed his fellow Montana journalists to Anaconda. Their numbers included Oliver S. Warden, the young Yankee publisher of the *Great Falls Tribune,* who, with partner William Bole, bought the newspaper cheap from Daly after the capital fight. Others in attendance included the press association's founder, "Captain" James Hamilton Mills, publisher of Deer Lodge's *New North-West.* Mills's newspaper career began in Virginia City in 1866 when he was persuaded to revive the wheezing *Montana Post,* the territory's first true newspaper. The sire of numerous newspaper ventures across the state, Mills was surely the father of Montana journalism, and, as such, he was accorded the irreverent digs that passed for respect among his peers. According to the Butte *Inter Mountain,* Mills "never told a lie when the truth would do just as well, and not even then except in a good cause."[8]

The crowd also included Hamilton's Miles Romney, the irreverent young Spanish-American War veteran and Mormon backslider whose weekly *Western News* would emerge as the most caustic and persistent critic of Daly's political machine and the corporate behemoth it would foster. Other Daly critics in attendance included John Read and Adelphus B. Keith, the wits behind the Butte *Inter Mountain.* Yet Daly's most prominent rival—and the most prominent member of the state press association—was most conspicuously absent. William A. Clark had already exchanged Montana for Washington, D.C., in preparation for assuming the Senate seat he had so flagrantly purchased earlier in the year.

To the assembled editors, William A. Clark's storied rise from the poverty of his Pennsylvania boyhood was as thrilling as Daly's. Fleeing the Civil War, Clark headed for the western goldfields in the early 1860s and rose quickly to prominence. With two thousand dollars from the sale of a Bannack-area placer claim, he built an empire in banking, mining, railroads, and real estate, amassing one of the country's largest personal fortunes, his springboard to political power within the Montana Democratic Party. More than any other man, Clark could claim to have blocked Anaconda's push five years earlier to become Montana's capital, so his absence from the convention was only fitting. It was enough that he was represented by his able editors at the *Butte Miner,* who would more than hold their own against Daly's upcoming push to have Clark tossed from the Senate. For the moment, though, an unseen flag of truce flapped over the convention, and both the *Butte Miner* and the *Inter Mountain* sent the *Standard* lovely birthday bouquets, which the *Standard* acknowledged with only a whiff of sarcasm. "The bloody chasm," it wrote, "is filled up with roses this week."[9]

The truce held as the journalists filed into the Margaret Theater, named for Daly's wife, for an evening of music and speeches that would officially kick off the most elaborate convention in the press association's fourteen-year history. Montana's premier musicians, members of the Boston and Montana Band, opened with rousing renditions of "My Old Kentucky Home" and "Georgia Camp Meeting" followed by brief welcoming remarks from Warren W. "Wally" Walsworth, the newspaper association's reigning president and chief of the *Standard*'s Butte bureau. For reasons never explained, the convention's keynoter, the editor of Denver's *Rocky Mountain News,* never made it past Butte, so the honor passed to Judge C. C. Goodwin, fiery editor of the *Salt*

Anaconda Standard *illustrators provided readers with an array of portraits of* Montana newsmen who attended the 1899 Montana State Press Association meeting.

Anaconda Standard, September 5, 1899

Lake Tribune. Goodwin's paper would eventually fall under the control of Utah mining baron Thomas Kearns, a future business partner of William A. Clark, but on this night Goodwin could still claim the credibility that went with independence. He dutifully praised Montana newspapermen while urging them to learn more about science and to always consider the tender sensibilities of their youngest readers.[10]

The evening's final speech featured the incorruptible, if tiresome, pillar of Montana's Republican Party, "Colonel" Wilbur Fisk Sanders. A former U.S. senator, a lawyer, and the nephew of Montana's first territorial governor, Sanders had burned himself into Montana's memory on a winter's night in 1864 when he stood in the back of a wagon and persuaded a nervous Virginia City crowd to hang a local bandit and thereby commence the gruesome work of making the territory safe for development. Sanders now reminded his audience that in that same vigilante winter, thirty-five years earlier, he had stood by a printing press hardly bigger than his hat and watched it issue "a little sheet of news" that he himself had written.[11] Sanders later witnessed the birth of the territory's first regular paper, the *Montana Post*, and boasted that for years he subscribed to every newspaper in the territory, but now, with more than forty papers statewide, his Helena home was too small to contain them all. He marveled at the growth of Montana's press, singling out the *Standard*'s birthday edition as "a milestone in the highway of intellectual life in the state," but as the evening concluded, Sanders also struck the evening's only awkward note, warning that Montana's journalists increasingly risked their credibility by acting as mercenaries in the state's copper wars. "We in this state have had many newspaper men who were birds of passage, who would sell their abilities to one side as quickly as another," Sanders said. "As a result of this there has grown up a sort of newspaper infidelity."[12]

Wednesday brought tours of Daly's smelter works and weighty professional discussions on such pressing worries as fraudulent advertising, the disturbing trend toward sensational crime reporting, and the challenges facing "The Independent Newspaper in Politics," but the evening's birthday banquet for the *Standard* was the convention's glittering high point. Shortly after 10:00 PM, the Boston and Montana Band, screened from the diners' view, struck up a march, the signal to open the doors to the Montana Hotel's banquet hall and seat the *Standard*'s two hundred guests. The newspapermen and an array of prominent Montanans, most in evening dress, strolled past the potted palms to find their places at the three long tables set with gleaming silver, goblets of cut glass, and bouquets of sweet peas, tea roses, and carnations. Beside each plate lay a cream-colored menu card featuring an embossed Cupid roasting a turkey skewered on an editor's pen. Inside, on heavy linen paper, it offered a menu fit for royalty: roasted mountain grouse, lobster "mayonnaise," sweetbreads, fresh peas and mushrooms, aspics of tomato and raspberry, rare cheeses, and sweet cakes—all to be washed down in courses with Spanish sherry, French wines, coffee, and cognac.[13]

To the assembled journalists, the notables among them must have seemed as intriguing as the fare. Joining Judge Goodwin and Wilbur Fisk Sanders as the *Standard*'s guests were Daly's most prominent allies in the battle to keep William A. Clark from occupying the Senate seat he had so flagrantly purchased. They included Populist governor Robert B. Smith, whose "free silver" stance ensured him the support of Daly's miners, smeltermen, and newspapers; former senator Lee Mantle, the politically ambitious publisher of the Butte *Inter Mountain*, whose shaky future required Daly's tacit support; and Congressman A. J. Campbell, principal leader of Daly's faction in the state Democratic Party. Joining them were Montana's attorney general, C. B. Nolan, and its Supreme Court chief justice, Theodore Brantly, both of whom had recently rejected bribes to drop disbarment proceedings against Clark's chief legal adviser and reputed bagman. Also in attendance was Christopher Powell Connolly, Silver Bow County's prosecutor and a future muckraker, whose investigative skills were even then providing Daly with evidence he would use to challenge Clark's ascension to the Senate.[14]

Presiding over them was Marcus Daly himself, who made a rare trip from his sprawling ranch in the Bitterroot Valley to entertain the state's opinion makers. His visits to his humming smelter town had been less frequent since the capital fight five years previous, during which he and Clark had flooded the state with cash and propaganda, setting a precedent for the corruption that would soon shock the nation. Stout and balding in his late fifties, with a thick mustache beneath his wide, round nose, Daly was more comfortable at the racetrack than in society, but many of the assembled journalists were employees, allies, and friends. By all accounts, Daly enjoyed the irreverent company of newspapermen. During his years as Anaconda's most prominent resident, he had been a frequent visitor at the *Standard,* where he delighted in passing on bits of news, scanning the next day's headlines, and watching the presses run. Blunt and plainspoken, he clearly relished his image as patron of the state's journalistic arts, a role the *Inter Mountain* had celebrated that very afternoon in its editorial columns: "The honorable Marcus Daly is an honorary member of the Montana State Press Association and is reported to have paid his dues regardless of the needs of his family. Though not personally engaged in newspaper work, he knows what newspapers are and what they cost. He has given away several newspapers on the grounds that he likes to see other people prosper as well as himself."[15]

At midnight, Durston raised his glass for a succession of toasts: to Montana and to its progress, to the vision of its pioneers, and to the bravery of its soldiers then steaming homeward from the conquest of the Philippines and the bloody insurgency that followed. Chief Justice Brantly toasted the press, while Arthur L. Stone, the *Standard*'s Missoula correspondent and future founder of the University of Montana's School of Journalism, touted the beauty and industry of western Montana. At last, the association's officers rose to offer resolutions of gratitude to the railroads for "transportation courtesies so kindly tendered"; to the hospitality of the *Standard*, "the greatest newspaper in the great state of Montana"; and to Marcus Daly for "the receipt of many courtesies." With that, the convention formally adjourned, though the gaiety extended well past the *Standard*'s press time. "The editorial columns of the Montana press were loaded full of sparkling material last night," the *Standard* reported on the morning after. "We refer of course to the editors' spinal columns." Sometime just before dawn, a light snow fell, and by mid-day the newspapermen began to filter from town, some to soothe their hangovers at nearby Gregson Hot Springs before moving the party to Butte.[16]

The press association would not record another convention for six years as Montana endured its turbulent copper wars. Within six months, Clark would be tossed from the Senate only to win reelection later that year, thanks in part to a spree of newspaper buying unmatched in the state's short history. Daly, backed by the Standard Oil Company executives behind the Amalgamated Copper Company, would respond in kind but succumb shortly to complications of kidney disease, living just long enough to witness his rival's political victory. Some journalists—Sanders's "birds of passage"—would sell their talents eagerly, often, and to both sides, while others would succumb reluctantly to economic coercion. Oliver Warden would be forced to sell his *Great Falls Tribune* to Clark, who threatened to start a competing daily. Warden's partner, William Bole, would escape to edit Daly's *Bozeman Daily Chronicle*, whose loyalties flopped profitably between Daly and Clark until Daly finally bought it. The *Inter Mountain* would struggle to remain free of the influence of copper kings, but its resistance would eventually crumble. As for the press association, its convention reports would resume in 1906 with the account of a boozy 1,700-mile junket from Butte to Los Angeles that traveled extensively over William A. Clark's new railroad, the San Pedro, Los Angeles, and Salt Lake. To the astonishment of the train's porters, the Montana scribblers ran out of whiskey somewhere near present-day Las Vegas, Nevada. Such horrors notwithstanding, the association later expressed its gratitude to its host, who, according to one prominent editor, had initiated the trip "unmindful of the fact that he may have political ambitions."[17]

Some publishers, mostly in remote rural areas of the state, would keep their independence. Men such as William K. Harber of Fort Benton's *River Press* and Miles Romney of the *Western News* in Hamilton would come to deplore the corruption that scrambled Montana's politics and corroded their profession's credibility. After the storm, they and other Progressives would argue passionately for reform—and Montanans would listen. But the stain on Montana journalism would linger for decades. The legend of the state's copper-collared press was no mere fiction, though the small, persistent, and often radical press that howled at its heels often exaggerated its details. The story, steeped in the partisanship and boosterism peculiar to American frontier journalism, would only grow as the company consolidated its industrial might.

Two unidentified newsmen, above, posed in 1899 while printing the weekly East Helena Record.

CHAPTER ONE

Raising the Standard

MARCUS DALY
BUILDS A
NEWSPAPER

O N A RAINY SPRING DAY IN 1889, a tall man in a canvas duster ducked into the clapboard offices of the *New North-West,* one of two weekly newspapers serving the small town of Deer Lodge. He leaned an elbow on the counter and asked for the proprietor, "Captain" James Mills. As Mills would recall years later, his visitor was athletic, his face bronzed by the high country sun. "My name is Durston," the man said. "I've been working a quartz mine over beyond Butte, but I used to do a little newspaper writing down in New York state. I am thinking of going into the newspaper business in Anaconda, and want to ask you if you think a daily could be made a success up there."[1]

In seeking out Mills, John Durston had done his homework. If anyone understood the vagaries of frontier journalism, it was Mills, whose two decades of Montana newspapering spanned most of the history of Montana's territorial press. A decorated Union veteran who had entered Lincoln's army as a private and left it with the brevet rank of lieutenant colonel, Mills left his native Ohio after the war and headed for Montana's fabled goldfields. His dream of striking it rich evaporated on the upper Yellowstone River in the summer of 1866 when a guide Mills and his partners had entrusted with their grubstake vanished during a run for supplies. Mills straggled into Virginia City with ten cents in postal currency to his name and found work as a bookkeeper, but he was soon enticed into the offices of the tri-weekly *Montana Post,* which sorely needed an editor. Impressed by an article Mills had written for an eastern journal and satisfied with his Republican loyalties, publisher D. W. Tilton offered the young veteran command of the paper's editorial desk—a rough pine table set alongside the paper's Campbell press. With that, Mills had become the third editor of Montana's first true newspaper, succeeding the

The sire of numerous newspaper ventures across the state, including the New North-West *in Deer Lodge, James H. Mills (seated) also served as state commissioner of agriculture. He is pictured here with his chief clerk A. C. Schneider circa 1895.*

MONTANA HISTORICAL SOCIETY PHOTOGRAPH ARCHIVES, HELENA

late Thomas J. Dimsdale, the fussy and tubercular British schoolteacher famous for his serial history of Virginia City's vigilantes, and Henry N. Blake, the Harvard-educated lawyer whose flamboyant editorship lasted all of five months.[2]

For two and a half years, until the paper was moved to Helena and eventually sold at a sheriff's auction in 1869, Mills edited the *Montana Post* for a scattered, shifting readership hungry for reading material. With its long columns of hand-set type, smallish headlines, and an occasional woodcut sponsored by that most rare and valued of frontier journalistic commodities—a regular advertiser—the *Montana Post* was hardly a paragon of the printer's art. Yet its pages bubbled with reports of mining discoveries, fractious territorial politics, hostile encounters with Indians, the comings and goings of a transient populace, and the splendid wares of local merchants. Above all, it exuded an unshakeable faith in the town's commercial and cultural destiny. Boosterism, unabashed and often laid on in inverse proportion to the camp's true hopes for lasting prosperity, was the frontier editor's principal responsibility. It could hardly have been otherwise, historian Daniel Boorstin would note. Like western railroads, a pioneer newspaper "had to call into being the very population it aimed to serve." Acting as one-man chambers of commerce, frontier editors promoted their communities so vigorously that virtually every town in mining country was pegged a future Paris or Athens of the West. Virginia City was no different, and James Mills touted its golden promise until the day he packed up the *Montana Post* and moved it to Helena's richer diggings in 1868.[3]

Promotion enticed advertisers and investors, but it was news and opinion, often inseparable, that distinguished early western newspapers. Rival editors eagerly exchanged subscriptions by mail, and through these "exchanges" they regularly engaged one another in spirited contests of wit and vituperation. The resulting parochial and personal feuds were sometimes playful, sometimes vicious, but almost always entertaining. "The Bozeman Courier is out again, printed in saddle-colored wrapping paper," the editor of Virginia City's *Madisonian* wrote in June 1876. "It contains Bozeman 'ads' and its usual amount of deplorable vulgarity."[4]

Politics, above all, stoked the editorial flames, and in the post–Civil War tension that colored much of Montana's territorial period, editors' battles over the efficacy and patronage of territorial government shared space with bitter exchanges over Reconstruction and race. Unionist editors like Mills were quick to "wave the bloody shirt," reminding readers of the war's toll, while rival Democratic papers serving Montana's contingent of Southern sympathizers from Missouri and other border states played to their readers' fears of racial integration. Montana Democrats formally opposed "the odious and pernicious doctrine of 'negro equality'" at their party's convention in 1865, and such sentiments found voice in Helena's weekly *Rocky Mountain Gazette* and the Deer Lodge *Independent,* whose first publisher, J. H. Rogers, had refused to take the Union loyalty oath at the first territorial legislature.[5] When debt finally forced the transplanted *Montana Post* to close in 1869, Mills, at the invitation of outnumbered Deer Lodge Republicans, moved to Deer Lodge to continue the Unionist fight beneath the masthead of the *New North-West.* Helena's Republican readers remained in the care of the combative *Helena Herald,* the Fisk brothers' new daily ably led by Robert E. Fisk, a "fighting editor" who learned his craft as a young compositor for the *New York Herald.*[6]

Fisk engaged the *Rocky Mountain Gazette* with some of the most intemperate ink slinging of the day, vilifying his Democratic rival as a "copperhead snotrag" and a "weekly sluice-head of obscene insults, abuse and calumny."[7] In response to a provocative *Gazette* editorial printed on June 8, 1868, the *Helena Herald* demonstrated its own special talent for vitriol:

> The organ of the 8th inst. rises from its foul nest, as much refreshed after its week's labor as a sow crawling from its mire, or a buzzard after feasting upon carrion. Its feathers were ruffled by the rude hand of the Herald on Saturday last, and like the gorged condor of South America, it vomits the disgusting contents of its stomach in the faces of its several readers, in a manner which is enough to sicken a dog.[8]

Robert E. Fisk and his brother ran the Helena Herald *from this downtown Helena building, pictured above in 1875.*

MONTANA HISTORICAL SOCIETY PHOTOGRAPH ARCHIVES, HELENA

In turn, the *Rocky Mountain Gazette* peppered its news columns and editorials with sneering jabs at the Republican "nigger lovers" who dared promote the rights of former slaves. "The spot of the leopard and the color and odor of Africa are too plain and palpable to deceive anyone," its editor wrote.[9]

Verbal pyrotechnics could help keep frontier paper afloat, but with subscribers and advertisers in short supply, survival often rested on political patronage and luck. The *Gazette*'s owners included such Democratic luminaries as Martin Maginnis, Montana's future territorial delegate to Congress, but it was the smell of wood smoke, not of Republicans, that signaled the *Gazette*'s demise. When the fires that periodically swept Helena's early business district destroyed the paper for a second time, on January 9, 1874, its owners gave up, entrusting their subscribers and Democratic vision to the newly established *Helena Independent*, whose publishers, Addison Smith and Hugh McQuad, had filled the political void by hauling their press over the mountains from Deer Lodge, where Mills's *New North-West* had proved a too-worthy rival.[10]

Mills's paper, like the *Helena Independent*, thrived in the bumptious mix of territorial politics and journalism in which editors understood their role as rousers of the party faithful and first skirmishers in the fight. Always among the best-known men in the territory, editors themselves served regularly as party leaders and candidates for office, a tradition that would linger well into the twentieth century. Mills supplemented his journalistic career by serving variously as Montana's territorial secretary; adjutant general of the militia; collector of federal revenues; state commissioner of agriculture, labor, and industry; and Powell County's first clerk and recorder.[11]

Political neutrality not only made for dull copy, it was bad for businesses. Partisan editors who backed the winning ticket often drew key political appointments, but the richest reward came in the form of government printing contracts that kept many papers solvent as they struggled to find readers and advertisers. Such patronage—the printing of ballots, ordinances, land claims, and the myriad official government forms—was crucial, and the competition for it could spark jealous rivalries among publishers of the same party. When the *Helena*

Herald lost a bid for several territorial printing contracts to Mills and the *New North-West* in Deer Lodge, its furious editor, Robert Fisk, sourly accused his brother Republican of taking "a sweet suck at the public titty-bag." The intra-party rivalry extended beyond matters of patronage. Fisk had been equally critical of Mills's failure, as the politically appointed head of Montana's militia, to prevent the march of Chief Joseph's Nez Perce across Montana in 1877.[12]

One of Montana's pioneer newsmen, "Colonel" Sam Gordon edited eastern Montana's first substantial newspaper, the Yellowstone Journal, *started in Miles City in 1879 by a son of one of Horace Greeley's partners in the* New York Tribune. *This photograph was taken in 1895.*

TAYLOR, PHOTOGRAPHER, MONTANA HISTORICAL SOCIETY PHOTOGRAPH ARCHIVES, HELENA

By 1889, Mills had weathered more than two decades of boom-and-bust partisan newspapering and witnessed the rise of such vibrant pioneer editors as the *Helena Herald*'s Robert Fisk, William W. Alderson of Bozeman's *Avant Courier*, Judge Frank Woody of Missoula's *Missoulian*, and brothers Robert and William Sutherlin of the state's principal agricultural newspaper, the *Rocky Mountain Husbandman*, based in White Sulphur Springs. The list also included John B. Read, the gentle wit of Butte's *Inter Mountain*, established in 1881 as a platform for Butte Republicans and the political ambitions of its owner and publisher, Lee Mantle. Others included Jerre Collins of Fort Benton's scrappy *River Press*, and "Colonel" Sam Gordon, editor of eastern Montana's first substantial newspaper, the *Yellowstone Journal*, begun in Miles City in 1879 by a son of one of Horace Greeley's partners in the *New York Tribune*. A founder of the Montana press association in 1885, Mills knew the pressures and demands of the business and had watched pioneer papers. His *New North-West* was on solid footing in Deer Lodge—for now—but he had also established early weeklies in Butte and Anaconda, only to sell them within a few years' time. By 1879, the *Butte Miner*, which Mills and a partner had founded three years earlier as a Republican weekly, was publishing daily. Two years later, its ownership passed into the hands of a quartet of new investors, among them the younger brother and principal business partner of William A. Clark.[13]

The elder Clark's interest in newspapering as a fiscal investment seems unlikely; as bankers, he and his brother may have acquired the property by financial default—a common fate of early papers. Whatever the reason, Clark clearly saw the paper's political potential, and his money made the *Butte Miner* the territory's preeminent Democratic voice. A vigorous daily required serious and continual investment, the kind of money few newspapermen or local politicians could muster. Increasingly, that money would come from industrialists like Clark, who saw more profit in a paper's influence than in its bottom line.

Such arrangements required the services of ambitious newspapermen, and it helped if their politics were flexible. Mills carefully maintained his Republican loyalties and his journalistic independence over the years, but the big money fueling Montana's development over the ten-year run-up to statehood in 1889 encouraged a more mercenary breed of journalist, men like Chauncey Barbour, onetime editor of the *Missoulian,* a weekly until its conversion to daily publication in 1891. Before the *Miner*'s emergence as Butte's dominant Democratic daily, Barbour had schemed to interest rail magnate Jay Gould in "a vigorous railroad paper in Butte." In return, the new daily would promote public subsidies for Gould's Utah and Northern Railway, then pushing north into Montana. In keeping with the sentiments of his readers, Barbour insisted the plan be kept secret because his own *Missoulian* opposed railroad subsidies. "So long as I remain in Missoula county it is my solemn duty to oppose all aid to railroads," Barbour wrote his confidant in the matter, former territorial governor Samuel T. Hauser. "A journalist is bound to reflect the sentiments of his immediate patrons. If he goes among another people he must reconstruct, so to speak."[14]

By the spring of 1889, with statehood just months away and the economic and political stakes never higher, James Mills surely understood the implications of the tall man's friendly visit to the offices of the Deer Lodge *New North-West*: Marcus Daly was about to enter the newspaper game, and it would never be the same.

"Could someone base a successful daily in Anaconda?" John Durston had asked.

"By putting plenty of money into it and making it the best newspaper in the state, yes," Mills replied.[15]

DALY CAME LATE TO JOURNALISM, but that was characteristic of the man who rarely took an unconsidered risk. By 1888, William A. Clark's *Butte Miner* reigned as Montana's premier Democratic daily, giving its owner an influential voice in the debates leading to statehood, a platform on which to build a political machine, and a tool to promote his varied businesses. Throughout his career, Clark carefully tended his image and those of his enterprises in the press. In time, he would own newspapers in Arizona and Utah but none as muscular or as devoted as the *Miner*, which would protect his reputation and burnish his vanity until his death in 1925. Daly's interest in newspapers was similarly pragmatic though—unlike Clark and other politically ambitious publishers such as the *Inter Mountain*'s Lee Mantle—Daly harbored no personal desire for office.

Yet there are signs Daly's interests in journalism ranged beyond the purely economic and the purely political. His curiosity may have been piqued through his long association and friendship with California millionaire George Hearst, a barely literate but savvy miner, businessman, and member of the San Francisco syndicate that bankrolled Daly's Anaconda venture. Hearst, who mentored a young Daly during Nevada's silver boom in the 1860s, bought the *San Francisco Examiner* in 1880, and though Hearst cared little for the publishing business, he found it perfectly useful in promoting his election to the U.S. Senate in 1887.[16]

Owning a newspaper—an institution held in greater esteem then than now—may have appealed to Daly's immense curiosity and soothed some measure of insecurity. For all his wealth and business acumen, Daly lacked formal education and his speech was described as "crude and faltering," yet he devoured newspapers. Accounts of his early days in Butte portray him relaxing after a day in the mines, his chair pulled close to the stove in a neighbor's cabin, poring over a weeks-old edition

of the *Irish World and American Industrial Liberator.* He clearly enjoyed the competitiveness and irreverent banter of newspapermen. As a
young miner learning to read silver veins in the Comstock Lode, Daly
included in his circle of friends Samuel Langhorne Clemens, the future
Mark Twain, then a young reporter for Virginia City, Nevada's raucous
Territorial Enterprise. Years afterward, though his name never appeared
on the *Anaconda Standard* masthead, Daly delighted in presenting its
editors with morsels of news gathered on his travels or pressed upon him
by neighbors during his strolls about Anaconda. He enjoyed watching
Standard employees scramble to meet the paper's late-night deadlines,
and he was proud and protective of the paper's reputation. On at least
one occasion, he upbraided a *Standard* editor for being late with a story
that had appeared in the previous day's *Butte Miner.*[17]

But Daly was nothing if not a practical man, and there were practical reasons for his foray into journalism. A daily newspaper with a
statewide influence would have seemed essential for nurturing the vast
investment he and his backers had made in mines and smelters and a
growing string of supporting enterprises that included lumber mills,
coal mines, railroads, and mercantile stores. By comparison, the cost
of a daily newspaper—even one as extravagant as Daly's—would have
seemed minor. By the winter of 1888–89, Daly had already built a political machine in preparation for the territory's transition to statehood
and the attendant scramble to locate key institutions of government
and to elect congressmen, legislators, judges, and local officials with
the power to tax or regulate industrial holdings. At the heart of Daly's
vision lay the smelter city of Anaconda. Already anticipating the competition over the location of a permanent state capital, Daly invested
heavily in the prerequisites: good water, rail service, a grand hotel, public parks, electric lights, and a regal hillside plot for the capitol itself.

But vision required a voice, and Daly's budding Democratic organization felt the need keenly as it struggled against a field of well-heeled
rivals, each with its own daily newspaper. The pressure increased in the
aftermath of the 1888 election for Montana's territorial representative to
Congress, which William A. Clark, the Democratic nominee and pre-
sumptive favorite, lost to Republican Thomas Carter. Butte's nominally
Democratic Irish miners, many of them Daly's employees, abandoned

the party to vote for the Irish-Catholic Carter. Clark, a Protestant and Anglophile, raised Irish doubts during the campaign with his support of free trade with England, his criticism of Irish nationalist leaders, and in a series of insensitive gaffes that included inviting his would-be Catholic constituents to a beef barbecue on Friday. Republicans, through the Butte *Inter Mountain,* gleefully exploited Clark's blunders, but Clark, through his *Butte Miner,* blamed the defeat on Marcus Daly, claiming that Daly had ordered his Irish workers to vote for Carter. Daly denied any role in Clark's embarrassment, but in months that followed, Clark's ire at Daly's "betrayal" dripped from the columns of the *Miner,* while Democratic editors in Helena and Great Falls pointed fingers at Daly too, firing the first journalistic salvos in a twelve-year feud that would cast a long shadow over Montana's political and journalistic history.[18]

Outgunned, Daly decided to build his own newspaper, and in the early months of 1889 his first task was to find an editor. Fortunately, he found one close by. In fact, John Durston, a former university professor and New York newspaper editor, had caught Daly's attention some months earlier through an article Durston had written on Montana politics for the *Anaconda Weekly Review.* Impressed, Daly sought out Durston, who with his wife, Mary, had become welcome additions to Butte and Anaconda social circles, which they increasingly preferred to their disappointing mining claim near Homestake, southeast of Butte. Childhood sweethearts who met over piano lessons in Syracuse, New York, the Durstons enjoyed playing duets at parties, and over the winter of 1888–89, mentions of their activities appeared regularly in the *Review's* society columns.[19]

The stories of Daly's wooing of Durston vary. The most-repeated account holds that Daly summoned the editor from New York to Anaconda and made him an offer, which Durston promptly rejected, arguing that the tiny city could never support the kind of daily paper Daly envisioned. When Daly promised to make good the inevitable losses, Durston insisted the mining baron had no concept of how much money a daily paper could lose. "It's more expensive than a steamship," he said. "Besides, I don't want to be 'kept.' I want to run a newspaper that will earn its way." Undaunted, Daly urged Durston to take a few days, tour Butte, and think it over. There was no reason, he added, that a daily published in Anaconda couldn't circulate in Butte, in direct competition with the *Miner,* the *Inter Mountain,* and the city's various weeklies. Durston went to Butte but returned to Anaconda a few days later determined to reject Daly again. While waiting in the lobby of the Montana Hotel, Durston supposedly read an article in a Butte newspaper detailing Daly's recent purchase of an untested colt from a famous Kentucky racing stable for the extravagant price of four thousand dollars. When Daly greeted him a few moments later, Durston asked if the story was true. Daly said it was. "Well," said Durston, "if you are that way; if you will sink four thousand dollars in a colt that may or may not grow into a racehorse, I guess you can put forty thousand into an outfit that may or may not become a newspaper." The colt's price and Durston's estimate of the *Standard*'s initial investment would grow with the story's telling. Other details were clearly inaccurate. Durston was already in Montana when Daly supposedly summoned him from New York, and he was reasonably familiar with Montana's mining communities, its territorial politics, and its newspapers. Nor could Durston—sitting in Daly's hotel in the center of Daly's city—have been surprised at the depths of Daly's pockets.[20]

A more credible, if paler, account published during Durston's lifetime and written by his longtime associate, Charles H. Eggleston, suggests Durston was hardly the coy suitor that some imagined. According to Eggleston, Durston's chief concern was that Anaconda's population of less than four thousand could never support a metropolitan-style daily, and he predicted Daly would eventually find the paper "an intolerable white elephant." But Daly brushed Durston's fears aside. "With characteristic decision Mr. Daly said his mind was made up—he was going to have an Anaconda daily, and if Mr. Durston wouldn't run it he would look around for a competent man who would," Eggleston wrote. Durston took the job.[21] Durston had pressing reasons to accept the offer. Two years had passed since he left his last newspaper post and sold his shares in the *Syracuse Standard,* and his adventure in Montana mining was quickly becoming a family joke. Although he and his wife had come to love Montana's rugged beauty, a fire that destroyed the family's Syracuse home in late 1888 may have clinched the decision. In any case, by the summer of 1889, Durston was busy laying plans for a daily newspaper, scheduled to make its debut before the fall's special election on Montana's newly proposed constitution.[22]

For Daly, Durston was indeed a fortunate find. Worldly and authoritative, with proven experience in journalism and politics, Durston was rare among frontier editors, few of whom could match his educational or professional attainment. Many, like Mills, were literate men who fell into newspapering, learning its peculiar skills on the run. Others, like Helena's Robert Fisk, came to journalism as young men trained to run presses and set type, skilled laborers who eventually found themselves composing articles to fill their newspapers' columns.

Durston's route was different. Born in Syracuse in 1848, he was the second of four sons sired by John Durston, an immigrant British shipwright who built boats for the Erie Canal. His Protestant Irish mother, Sarah Hurst, played the organ for the Syracuse Episcopal Church and directed its vocal quartet, composed entirely of her sons. By all accounts, the Durstons led a comfortable, middle-class life centered on religion and the Republican politics of upstate New York. When a neighbor, Durston's future father-in-law, offered the boy full access to his extensive private library, young Durston revealed a wide-ranging curiosity and bookish bent. An excellent student, he finished Syracuse High School by age sixteen and enrolled at Yale University in the fall of 1864, but found Connecticut and his classmates dull. He left New Haven in his junior year and, thanks to the success of his father's business, sailed for Europe to enroll at the University of Heidelberg, where for the next three years he specialized in the study of language and literature. In 1870, at age twenty-two, Durston completed a doctorate in philology and returned to Syracuse as chairman of the modern languages department at the newly founded Syracuse University, where he tried to hide his distinction of being the school's youngest professor behind a mustache, sideburns, and the requisite black frock coat. Within a year, he married Mary Harwood, the girl next door, and the couple quickly settled into academic and family life, punctuated by the birth of two daughters and summer trips to Paris, where Durston polished his languages and added the study of civics and political economy to his academic résumé.[23]

By 1880, however, and for reasons unclear, Durston resigned from the university to purchase the struggling *Syracuse Standard*. Whatever his motives, journalism clearly suited his temperament, talents, and growing interest in politics. The thirty-two-year-old Durston quickly revived the paper's stagnant circulation and made himself a respected player in upstate Republican politics. Family lore holds that early in his editorial career, Durston, ever the professor, had hushed a young man whose animated whispering was distracting speechmakers during a session of the state's GOP convention. Unruffled, the youth introduced himself as Theodore Roosevelt, and the two struck up a conversation that Roosevelt would recall with amusement years later during a presidential sweep through Montana. Under Durston, the *Syracuse Standard* flourished over the next seven years, and its political endorsements carried increasing weight. To improve his paper and expand its reach, Durston took on wealthy local businessmen as partners and increased his staff of bright young reporters and editors, many of them college educated, with some, like Charles Eggleston, recruited from among his former students. The educational attainment of the *Standard*'s staff set it apart from many small-city newspapers of its day.

By all accounts, Durston threw himself into journalism with all the energy and idealism he could muster, but his vision of editorial independence would soon explode in the volatile mixture of politics and business. The spark came in 1887 as Syracuse debated whether to subscribe to a privately owned water system or finance a public utility. Though his new partners were investors in the private franchise, Durston refused to mount a crusade for what he saw as an unpopular monopoly, arguing that it would ruin the paper's credibility. In the end, the partners forced Durston to sell out. Voters rejected the private franchise by a margin of nine to one, confirming Durston's political instincts, but by then he was out of journalism with no plans reenter it soon.[24]

At loose ends, Durston took a pleasure trip on the Great Lakes with a former student, a businessman considering investments in western mines. When the man pressed Durston to extend his vacation and travel with him to inspect mines in Montana and western Washington, Durston agreed, and by the spring of 1888 he was co-owner and manager of the Gold Flint Mine near Homestake. That Christmas, Durston sent for his wife, who left the couple's children with relatives in Syracuse and traveled west, arriving in time to fight through nine-foot snowdrifts to reach her husband's cabin door. By mid-January of 1889, the couple's daughters had joined them, though by then the mine had already proved a disappointment.

But the country's raw beauty and the possibilities it offered on the eve of statehood impressed them all.[25]

Daly proved to be a generous, supportive, and interested newspaper owner who backed Durston's judgment in matters of journalistic craft and fashion with his extravagant wealth. This would be no typical frontier newspaper enterprise, susceptible to the whims of local subscribers and advertisers. Durston was responsible for the breadth and dash of his paper's news report, for its state-of-the-art appearance, and its attention to detail, but the paper's existence clearly rested on Daly's money, its politics on Daly's whims, and its future on the health of Daly's industrial empire.

In 1881, the Butte Miner, *which James H. Mills and a partner had founded as a weekly, passed into the hands of new investors and eventually to William A. Clark, who turned it into a weapon in his fight against Marcus Daly and his* Anaconda Standard. *That same year saw the creation of a Republican daily, the* Inter Mountain. *The Butte papers were neighbors in the building pictured here in about 1886.*

T. H. RUTTER, PHOTOGRAPHER, WORLD MUSEUM OF MINING, BUTTE

"HERE GOES FOR A DAILY NEWSPAPER."[26]

With those words, the first issue of the *Anaconda Standard* rolled off a new ten-thousand-dollar press on Wednesday morning, September 4, 1889, a month before the special election on the territory's freshly drafted constitution and two months shy of statehood. On the day of its debut, the *Standard* ranked among Montana's best newspapers, though at first it published only six days a week and had yet to establish its Butte bureau, the future heart of its statewide report. Still, it dwarfed the local Republican paper, the *Anaconda Weekly Review,* and stood alongside Daly's smelter, railroad, and grand hotel as a remarkable bit of overachievement for a town with fewer than four thousand residents, no sewers, and a smattering of streetlights. On the night before the *Standard's* inaugural issue, town officials had refused to ban livestock from the city's streets, "the opinion of the aldermen being that at this season of the year no harm can result to lawns or gardens from the presence of cattle."[27]

At eight pages, with each page divided into six neat columns, the *Standard's* makeup and presswork rivaled that of the *Helena Journal,* the smart Republican sheet owned by lawyer and rancher Russell Harrison, son of former U.S. president Benjamin Harrison. The *Standard's* advertising, often illustrated with exquisite woodcuts, was sophisticated and alluring, and no territorial paper could outdo its sweeping news report, most of which arrived through a special telegraph wire strung directly to the *Standard's* editorial offices at the corner of Main and Third streets.[28]

The inaugural front page featured national news concerning the arrest of two men suspected of fleecing a prominent New York socialite, a brutal Louisiana race riot, a baseball-related death in New Jersey, a congressional inquiry into price-fixing by meat packers, and fresh results of trotting races in Springfield, Massachusetts. The page offered plenty of local and regional fare too. Rail tycoon James J. Hill stood in danger of losing his grip over the Great Northern Railway, while lawsuits threatened to strangle Butte's productive Blue Bird Mine. Meanwhile, a shipment of eastern brook trout, rainbow trout, and "English trout" was speeding toward Yellowstone National Park, and a fortunate early-season snowfall had snuffed forest fires near Helena. Philipsburg, the prosperous silver town just over the Pintlers, reeled from the failure of its Silver Bank, while Republican officials in nearby Beaverhead County allegedly tried to prevent Democratic voters from registering.[29]

Inside, slotted alongside ads touting Kentucky whiskies, patent medicines, and "teeth extracted without pain," the paper reported train and mail schedules, quoted stock prices and weather reports, and recounted a Boston lecture by Charles Dickens. Readers were offered a primer on the state's proposed constitution, which the *Standard* wholeheartedly supported. The paper also noted that William A. Clark's *Butte Miner* "is to be enlarged at once and its editorial staff increased," an obvious response to the *Standard*'s challenge.[30]

But it was on its muscular editorial page, beneath its masthead and a listing of the Democratic ticket for Montana's first statewide election, that the new state's newest daily declared its ambition as a "vigorous child of a wide-awake town":

> The STANDARD entertains no doubts regarding the field before it. Into that field it steps hopefully and with good cheer. Its plans are broad. Knowing how much the intelligent public demands of the press, it has prepared itself to meet that demand, and its ambition is to rank as the best newspaper in the commonwealth. It proposes to be tidy in dress and hopes to be attractive in style. In manner and matter it will surely be clean.
>
> The first business of the STANDARD will be to give the world's news to its readers. It has secured better telegraphic facilities than are at the command of any other newspaper in the Northwest. In turning these resources to account, it will have in mind the reasonable demands over every class of readers. It will work hard to secure a constituency. Its business office solicits generous patronage and expects to get it.[31]

In a neat feat of verbal gymnastics that would have fooled no one familiar with the paper's parentage, Durston pledged both fealty to the Democratic Party and independence of its factions and leaders. The *Standard* would not be "blindly partisan, its politics will be in no sense personal." Yet without naming his employer, Durston also addressed Marcus Daly's contribution, urging its readers to give credit to "those whose muscle and brain, purse and public spirit have made Montana fit to be a state."[32]

It was an extravagant beginning that caught the attention of editors throughout Montana. The *Anaconda Weekly Review* described the *Standard* as "an exceedingly neat and pretty sheet," and even the rival

Butte *Inter Mountain* was forced to acknowledge that Durston, whose name the paper would forever maliciously misspell, had built the "finest fitted newspaper plant in this northwestern country."[33] Cost, the *Inter Mountain* concluded, had apparently been no object:

> The Standard occupies its own commodious two-story and basement brick building, and any one office occupies about as much room as the ordinary newspaper office, where there are so many conveniences provided for softening the hard lines of the newspaper life that an old-time Montana [editor], were he to wake up some morning and find himself in the Standard quarters, would imagine himself in newspaper heaven. The business office looks like a banking house, the editorial rooms are actually carpeted, and Editor Durstan [*sic*] sits in an upholstered chair. The composing room is large and fine enough for a ball room [*sic*], while the press room, with its steel-plated floor, would not be too cramped for a skating rink if the $10,000 perfecting press and a few other similar mechanical trifles were set out in the alley.[34]

Even Clark's *Butte Miner* doffed its hat to the latest debutante in "an era of journalistic bubbling over in Montana," and it welcomed Durston to the fraternity with the ritual mangling of his name:

> The "Anaconda Standard" is the most pretentious of the new publications. It is the much-talked of daily for the Democrats in Anaconda, and made its appearance Wednesday morning. Its editor is Mr. J. H. Durstan [*sic*], an able and versatile writer, and an old eastern newspaperman. The handicraft of a veteran artist is apparent in every page of the "Standard," which is a six-column quarto, printed on good paper from handsome type, and its general appearance in every way commends it to popular approval. Above all, it is Democratic, and will fight a vigorous battle for the success of the party this fall. The "Standard" is a well-equipped newspaper, with plenty of money and brains at its back, and will doubtless succeed.[35]

If the equipment was first rate, so was Durston's staff. On a trip east to buy equipment, Durston raided his old paper, the *Syracuse Standard,* for talent. Among those lured west were some of paper's best printers and two bright former protégés destined to serve as the pillars of Durston's new publication. Wally Walsworth would establish the *Standard*'s Butte bureau offices and ride herd on the paper's network of state and regional correspondents. Charles Eggleston, who had also been Durston's student at Syracuse University, would serve as Durston's chief deputy, gathering

Determined to build a newspaper that would provide him a voice in the state's Democratic politics, Marcus Daly found the talent he needed in editor John Durston. Durston made the Anaconda Standard *exceptional for a paper its size, but its existence clearly rested on Daly's money, its politics on Daly's whims, and its future on the health of Daly's industrial empire. Two unidentified men pose in front of the newspaper's office, probably in the 1890s.*

World Museum of Mining, Butte

and editing local news and writing the poetry and clever "paragraphs" that leavened Durston's thunderous editorial page. In time, Eggleston would also serve as Marcus Daly's point man in the Montana legislature.[36]

For Durston and the young newspapermen gathered around him, the *Standard* promised to be an exhilarating adventure, a chance to build a dream newspaper with little concern for cost, to wield instant influence over a sprawling new state, to be both pioneers on the vanishing western frontier and vanguards of the industrial age. The price was unshakable loyalty and a certain nimbleness of principle that put personal allegiances ahead of politics.

From the start, Daly's ownership raised suspicions regarding the lofty principles outlined in Durston's inaugural editorial and the depth of its commitment to the Democratic Party. The *Inter Mountain* rarely skipped an opportunity to remind readers of Daly's role or comment on Durston's convenient political conversion, writing in January 1891, for example:

> Within the past six years Mr. Daly has taken an active and unselfish personal interest in the growth and well-being of the town of Anaconda. He has erected a magnificent hotel there at a cost of $200,000, organized a race track association, built a fine race course, with grandstand and stable; brought in an abundant and wholesome water supply; started a newspaper at a cost of $30,000, and in order that it might satisfy both political parties, engaged a republican editor and instructed him to make the paper democratic.[37]

Indeed, at its heart, the *Standard* was Daly's paper. Throughout their careers, *Standard* employees would remain remarkably loyal to Durston and Daly and skillfully play their dual roles as journalists and political operatives for an organization devoted to the mining and refining of copper. Daly expected his journalists to be vital, interesting, provocative, and entertaining, and he gave them ample means to do the job. In turn, they were his boys in a fight, and as Montana entered its first decade as a state, major battles loomed just ahead.

Over the next decade, and throughout the "war of the copper kings," the *Standard*'s circulation would soar, and it would earn its reputation as one of the West's finest newspapers. It would suffer spectacular defeats as well, losses rooted, as were its successes, in the blunt fact of Marcus Daly's patronage.

HELENA'S VICTORY

THE CAPITAL QUESTION SETTLED BEYOND A DOUBT.

MEAGER ELECTION RETURNS

POPULISTS ELECT SIX MEMBERS OF THE LEGISLATURE IN LEWIS AND CLARKE COUNTY AND ONE IN MISSOULA— OTHER COUNTIES.

can. The fight for audito tween Pat Campbell, Pop S. Featherly, Republican, ter a little ahead, but w precincts to hear from. F torney, S. A. Baliet, (Repu Crutcher, (Populist), and I (Democrat), are running apart, with the chances maining precincts will ele Jake Fischer, Democrat, lead over Harry Tilton, R assessor, and it will not b the official count. Paul B lican, leads A. Z. Lombard, surveyor, about 50 votes, maining precincts will pr Lombard.

MISSOULA.

William A. Clark's Butte Miner *celebrated voters' choice of Helena over Anaconda as the location for the state capital by decorating its front page with a row of crowing roosters.*

BUTTE MINER, NOVEMBER 8, 1894

CHAPTER TWO

Slinging Ink

"Copper Editors"
in the Capital
Fight

Fireworks glittered and popped against the mountainsides as thousands of residents lined Last Chance Gulch for the greatest celebration Helena, Montana, had ever known. Despite the crisp late afternoon air of November 12, 1894, hundreds more swamped the depot as a special train from Butte lurched into view. They pressed closer in the steam and smoke as the passenger cars came to a stop, and cheering erupted as the dapper little man with brushed-up beard and mustache disembarked. Breaking from the crowd, several strong men hoisted the wiry William A. Clark to their shoulders and hauled him through the adoring crush to a decorated carriage, whose horses had been unhitched and led away. Placed aboard, Clark settled next to his companion for the noisy, fawning parade up the gulch.[1]

A changing cast of men and boys tussled for the honor of pulling the millionaire's carriage up the crowded central street of what would forever be Montana's capital. Later that evening there were speeches at the auditorium, where thousands savored the wonder of Helena's narrow victory over Anaconda in the election to decide which city would be the state's permanent capital. Eventually, the celebrants moved to the saloons, where only Clark's money—thirty thousand dollars by one reckoning—was any good. Overwhelmed, bartenders quickly abandoned the formality of pouring drinks and simply tossed bottles to the mob. From across the Prickly Pear Valley, farm families gazed at the flickering bonfire atop Mount Helena.[2]

Most chroniclers of the parade would recall the night's fireworks, the cheering crowds, and the joyful blare of the marching band, but only a few would note that the man sitting beside Clark in the giddy procession up the gulch was no politician or captain of commerce, but

39

Helena's champion William A. Clark and Butte Miner *editor John M. Quinn rode in this decorated carriage in the procession celebrating the city's victory in the capital fight on November 12, 1894.*

J. P. BALL & SON, PHOTOGRAPHERS, MONTANA HISTORICAL SOCIETY PHOTOGRAPH ARCHIVES, HELENA

John M. Quinn, the editor of Clark's newspaper, the *Butte Miner*. Over the campaign's final weeks, Quinn's editorials in the *Miner* and Clark's cash had combined to frustrate Marcus Daly's hopes of delivering an overwhelming majority of Butte's votes to Anaconda, which finished 1,900 votes short.

Quinn's chief editorial rival, John Durston, was in no mood to be gracious. In a remarkable display of pique, the *Anaconda Standard,* having poured its ink and heart into the campaign, refused to acknowledge Helena's triumph until the eve of the new capital's wild celebration several days later. Even then, it did so obliquely, sourly accusing Butte's miners of having sold their votes to Clark and Helena:

> It is to be hoped that in the big excursion to Helena will be included all those union men, members of labor organizations, who on election day stood on the street corners and refused to vote until they had been bribed. . . . And then there are the imported thugs, repeaters and

detectives from Spokane whom the Helena Capital Committee sent to Butte for the campaign. They should not neglect to take the train for Helena and march in the big procession.[3]

On the morning after Helena's revelries, the *Standard,* which prided itself on its statewide news report, barely bothered to report the historic celebration, confining its coverage to one petulant paragraph buried deep within the paper: "The ovation which William A. Clark received early in the evening upon his arrival from Butte showed that Helena thanks Clark for sacrificing his own city for Helena. He rode in a richly decorated carriage."[4]

IN 1889, MARCUS DALY'S HOPES for his newspaper were entangled with his hopes to make Anaconda Montana's capital.[5] As Durston worked through the summer to launch the *Standard,* Daly's delegates to the state's constitutional convention forced multiple ballots on the question of whether Helena or Anaconda would serve as the interim capital until voters could permanently decide the question. Helena won the temporary honors, but within months of its debut Durston's newspaper was charging that Helena had won its temporary status through bribery, which the *Standard* found "offensive to the very large majority of the people of Montana and we look forward with confidence to see it uncrowned two years hence."[6]

Meanwhile, Durston worked to improve his newspaper, hiring additional reporters, editors, compositors, and pressmen; overseeing installation of the latest printing equipment; and establishing a statewide network of correspondents under the direction of its Butte bureau. Within months of its launch, the *Standard* expanded its publication schedule from six days a week to seven and distributed it as far as the rails and mail could take it. By the end of its first year, the *Standard* was already the envy of publishers throughout the region. The Butte *Inter Mountain,* in its annual "progress" edition published at the year's close, gushed that its rival had become "the finest fitted newspaper plant in this northwestern country." Of course, the presses and the paper's luxurious appointments—the carpeted editorial offices, a spacious composing room, and a steel-floored pressroom—were all due to Daly's money. "The question of cost seems not

The Anaconda Standard*'s excellence rested on the talents of its employees, includ-ing the members of the production staff (above) photographed in 1893.*

Marcus Daly Historical Society, Anaconda, Montana

to have been taken into consideration when this paper was founded," the *Inter Mountain* wrote.[7]

Because most of the *Standard*'s readers lived in Butte, Durston established the paper's central news bureau there and devoted at least two pages per issue, often more, to news emanating from the city whose fortunes were so linked with Anaconda's own. The *Standard* waded into Butte's raucous politics, centered on the growing rivalry between Clark and Daly factions within the city's dominant Democratic Party. Editorially, Durston faced the delicate challenge of boosting his master's party while providing cover for Daly's on-and-off dalliances with Republicans, who held the key to local and statewide political success throughout the 1890s.[8]

That tension, and Durston's need to establish his credentials as both a Democrat and a fighting editor, no doubt fueled the *Standard*'s special ire toward the *Inter Mountain* and its politically ambitious publisher Lee Mantle. Within two weeks of the *Standard*'s debut, Durston shattered the journalistic peace and attacked Mantle and his paper for insinuating that Daly loyalists were behind the publication of an anonymous and perhaps libelous pamphlet accusing prominent Republicans of making illegal profits on contracts to provision Montana Indian tribes. For the first time, Durston's editorial temper boiled over:

> No decent community was ever afflicted with libelous journalism more cowardly in manner or meaner in methods than was exemplified in the editorial columns of the Butte Inter Mountain. That indecent sheet, owned by Mr. Lee Mantle, dares to assail reputable men in a manner which this newspaper will no longer tolerate and which must stop here and now. . . .
>
> We are not unmindful of the crawling compliments by which the Butte Inter Mountain seeks to conciliate Mr. Daly, in an editorial which follows the slinking epithets with which it assails him. It must disgust any reputable man to be the object of a prostitute's compliments; it must insult any man to be made the object of pleasant mention in a newspaper so base in its purpose, so contemptible in its methods and so outrageous in the deliberation of its false testimony as the Butte Inter Mountain has proved itself to be.[9]

John Durston was especially acrimonious in editorials describing Republican Lee Mantle, pictured here in 1895. Mantle published the Butte Inter Mountain, *which Durston accused of libel.*

J. P. BALL & SON, PHOTOGRAPHERS, MONTANA HISTORICAL SOCIETY

Durston's editorials quickly became required reading in Butte, and the *Standard* soon surpassed the *Butte Miner* in circulation. When demand for copies occasionally outstripped supply, crowds gathered beneath the steps of Clark's Butte bank to hear Durston's latest broadside read aloud.[10]

The paper also attracted attention with its aggressive local reporting, and in the dark, smoky winter of 1890–91 Durston launched what may have been Montana's first journalistic crusade against mining-related pollution, an unlikely subject for a newspaper owned by a copper king. The target was smoke, great yellow-gray layers of it, so thick at times that Butte seemed to swim in it. A *Standard* reporter who climbed the mountains overlooking the city on one cold but windless November day described it as a "silent mysterious sea" that lapped at the flanks of Butte Hill, obscuring most of the city and all but muffling the usual urban, industrial cacophony. Beneath it, Butte residents crept through a fog so dense that, according to one account, miners sometimes lost their way from home to work and conductors carrying lanterns walked ahead of street trolleys to prevent collisions with pedestrians and horse-drawn carriages. Laden with arsenic and sulfur, the hellish smoke killed vegetation for miles around and took a toll on Butte's residents, many of whom wheezed, vomited, or bled from the nose when the smoke was heavy. Others, already

In winter 1890–91, the Anaconda Standard *launched what may have been Montana's first journalistic crusade against mining-related pollution, an unlikely subject for a newspaper owned by a copper king. The target was smoke, great yellow-gray layers of it, so thick at times that Butte seemed to swim in it. Even the end of open roasting did not solve Butte's smoke problem; the city's air pollution would worsen as more smelters processed increasing amounts of ore in and around the city. This scene shows Butte viewed from the southwest, circa 1895.*

Montana Historical Society Photograph Archives, Helena

suffering from the pulmonary ailments common to crowded western mining camps, simply died. In the early 1890s, Butte's death rates from respiratory illness equaled those of New York and Paris and exceeded Chicago's and London's.[11]

For years, smoke had billowed from the smelters and mills below the city, but the practice most frequently blamed for its prevalence was the open-air roasting of thousands of tons of ore over enormous bonfires, a process that greatly reduced the cost of hauling the mineral-rich rock to smelters. Until the development of cleaner smelting practices, Butte was enshrouded for weeks each year, particularly during winter inversions. To many, the smoke was the unavoidable price of industrial progress, and a local physician's struggling campaign to end open-air roasting might have died without the enormous boost it received from the *Standard* in late autumn of 1890.[12]

By contrast, Clark's *Butte Miner* downplayed the issue, meeting the complaints with humorous condescension, specious science, and the overriding economic argument. Clark, himself a partner in many of the ore-roasting ventures, had long defended Butte's smoke. During the constitutional convention debate over a permanent location for Montana's capital, Clark dismissed the concerns about the healthfulness of Butte, arguing that the city's sulfurous smoke actually served as "a partial disinfectant" against the germs of disease and insisting that Butte's ladies owed their beautiful complexions to a touch of arsenic in the air. Smoke was a small price to pay for the economic and health benefits. "Although disagreeable in some respects, it would be a great advantage for other cities . . . to have a little more smoke and business activity and less disease," Clark told his fellow delegates.[13]

With Daly's own smelters miles away in Anaconda, the *Standard* hammered away at the companies practicing open-roasting in Butte. Wally Walsworth, the paper's Butte bureau chief, pursued the story almost daily in the *Standard*'s news columns and wrote mock sermons on the cause for the paper's Sunday feature sections under the guise of "Reverend Jerry Rounder." Durston contributed his editorial blasts, which grew louder in the hellish month of December, when intense smoke covered the city for twenty-eight days. Backed by local doctors, the *Standard* attributed the month's thirty-six deaths to breathing-related illnesses, most of them aggravated by the smoke. "It is the opinion of good physicians that but for the smoke, several, if not most, of the sick with pneumonia would have recovered," the paper reported.[14]

Joined occasionally by the Butte *Inter Mountain,* the *Standard* pressed its "War of Wealth Against Health" for more than a year, encouraging city officials to ban open roasting and suggesting that smelters experiment with new processes or install taller smokestacks such as those that graced Marcus Daly's expanding works in Anaconda. It dismissed the roasters' threats to ignore any such ban or shut down their operations, arguing that Butte's economic vitality, especially its property values, rested as much on the health of its populace as it did on its smelters and mines. "If there is going to be a contest, we ardently hope that it will be a fight to the finish," Durston wrote. "Life, health, comfort and the comparative value of millions of dollars of property, outside of the smelting plants, are involved." When the Parrot Smelter shut down briefly in late January 1891 to protest the city's ban on open-air roasting, the *Standard* reported that the closure was actually due to a glut in the copper market and urged anti-smoke campaigners to push on, even at the risk of closing all of Butte's smelters.[15]

Other smelter owners defied the ban, but in late 1891, when city crews finally smothered the last of Butte's burning ore heaps, the *Standard* declared victory with a magnanimous nod toward chastened smelters who had agreed to build smokestacks and otherwise treat their ore indoors. "Peace on honorable terms is in sight; pure air has made its conquest," Durston wrote. Despite the paper's celebratory language, the end of open roasting did not solve Butte's smoke problem; the city's air pollution would worsen as more smelters processed increasing amounts of ore in and around the city. But the *Standard,* which had invested a year's effort and barrels of ink in the fight, seemed to lose its taste for the crusade as abruptly as it had found it. Perhaps its zeal withered with the realization that the costs of a real solution were more than most smeltermen, including Marcus Daly, were willing to pay. In any case, the *Standard* would take a much different stand a decade later when the poisonous smoke billowing from Anaconda's own smokestacks came under fire.[16]

The paper had more pressing business to consider as 1892 unfolded. It was a presidential election year, with crucial contests for governor and the state's lone congressional seat being decided as well, but Durston made it clear in his New Year's Day editorial that Montana's paramount issue would be the selection of a permanent state capital. He predicted a boisterous scramble among the seven cities that had petitioned for a spot on the ballot: Anaconda, Boulder, Bozeman, Butte, Deer Lodge, Great Falls, and Helena. Any city receiving a majority of votes would win the capital outright; short of that, the top two vote-getters would face off in 1894. Durston braced his readers for the coming campaign, lamenting that the excitement was sure to obscure "a good many important matters."[17]

Marcus Daly provided much of the excitement himself, opening his purse to finance "Anaconda for Capital" clubs in cities across western Montana, while operatives worked behind the scenes, offering other cities Daly's support in landing key state institutions in exchange for their votes on the capital question. The *Standard* and its employees played crucial roles as well. Durston, his deputy Eggleston, and a talented new *Standard* reporter, Arthur Stone, signed Anaconda's nominating certificate, while Durston and Daly took personal charge of the city's booster club. *Standard* correspondents statewide provided regular coverage of the various Anaconda clubs' activities, while Durston's editorials preached Anaconda's virtues and tactfully explained the hopeless prospects of other suitors—especially Butte, whose physical squalor, unhealthy environment, and political unpredictability made it a poor choice, despite its wealth and energy. With the transportation and civic improvements on tap for Anaconda, Durston predicted it would soon be the "peer of Butte and superior of any other city in Montana." In wooing far-flung voters, the *Standard* stepped cautiously in its characterizations of most of Anaconda's competitors, but neither Durston nor Eggleston could resist tossing darts at Helena, which they considered to have stolen Anaconda's rightful appointment as the state's temporary capital.[18]

In arguing the respective merits of their cities, both the *Standard* and Clark's *Butte Miner* warned readers that Helena's supporters would stop at nothing, including bribery, to keep the capital. The *Miner* went so far as to list Helena's going rate at thirty dollars a vote, while Durston accused Helena's capital committee of buying the support of weekly newspapers it declined to name. "We have figures which show at how ridiculously cheap a price some of the newspapers of the state bargained to boom Helena—we will print the figures on call," the paper charged, adding, "still, it is Helena's money, and as long as we get the votes we don't care particularly who gets the squandered money."[19]

The *Standard*'s concern for purity of the press drew hoots from the *Helena Journal*, which couldn't help but point to the source of the complaint. "A newspaper maintained as a plaything and tool of a millionaire, without reference to its right to exist as a business proposition, is in mighty small business when it attacks the weekly press of Montana," the *Journal* wrote.[20]

The epithets flew. Eggleston, who at Daly's order was also running for the state senate, scored literary points with parodies and tinny doggerel appealing to Butte's working-class prejudices by portraying Helena as Montana's swinish and elitist "Hogopolis," the domain of bankers, politicians, and hangers-on who profited unfairly from workers' sweat. In response, Helena's supporters scored the campaign's most imaginative coup by somehow managing to affix Helena-for-capital stickers to hundreds of mailed copies of the *Standard*. Still, on Election Day, Durston confidently predicted that Butte would lean Anaconda's way, regardless of the pressure applied by Helena's ruling clique of developers, bankers, and railroad promoters.[21]

No race on the ballot, not even the presidential rematch between Grover Cleveland and Benjamin Harrison, received as many votes as the capital question. Despite its small population, Anaconda finished second with 10,183 votes to Helena's 13,983, with both cities qualifying for a runoff two years later. Although Butte had been in the running too, Anaconda captured almost a third of the vote in Silver Bow County and more than half of the votes in Missoula and Deer Lodge counties as well, a testament to Anaconda's strong campaign. Daly and Durston took the loss hard but were determined to win in 1894.[22]

First, however, the *Standard* had to negotiate Montana's increasingly fractured political landscape, torn apart by the nationwide depression of 1893, the emergence of a rapidly growing Populist Party, and the growing rivalry between Democratic factions loyal to Clark and Daly. Butte served as the principal battleground as the Clark-Daly feud began to color nearly every political controversy, no matter how mundane. Clark, still blaming

Daly for his failure to become Montana's territorial delegate in 1888, bested Daly in a municipal fight for control of Butte's water supply. In retribution, Daly Democrats allied themselves with Lee Mantle and local Republicans in the 1892 elections, and as a result Butte sent a hopelessly deadlocked delegation to the 1893 legislative assembly, whose chief duty was to elect a U.S. senator by a clear majority. In a contest tainted by bribery on all sides, legislators ultimately rejected Clark's Senate candidacy. Throughout the voting, Daly Democrats led by a freshly elected Senator Eggleston remained solidly opposed to Clark. On the final day's balloting, a grim but confident Clark, sitting in the capitol with his acceptance speech tucked in his coat, endured the humiliation of falling several votes short.[23]

The *Butte Miner* screamed foul, the Butte *Inter Mountain* cheered, and the *Anaconda Standard* absolutely crowed at Clark's defeat. "THEY FELL DOWN," the *Standard*'s main headline declared. "Money Couldn't Buy Enough Votes," read the second deck. "It was a death struggle between corruption and honesty for the honor of the state," wrote the *Standard*'s reporter on the scene. "And from the terrible crisis, Montana emerged triumphant. . . . With all the forces of corruption doing their utmost for weeks, the legislature, in a joint assembly today declared by a vote of thirty-seven to thirty-two that the majority of the legislature is honest and that a seat in the U.S. Senate cannot be bought." With the lawmakers unable to muster a majority for any candidate by the session's end, Montana's Republican governor John E. Rickards appointed Lee Mantle to the U.S. Senate, whose Democratic majority promptly refused to seat him. The seat remained vacant for two years. As Montana sank into the depression that followed the collapse of national money and metal markets in 1893, its politics remained mired in the rivalries of copper kings. Yet the political fights of 1892 and 1893 were little more than skirmishes compared with the battles yet to come.[24]

As the stakes in Montana's political contests grew, Durston continued to strengthen his paper, dipping into Daly's seemingly depression-proof pockets for the latest in newspaper technology and riding herd on an expanding staff of editors and reporters who filled the *Standard*'s columns with the region's brightest and broadest assortment of news and commentary. In 1894, the *Standard*, along with the Portland's *Oregonian* and Spokane's *Spokesman-Review,* installed some of the

Northwest's first Mergenthaler Linotypes, the ingenious typesetting machines that spelled the most revolutionary advance in printing since moveable type. No longer would compositors stand hunched over vast cases of type, painstakingly selecting individual letters and arranging them into sentences and columns on hand-held type sticks. A Linotype operator could set entire columns of type in a fraction of the time it had once taken a skilled compositor to handset a few sentences. The machine brought wholesale advances to the newspaper industry, permitting editors to stretch deadlines and publish more news and multiple editions. Other western papers had installed typesetting machines before the *Standard*—the *Helena Journal* purchased the region's first in 1891—but by the mid-1890s the *Standard* could honestly boast that no New York daily had more modern equipment.[25]

Greater production capacity meant more pages, and Durston jumped at the opportunity to add feature services, fattening the *Standard*'s already impressive Sunday edition with serial fiction and articles on the latest national and international trends in fashion and the arts. Circulation gains led to increased advertising revenues, and by the autumn of 1894 Durston boasted that he oversaw "the most important newspaper property between San Francisco and Chicago, along the northern routes." Financially, he reported, the paper was finally turning an operational profit, no small accomplishment given the nation's slumping economy. "It is prosperous," he wrote. "It pays and it has never failed to pay, month by month, since the autumn of 1893."[26]

Among the stories *Standard* editors followed closely as Montana slipped deeper into depression was the growing tension between labor and industry. Bloody strikes and repression in Idaho's Coeur d'Alene mining district, in Tennessee's coal mines, and the steelmaking town of Homestead, Pennsylvania, caught the attention of Butte and Anaconda's unionized workers and their employers alike. Surprisingly, the *Standard*'s sympathies ran largely with those of workers, a reflection of the public's mounting suspicion of "trusts," the powerful business combines that suddenly seemed to dominate the American economy. The newspaper's attitude also reflected Daly's qualified support of unions, an attitude largely dependant on their compliance but also rooted in his early experience as a miner, his solidarity with the pro-labor Irish nationalist community, and his need for labor's support in the capital fight and other political contests. In the aftermath of labor violence in northern Idaho, Durston took pains to explain the aims and motives of unionized miners, the majority of whom "are conservative citizens who have homes and families and who would not resort to a measure likely to result in a riot unless forced by tyrannical measures to do so." "The fact that a man is a union man is not sufficient means for his discharge," he wrote.[27]

The *Standard*'s stance on unions and its ability to serve its readers faced a serious test in the summer of 1894 when Eugene Debs's American Railway Union struck at the Pullman Palace Car Company near Chicago. Railroad workers nationwide walked off the job in sympathy, including Montana employees of the Northern Pacific, the Union Pacific, and Montana Union railroads. Though the strike all but stopped the state's travel and commerce, Montana rail workers found support among those farmers, ranchers, and miners who saw railroads as predatory monopolies. Despite the economic hardship it caused, and no doubt in sympathy with Daly's frustration over freight rates paid by his mining and logging operations, the *Standard* supported the strike, which had also hampered the paper's statewide distribution. In a mindboggling feat of organization and human locomotion, *Standard* officials recruited relay teams of workmen who pumped handcars or pedaled smaller carts known as "velocipedes" to deliver the *Standard* as far west as Missoula and eastward, over the Continental Divide, to Livingston. By the end of the four-week strike, the *Standard*'s "Handcar Limited," working in conjunction with a specially arranged pony express, managed to deliver the paper to news-hungry tourists—including a contingent of stockbrokers—stranded for weeks at Mammoth Hot Springs in remote Yellowstone National Park. The service was slow but effective, and *Standard* editors could hardly believe they had pulled it off.[28]

NOTHING IN THE *Standard*'s brief experience, however, could compare with the final stages of the capital fight, which kicked into high gear that fall. The contest—part circus, part modern mass-marketing campaign—showered the state in pamphlets, trinkets, booze, and, above

In summer 1894, railroad workers nationwide walked off the job, nearly stopping travel and commerce across Montana and hampering the Anaconda Standard's *statewide distribution. To deliver the paper, teams of workmen pumped handcars as far west as Missoula and east, over the Continental Divide, to Livingston.*

ANACONDA STANDARD, SEPTEMBER 5, 1899

all, cash. By its end, Daly and Clark had spent an estimated fifty dollars a vote—the equivalent of nearly one thousand dollars in twentieth-century currency. Few Montanans escaped the debate, much less the debauchery that would set a tone for Montana politics in the following decade. From their pulpits, pastors preached sermons on the relative virtues of Helena versus Anaconda, while families argued the cities' merits over dinner. Miners and smeltermen were reminded of their sources of income, while opportunistic castabouts shifted their allegiance regularly based on the availability or quality of Helena hooch or Anaconda cigars. At issue was more than the erection of a capitol building on a hill. In terms of jobs, investment opportunities, and the ultimate disbursement of state institutions, the stakes were immense. Prestige, and the political and economic influence that follows it, were on the line as well, and Daly and Clark determined to spend whatever it took to win.[29]

In the debate itself, Clark held much of the rhetorical high ground. Through the *Butte Miner,* he had loyally backed Butte in 1892, but Helena's business and political leaders made powerful allies, and Helena's cause, colored by self-interest and tinged with ethnic and social prejudice, nevertheless drew vital support from Montanans whose objections to setting the capital in Daly's company town outweighed their suspicions of Clark.

Both sides expected a roaring fight, and both viewed newspapers as essential weapons in the contest. Months before the voting, Clark and Daly competed for the support of papers statewide, especially in areas where each considered the other vulnerable. Daly expected strong support in areas where he ran mining, smelting, or logging operations— namely Silver Bow, Deer Lodge, Flathead, and Ravalli counties—but he lacked a voice in Great Falls, home to hundreds of smeltermen employed by the Boston and Montana Company, whose executive, Albert S. Bigelow, declared for Helena. Daly promptly purchased the town's Democratic daily, the *Great Falls Tribune,* and imported a special editor to argue that it was Daly, not Bigelow, who had maintained union wages during the Panic of 1893. Meanwhile, the competing *Great Falls Leader* carried Helena's banner, predicting—wrongly as it turned out—that the temporary capital would receive 75 percent of Cascade County's vote. "It is not the howlers for money who do all the voting," the *Leader* argued. Other newspapers supporting Anaconda included the weekly *Bozeman Chronicle,* which argued that the food markets of Butte and Anaconda meant more to Gallatin County's industrious farmers than Helena's. Publisher A. K. Yerkes, who maintained close ties to Daly throughout the 1890s, also fumed at Helena's supposed superiority and indifference to outlying communities.[30]

Helena's papers would serve their own interests, but Clark over-looked no constituency in the fight, not even Montana's tiny African-American population. With Clark's financial backing, the *Colored Citizen* debuted in Helena on September 3, 1894, with editor J. P. Ball Jr. proclaiming his paper's devotion to "the social, moral and industrial interests" of the state's black population. Under such headlines as "The Anaconda Company Employs Only White Men and Dagoes," Ball urged his readers to resist Anaconda's blandishments. "He [Daly] will hobnob and coddle us now, for he says to himself, 'I'll give the niggers a little taffy and lots of promises now in order to get their votes, and then they can go to Helena.'" Clark's own motives, however, were no less mercenary; with thanks to those who had supported the paper, the *Colored Citizen* folded the day before the election. Helena's other papers drew on Clark's financial support as well, especially the daily *Helena Independent,* which described Anaconda's supporters as "morally rotten, oblivious to their own interests, lost to all sense of decency."[31]

Missoula, less than one hundred miles downstream from Anaconda, proved more difficult to gauge. Although Daly had promised Missoula the state university in the logrolling that preceded the 1892 capital fight, Helena found an important ally in Republican timber baron and merchant Andrew B. Hammond, whose testy business dealings with Daly made him suspicious of Anaconda's power. Like Clark and Daly, Hammond owned a daily newspaper, the *Missoulian,* purchased two years earlier from an ailing political rival. Fearful that Missoula would shrink in commercial importance between a more powerful Anaconda and Hamilton, Daly's home base in Ravalli County, Hammond loaned the *Missoulian* to Clark's agents, who imported Helena publisher George Boos to run the capital campaign. Though the *Anaconda Standard* declared the Montana's "West Side Men Solid" for Anaconda, and though Daly's logging enterprises assured him of friends in the city, the *Missoulian* whittled away at the margins. "What has Anaconda ever done for Missoula anyway?" the paper asked. "If Christ came to Anaconda, he would be compelled to eat, sleep, drink and pray with Marcus Daly." Fear of corporate power also proved a compelling argument in eastern Montana, where the young *Billings Gazette* argued against setting the capitol dome "amid the smelter chimneys of Anaconda."[32]

As always, the crucial battleground was Butte, where Clark's *Butte Miner* squared off against both the *Anaconda Standard* and the *Inter Mountain*. In a continuation of the alliance formed with Daly two years earlier, the *Inter Mountain*, "with charity for all and malice towards none," argued that Butte's interests would be better served by nearby Anaconda, a city whose well-being would always be linked to Butte's. Hotter words flew between the *Standard*'s Durston and *Miner* editor John Quinn, whose editorials echoed through the statewide grapevine of newspaper exchanges. There were reasonable issues to discuss—each site's relative merits in terms of transportation, communications, accommodations, services, and prospects for future growth—but the newspaper wars quickly degenerated into a contest of personalities, distorted history, social and ethnic stereotypes, and accusations of corruption.[33]

As it had two years before, the *Standard* portrayed Helena as the "Hog"—selfish, superior, and disdainful of labor and the welfare of Montanans outside their city. Durston, who usually scribbled his editorials over a composing stone next to one of the *Standard*'s new Linotypes, kept its operator busy translating the editor's uphill scrawl into legible indignation at Helena's numerous slanders. As the campaign headed toward its final weeks, Durston portrayed Helena as a maniac, "made mad by the wreck of her prosperous pretense" and "muttering the imprecations of an imbecile against all who oppose her."[34]

The *Standard*'s most entertaining assaults, however, came from Eggleston, whose sarcastic allusions to Helena's corruption and supposed social graces delighted readers on both sides of the question. For weeks, Eggleston peppered the *Standard*'s editorial pages with biting single-sentence shots, many of which depicted Helena in the clutches of what the *Standard* viewed as Montana's true corporate villain: the Northern Pacific Railroad, with its vast land holdings and exorbitant freight rates. The *Standard* chided the railroad for offering free passes to Helena's promoters who traveled the state giving speeches, and Eggleston tried to discount their effect. "The Northern Pacific Railroad owns 47,000,000 acres of land, but it doesn't own quite that many people," he wrote.[35]

In response to Helena's portrayals of Marcus Daly as Montana's "would-be king," Eggleston concocted the campaign's most memorable piece of propaganda, a slick, Swiftian pamphlet titled *Helena's Social*

Supremacy, in which he feigned agreement with Helena's cause and its supposed belief that "no man in Butte or Anaconda may kiss his wife, spank his child, throw a stone at his cat, cut a watermelon, string a clothes line, or bark his shins without first obtaining permission from the Anaconda company in writing."[36] Eggleston also mocked Helena's supposed pretentiousness, sophistication, and distaste for Montana's working class. In Helena's eye, Eggleston wrote, Anaconda was a "rude, rough smelter town, rooted in vileness and vulgarity . . ."

> a town nine-tenths of whose population toil the year around in manual labor; big, strong, coarse workingmen, who could not tell a german [*sic*] from a wheelbarrow; with so erroneous a conception of the proprieties that, so far from exhibiting a sense of mortification and chagrin, they seem to take a sort of conscious pride in going to and from their work in soiled overalls and with huge dinner buckets; laborers, mechanics, artisans, bricklayers, copper dippers, whose average wages reach only $105 a month; living in small cottages with ridiculous wives and children; spending their spare time in cultivating their little, sawed-off gardens, going to low picnics, and organizing and perfecting labor unions, which, as Helena is informed and believes, are the greatest curse to the modern world.[37]

In the campaign's final weeks, the *Standard* devoted its entire editorial page to the capital contest, while its news staff reported the enthusiasm of the state's various Anaconda-for-capital clubs and accommodated favorable exchanges from pro-Anaconda newspapers. It was a prodigious effort and Durston made the most of Daly's money, but Clark's newspapers, with Quinn's *Butte Miner* in the lead, made the best of Helena's chief argument that state government belonged beyond the shadow of a single corporation. Quinn, whose future would include a successful career in New York politics, drove the message home relentlessly, offsetting the *Standard*'s advantages in manpower and money with sheer energy. *Standard* newsmen would forever hold Quinn in the special regard reserved for honorable foes, but during the fight he was an enemy to be reckoned with, feverishly filling his paper with warnings to Butte's workingmen that Marcus Daly's tolerance of unionism would surely evaporate if the company gained political power. Quinn asked his working-class readers to imagine magnates such as Carnegie and Pullman asking voters to relocate the capitals of Pennsylvania and

Illinois in their company towns. Any advocate of such a move "would be considered a subsidized representative of the company or a subject fit for the lunatic asylum," he wrote.[38]

Appealing directly to Daly's miners, Quinn urged those who had supported Anaconda for fear of company retribution to redeem themselves on Election Day. He ridiculed the ubiquitous "cabbage leaf Havanas" and "kill-me-quick whiskey" that Anaconda operatives doled out across the state, and like Durston, he warned miners against the morally corrosive effect of trading their votes for cash. He wrote:

> It is the kind of money that is dangerous to touch. It would burn holes in your pockets and conscience; put blushes of shame upon your cheek, the weight of regret in your heart and the chains of guilt upon your intellect. It is money with which to buy your manhood and self-respect, and give the devil a mortgage on your soul. It is being used to buy a yoke to put upon your children and shackles with which to enslave the men and women of the future.[39]

Quinn also warned Butte's businessmen and real-estate developers that Anaconda's future prominence, should it become the capital, would come at their expense. "What Butte merchant who signed his name to the roll of the Anaconda capital club could remove to Anaconda and do business without becoming a toady to the Anaconda corporation?" he asked.[40]

The rhetorical clash of the copper kings' newspapers echoed in small-town weeklies across the state and were noted by journalists beyond Montana's borders. At its meanest, the journalistic brawl also reflected the prevailing racial and ethnic prejudices, with Helena's dark warnings against the "foreigners" drawn to Anaconda's cause and the *Standard*'s repeated references to the gambling dens and opium joints in Helena's Chinatown. The *Standard* proudly reported that "the people of Anaconda have succeeded in reducing the total number of pigtails in this city to less than a dozen all told." Newspapers served as obvious targets themselves, though the criticism sometimes ran deeper than the usual digs about the veracity or sanity of a particular editor or the correctness of a paper's political views. The *Standard* drew blood when it accused both the *Helena Herald* and *Helena Independent* of cramming their pages with innocuous pre-printed features called "boilerplate," insinuating that both papers were either too cheap or too lazy to produce

their own news. When the *Independent* complained that "morally rotten" Anaconda spies had infiltrated Helena, the *Standard* sarcastically
suggested that Helena residents "shoot them on the spot." "Kill every
last man of them!" the paper wrote. "Get the Independent to fire deadly
boiler plate at them! That should kill anything. What claim on life has
any man who won't vote for Helena for the capital?"[41]

Journalists outside Montana could only shake their heads. "In
Montana a disgraceful fight is going on," wrote C. C. Goodwin, the
respected editor of the *Salt Lake Tribune*. "The interests of the country are subordinate to the question of whether the capital of the state
should be moved to Anaconda or not. The real question is whether the
Anaconda Company has the state in its pocket or not."[42]

In the days before the vote, Durston's confidence soared. On October
27, five thousand Anaconda supporters marched through Butte in a
torchlight parade, their numbers representing a mere fraction of the
vote Durston anticipated from Silver Bow County. On Election Day,
the *Standard*'s front-page headline predicted the result: "HELENA IS
COMPLETEY ROUTED, She Can't Come Within Four Thousand
Votes of Winning the Capital." Even so, Durston urged his readers to
mark their ballots carefully and to avoid the thugs Helena was sure to
send over to disrupt the voting.[43]

The vote was close. Of the fifty-two thousand ballots marked statewide, Helena won by less than two thousand. While the *Standard*
pouted in silence, Quinn decorated the *Butte Miner*'s front page with
woodcuts of crowing roosters. The stacked headlines atop its editorial page shouted the news: "Three Cheers! The people are supreme!
The Citizenship of Montana is vindicated! Tyranny has reached its
Waterloo!" Within days, Quinn would share Clark's celebratory ride
up Last Chance Gulch.[44]

For all the money, ink, and energy expended, the newspapers' influence over the outcome remains difficult to gauge. Most Montanans voted
for the nearest city, just as they had two years earlier. But there were exceptions. Great Falls bucked the trend and voted for Anaconda, a reflection perhaps of the *Great Falls Tribune*'s influence among smelter workers, though other inducements may have carried greater weight. Though
it failed to carry Silver Bow, Deer Lodge, and Missoula counties—areas

with strong ties to Anaconda—Helena siphoned more than six thousand votes from those regions—three times its margin of victory—a testament perhaps to the vigorous campaigns waged by Clark's *Butte Miner* and the *Missoulian,* if not also to Clark's liberal application of cash.[45]

The campaign clearly solidified the role of newspapers as essential weapons in Montana's political warfare. Both Clark and Daly learned how to wield and influence the press, and those lessons would be applied with increasing vigor as the copper wars raged on. But the corruption of Montana's press did not go unnoticed, even in the thick of the fight. William Greene Eggleston, the pro-Helena editor of the Marysville *Mountaineer,* lamented the fact that nearly all of Anaconda's newspaper support appeared to have been purchased. "This fact shows the potency of money, the venality of the press and the true sentiments of the people of Montana regarding the capital question," he wrote.[46]

Beyond the corruption, the clash also fed a growing tenacious strain of anti-corporate suspicion that would run through Montana's politics and journalism for generations. Though few seemed to notice, it also demonstrated the limited credibility of the corporate press.

MARCUS DALY'S CITY WOULD NEVER become the political and cultural nexus of Montana, but his newspaper would come close. Despite its failure in the capital fight, the *Standard* never lost Daly's support, though he all but abandoned the city for his Bitterroot Valley farm, with its exquisite mansion and stable of thoroughbred horses. With Daly's encouragement, Durston continued to improve the paper, expanding its reach and ensuring that it kept pace with metropolitan standards for content, appearance, and advertising—standards no other Montana newspaper could match. At the height of the capital fight, Helena's daily *Independent* had kept four employees setting type at a furious pace; the *Standard,* by contrast, employed thirteen. Over the next two years, regular front-page stories kept *Standard* readers abreast of each new technological marvel, including the anticipated arrival of a new "fast press" capable of printing larger sections in record time. Commercially, the *Standard* boasted the best advertising agency between Omaha and

San Francisco, and the paper profited from a growing national mass market, epitomized by the ubiquitous patent-medicine ads that promised relief of every affliction from gout to "the vapors."[47]

The paper's circulation continued to climb, a reflection of its ever-expanding news and feature coverage, still grounded in the state's best regional report supplied by talented correspondents in Butte, Missoula, and Great Falls. In exchange for advertising, the Great Northern Railway supplied the *Standard* with free rail passes, allowing its editors and reporters to roam far and wide for news. Its Sunday feature sections—packed with serialized fiction and articles on sports, society, the arts, and fashion coverage—were unrivaled, as was its coverage of mining news, including the latest prices from the nation's metal markets and detailed reports on legal disputes that bedeviled the industry. To leaven the paper's news-heavy coverage, *Standard* reporters were encouraged to write in a lively and elaborately detailed style, and reporters such as Arthur Stone—"a good man at anything from a funeral to a cat fight"—found time among his daily reporting chores to contribute lengthy, colorful features on pioneer life and Indian lore for the fat Sunday paper. Though politics cut increasingly into his production, Senator Eggleston continued to delight *Standard* readers—or at least its Anglo-Saxon ones—with what passed for nineteenth-century American comedy, chiefly the scrambled-English misfortunes of Montana's hapless Indians, African-Americans, Chinese, and assorted recent immigrants. Yet it was with grave formality that the *Standard* reported the eighteen-month prison sentence meted out to a "colored" waiter for visiting a white prostitute whose name he would not divulge.[48]

As befitted the state's leading newspaper, national issues dominated the *Standard*'s front page and editorial thoughts, and in 1896 no issue meant more to Marcus Daly and his paper than the cause of "free silver." The federal government's 1893 decision to stop buying silver had staggered the western mining industry, which was still turning profits from silver despite the eclipsing importance of copper and other metals. As Republicans and Democrats struggled to cope with the financial panic and depression that followed, Populists grabbed power in the West by promising to restore silver as the basis for the nation's money. Montana's mining barons lent their cash and their newspapers to the national crusade for the "free coinage of silver," an effort culminating in the 1896 presidential campaign of William Jennings Bryan of Nebraska. Durston threw the *Standard* into the "free silver" fight with energy and bombast. From the paper's masthead, he urged Republicans and Democrats to unite in the cause, "subordinating all political preferences and all partisan bias to the one issue that engrosses public attention in Montana."[49]

The Clark-Daly feud still simmered in the background. In local elections that year, the *Butte Miner* assailed the *Standard*'s choice for Silver Bow County district judge as "an agent for the Anaconda," while the *Standard* accused Clark's man of membership in the anti-Catholic, anti-Irish American Protective Association. Even so, the copper kings and "Silver Republicans" such as Lee Mantle set aside their differences for "free silver" and Bryan. Daly poured an estimated three hundred thousand dollars into Bryan's campaign against William McKinley— an immense sum for the time—while Clark reportedly chipped in fifty thousand. Another sixty thousand dollars came from Anaconda's employees, though their donations were not always voluntary. "We have adopted a rule at the mines that each man contribute a day's pay to the silver cause," Daly wrote the manager of his smelter that spring.[50]

Though Bryan lost, Montana's Populist-Democrat alliance swept the statewide elections, and Bryan repaid his Montana supporters the following August with a grand visit that prompted wild celebrations all along his route, especially in Butte, where residents lined the rooftops, hung from windows, and packed the streets so densely that Bryan's carriage could barely move. Bryan, reveling in the adulation, paid personal calls on both Clark and Daly, and the *Standard* covered every step. Eggleston captured the hoopla's spirit with a five-stanza poem, "When Bryan Came to Butte," which covered almost all of a page on August 13. When demands for reprints finally overwhelmed the newspaper's supply and patience, the paper republished the poem as a pamphlet, selling thousands of copies over the next fifteen years.[51]

Montana's politics enjoyed a brief and spotty truce around the mutual cause of "free silver," but Clark and Daly were headed for a more spectacular clash that would taint the state's politics and journalism for decades to come.

OFFENDED MONTANA PRONOUNCES SENTENCE UPON THE MAN-BUYER.

No one knows exactly how many newspapers were bought, rented, or subsidized in the spree of bribery and newspaper buying that accompanied William A. Clark's push for the U.S. Senate in 1899–1900. A chief player in the ensuing editorial fights, the Anaconda Standard *lampooned Clark's efforts to buy the election.*

ANACONDA STANDARD, NOVEMBER 4, 1900

CHAPTER THREE

The Longest Purse

CORRUPTION AND
COERCION OF
THE FREE PRESS

FOR OLIVER WARDEN AND WILLIAM Bole, the choice was no choice at all. Five years had passed since the transplanted New Englanders had purchased the *Great Falls Tribune* for two hundred dollars cash and a loan secured with the books in Bole's personal library. Marcus Daly's asking price had been six thousand dollars, but given the circumstances, he could afford to be generous. As Daly's local proxy in the capital fight, the *Great Falls Tribune* had proved useful, but Anaconda's defeat rendered Daly's ownership moot, and the money, after all, was meaningless. It was enough to place the paper with two loyal Democrats, practical men who understood copper's importance to their growing smelter town on the shores of the Missouri River.[1]

Such benevolence deserved loyalty, but now, in the spring of 1900 and after less than six years at the *Tribune*'s helm, Warden and Bole faced a new proposition from a different copper king. Once again, as Bole told his readers, the offer had been impossible to refuse. "From any purely business standpoint, and in the nature of things, a struggle for existences must ensure with the odds in

William A. Clark, seen here in an 1898 portrait, purchased the Great Falls Tribune *and the* Helena Herald *to promote his campaign.*

WILHELM, PHOTOGRAPHER, MONTANA HISTORICAL
SOCIETY PHOTOGRAPH ARCHIVES, HELENA

Forced to sell the Great Falls Tribune, *Oliver S. Warden (left) and William Bole (right) nonetheless secretly understood that they would be allowed to repurchase the paper once Clark was through with it.*

WARDEN: SCHOOL OF JOURNALISM, UNIVERSITY OF MONTANA, MISSOULA
BOLE: HEYN KEELEY PHOTOGRAPHER, MONTANA HISTORICAL SOCIETY
PHOTOGRAPH ARCHIVES, HELENA

favor of the longest purse in the end," Bole wrote. "Confronted with these facts, the owners of the Tribune chose the first alternative and named a price that was accepted yesterday."[2]

Bole carefully omitted the new owner's name, but readers would figure it out as soon as the paper began trumpeting William A. Clark's latest campaign for the U.S. Senate. Nor had Bole mentioned the $45,000 sale price or the secret understanding that the partners would be allowed to repurchase the paper once Clark was through with it. Under the terms of the deal, Warden would remain as the *Tribune's* business manager, overseeing significant improvements to its plant. Bole, however, gathered his family and his books and headed for Bozeman as editor of the *Chronicle,* a Democratic weekly performing its own tango with copper kings. Only a year before, the pro-Daly paper had been sold, and its new owners had accepted $2,500 to throw their support to Clark. Daly promptly bought the paper back for $11,000 and placed it in Bole's capable hands.[3]

Years later, when the smoke of Montana's copper wars finally cleared, Warden and Bole repurchased the *Great Falls Tribune* and steered it on a cautious course of editorial independence. Yet shadows of the paper's brief captivity would linger. In 1959, as the *Tribune* celebrated its Diamond Jubilee, Warden's heirs still felt compelled tell their readers that "at no period since 1905 has the Tribune been subsidized by anyone, any organization or industrial company. It has been privately owned for 54 years."[4]

NO ONE KNOWS EXACTLY how many newspapers were bought, rented, or subsidized in the last, furious innings of Montana's copper wars. Newspapers were not required to publish meaningful statements of ownership as a condition for using the U.S. mails until 1912, and even then, many publishers ignored the toothless law, content to keep their readers guessing. Partisan editors regularly published lists of the opposition's "hireling" press, but such accounts were often exaggerated to include independent papers with honest objections to one faction or another. Still, the claims held enough truth to give some observers a sense that battling industrialists controlled nearly every newspaper in the state. The spree of bribery and newspaper buying that accompanied William A. Clark's push for the Senate made most charges of journalistic prostitution seem plausible, and in such a cynical climate editors who professed independence only drove the prices higher. Inquiries into Montana's notorious scandals of 1899–1900 would count newspapermen among the fixers as well as the fixed.[5]

Clark's long-frustrated political ambition flared anew in the summer of 1898 when prominent Democrats, including former governor Sam Hauser and John S. M. Neill, publisher of the pro-Clark *Helena Independent*, convinced the supposedly reluctant millionaire that only he could save the state from the "one-man rule" of Marcus Daly, who had placed his corporate resources and his press behind the successful "fusion" of Populists and so-called "Silver Republicans" two years earlier. In the 1898 campaign for all-important legislative seats, Clark's *Butte Miner* and Neill's *Helena Independent* focused their editorial fire on Daly's *Anaconda Standard* and a sprinkling of pro-Daly, "free silver" weeklies like the *Butte Times,* a "Silver Republican" sheet so enthusiastic in its flaying of Clark, the "monied shylock," that its editor was served a federal warrant for publishing indecent reading material. Among the *Butte Times*'s claims was that smoke from Clark's sulfurous "stink pile"— his Butte Reductions Works— had caused at least sixty deaths, "more innocent lives than all the corporations in Butte City."[6]

John S. M. Neill, publisher of the Helena Independent, *lined up with William A. Clark against Democrat Marcus Daly, who had thrown his support behind a successful "fusion" with Populists and so-called "Silver Republicans" two years earlier.*

C. P. CONNOLLY, "FIGHT OF THE COPPER KINGS," *McCLURE'S MAGAZINE*, MAY 1907, P. 639

Vanity and a hunger to avenge past humiliations surely lay at the heart of Clark's reasons for seeking office, but his supporters' motives were complex. For many, Clark, the self-made, independent businessman, offered a compelling antidote to corporate power. Meanwhile, conservative and loyal Democrats, resentful of Daly's willingness to dally with Republicans and Populists, saw Clark as the only true Democrat standing. In an era of heavy immigration, Clark's nativist, anti-Irish prejudices no doubt appealed to still others. The mixture of motives, wrapped in Clark's money, would prove unstoppable.

Yet for all of their power, neither Clark nor Daly could produce a clear Democratic majority in the legislative session of 1899, effectively placing the election of Montana's U.S. senator in the hands of fifteen Republicans. The *Anaconda Standard*, which counted three of its own staffers among the assembly's members, immediately raised the specter of wholesale bribery, declaring that Clark's cash had already lined the pockets of legislators the paper declined to name. Without bribes, Durston wrote, Clark could not win six votes, and as the session opened the *Standard's* lead headline—"Air Thick with Boodle"—set the theme. Daly forces also reprinted a *New York Herald* article recounting the alleged purchase of U.S. Senate seats by millionaires in other states and placed a copy on each lawmaker's desk. An investigation would later expose the *Herald's* anonymous correspondent as Charles D. Greenfield, editor and publisher of the *Montana Stockman and Farmer,* a Helena-based agricultural paper experiencing temporary cash-flow problems. According to testimony, Daly's operatives paid Greenfield five hundred dollars to write the story.[7]

The anticipated scandal erupted dramatically when Republican senator Fred Whiteside, a Kalispell-based building contractor, rose on the first day of senatorial voting and, with an envelope of cash in hand, declared that Clark's agents had offered him thirty thousand dollars for his vote and those of three fellow Republicans. "Clark Bribers Caught At It Red Handed," the *Standard* boomed amid the uproar. The *Great Falls Tribune,* still siding with Daly these days, vouched for Whiteside's character and credentials, while Helena's dailies, the Democratic *Independent* and Republican *Herald,* painted him as a Daly tool and noted his business ties to the Anaconda Company. Clark's *Butte Miner* set a shriller tone; its next-morning headlines declared Whiteside's accusations "A DAMNABLE CONSPIRACY," an elaborate "Daly Trick" designed to "stampede" legislators from Clark.[8]

As the factions wrestled for control of the official investigations that followed, they also fought the battle for public opinion, concentrating on small dailies and weeklies, whose combined circulations easily outnumbered those of the noisy dailies of Helena and Butte. With no objective source of news—an independent Associated Press bureau was still two decades away—statewide coverage of Montana's most infamous political scandal rested largely on partisan editorial exchanges and dispatches filed by Helena's daily reporters, who fed their work to the wires. To make his case to the state's independent, if hardly neutral, press—and to provide hometown cover for legislators supporting his election—Clark launched a media blitz. Small-town editors were brought to Helena

When the election fell to state legislators to decide, Kalispell state senator Fred Whiteside (left) denounced Clark's agents for offering him thirty thousand dollars for his vote and those of three fellow Republicans.

C. P. Connolly, "Fight of the Copper Kings," *McClure's Magazine*, May 1907, p. 629

for informational talks, while operatives scurried across the state to buy what editorial favors they could. The arrangements varied. The short-lived *Montana Bulletin*, a pro-Clark weekly in Butte, owed its existence to the three-thousand-dollar bond Clark posted for its establishment. John Neill, the *Helena Independent* publisher and a go-between in the Clark bribery scandal, later admitted that Clark held a twenty-five-thousand-dollar mortgage on his paper. Some newspapers that resisted both argument and subsidies were purchased outright. At more amenable papers, Clark's operatives paid the salaries of special editors assigned to do nothing but boost their patron's defense.[9]

Clark's efforts clearly paid off. The result was an overwhelming denunciation of Whiteside from every corner of the state, and the chorus included editors who suspected that neither Daly nor Clark was immune to bribery. The *Butte Miner* could call Whiteside a "masculine strumpet" and "well-paid harlot," but to most Montana editors he was simply a "sneak," "spy," or "informer." In testimony later before a U.S. Senate committee, both Clark and Daly supporters agreed that fifty-two of the Montana's fifty-six daily and weekly newspapers had criticized Whiteside's methods or motives. Among them, the *Libby News* offered perhaps the most cynical observation, questioning whether any Montana politician could have resisted "thirty-thousand plucks in his strong right arm" without a promise of more cash from the other side. "This does violence to all legislative precedent and tradition in this state," the *News* wrote, "and it is likely to create an entirely unwarranted bull market in the price of statesmen."[10]

With much of the state's press providing cover, Clark's minions pressed on, winning legislative support by means that may have included envelopes stuffed with cash but more often involved sweetheart business deals, lopsided land swaps, or a touch of financial blackmail. In the case of Representative Edward H. Cooney, a Cascade County Democrat and the *Anaconda Standard*'s Great Falls correspondent, the lure was professional as well as financial. For his vote, Clark's agents offered $2,500 a year for five years and a job as the *Butte Miner*'s Great Falls circulation agent. Cooney rejected the bribe, and an additional $10,000 sweetener, and loyally held out for Daly's candidate, the prominent banker and rancher William G. Conrad. But it was a sinking cause. Clark partisans derailed both legislative and grand jury probes into Whiteside's charges, then had the senator expelled on specious charges of improprieties in Whiteside's own election. On the final ballot, Clark rolled to victory and "vindication" with votes to spare. That night Helena celebrated yet another Clark victory with sparkling rockets, bonfires, bands, speeches, and free champagne. In Butte, from the basement of the *Miner*, Clark's partisans commandeered an old cannon, reputedly a veteran of Bunker Hill, and fired a salute. For historian Forrest L. Foor, the editorial barrage laid down by Clark's newspapers had been decisive. "In its accomplishment," he wrote, "the power and influence of the press had been second only to money."[11]

Outmaneuvered in the statehouse and in the press and furious with Clark's success in dismissing Whiteside's allegations as a frame-up, Daly fought back. Through the summer and fall of 1899, Daly's forces laid the groundwork to have Clark expelled from the U.S. Senate. While his

LEFT SHAPELESS IN THE BOODLE BARREL'S PATHWAY.

William A. Clark's purchase of the U.S. Senate seat in the 1899 election prompted biting political cartoons (above and facing page) from the Anaconda Standard, *depicting Daly's rival as Montana's "man-buyer" and "boodler."*

ANACONDA STANDARD, NOVEMBER 4, 1900

lawyers collected evidence of bribery, Daly renewed his own courtship of Montana's press. As Daly's personal organ, the *Anaconda Standard* was easily the state's best and most widely distributed paper, but its credibility suffered by association. Durston leveled a withering editorial fire against Clark, supplementing the paper's news coverage and editorials with biting political cartoons depicting Daly's rival as Montana's "man-buyer" and "chief boodler." But Clark's faction had demonstrated the value of a broader network of newspaper support, and within months of Clark's victory Daly started shopping for smaller newspapers across

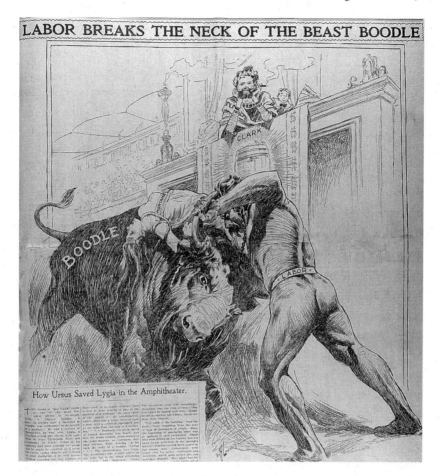

LABOR BREAKS THE NECK OF THE BEAST BOODLE

How Ursus Saved Lygia in the Amphitheater.

Another of the Anaconda Standard's *political cartoons showed Clark forcing organized labor to save the state from his graft.*

ANACONDA STANDARD, OCTOBER 28, 1900

the state. He bought the *Bozeman Chronicle* for eleven thousand dollars, and he either purchased or subsidized the *Carbon County Democrat* in Red Lodge, Virginia City's *Madisonian,* Hamilton's *Ravalli County Democrat,* and Helena's *Montana Stockman and Farmer.* Daly also acquired the Republican *Livingston Enterprise,* placing it in the hands of local supporters but holding its stock as collateral for the "loan." As attorney general C. B. Nolan, a Daly loyalist, would later testify, a paper's politics mattered little. Nor was Daly interested in absolute control of a paper's editorial policy—so long as it attacked Clark. Daly's aim, Nolan said, was merely "to get some papers that would advocate decency and speak disparagingly of the use of money illegally in politics."[12]

For some editors, shifting loyalties ran both ways. Walter Aitken, editor of Big Timber's tiny *Weekly Express,* initially supported Clark's election as a means of teaching Marcus Daly "once and for all that he is not the state of Montana." But Aitken's tune softened nine months later when he reported that Clark had tried to buy an anonymous publisher's weekly—perhaps Aitken's own—for about half of what it was supposedly worth. Clark's offer had been blunt: the publisher could either sell out or face the competition of a new weekly to be published by a Republican state senator whose vote had been critical to Clark's 1899 election. At least Daly paid "good, honest prices" for his papers, Aitken wrote.[13]

Daly's efforts to cultivate support among Montana's independent editors extended to his lavish treatment that fall of newspapermen attending the Montana State Press Association's 1899 convention in Anaconda, a celebration of professional camaraderie that broke all association records for subsidized hospitality. Daly himself joined the festivities, along with a bipartisan group of Montana luminaries, all of whom would play key roles in the fight to unseat Clark. Attending along with Republican senator Lee Mantle, whose Butte *Inter Mountain* was again siding with Daly, were Populist governor Robert B. Smith, Democratic congressman A. J. Campbell, Montana Supreme Court chief justice Theodore Brantly, Democratic attorney general C. B. Nolan, former Republican senator Wilbur Fisk Sanders, and Silver Bow County attorney Christopher P. Connolly, a future muckraker who was helping Daly gather evidence for the eventual Senate investigation of Clark's election. On the excuse of clearing Whiteside's name, Daly's lawyers had filed libel suits against both the *Butte Miner* and *Helena Independent,* but the effort's real aim was to depose Clark and his lieutenants. Daly's lawyers also instigated successful disbarment proceedings against Clark's chief agent, Helena attorney John Wellcome, widely suspected as the principal bagman in Clark's bribery schemes.[14]

As Montana editors rubbed shoulders with players in the state's consuming drama, Durston dazzled them with demonstrations of the latest journalistic arts. On this, the *Anaconda Standard*'s tenth anniversary, the paper refrained from partisan swipes at Clark and his newspapers,

New technology that reduced the time it took to transfer a drawing from an artist's pen to the press sparked a golden age of political cartooning. It enabled the Anaconda Standard*'s famous artists (above) to ridicule Clark in scathing cartoons.*

MARCUS DALY HISTORICAL SOCIETY, ANACONDA, MONTANA

but in unveiling its spectacular anniversary issue, it served notice that it had acquired new and potent propaganda weapons for the coming fight: cartoons and illustrations, made possible by a new engraving process that drastically reduced the time it took to transfer a drawing from an artist's pen to the press. The techniques, pioneered in the East and used to sensational effect by New York's "yellow press," sparked a golden age of political cartooning, and in that, as in most aspects of the craft, the *Standard* was amazingly up-to-date. Columns of text and small headlines suddenly gave way to vivid representations of the news and caricatures of newsworthy people, images that lingered in readers' minds long after the accompanying words had faded. The work of the *Standard's* new art department, under the direction of J. W. Trowbridge, freshly recruited from the *New York Herald,* held conventioneers in awe.[15]

The editors left Anaconda in fine spirits. They enjoyed Daly's town, marveled at his newspaper, and toasted his hospitality, but it was little more than an intermission in the fight that now shifted from Montana to Washington, D.C. On December 7, 1899, three days after Clark took the oath of office, the Senate's Committee on Privileges and Elections began its probe into his election. Over the next three and a half months, a stream of Montanans on both sides of the Clark-Daly feud embarked for Washington, where their confessions of bribery, fraud, and perjury shocked the nation. It was hardly the first time a senator stood accused of buying his office, but the flagrancy and frequency of Montana's corruption, combined with the casual frankness of those who confessed it, gave the state a singular reputation for political depravity. Editors from Chicago to Boston bemoaned Montana's degeneracy, arguing that it had stained not only the state, but the integrity of the U.S Senate as well.[16]

Montana newspapers followed the story closely. By January, both Durston and Charles Eggleston, Durston's chief lieutenant and a state senator, were in Washington covering the hearings for the *Standard,* and the *Butte Miner* hired a special correspondent. When the committee eventually recommended Clark's expulsion, more than fifty Montana newspapers condemned the action. Many cared less about Clark's bribery than the shame Daly's investigation had brought upon the state, arguing lamely that Montana politics were no more corrupt than politics elsewhere. Others noted that the testimony ultimately favored neither Clark nor Daly and that Daly's forces had also resorted to bribery and coercion in soliciting evidence against Clark. The *Billings Gazette* presumably spoke for many independent editors when it suggested that Daly "and his crowd are just as corrupt as Clark and we will never have any decent politics in Montana until both are shorn of power." A few, like the *Townsend Star,* acknowledged the wrongdoing of Daly's faction but backed the committee's recommendation nonetheless. Clark's crimes, the *Star* wrote, should not be overlooked just because "a thief is caught by a gang of thieves."[17]

Tearfully maintaining his innocence, Clark resigned rather than face a Senate vote on expulsion, but that same day Clark's operatives lured Governor Robert Smith out of state and had his lieutenant governor A. E. Spriggs—a Clark man—appoint Clark to the seat he had vacated just hours earlier. Smith, racing back to Montana, promptly squelched the bizarre and desperate scheme. Humiliated and bitter, Clark returned to Montana determined to elect an overwhelming legislative majority that would send him back to Washington without the antics that had marred the 1899 session.[18]

Dramatic changes in Daly's economic empire worked in Clark's favor. Nearly lost in the noise over the Senate fight was the sale of the Anaconda Company's mining, smelting, and logging operations to a Wall Street consortium controlled by a clutch of Standard Oil Company executives. With Daly still aboard as president, Anaconda's new owners sought nothing less than to control the American copper industry, beginning with the rich Montana properties Daly had developed with his California backers. With the *New York Times* portraying the sale as the "the biggest financial deal of the age," Anaconda fell under the corporate umbrella of a powerful new holding company, the Amalgamated Copper Company. Daly would oversee Amalgamated's mining and smelter operations, but Henry H. Rogers, Standard Oil's chief executive since the retirement of John D. Rockefeller, held the financial power. Although the elder Rockefeller took no part in the venture, his brother William did, and so did other noted Wall Street players with close ties to one of the country's most powerful—and hated—trusts.[19]

For years Anaconda's critics had portrayed Daly's company as a corporate "octopus," but here was the real thing, a copper trust, modeled, as many of the great holding companies of the era were, on Rockefeller's monolithic Standard Oil. By 1900, two years before the publication of Ida B. Tarbell's muckraking exposé in *McClure's*, Standard Oil had already earned a reputation for ruthlessness among an array of mysterious and powerful combines consolidating their grip over industries ranging from steel and farm machinery to ice, beef, and kerosene. In the West, only railroads drew more suspicion from fearful consumers and producers who found themselves increasingly subject to an economy organized along national rather than local or regional lines and controlled by New York and Boston banks.

Montana was the first step in Amalgamated's plan to consolidate the American copper industry. After Daly's holdings, Amalgamated's objectives included those major mining properties owned by a group of Boston financiers, William A. Clark, and a brilliant and nervy young mining engineer named F. Augustus Heinze, who rose to prominence with a keen understanding of both mining and mining law and a flair for politics and publicity. Since 1898, Heinze's lawsuits contesting Anaconda's mining claims and those of other mining companies had clogged Butte's courts, where judges sympathetic to Heinze held sway.[20]

More than merely annoying, the suits posed real threats to Butte's principal mining company. By January of 1900, Marcus Daly had had enough of Heinze's antics and ordered Durston to have the *Standard*'s Butte bureau chief, Wally Walsworth, and William Scallon, Amalgamated's attorney, launch a full-scale journalistic investigation of the man he regarded as "a blackmailer, a thief and a most dangerous and harmfull [sic] man to the business and property interests of Butte." They were instructed to detail Heinze's attempts to steal ore from adjacent claims

Marcus Daly regarded F. Augustus Heinze, the third power broker in the copper king battle, as "a blackmailer, a thief and a most dangerous and harmfull [sic] man to the business and property interests of Butte" because he contested mining claims and formed alliances contrary to Daly interests.

C. P. CONNOLLY, "FIGHT OF THE COPPER KINGS," *MCCLURE'S MAGAZINE*, MAY 1907, P. 318

while using Butte courts to shut down competitors. "[S]how the possibilities that might follow his operations, based in every case entirely on blackmail, attempted intimidation and robbery, and not in a single instance on legitimate business reasons," Daly ordered. "Make the denunciation of his methods as definite and scathing as possible."[21]

The *Standard* complied, but Amalgamated suffered most as the company fell under attack from what the paper described as the "Fusion" campaign of Clark and Heinze, whose interests dovetailed neatly. Both needed Butte's votes: Clark to smash Daly's bloc in the legislature and thereby win election to the U.S. Senate, and Heinze to gain control of Silver Bow County's local government, especially its courts. In the Standard Oil Company's reputation for ruthlessness, Clark and Heinze found the issue they needed to woo workers personally loyal to Daly, whose status in Butte was by now undermined by long absences and the debilitating effects of diabetes. As Amalgamated lumbered to get its bearings for the 1900 elections, Heinze and Clark attacked through their respective newspapers. Firing alongside Clark's *Butte Miner* was Heinze's crude weekly, the Butte *Reveille,* or as critics would come to call it, "the Reviler." Edited by Patrick A. O'Farrell, an itinerant Irish journalist with a genius for invective, Butte's most scurrilous sheet was

WHAT FUSION MEANS IN BUTTE.

INTERMOUNTAIN NOVEMBER 5 1904

Clark's and Heinze's interests dovetailed in the "Fusion" campaign. Both needed Butte's votes: Clark to smash Daly's bloc in the legislature and win the U.S. Senate election and Heinze to gain control of Silver Bow County's local government, especially its courts.

Butte *Inter Mountain*, November 4, 1904

established in 1898 as Heinze's personal organ and devoted much of its meager space to coverage of its benefactor's business, social, and political activities, though it rarely acknowledged Heinze's patronage.[22]

Meanwhile, Clark expanded his statewide newspaper holdings, purchasing two important dailies: Warden and Bole's *Great Falls Tribune,* a Democratic paper, and the *Helena Herald,* the Fisk brothers' venerable Republican paper, which now stood alongside publisher John Neill's Democratic *Helena Independent,* which Clark continued to bankroll. Clark's agents immediately stocked all three papers with editors and paid them top wages for the duration of the campaign.[23]

Beyond putting his paper at Clark's service, Neill also scouted other newspaper publishers for their willingness to take on Clark as a business partner, at least through the election. Typical of the approach was Neill's suggestion that Clark's eldest son and principal operative, Charles, invest in T. J. Johns's short-lived campaign weekly, the *Lewistown Eagle.* "At present he is publishing the best weekly paper in the state, and I believe it would be in the interest of your father and yourself to assist him by taking stock in his paper," Neill wrote the younger Clark. "If Johns is with you, you can always rely on his county being with you."[24]

In his effort to woo former Marysville *Mountaineer* editor William Eggleston to edit the *Helena Independent,* Neill offered $60-a-week salary and agreed to pay a $3,500 bonus, princely pay for the era. Sensing Clark's urgency, Eggleston, then editor of North Carolina's weekly *Ashland Citizen* (and no relation to the *Standard*'s Charles Eggleston), promptly raised his price to $5,000, adding "and what is that to Clark?"[25]

Meanwhile, other newspapermen confirmed Eggleston's gauge on the depths of Clark's purse. Amalgamated's loyalists estimated that by August Clark had control or the sympathies of all but four of the state's Democratic papers. Beyond what it cost him to run the *Butte Miner* and support the *Helena Independent,* Clark reportedly spent three hundred thousand dollars on newspapers for his campaign. The estimate included one hundred thousand dollars to buy the *Helena Herald,* one hundred thousand dollars for the *Great Falls Tribune,* fifty thousand dollars for the *Libby News* and other weekly newspapers, twenty-five thousand dollars in newspaper advertising, and another twenty-five thousand dollars to distribute free copies of the *Butte Miner* throughout the state. Such reports may have been exaggerated, but the price would have been rich at half the amount.[26]

Yet the sum Clark spent on his newspapers paled compared with the $1.5 million Henry H. Rogers reportedly authorized Amalgamated to spend on its newspaper campaign. In addition to the papers whose support Daly had purchased earlier, the company now added several more, focusing mostly on Republican papers that had supported Clark in 1899.[27]

In Butte, Amalgamated "persuaded" Lee Mantle's *Inter Mountain* to abandon its vacillating independence by threatening to establish a competing Republican daily. To prove its seriousness, Amalgamated shipped five Mergenthaler Linotypes to Butte and reportedly hired a staff of reporters and editorial writers. The *Inter Mountain's* ambivalent tone quickly changed, though within a year Amalgamated would absorb the paper completely. The *Billings Gazette,* which had wished both Daly and Clark out of Montana politics a few months earlier, received an infusion of Amalgamated cash, enough to make it suddenly comparable in size and appearance to Helena's dailies. The *Great Falls Leader* obtained a similar boost in return for seeing things Amalgamated's way in 1900, and the *Missoulian* was rumored to have received company support as well.[28]

Smaller papers received Amalgamated money too, but the company's most ambitious project was the establishment of the *Montana Daily Record,* a Republican organ for U.S Senator Thomas "Oily Tom" Carter, a crucial Daly ally, in Helena. The paper aimed to compete with Clark's daily *Helena Herald* and Neill's *Helena Independent,* but because Clark's dailies already controlled Helena's morning and afternoon Associated Press franchises, the *Montana Daily Record* was forced to lease a special news wire at enormous expense. When the *Daily Record* tried to cut costs by simply clipping Associated Press stories from the *Anaconda Standard,* Clark's newsmen exposed the scheme and tried to have the *Standard* stripped of its wire service.[29]

The enormous sums of money thrown into Montana's newspaper war of 1900 made mercenaries of journalists across the state. Most took their cues from Clark and Daly's flagship dailies. Amalgamated editors echoed the editorial rants of the *Standard's* Durston, who railed

against Clark and Heinze, their damnable "fusion," and their transparent inducements to Montana's laborers. The pair's inspired decision to grant their mine and smelter workers an eight-hour workday
sent Durston into flights of vitriol, but so did their liquid generosity
in Butte working-class bars and their sponsorship of vaudeville acts,
parades, and prizefights—anything, it seemed, to draw a crowd. Only
Clark's money kept him in the race, Durston snapped. "[H]e surrounds
himself with an aggregation of hitters who for his money, it can be said
in all sobriety, have made of Mr. Clark a freak and of his political ambitions, a howling travesty."[30]

Durston warned workers not to fall for the temporary allure of
higher pay and shorter days, for the practice would only drive mining
enterprises out of Montana and encourage layoffs and closures. At its
heart, he added, the eight-hour day was merely another form of bribery. Durston's fury leached into the *Standard*'s news columns, and as
the campaign heated up the paper abandoned all pretense of objectivity. The opening of a Butte headquarters for the Clark-Heinze "Fusion
party" elicited a blistering front-page story in the next morning's
Standard, under the headline "A PLAIN COMMON SENSE TALK/FOR
WORKINGMEN WHO THINK. According to the report, the offices
were convenient to Clark's bank, but Clark's business offices nearby
were where the political payments were made. "That is the place to go
if you want to sell yourself," the story concluded.[31]

The newly cowed Butte *Inter Mountain* chipped in as well, charging
that the Clark-Heinze partnership "means destruction to enterprise and
industry in Montana," while back at the *Standard,* Charles Eggleston contributed his trademark "paragraphs"—short, one-sentence darts, many
of them aimed at Clark's purported hold over Montana's press. As Clark
vacationed in Europe just before the fall campaign's final push, Eggleston
urged the copper king to add a few European newspapers to his stable. "It
would be an exceedingly novel and pleasing experience to Mr. Clark to find
himself eulogized by a few newspapers other than the various Montana
publications he owns outright or controls by mortgage," he wrote."[32]

Arguably, the *Standard*'s most potent weapons, however, were its
merciless political cartoons and extravagant illustrations—some of which
covered most of the paper's front page. Standard artists repeatedly por-

THE BOSS BOODLER IS HANDY AT IT.

Among Marcus Daly's most potent weapons were the Anaconda Standard's *merciless illustrations that repeatedly portrayed Clark as an elfish, bristle-faced dandy, blithely dispensing cash from a ubiquitous boodle bag or barrel.*

ANACONDA STANDARD, OCTOBER 28, 1900

trayed Clark as an elfish, bristle-faced dandy blithely dispensing cash from a ubiquitous "boodle bag" toted by a black servant. On other occasions, Clark was depicted trying to operate a fantastical mechanical bogeyman labeled "Standard Oil Bogie" or, dressed in his "vaudeville nightshirt," tossing cash from the balcony of his hotel to crowds in the street. One fanciful *Standard* cartoon showing Clark tossing bundles of cash over the

Now and Then "Kerosene" Catches a Lonesome Sucker.

The Anaconda Standard *also showed Clark creating a bogey of Standard Oil, offering to destroy the "Great Alamagoozumm—Amalgamated Copper Company—the Standard Oil–owned company trying to take over Montana's copper industry.*

Anaconda Standard, November 3, 1900

transoms of legislators' hotel rooms would fix the image as fact in the minds of Montanans for generations.[33]

The *Standard*'s artists—Loomis, Thorndyke, Johnstone, and others known to readers only by the last-name signatures on their cartoons—were the best money could hire, but surprisingly, the *Butte Miner* and Butte *Reveille* may have carried the campaign's most effective cartoons. What they lacked in artistry, they recouped in emotional impact by playing to working-class fears of a state owned and controlled by Standard Oil—the "Kerosene" gang—and its "reptile press." In the campaign for blue-collar votes, one *Butte Miner* cartoon set the theme clearly by depicting a cow labeled "Montana industries" being fed by Montana workmen and milked by eastern capitalists.[34]

Avoiding attacks on Daly, whose personal popularity remained high among the Irish workmen he favored, the Clark-Heinze press found better targets in Standard Oil's John D. Rockefeller and Henry H. Rogers, whom they variously portrayed as predators of small businesses and corruptors of politicians like Senator Thomas Carter. Under Amalgamated, they warned, Montana would become a collection of company towns, its workers forced to spend their scant wages, paid in company script, at the thieving company stores. When they emphasized

A Butte Miner *cartoon depicting a "Montana industries" cow being fed by Montana workmen and milked by eastern capitalists established a theme that appeared often in political cartoons of the era.*

MICHAEL P. MALONE, *THE BATTLE FOR BUTTE: MINING AND POLITICS ON THE NORTHERN FRONTIER, 1864-1906* (HELENA, MONT, 1981), P. 154

the point by printing phony Amalgamated currency, the *Standard* shot back with articles depicting the supposedly sordid conditions in Clark's own company town, the copper-mining camp of Jerome, Arizona.

The Clark-Heinze combination proved unbeatable in the November voting. Besides their edge in newspaper circulation, the duo had captured most of the state Democratic Party machinery along with the support of minority Populist and labor organizations. Leaving Daly with the backing of a handful of so-called "Independent Democrats" and lukewarm Republicans, they rolled to victory, with Clark easily winning his legislative majority and Heinze gaining control over Silver Bow County's local government, most critically its judges.

As they had in the capital contest and again in 1899, Clark's newspapers crowed. The *Helena Independent* basked in its earlier predictions that voters would provide a "rebuke to the liars and trust hirelings who went into the campaign with the battle cry: 'Clark is a boodler and briber.'" In the dwindling days before the election, the *Standard's* awkward attempt to denounce the eight-hour day and still pose as labor's friend offered the Clark-Heinze press a fat target. So desperate was the situation on the election's eve that an ailing Marcus Daly had made a rare front-page appearance in his own newspaper, imploring voters to consider the consequences in an election that would decide "whether justice shall be honestly administered and rights given the protection provided for in the law, whether employment is to be secure." But such arguments only underscored the *Helena Independent's* repeated assertion that Amalgamated's workers were merely pawns. "From its first issue the Standard has never been in favor of any state measure for the benefit of the people," one of the paper's employees wrote. "With the faithfulness of a spaniel it has worked the workers for the benefit of the granters."[35]

Durston's understanding of the forces arrayed against Amalgamated left him unusually philosophical in defeat; for once he failed to summon his famous indignation. So thorough was the Clark-Heinze victory—"if there is anything they wanted and didn't get, the Standard does not know what it is"—that Durston could hardly attribute it to bribery or ballot stuffing alone. The voters, he conceded, knew what they wanted. "In this instance they got it plenty; their will, expressed through the agency of ballot, was so emphatic that is stands, with no doubt about it."[36]

As if to mirror his superior's mood, Eggleston's staccato "paragraphs," which punctuated the campaign like daily drumbeats, stopped cold on Election Day. They returned a few days later, bedraggled and hung-over in spirit. "For sale, cheap," he wrote, "A prophet's mantle. Inquire at this office." Other pro-Daly papers were not so chastened. Hamilton's *Ravalli County Democrat* could barely choke back its spleen. "If the majority of the people of any given state are horse-thieves," it wrote, "it would seem that they should have the right to select, as their representative, the leading horse thief among them."[37]

Daly's supporters suffered their hardest shock in the week after the election. On November 12, Marcus Daly died in a room at New York's Netherlands Hotel, a victim of the diabetes-related kidney and heart ailments that had frustrated doctors on both sides of the Atlantic. As he drifted in and out of consciousness in the final days of his life, family and friends withheld the news of Clark's victory, but his aides felt that somehow he knew. Thousands attended Daly's New York funeral service and memorial events in Montana. On November 13, Durston devoted the *Standard's* entire front page to news of Daly's death. Two hundred column-inches of news copy surrounded a three-column photograph of Daly. Column rules were inverted in mourning. Durston's personal farewell to his mentor took up nearly a third of the editorial page.[38]

For all its fury, the election of 1900 proved to be little more than an expensive, noisy aside to Amalgamated's push to consolidate its power over Montana's economy and it politics. Yet for Montana's press, it proved the primacy of money over journalistic principle in a land where both were often scarce. It had shown how easily the state's independent, if hardly neutral, press could be manipulated to serve powerful economic interests.

Yet support did not always imply editorial control. In fairness, some editors backed Clark on principle and sometimes at great professional risk. Miles Romney, the iconoclastic editor of Hamilton's *Western News,* was a

The November 13, 1900, edition of the Anaconda Standard *announced the death of its patron Marcus Daly. Two hundred column-inches of news copy surrounded a three-column photograph on the paper's front page.*

ANACONDA STANDARD, NOVEMBER 13, 1900

staunch Democrat and populist who hated trusts and detested Daly's convenient flings with Republicans. Despite Clark's millions and penchant for bribery, Romney and other pro-Clark editors viewed their champion's fight as a reflection of their own struggles as independent Montana businessmen in the face of corporate power. In Romney's case, the argument was no abstraction. Throughout the campaign, his paper faced overwhelming competition for subscribers and advertisers from two pro-Daly papers, one Republican, the other Democratic, both crammed with Amalgamated advertising and further nurtured by the profitable commercial printing business supplied by the company's local lumber mill.[39]

Yet with characteristic bravado, Romney welcomed the fight. "The more the merrier," he wrote. "The Western News can stand the pace if the other fellows can." Nor was Romney much bothered by Amalgamated's "long, drawn, doleful howl" about Clark's bribery. "Stamped upon the forehead of every one of the company stump speakers and across the pages of its chattel newspapers in vivid outline and plainly discernable is the legend 'you, yourself are bought,'" he wrote. "Yet these are the fellows that are so strong for 'purity in politics.' Wouldn't that jar you?"[40]

In a similar vein, the *Forsyth Times* equated "Dalyism and despotism" and predicted early and accurately "that the opinion held by the U.S. Senate will not change the state of Senator Clark before the people of this state." Other pro-Clark editors plainly feared an Amalgamated takeover of the state's Republican Party. The editor of the tiny *Garnet Mining News* warned its readers that Republicans, with Amalgamated's "slimy support," would easily win "unless the real democrats get together" and use their brains as well as their money. Still others may have shared the *Butte Miner*'s appeals to Americanism and its barely veiled suspicions concerning the Irish-Catholic loyalties of much of Amalgamated's workforce and of its "white czar," Marcus Daly, "a man who has never considered American citizenship a boon worth applying for." The charge was patently false, but the *Miner* persisted in portraying the election as a "fight of the American people against an inhuman and unholy thing conceived in sin and sharpened into iniquity." Montanans "who are American people—and by American people is meant those who have some idea of what American citizenship means—must stand by Clark," it added.[41]

However, John Neill's predicament at the *Helena Independent* illustrated the difficulty inherent in maintaining editorial independence while accepting a copper king's cash. A prominent civic booster and developer as well as a newspaperman, Neill had been among the handful of prominent Montanans who had begged Clark to enter the Senate race in 1898, arguing that keeping the state's political machinery out of Daly's hands "is not only a duty you owe to the people, but a duty you owe to your family." Neill's sentiments were rooted in his opposition to the growing influence of out-of-state corporations, but the twenty-five-thousand-dollar note Clark held on the *Independent* was never far from his mind. Nor was Clark's enormous wealth. In courting an editor to oversee the *Independent*'s 1900 campaign coverage, Neill carefully spelled out his relationship with the flinty millionaire. "You know my feelings in regard to Clark," he wrote. "While he is very selfish and very close, still he represents an idea in this state. He is the only man who has sufficient wealth to combat the tyranny of Daly and his crowd, hence I am for him and had always been."[42]

Neill proved loyal throughout Clark's drive for the Senate, but such fealty was not without cost. Close to the principal players in the Whiteside bribery scandal, he had been summoned to testify in the Senate investigation. Though Neill was never accused of bribery, his testimony and that of others clearly illustrated his role as one of Clark's chief lieutenants and a go-between in the Clark camp's various intrigues. In fact, Neill himself suggested Clark's bizarre, almost comical, plot to lure Governor Smith from the state so Clark could be reappointed to the Senate.[43] In return for such devotion, he felt entitled to the copper king's financial support, and his correspondence with Clark throughout 1899 and 1900 reveals his anxiety over the costs of maintaining a daily newspaper in such an intense campaign. On one occasion, Neill complained to Clark that his criticism of a pro-Daly member of the State Capitol Commission had cost him seven thousand dollars in state printing contracts, and he later reminded Clark that he had turned down twenty thousand dollars to throw the *Independent*'s support to Daly during the 1899 legislative session. "My efforts in a political way have been entirely for others," he wrote. "For a man without means to devote all his energies and his life to produce a democratic paper for the use of the party and political associates, it is a dog's task. I may be here a number of years, but in all reason it must be evident to you, that I never can make a considerable sum out of a newspaper in this state."[44]

Neill's complaints drew a cool response from his benefactor, who reminded him of the political realities in a city that owed Clark its status. "I recon [sic] that in making up your mind to decline such a magnificent offer, you probably considered the sentiment of the community in which you are doing business, at least to some extent," Clark wrote. The gentle tug-of-war over money and editorial control would persist, and so would Clark's measured support. When Daly's attorney's sued the *Helena Independent* for its alleged libel of Fred Whiteside, Clark generously paid for the paper's successful legal defense.[45]

Occasionally, Neill did bite the hand that fed his newspaper. Shortly after Clark's disputed election to the Senate in 1899, lawmakers debated a bill aimed at preventing minority stockholders from blocking corporate mergers and consolidations. It was legislation crucial to Amalgamated's formation, but its supporters also included the Northern Pacific Railroad, whose policies and influence Neill had long opposed. Demonstrating just how little he really thought of the anticorporate fight his supporters had waged on his behalf, Clark urged Neill to endorse the bill as a means of currying favor with the railroad. "I expect the friendship of the Northern Pacific railroad company," Clark wrote. "[I]f the friendship is carried up to Washington, as it may be, I think it unwise for any of my friends to take any position against the interest of that company at this time."[46] When Neill balked, Clark spelled it out more explicitly:

> It's a matter of great concern to me. The First National Bank of New York, Northern Pacific railroad company, Senator Carter, and the Standard Oil people are all working hard to get this bill through, and I am sure it will be very much to my interest if we can succeed. . . .
>
> The influence these people exert at Washington, if a contest should be made there, is a matter of very great importance. I certainly expect you . . . [would] not do anything against the bill after we worked so hard for victory.[47]

Neill stood his ground. For years, his newspaper had been a prominent critic of Montana railroads, which it blamed for exorbitant freight rates and poor service. He was an early proponent of a state commission to regulate railroads, which also exerted influence through their ownership of vast tracts of what had once been public lands. As Neill and others saw it, the corporation bill not only violated the state's constitution, but forced injured or abused Montanans to seek damages against such corporations in federal rather than state courts, where the odds against recovery were longer and where judges were often the handpicked protégés of powerful interests. Despite such arguments, the legislature approved the bill by an overwhelming margin.[48]

The tug-of-war between Clark and Neill over the corporation bill demonstrated not only the boundaries of their relationship, but also the extent to which each needed the other. Clark must have been furious at Neill's refusal to back the merger legislation, but the copper king and his Helena newspaperman faced battles still to come. Tensions, however, would continue to build. Shortly after Clark's purchase of the *Great Falls Tribune*, Neill complained bitterly that his paper was languishing while Clark poured cash into improving the *Tribune*, which was suddenly beginning to land state advertising and printing contracts that had once gone to the *Helena Independent*.[49]

The relationship strained to the breaking point after Clark's election to the Senate and Daly's death. Ever the practical man of business, Clark quickly abandoned the alliance with Heinze and sided increasingly with Amalgamated, whose conservatism and business interests essentially reflected his own. Neill, meanwhile, continued to press Clark for money. In a letter pleading for a new twenty-five-thousand-dollar loan, Neill claimed he had recently turned down Amalgamated's generous offer of seventy-five thousand dollars for a 49 percent share of the *Helena Independent*'s stock. "I could not accept it at that time as we had not completely broken with the Heinze crowd and I did not feel that I could take it."[50]

Whatever the case, Neill suddenly found himself in the cold, railing against corporate power while his paper continued to hemorrhage money in its competition with Amalgamated's Helena daily, the *Montana Daily Record*, which by Neill's own calculations was losing more than one hundred thousand dollars a year. Neill boasted to friends that the *Helena Independent* was thriving, but in truth it was sinking in debt. In

August 1902, when Clark offered the publisher more than one hundred fifty-two thousand dollars and commercial property worth seven thousand more for his paper, Neill was in no position to refuse.[51]

Even so, Neill had no intention of surrendering to Amalgamated—at least not yet. "I am not going to quit fighting as you suggest, but expect to start in Helena shortly the finest semi-weekly paper ever published in the Northwest," he wrote an acquaintance shortly after the *Independent*'s sale. With the talented William Eggleston as editor, Neill launched his new Helena paper, the *Press*, in the fall of 1902, and for the next two years he came close to fulfilling his promise to publish the region's finest weekly. Independent and smart in both content and design, the *Press* exempted no one from its editorial gaze, not even Clark, whom it considered a sellout in the crusade to spare Montana's government and economy from Amalgamated's ever-tightening grip and to advance an impressive array of Progressive reforms.[52]

Both struggles would dominate Montana's politics—and divide its press—in the years leading to World War I.

WHAT THE DOMINATION OF HEINZE IN BUTTE
WOULD MEAN.

After Marcus Daly's death and William A. Clark's election to the U.S. Senate, Clark quickly abandoned his alliance with F. Augustus Heinze and sided increasingly with Amalgamated. Clark's newspapers followed suit: the Butte Miner *portrayed Heinze and his United Copper Company as bad for workers and families.*

BUTTE MINER, OCTOBER 23, 1902

CHAPTER FOUR

Reform and the "Reptile Press"

CORPORATE POWER AND A PROGRESSIVE BACKLASH

The celebration began to the sound of steam whistles. In Great Falls, pedestrians initially mistook the noise for an alarm, but their worry turned to joy as its true significance spread through town; the city's smelter, shut down for three dreary weeks on the eve of winter in 1903, was back in business. The news chattered across the *Great Falls Tribune*'s wires at 3:00 PM, and by 4:00 the city was giddy. "There was nothing but smiling faces on the streets, in the stores, in street cars and every conceivable place where people congregate," the *Tribune* reported. It seemed as if "this whole town had taken a foolish powder." The whistles meant the return of regular paychecks for nearly 1,500 smelter workers and the thousands more whose jobs depended indirectly on Amalgamated's Boston and Montana works at Black Eagle. The Montana Central Railroad immediately recalled dozens of laid-off workers, and the news brought instant hope to scores of out-of-work shop clerks and servant girls, many of whom had spent recent days knocking on doors in the city's better residential neighborhoods, begging for odd jobs. For those who had already fled town rather than face the winter without work, the whistles came too late. For those who remained, the November sun had finally broken through.[1]

The news came like a pardon to a condemned man, the *Tribune* reported, and the party took to the streets and taverns, where celebrants "banked three deep around the bars" and fortified their joy with "large three finger drinks." Later that night, several hundred smeltermen, led by the Black Eagle band, marched, or rather lurched, through the city's streets, stopping frequently to offer their heartfelt serenades. "Their

In 1903, to protest Heinze-influenced unfavorable court decisions, Amalgamated shut down its mining and smelting in Montana, crippling much of the state's commerce. Only the company newspapers continued to operate. Great Falls's Boston and Montana smelter, pictured here in March 1903, was among the idle plants.

MONTANA HISTORICAL SOCIETY PHOTOGRAPH ARCHIVES, HELENA

music was rather discordant but it sounded good to them," the paper said. By then, the word had reached the unemployed coal miners of nearby Belt, Stockett, and Sand Coulee as well as the jobless men who worked the limestone quarries at nearby Albright.[2]

The news echoed across the state, and nowhere was the rejoicing more boisterous than in Butte, where Amalgamated's statewide shutdown had tossed an estimated 6,500 local miners and smeltermen out of work. Hungry for specifics, excited crowds pressed against bulletin boards outside the city's three dailies, while mine foremen scrambled to assemble work gangs for the ensuing labors, which would include the lowering of dozens of horses and mules into the damp tunnels beneath the city. But that night was for celebrating, and Butte's thousands joined thousands of workers across the state in raising their glasses to a future of steady paychecks and the eternal beneficence of Amalgamated Copper Company.[3]

The shutdown of 1903—the company's protest against court decisions undercutting its ownership of key mining properties—was a major victory in Amalgamated's ongoing consolidation of Montana's copper industry. The closure forced a reluctant governor and legislature to meet in emergency session to pass the company's "fair trials" bill, allowing Amalgamated to move its court battles with F. Augustus Heinze beyond the reach of Butte's corrupt, unsympathetic judges. But its effects were psychological as well as legal. In forcing a sovereign state to its knees, the company sent a message that would reverberate down the years. "Whatever its motive," Spokane's *Spokesman-Review* wrote, "the fact stands out like a gigantic mountain rising from the plain, that the Amalgamated company has the power to throw 15,000 to 20,000 men out of employment, paralyze the chief industry of a state of American union, and depress, if not ruin, may other industries in that state." Whatever the company's reasons, Montanans would never forget it methods.[4]

This worker skimming the reverberatory furnace at Great Fall's Boston and Montana facility may have been among the 1,500 smelter workers and thousands of others who celebrated when Amalgamated's three-week shut down ended.

MONTANA HISTORICAL SOCIETY PHOTOGRAPH ARCHIVES, HELENA

Nor could they fail to see that the only company businesses allowed to operate through the shutdown were its newspapers, which took pains to explain the reasonableness of Amalgamated's position and fix the blame for the state's hardship on Heinze, the governor, and a reluctant legislature. When Clark's dailies, now free of their anti-company animus since their owner's election to the Senate and his break with Heinze, chimed in, observers at the Spokane *Spokesman-Review* and elsewhere could hardly be blamed for assuming that Amalgamated had Montana's press "practically at its beck and call."[5]

In Great Falls, the *Tribune's* tacit support for the shutdown confirmed the view. Just three years earlier, the paper had added its editorial weight to Heinze's attacks on Amalgamated's growing power. But with its owner safely in the Senate and despite the hardships caused by the shutdown, the newspaper asked readers to consider the "justness" of Amalgamated's demands, "not how they are made."[6] Other dailies fell in line. The *Missoulian,* a struggling Republican daily now owned in part by the state's rising political star, Congressman Joseph M. Dixon, blamed no one but Heinze for the shutdown and its consequences: "He takes food out of the mouths of children, dresses from the backs of women, and shoes from their feet. He withdraws thousands of dollars from the savings banks of the state. He caused a reduction of the forces in stores and shops and will eventually close their doors. He takes children out of schools and positions away from school teachers. Will he gloat over the ruin he has wrought?"[7]

Amalgamated's battle with Heinze—the last act of Montana's copper wars—would fix an enduring image of the "copper-collared press" on the state's collective memory, but it would also foster a small but influential opposition press, whose progressive views would nudge Montana toward reform.

IN THE YEARS BETWEEN Clark's election to the U.S. Senate in 1900 and the Amalgamated shutdown of 1903, Montana's press underwent a significant reshuffling. Amalgamated divested itself of some of the papers it had purchased during the campaign, selling them to allies whose allegiance the company maintained through mortgages or generous

WILL HER CHILDREN COME TO HER RESCUE?

With Amalgamated and Clark in a state of respectful coexistence—and in control of the daily press in Anaconda, Butte, Helena, and Great Falls—F. Augustus Heinze faced the last great battle of Montana's copper wars with the small but feisty Butte weekly, the Reveille, which he frequently used to attack the "Copper Trust Gang." In 1904, Heinze launched a daily, the Butte Evening News.

BUTTE *REVEILLE*, NOVEMBER 27, 1903

contacts for printing and advertising. But in Butte, where Heinze re-
solved to fight on despite Clark's easy abandonment of their former
"fusion," the company strengthened its grip on the city's daily press by
commandeering Lee Mantle's *Inter Mountain.*

For years, the paper's nominal independence of any copper faction had made it a wild card in the fractious politics of Silver Bow
County. Mantle tried to keep the paper on a cautious course, but
Amalgamated patience had worn thin even before the high stakes election of 1900. That summer, the *Inter Mountain* had reported the rumors of Amalgamated's aim to establish a competing Republican daily
in Butte. The prospect even had a name—the *Butte Sun*—but more
important, Amalgamated had imported a press and five Linotypes,
which it kept in a local warehouse while it made a noisy search for
an editor and staff. The *Inter Mountain* maintained a careful neutrality in the fall election, but neutrality was not enough. In February
of 1901, Mantle and two nephews accepted the company's ultimatum
and resigned as trustees of the Inter Mountain Publishing Company.
Officials representing the Daly Bank and Trust Company immediately replaced them on the paper's masthead while the newspaper's employees reviewed their options. Adelphus Keith, the *Inter Mountain's*
managing editor and for years a clever critic of Daly and his ventures,
jumped to Clark's *Butte Miner,* conveniently located in the building
next door. From there, Keith could still boast a nominal independence
of the company, though in reality, Clark's dailies in Butte, Great Falls,
and Helena now stood squarely with Amalgamated on most issues of
business and politics.[8]

In Helena, John Neill's *Independent* suffered a different set of con-
tortions in the aftermath of Clark's victory. When Clark's allegiance
with Amalgamated became too obvious to ignore by 1902, a betrayed
Neill faced a bleak future. Unable to repay the mortgage Clark still held
on the paper, and with his paper leaking money, Neill grabbed Clark's
offer of some one hundred sixty thousand dollars in cash and property.
For Neill, who claimed to have paid forty-one thousand dollars for the
paper just five years earlier, the deal was a godsend. As in Clark's earlier
purchase of the *Great Falls Tribune,* the deal almost certainly included a
provision allowing Neill to repurchase his paper when Clark no longer

found it useful. To run his new Helena daily, Clark imported the *Butte Miner's* city editor J. Larry Dobell, an English-born journalist and ex-lawyer who would serve as both Clark's chief newsman and political agent for the next twenty-three years.[9]

With Amalgamated and Clark now in a state of respectful coexistence—and in control of the daily press in Anaconda, Butte, Helena, and Great Falls—Heinze faced the last great battle of Montana's copper wars with one small but feisty weekly and the sympathy of a cadre of progressive country editors in Montana's farm country.

OF ALL THE EDITORS WHO NIPPED at Amalgamated's heels, none would annoy it quite like Patrick A. O'Farrell, the mysterious editor of Heinze's weekly Butte *Reveille.* Tall and wide, a barrel of a man with overgrown eyebrows set over piercing eyes and an opulent handlebar mustache, O'Farrell exuded intrigue. His father, he claimed, had known the Irish patriot and Montana territorial governor Thomas Francis Meagher in the old country, and O'Farrell himself claimed acquaintance with Charles Parnell, Michael Davitt, and other heroes of the Irish independence movement. Educated in Ireland, O'Farrell had worked his way around the globe as an itinerant journalist, with extended stays in Europe, Egypt, and Australia, where he had witnessed, by his own account, "the fierce struggle for existence, the heartbreaks, the hunger, the wants and poverty of millions and the helplessness of governments or philanthropists in the face of human suffering."[10]

O'Farrell met Heinze in a soggy mining camp in British Columbia, where O'Farrell's rhetorical gifts meshed with the brash mining engineer's genius for exploiting his competitors' weaknesses. In 1895, Heinze spotted opportunity in the rich lead and silver mines near Rossland, British Columbia. Twenty miles away at Trail Creek on the Columbia River, Heinze built a profitable smelter. He also bought the weekly Rossland *Miner* and hired O'Farrell to campaign against the monopolistic practices of the Canadian Pacific Railroad while touting Heinze's audacious scheme to build his own railway to the sea. The crusade struck such a responsive chord that the provincial parliament awarded Heinze

a six-hundred-thousand-acre
land grant to support construction of his Columbia and
Western Railway. Alarmed,
the Canadian Pacific bought
Heinze out in 1898.[11]

Heinze's Canadian esca-
pade brought him nearly $1
million in cash and valuable
land holdings, in addition to
the rich mine properties he
and a brother were developing in Butte. Beyond a keen
eye for ore, Heinze also displayed an intricate knowledge of mining law, and
when Amalgamated's push
to consolidate Butte's mining
industry threatened independent operators, Heinze fought
back with a blizzard of law-

Of all the editors who nipped at Amalgamated's heels, none would annoy it quite like Patrick A. O'Farrell, editor of Heinze's Reveille. *His attacks against Amalgamated still stand among the most memorable anti-corporate propaganda campaigns in Montana history.*

COURTESY THE AUTHOR

suits challenging the company's mineral claims. While Heinze's lawyers mined Butte's courts and his miners pirated ore from disputed
claims, O'Farrell again proved his worth as a fighting journalist. The
contest this time was for control of the Silver Bow County's judge-
ships, and O'Farrell's weapon was the Butte *Reveille*. The success of
the Clark-Heinze "fusion" in the elections of 1900 owed much to
Heinze's flair for showmanship and to the *Reveille*'s self-styled role
as an "ardent advocate for the greatest good and the best interests of
the toiling masses as against the ruling class." Clark and Heinze's master-
stroke had been to grant Butte's miners and smeltermen the eight-
hour workday, while both the *Miner* and *Reveille* gleefully exploited
Amalgamated's reluctance to follow suit. With the *Miner* exalting
Clark's largesse and defending his reputation, the *Reveille* devoted
itself to promoting Heinze's personal, political, and business activities
while fraudulently denying any link to the man himself. Accused on

one occasion of criminal libel, O'Farrell testified that he was not the paper's editor and defied anyone to prove otherwise. The ruse fooled no one but the law.[12]

O'Farrell's attacks against Amalgamated still stand among the most memorable anti-corporate propaganda campaigns in Montana history. In his colorful lexicon, Amalgamated loomed as the evil "copper trust," the spawn of Standard Oil's "Kerosene Gang" led by the "arch monster" of American capitalism, John D. Rockefeller, who, despite the portrayal, owned no part of Amalgamated and had in fact warned his colleagues away from the venture. To the *Reveille's* readers, Amalgamated's newspapers became "the reptile press," and the Associated Press, which relied on reporters from the "Standard Oil subsidized press" for its Montana news, became the "Standard Oil press bureau." After the break with Clark, O'Farrell turned his pen on the *Butte Miner's* editors as well. When *Miner* editor Adelphus Keith railed against "the hoodlums, the maudlin wretches, the salaried thugs, the repeaters and penitentiary birds that Heinzism represents," the Butte *Reveille* responded by describing Keith as "the high priest of theosophy in Montana, the mouthpiece of Boodler Clark, and most asinine scribe in the editorial chair on any newspaper."[13]

Compared with the metropolitan stylings of Butte's daily papers, the *Reveille* was crude and nearly void of news concerning national or international events. But it made a loud noise on the street, where the city's roving newsboys hawked it with special fervor because Heinze shrewdly allowed them to pocket an extra penny or two from each sale.[14] Like a mutt in a pedigreed dog show, the *Reveille* stood out as a scrappy, irreverent, and outrageous alternative that provoked company officials and editors into indignant rebuttals, which O'Farrell then gleefully deconstructed for his readers. Above all, the *Reveille* claimed that it stood alone for a free and independent press in Montana, whose dailies, it asserted, were "entirely owned by the Standard Oil Trust and its allied interests."[15]

In the weeks before Amalgamated's great shutdown, the *Reveille's* incessant attacks on the "muzzled press" even goaded the Butte *Inter Mountain* into a rare admission and defense of the company's newspaper ownership:

It is true that some corporations have made investments in newspapers in Montana, but it is not true that this action was in pursuit of a purpose to possess the government and to prey upon the commonwealth. It appeared to be the safest means to protect the public as well as the corporate interests from misrepresentation, and was and is a necessary defense of their vast interests—the safeguarding of [which] is vital to the welfare of the state, and to such ownership the people of Montana are indebted for the most complete newspapers furnished to a clientele so limited in numbers anywhere on earth. Without exception, these newspapers uphold the laws, advocate and support every institution and every policy designed to make the state more prosperous and intelligent and respectable.[16]

The *Inter Mountain's* words would stand for decades as the company's only public justification of its newspaper ownership, and they drew predictable howls from independent editors across the state, including the flabbergasted editor of Fort Benton's *River Press,* William Harber. "Is it not the mission of these newspapers to serve their masters?" he asked readers. "Do not the latter expect to get value for their money? When the interests of the corporations and the general public conflict, is it not reasonable to assume that corporation-owned newspapers will work for the success of their proprietors?"[17]

The Butte *Reveille* pounced as well, asking its readers to imagine the Butte *Inter Mountain,* the *Anaconda Standard,* the *Butte Miner,* the *Helena Independent,* the *Great Falls Tribune,* the *Great Falls Leader,* the *Missoulian,* and a number of "small fry that, parasite-like, cling to the Standard Oil barrel in campaign times 'protecting the public!'" "Here are four republican newspapers, four democratic newspapers and one socialist newspaper, purchased at a cost of at least a million dollars and entailing an annual expense of not less than a million more, conducted by the Standard Oil Copper Trust and its ally, William A. Clark, as 'the safest means to protect the public!'"[18]

Of course the Butte *Reveille's* own politics were an unabashed blend of whatever it deemed useful to Heinze's cause. It touted Heinze's affection for Jeffersonian democracy but endorsed Republican Theodore Roosevelt for president in 1904. It championed the cause of the "toiling masses" against their corporate masters but attacked Montana's budding Socialist Party, which had surprised political observers in the spring of 1903 by winning control of Anaconda's municipal government and drawing respectable numbers in Butte's city election. Although the *Reveille* endorsed some Socialist-backed reforms, such as the initiative and referendum and public ownership of utilities, O'Farrell and his editorial deputy, Richard Kilroy, variously equated Socialists with "free love" and forced mediocrity and claimed they were intent on undermining the church and "the beauty and sanctity of family life." From Heinze's view, and not entirely without evidence, the *Reveille* considered the Socialists' emergence an Amalgamated plot to split Heinze's working-class support, noting that the *Labor World,* an early Montana labor organ with Socialist sympathies, had been published initially on the *Anaconda Standard*'s press.[19]

In its attack on Socialists, the Butte *Reveille* carefully avoided any direct criticism of workers themselves, and it found ample reason to back their complaints against the bosses, company stores, labor spies, and "thugs" whose targets for assault reportedly included both O'Farrell and his deputy, Kilroy, who claimed to have beaten off his attackers with a cane. O'Farrell also charged that Amalgamated's Irish leaders— men such as attorney William Scallon, now president of the company's Montana operations, and Dan Hennessy, manager of the company's general stores—were traitors to their people, "hired to gull, to foil and to betray the Irish toilers on the hill into supporting Standard Oil's schemes of villainy."[20]

At its cynical heart, the struggle between Heinze and Amalgamated had little to do with political philosophy or the purity of the press. Tensions boiled over in October of 1903 when Silver Bow district judge William Clancy, a colorful Heinze partisan, issued two rulings that threatened not only Amalgamated's push for consolidation, but also the trust's very existence. In the first, Clancy gave Heinze title to a rich but disputed mine, the Minnie Healy, which bordered key Amalgamated holdings. In the second, sparked by a Heinze-inspired challenge by minority stockholders against the consolidation of key Amalgamated holdings, Clancy authorized injunctions that effectively stripped the trust of its ownership and earnings. Exasperated, Amalgamated shut down its operations statewide on October 22.[21]

The shutdown, which lasted only eighteen days, would leave a lasting mark on Montana's relations with the company. Though many sympathized with the company's frustration with Butte's corrupt courts, the shutdown on the brink of a bitter Montana winter drove home the blunt reality of Amalgamated's power. Beyond the copper press, some independent newspaper editors like William Harber, the English-born, Republican editor of Fort Benton's daily *River Press,* saw the shutdown for exactly what it was—a power play. Harber's criticism of the company and newspapers carrying the company's water rang loudly in rural areas beyond Anaconda's direct influence. "Corporation ownership of Montana newspapers and corporation interference in Montana politics are not dictated by an unselfish desire to promote the welfare of the general community," Harber wrote.[22]

In Hamilton, Miles Romney, the anti-company editor of the Democratic *Western News,* stepped up his attacks on the company throughout the shutdown. Despite the closure of his town's company sawmill and Amalgamated's underwriting of his local newspaper competitors, Romney urged his readers to resist the company's pressure. "The fair-minded people of Montana want to see the Amalgamated company keep its mines and prosper," he wrote. "They want to see them get a square deal, but they can never be starved or intimidated into giving that or any corporation any inequitable advantage."[23]

As Montanans pondered the abyss and searched for news, the weekly *Lewistown Democrat* expressed its "utmost contempt" for the company for throwing thousands of Montanans out of work "for the sole purpose of securing political advantage." It also complained that it was Montana's "misfortune" that none of its major cities published a "single free and independent daily newspaper."[24]

Though it lacked the staff and equipment of its rivals, the Butte *Reveille* led Heinze's defense during the shutdown with energy and flair. With O'Farrell traveling in Europe, the task fell to his acerbic deputy, Richard Kilroy, who focused the paper's wrath on Standard Oil chieftain Henry H. Rogers, whose ruthless methods were then on national display in muckraker Ida Tarbell's sensational rendering of Standard Oil in the current issues of *McClure's.* With headlines blaring "ONCE MORE H. H. ROGERS RESORTS/TO THE MAILED FIST IN MONTANA," the *Reveille* even claimed the shutdown was at heart Roger's plot to manipulate Amalgamated's stock and raise the price of copper.[25] The Butte *Inter Mountain,* the company paper most closely associated with Amalgamated's Montana president William Scallon, responded by accusing the Butte *Reveille* of publishing "the wickedest and foulest slanders," against Rogers, but such umbrage only egged Kilroy onward.[26]

Throughout the ordeal, Heinze's weekly pounded away, publishing lurid "extras" detailing the standoff's most dramatic moments, and none was more dramatic than Heinze's October 26 speech to ten thousand worried citizens gathered at the steps of the Silver Bow County courthouse, most of them hoping to hear that Heinze and Amalgamated had reached a deal. Instead, he implored his listeners to support him, warning them that only he stood between them and their complete domination by the Standard Oil trust. "They will cut your wages and

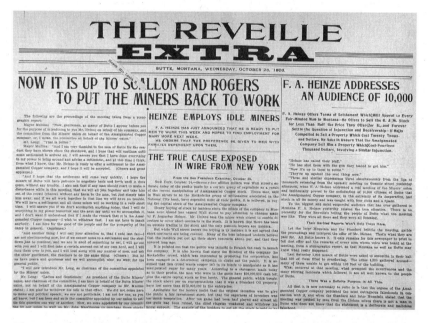

Throughout Amalgamated's shutdown, Heinze's weekly published lurid "extras" detailing the standoff's most dramatic moments. None was more dramatic than Heinze's speech to ten thousand worried citizens gathered at the steps of the Silver Bow County courthouse. "They will cut your wages and raise the tariff in the company stores on every bite you eat and every rag you wear," Heinze told them.

BUTTE *REVEILLE,* EXTRA, OCTOBER 28, 1903

raise the tariff in the company stores on every bite you eat and every rag you wear," Heinze told them. "They will force you to dwell in Standard Oil houses while you live, and they will bury you in Standard Oil coffins when you die." A *Reveille* "extra" carrying Heinze's speech in full was distributed free to thousands of Silver Bow households. Thousands of additional copies were distributed statewide over the rails, though the *Reveille* complained later that Amalgamated officials in Bozeman, Great Falls, and Missoula bought up huge lots of the papers and had them destroyed.[27]

For all their bluster, Heinze's bravado and the *Reveille*'s assaults on the "muzzled press" only seemed to harden Amalgamated's resolve. The shutdown ended when Governor Joseph K. Toole buckled beneath massive public pressure and called legislators into emergency session to pass legislation allowing the company to move its legal fights from Butte's courts to those in Helena. Though the shutdown seriously undermined his political clout, Heinze continued to pour money and ink into the battle for Butte's hearts and minds throughout the treacherous year of 1904. Beneath the city, miners loyal to Heinze and Amalgamated fought each other with steam drills and dynamite. Above ground, the company and its rival fought through the courts and the press.

For once, the *Anaconda Standard* and *Butte Miner* found themselves on the same side, and their shared targets included not only Heinze and his newspaper, but Socialists as well. In 1900, Amalgamated had reportedly tolerated Montana's fledgling Socialist Party as a means to fracture Clark and Heinze's working-class support, but the Socialists' strength in the Anaconda and Butte city elections in 1903, coupled with an attempt by Deer Lodge County's Socialist assessor to raise taxes on Amalgamated's smelters, led to a ruthless repression. With the *Standard* providing rhetorical cover, the company fired as many as seven hundred suspected Socialists among its workforce. By the spring of 1904, *Standard* editor John Durston boasted that his city had been wiped clean of the party's influence. "In all likelihood nothing more will ever be heard of the Socialist Party in Anaconda," the *Standard* predicted. "Its fate suggests the epitaph on the tombstone over the grave of a three-year-old child in the Cheltenham churchyard: It is so soon that I am done for, that I wonder what I was begun for."[28]

ROUNDING 'EM UP.

THE MASTER OF THE HOUNDS AND HIS PACK.

Campaigning in the election of 1904, Heinze barnstormed the state while the Reveille *cranked out propaganda in Butte, much of it in the form of scathing political cartoons that rivaled any in the state for sheer impact.*

BUTTE *REVEILLE*, JANUARY 29, 1904

Durston's predictions were premature; the Socialists would pose a more serious challenge eight years later, and their efforts in 1903–4 resulted in the publication of Montana's first Socialist newspaper, the *Montana News.* The paper began in Lewistown in 1903 as the *Judith Basin News,* a weekly owned and edited by J. H. Walsh, a future organizer for the radical

Industrial Workers of the World (IWW) and future leader of the IWW's "free speech" fight in Spokane in 1909. In the spring of 1904, Walsh changed his paper's name to the *Montana News,* moved it to Helena, and donated it to the party for use in the fall elections in which Socialist Eugene Debs collected a respectable 9 percent of Montana's presidential vote.[29]

For all its undercurrents, the election of 1904 figured largely as a test of Heinze's ability to retain some of the clout he and Clark had won four years earlier. Hoping to bolster his machine's legislative representation, Heinze barnstormed the state while his weekly cranked out the propaganda. More memorable than its words, however, were its scathing political cartoons, which rivaled any in the state for sheer impact. Cartoonist Thomas Nast had demonstrated the art's power against New York's corrupt Tammany Hall as early as the 1870s, but with advances in the fast and accurate zinc engraving process, barbed cartoons burst on the national newspaper scene in the campaign of 1896. In Montana, the *Anaconda Standard* used them extravagantly at the height of the Clark-Daly feud, and for artistry the *Standard's* illustrations were peerless. But the Butte *Reveille's* hired-gun cartoonists took the prize for emotional power. From 1900 to 1905, the *Reveille* employed five editorial artists, whose work appeared periodically and mainly around election time. At one time or another, the weekly's ever-changing stable of cartoonists included T. O. McGill, Tom Thurlby, A. F. Wilmarth, Alfred M. Dutton, and a mysterious artist known only as "de. Q." Of them all, Dutton had the longest tenure, and his career illustrated not only the state's shifting politics, but also the mercenary nature of the job. He joined Clark's *Butte Miner* in 1900 and made Amalgamated his target, but when Clark's allegiances changed after his election to the Senate, Dutton jumped to the Butte *Reveille* in time for the 1904 elections. Afterward, Dutton danced back to the *Miner* and turned his pen on Heinze.[30]

The *Reveille's* cartoonists were quickly forgotten, but their theme—Amalgamated's intent to enslave Montana—would endure through their stark and withering portrayals of the company and its leaders. In one classic illustration, an enormous buzzard, its bald head a wicked caricature of John D. Rockefeller, cast its shadow over the entire state. In others, Rockefeller slipped a copper collar around the neck of

In this classic political cartoon, an enormous buzzard, its bald head a carica-ture of John D. Rockefeller, casts its shadow over Montana. Despite such vitriol, Heinze sold out to Amalgamated in 1906, bringing the copper wars to an end with the company firmly in control of Montana's mining industry.

BUTTE *REVEILLE*, FEBRUARY 26, 1904

an unconscious female representing Montana or dispensed goods and advice at the company store. In still others, Amalgamated's William Scallon, dressed as master of the hounds, held the reins to a pack of muzzled company newspapers, and a haggard working-class couple surveyed Butte's bleakness from the door of their dilapidated shack while their emaciated child reached to play with a rat.[31]

While the *Reveille* employed its demagoguery, Heinze's most ex-travagant journalistic pursuit for the 1904 election was the creation of a new daily newspaper, the *Butte Evening News*. With the dyspeptic Kilroy in charge, it shouldered its way onto Butte's streets as the city's fourth daily, and though its staff was barely a shadow of those at the *Standard,* the *Miner,* and the *Inter Mountain,* the *Evening News* offered a sensational alternative, with bold headlines, modern layout and type-faces, photos of celebrity belles, vivid accounts of bizarre crimes, and national sports stories plucked from its Scripps News Service wire, the service's first appearance in Montana. Compared to its younger daily sibling, the *Reveille* seemed crude and certainly heavy handed.

Among Butte's dailies, the *Evening News* developed a reputation for the swagger of its young, hungry staff, which included the likes of E. G. Leipheimer, a young reporter and subeditor whose enterprising coverage of IWW founder William "Big Bill" Haywood's Idaho murder trial in 1907 captivated Butte and impressed the national press in attendance. Leipheimer would later serve the Anaconda Company as one of its most influential editors, but the most illustrious staffer at the *Evening News* was Berton Braley, a fledgling poet who had traded the "blue waters and spreading maples" of Madison, Wisconsin, for the "gawd forsaken hole" of Butte and a twenty-five-dollar-a-week reporting job at the Butte *Inter Mountain.*[32]

Braley fell in love with Butte's raw charms, even its sulfurous smoke, which he said had to be "brushed aside in order to see the waiter to whom you were giving your breakfast order." He was less inspired by the *Inter Mountain,* which discouraged his poetry that would later grace New York's top newspapers and magazines such as the *Saturday Evening Post, Collier's,* and *Puck.* Braley soon joined the *Butte Evening News,* which tolerated not only his poems and news copy, but his mixed-breed dog, Solomon, who followed his master throughout the city in the search of tales of crime, intrigue, graft, and romance. Though its existence was relatively short, the *Evening News* earned a lasting place in Montana newspaper lore when its employees discovered that a hose from an adjacent beer hall's kegs ran through a corner of the newspaper's basement. Staffers secretly tapped the line and made frequent use of it in a process known as "visiting the Dutchman." A printer's failure to close the tap one day led to its discovery by the bar's owner, whose anger Kilroy reportedly soothed with six months of free advertising.[33]

With all their color, Heinze's newspapers gave him an influential voice in Butte but his dream of statewide power crashed in the 1904 elections. His machine ran strong in Butte and Silver Bow County, but rumors that Heinze was secretly negotiating a sellout to Amalgamated gradually eroded loyalties there as well. Among the signs of Heinze's demise was the Butte *Reveille*'s steady decline. O'Farrell quit Butte shortly after the election amid rumors that he had quarreled with Heinze over a game of bridge and his disappointment at not being named editor of the *Butte Evening News,* but his occasional political or travel pieces for the paper suggest he had merely decided to indulge his old wander-lust. Whatever the case, the *Reveille* slipped steadily into an editorial coma, its meager pages increasingly filled with copy scavenged from the *Evening News.*[34]

THE BUTTE *REVEILLE* WAS HARDLY the only Montana weekly to chal-lenge the Amalgamated press and its allies during the company's suc-cessful drive to consolidate its power between 1900 and 1906. A more credible, if less sensational, voice came from John M. Neill's thoughtful Helena weekly, the *Press.* Stylish and modern in appearance, and as lit-erate a weekly as Montana would ever see, the tiny paper offered a rare independent Democratic viewpoint, distinguished by its willingness to criticize both Clark and Amalgamated whenever it saw fit. More jour-nal of opinion than chronicle of events, the *Press* made its fight on is-sues of reform. In its inaugural issue in 1902, editor William Eggleston devoted his paper to the anti-corporate cause Senator Clark had so enthusiastically endorsed in his drive for the Senate—and so cynically abandoned after his victory. "Those who know corporation methods in politics saw that the political battle of 1900 was but the beginning of the fight between the people of Montana and the Amalgamated Copper trust for the control of this state," Eggleston wrote. The *Press* would continue to oppose the naming of state and local officials by "monopolist millionaires" sitting in New York offices. "It has no more respect for these men or their spies and corruptionists in this state than it has for the commonest thief or highwayman."[35]

Moreover, Eggleston demanded specific political reforms, including a direct primary law, "so as to remove the nomination of Judges and all other public officers from the influence of Fraud, Boodle and Trickery in Primaries, Caucuses and Conventions." The paper supported the enactment of initiative and referendum laws, "so that the People may Veto Bad Legislation at the Ballot Box, prevent Corporations from killing good measures in the legislature and put an end to Corporate Ownership of Legislators." Other progressive measures endorsed by the *Press* included the creation of a state commission to regulate the rail-roads' "Excessive Freight and Passenger Rates" and the formation of a state board empowered to assess property uniformly and "put an end to Tax-dodging and crooked assessment." In view of the corruption that tainted Senator Clark's election, the paper also backed the direct election of U.S. senators.[36]

Throughout its brief life, the *Press* also poured its steady fire at the copper press, the "corporation organs," including Clark's, for their opposition to most reforms. "These papers, which include the two in Great Falls, the two in Helena, the two in Butte, and the Anaconda Standard, are owned and controlled by corporations that have so far gone outside of their legitimate business as to meddle in the politics of the state, trying to control it," Eggleston wrote.[37] Beyond its own attacks, the *Press* frequently reprinted criticism of Montana's "coal oil press" from other newspapers, including the Marysville *Mountaineer*, a Republican weekly that saw little difference between the Amalgamated's Republican and Democratic dailies, "each and all dominated by the same influence."

> Not a single word is ever spoken in any of them, Democratic or Republican, in criticism of Senator W.A. Clark. No Republican daily in Montana dare say a syllable against the leader of the Democratic party of the state! Pleasant condition of public affairs, isn't it.
> Why is this so, do you ask? Simply because Senator Clark has formed an alliance with the owners of the Republican dailies of Montana, that is the Amalgamated Copper company and the Standard Oil company.
> What a condition [of] politics it is when the Republican daily press of a great state are ordered not to criticise [sic] the leader of the opposition party![38]

Eggleston and "Colonel" Sam Gordon, the venerable editor of Miles City's small but influential Republican daily, the *Yellowstone Journal*, often traded partisan blows over national politics, but they found common ground in their vilification of the copper press. When Gordon fumed against the company's "parroty mouthpieces" in Butte, Helena, and Great Falls, Eggleston reprinted his diatribe in the *Press*. "As mentors of the people, as reputable and honest moulders [sic] of public opinion, they are—with one or two exceptions noted—the rankest frauds that ever soiled white paper," Gordon wrote.[39]

Like many a nineteenth-century American editor, Gordon expected newspapers to be fiery partisans, duty-bound to incite rousing debate, even when their opinions were "more or less specious." "But not so with your corporation newspaper," he wrote.

> [I]t has no views; it never gives expression to an idea that has not been kneaded and moulded [sic] and baked before delivery to the editor; it is the puppet of the most transparent and ridiculous manufacture; a living shame to the intelligent men who, for a stipend, permit people to think that they are the inspired authors of the flabby and imbecile discussions of 'matters of state' that appear in the editorial columns.[40]

Eggleston agreed with Gordon's assessment, but chided him for thinking that editorials in the copper press actually resonated with readers. It was Montana's journalistic paradox, he argued, that its biggest and best newspapers also provide the least nourishment in terms of thoughtful editorial debate. Readers bought them for national and international news, entertaining feature sections, the latest advertising, and the colored comics only major dailies could offer—not for their "editorial pabulum."[41]

Eggleston could be similarly critical of Heinze's journalism, which he found lurid and self-serving, but Clark's *Butte Miner,* which he saw as nearly devoid of public spirit, was even worse. "The Reveille does not pretend to be decent; the Miner does," he wrote. The *Miner's* failure to report Governor Toole's reformist program during the 1903 legislative session reduced it to little more than "a shield for corruption."[42]

In such respects, the *Press* echoed the bipartisan sentiments of the independent weekly editors such as Hamilton's Miles Romney and William Harber of Fort Benton, who in turn reflected the aims of the growing Progressive movement, with its disdain for corporate scandal and government corruption. The editors frequently excerpted the work of muckrakers Ida Tarbell, Lincoln Steffens, and Thomas Lawson, whose book *Frenzied Finance,* an exposé of the stock manipulations that accompanied Amalgamated's creation, attracted Montana's special attention. With support from urban civic clubs, churches, farm organizations, labor unions, and factions within both major political parties, the Progressive movement grew rapidly in Montana, where newspapers, especially the fast-sprouting farm-country weeklies, pushed it along.

In the wake of the 1904 elections, Montana's daily newspapers underwent another reshuffling. Clark's decision not to seek a second term freed him of the need for a string of money-leaking papers, and he returned both the *Helena Independent* and the *Great Falls Tribune* to their original owners. John Neill, who had sold his *Helena Independent* to Clark in 1902, repurchased his daily in late November 1904 for a price and reasons that remain elusive. However, hints by Amalgamated officials that the company was through with politics—and by extension journalism—may have encouraged Neill to re-enter the daily newspaper business. By 1905 Neill was corresponding with Amalgamated officials, inquiring into his chances of buying the competing *Montana Daily Record* in Helena and the stock Marcus Daly's widow still held in the *Anaconda Standard*.[43]

In Great Falls, Clark sold the daily *Tribune* to William Conrad, a Democratic stalwart, who in turn sold it back to Oliver Warden, the *Tribune's* business manager and former owner. Warden and partner William Bole, whose partnership had been disturbed by the copper wars, recovered not only their newspaper, but Amalgamated's Great Falls daily, the *Leader,* and thereby emerged as publishers of the city's Democratic and Republican dailies. Clark, who had once purchased newspapers as blithely as he purchased legislators, kept his *Butte Miner,* which he continued to publish as his personal organ until his death in 1925, long after he sold most of his Montana mining properties to Amalgamated.[44]

Even as it expanded its economic power, Amalgamated tried to soften its reputation as a political juggernaut, an image the company's rivals had exploited with some success since the days of the capital fight. Beyond pronouncements that it was out of politics, the company sold off some of its newspapers, though in most cases the papers went to trusted political allies. In Helena, the company's efforts to sell its Republican daily newspaper, the *Montana Daily Record,* offered a rare glimpse behind the curtain. Established in the campaign of 1900, the *Daily Record* had been Daly's counterpoint to the pro-Clark *Helena Independent* and attempt to subjugate one of Montana's pioneer Republican dailies, the Fisk brothers' *Helena Herald.* The *Record* absorbed the *Herald* in 1902, but by the fall of 1905 the company was eager to divest itself of its Helena daily—or at least to appear to have done so. In a contorted transaction detailed by a former company editor-turned-muckraker,

Jerre C. Murphy, Amalgamated agreed to sell the paper for twenty-five thousand dollars to a clique of conservative Republicans supporting Senator Thomas Carter, Amalgamated's principal ally in Congress. Yet when the group's leader, physician Oscar "Doc" Lanstrum, managed to sell only five thousand dollars in *Daily Record* stock to the party faithful, the company reportedly furnished the remaining twenty thousand dollars through individuals who agreed to act as its trustees. Though the paper promised to "cater to no faction, individual, corporation or special interest," few believed it. In the years immediately following the copper wars, Lanstrum appeared to publish the paper with little day-to-day influence from the company, though its conservative politics were impeccable and company lobbyists reportedly helped it land government printing contracts that helped keep it afloat.[45]

Heinze's sellout to Amalgamated in 1906, long rumored in the Amalgamated press, brought Montana's copper wars to an end with the company firmly in control of Montana's mining industry and with a potent political machine to promote its interests.

Heinze left Montana for New York with an estimated $10 million of the company's cash, which he proceeded to lose in a series of disastrous Wall Street maneuvers and dissipation.[46]

Back in Butte, the *Reveille,* defanged and shorn of purpose, limped to its unacknowledged death in 1909. The *Butte Evening News,* Heinze's much subdued daily, soldiered on as well, but when its benefactor finally withdrew the last of his financial support in 1910, the paper was doomed. Kilroy tried to keep it running as an independent Republican sheet, but competition from the *Anaconda Standard,* Butte *Inter Mountain,* and *Butte Miner* proved too strong. The *Evening News* died early in 1911 with a terse farewell from its publisher, who wrote: "Conditions with which the local public is sufficiently familiar to need no recital make it impossible for four daily newspapers to maintain an independent existence in this community."[47]

MONTANA'S COPPER WARS SETTLED the question of industrial dominance, but their corruption and flagrant abuse of corporate power also fueled Montana's Progressive movement, which reached critical mass in 1906. Over the next decade, the movement's emphasis on reforms struck a resonate chord with Montanans weary of the political and economic warfare waged by industrialists. But unlike that contest, spearheaded by daily newspapers loyal to their copper-king owners, Montana's campaign for political reform was championed largely by independent newspapers scattered across the state, and it took on a decidedly rural cast as Montana's agricultural population blossomed.

By 1900, the number of Montanans living in farm and ranch country finally eclipsed those in mining areas, and agriculture would soon replace mining as the state's most prominent industry. By 1909, the homestead boom was in full roar, and with each new rural farm settlement came at least one, but often two, small weeklies, each staking out its political turf in the contest for readers, advertisers, and printing patronage. Many of the new publishers were printers by trade, whose talents as writers and editors varied widely. Through exchanges, they tracked each other carefully and regularly clipped, republished, and replied to one

The homestead boom between 1900 and 1920 changed Montana's demographics, and with each new rural farm settlement came at least one, but often two, small weeklies. Newsmen with the weekly Columbus News *posed for this photograph with the tools of their trade circa 1910.*

another's editorials with regional pride and partisan bombast, but regardless of party affiliation, most supported political reforms designed
to ensure farmers a share of power in a state seemingly ruled by industrialists and the owners of vast ranches. Harry Brooks, editor of
the *Chinook Opinion,* an influential Republican weekly on Montana's
High Line, no doubt spoke for most rural editors when he wrote, "The
day has dawned when the small farmer and stockman will dominate
Montana." As local opinion leaders who often doubled as officeholders
or leaders of local political factions, rural weekly editors clearly recog-
nized that such reforms bolstered their influence as well.[48]

Joined by small-town editors
who survived the copper wars
with their papers and integrity
intact, Montana's bipartisan
corps of Progressive editors included Fort Benton's William
Harber, Lewistown's Tom Stout,
Hamilton's Miles Romney, and
William Eggleston, who returned to edit the Marysville
Mountaineer when John Neill
folded the Helena *Press.* With
few exceptions, they embraced
a Jeffersonian vision of a society
grounded in the supposed virtues
of small, self-sufficient farms, so
unlike mining and ranching
with their dependence on outside capital investment and a
rootless workforce. As a group,
they supported an impressive
array of Progressive reforms
designed to popularize democracy. Chief among them were
the initiative and referendum,
which would give citizens the

*Of Montana's weekly editors, none displayed
more reformist zeal than Miles Romney Sr.
(above), editor and publisher of the* Western
News *of Hamilton, who quickly established
himself as one of Montana's most caustic and consistent critics of Amalgamated
and its corporate successor, the Anaconda
Copper Mining Company. He is pictured
here in 1909.*

MONTANA HISTORICAL SOCIETY PHOTOGRAPH
ARCHIVES, HELENA

power to make or reject laws in the face of legislatures controlled by corporate interests. Likewise, they fought for women's suffrage to expand the franchise and direct primaries to circumvent political bosses and lobbyists who often dominated party nominating conventions. And with Clark's bribery and Heinze's corruption still fresh in mind, they urged the direct election of U.S. senators, the election of nonpartisan judges, and limits on campaign spending. Progressive editors also backed limits on child labor, the eight-hour workday, pure food laws, and a separate judicial system for delinquent youth.

Such reforms were hardly unique to Montana, and the copper dailies endorsed many of the ideas themselves, though they maintained an aversion to industrial safety laws, compensation for injured workers, and the regulation of utilities. The 1906 ballot issue that placed Montana among the first states to adopt the initiative and referendum enjoyed overwhelming support from the state's press, including the *Anaconda Standard* and Helena's *Montana Daily Record.* Weekly editors such as Will Kennedy of the *Boulder Age* and William Eggleston of Marysville's *Mountaineer* had promoted the idea of "direct legislation" for years, but it gained momentum in the wake of the Amalgamated-Heinze fight. According to one study, only two of Montana's seventy-seven newspapers opposed it: the weekly *Meagher County Republican* in White Sulphur Springs, which called it a "vicious" piece of "class legislation" espoused by labor unions and Socialists, and the Helena-based Socialist weekly *Montana News,* which protested its exclusion of spending measures and amendments to the state's constitution. With the law's passage, the *Montana Staats-Zeitung* in Helena, the state's leading German-language weekly, surely spoke for most Montanans when it proclaimed that the power of "boodler" had been broken.[49]

Of Montana's weekly editors, none displayed more reformist zeal than Miles Romney, editor and publisher of Democratic *Western News* in Hamilton. A son of Mormon pioneers who moved to Montana's Bitterroot Valley in 1881, Romney spent his youth working as a ranch hand and laborer, his education limited to local schools and a brief course in business at Ohio Northern University. With no prior journalistic experience, he bought the *Western News* in 1895 and quickly established himself as one of Montana's most caustic and consistent critics of Marcus Daly's Anaconda Copper Mining Company, and its corporate successor, Amalgamated. Given Daly's influence in Hamilton, so close to his Bitterroot Stock Farm and home to one of the company's major lumber mills, Romney's stance was gutsy. Like many Montana Democrats, he supported Clark's drive for the Senate in 1900, his reasons grounded in prevailing anti-trust, anti-corporate attitudes and party loyalty. Newspapers across the state reprinted his fiery editorials against the company and its press, and Romney frequently made news with his own forays into politics. Though he ran unsuccessfully as the Democratic nominee for secretary of state in 1904 and 1908, he won a term as Hamilton's mayor in 1902, and in Montana's pivotal Progressive year of 1906, Romney won election to the state senate.[50]

For Romney, the day's burning question was whether "the corporations shall control the people or the people shall control the corporations." Like most Progressives, Romney believed the ills of unbridled capitalism could be cured by placing more power in the hands of a more educated electorate. "The railway corporations, the beef trust, the timber trust and every other predatory adjunct of capitalism that seeks special privileges and to unjustly tax the public will be brought up with a short turn and caused to obey the laws." The solution, he argued, was "enlightened public opinion."[51]

Reprints of President Theodore Roosevelt's speeches and articles from popular muckraking magazines that appeared in Romney's paper and other rural weeklies kept Montanans in tune with Progressive sentiments nationwide. A resolution adopted by the rancher members of the Northern Montana Roundup Association in 1906 blamed many of the nation's problems on arrogant and oppressive "captains of industry, who ought to be wearing stripes and doing time in penal institutions." The ranchers also praised journalist Ida Tarbell by name and applauded Roosevelt's efforts at trust-busting but also denounced the president's criticisms of muckrakers whose targets occasionally included Roosevelt's political friends.[52]

Railroads were a favorite target of western Populists and Progressives, and criticism appeared regularly in the state's dailies, including John

Neill's *Helena Independent*. Neill and others complained of the accidents that regularly killed and maimed railway employees and passengers, but they also criticized the railroads for their vast land and mineral holdings, high freight rates, and frequent railcar shortages that raised the cost of manufactured goods and made it difficult for Montanans to export their produce. Farm-country editors across the state favored railroad rate regulation, more equitable taxation of railroad lands, and the abolition of the railroads' practice of granting sympathetic legislators, journalists, and state officials free railroad passes, an expensive if genteel form of bribery. Neill even advocated government ownership of the rails.[53]

For Romney, however, Montana's chief obstacle to reform remained the Amalgamated Copper Company, with its "meddling" interference in both major political parties and its continued ownership of key Democratic and Republican daily newspapers. Romney's criticism of the copper press was integral to his newspaper's campaign for reform and to his personal political agenda. After one disappointing term in the state senate, Romney organized and led the People's Power League, an influential and bipartisan statewide Progressive forum founded in 1910 to promote reform through voter initiatives. By 1912, the league's work led to the state's first primary elections to end corporation-controlled party nominating conventions and a "corrupt practices" law that limited campaign spending. Two years later, Romney promoted successful initiatives granting women the right to vote and offering farmers a low-interest, state-backed alternative to the high interest rates bankers charged for agricultural loans.[54]

The People's Power League also supported an unsuccessful initiative calling for a robust system of compulsory compensation for industrial workers injured or killed in hazardous occupations like mining, smelting, and logging. The league's initiative intended to supplant a watered-down state workers' compensation law enacted in 1909, which had actually made industrial workplaces more dangerous by encouraging the selective hiring of inexperienced, unmarried immigrants whose survivors were prohibited from collecting death benefits. Romney's reform measure failed at the polls with strong opposition from the

Amalgamated-sponsored Montana Development Association and the copper press, which managed to convince farmers—and many farm-country editors—that they too would be forced to compensate itinerant farmhands and tramp printers for job-related injuries.[55]

More ominous from the company's view were the increasing demands by Romney and others that mine owners shoulder more of the state's property-tax burden, a reform first suggested by Governor Joseph K. Toole in 1903. When such legislation finally surfaced in 1907, it drew widespread endorsements from eastern Montana's Republican papers, including Fort Benton's *River Press,* the Malta *Enterprise,* Glendive's *Dawson County Review,* and Glasgow's *Valley County News.* The daily *Billings Gazette* endorsed it too, in stark contrast to Montana's mine-country dailies, which met the subject with near-total silence. The lone exception was Clark's *Butte Miner,* which argued that current mine taxes were more than fair and complained the effort to raise them was rooted in the prejudices that farm-country lawmakers and newspaper editors held against mining in general. Amalgamated's Helena lobbyists ensured the bill's quick death, but the issue would dog the company for most of its existence.[56]

Romney's battles with company lobbyists, both in the legislature and on the stump, hardened his revulsion for the company and its press, but he was hardly alone in his desire to reduce the company's political influence. In 1912, a string of small-town Montana editors endorsed a successful direct primary initiative designed to put the nomination of political candidates in the hands of citizens, whose votes, the Fort Benton *River Press* argued, could not be "controlled or traded by schemers who frequently directed the proceedings of old-time conventions." Papers such as Helena's *Northwestern Stockman and Farmer,* the Havre *Herald,* the Havre *Plaindealer,* and the *Red Lodge Picket* joined the fight.[57]

Romney claimed his newspaper was the first to promote a direct primary law, but others credited Fort Benton editor William Harber, who made an elegant spokesman for Progressive Republicans east of the Continental Divide. The son of an English country pastor, Harber was working as a printer and writer in London when his brother, who had immigrated to the United States, asked him for a loan to purchase Fort

Benton's *River Press.* When the paper faced a serious competitive threat from the rival Fort Benton *Record,* Harber shipped to Montana to protect his investment. In the brief but lively newspaper war that followed, both papers converted to daily publication, giving Fort Benton the short-lived distinction of being the country's smallest two-daily town until the *Record* eventually folded. In 1891, Harber became editor and manager of the *River Press,* titles he held until his death in 1922. Over the years, he earned a reputation as being a clear and fearless thinker who rarely ventured an opinion on statewide issues; when he did, it invariably made the rounds of the weekly newspaper exchanges.[58]

William K. Harber, editor of Fort Benton's weekly River Press, *earned a reputation as being a clear and fearless thinker. He especially despised what he saw as Amalgamated's continual interference in Republican politics.*

SCHOOL OF JOURNALISM, UNIVERSITY OF MONTANA, MISSOULA

Essentially conservative, Harber nonetheless supported a number of Progressive reforms, including compulsory compensation for injured industrial workers, women's suffrage, higher mining taxes, and legislation by initiative. He especially despised what he saw as Amalgamated's continual interference in Republican politics. In 1910, when company lobbyists maneuvered lawmakers into electing Ravalli County Judge Henry L. Myers to the U.S. Senate, Harber charged that the move was really an effort to sink the 1912 reelection of one of Amalgamated most powerful critics, Senator Joseph Dixon from Missoula County. In backing Myers, Harber wrote, company lobbyists knew the next legislature would shy from Dixon and the prospect of having both of Montana's senators hail from the same corner of the state. Harber also chided the *Great Falls Tribune* in 1913 when it complained that Montanans were developing an unfortunate habit of blaming Amalgamated for all of the state's ills.

Harber conceded that anti-company sentiment had been "over-worked" in recent campaigns but argued that the company's powerful lobby and "frequent interference in political affairs" encouraged such abuse.

> It is unfortunate that the Amalgamated or any other interest should be the victim of unjust accusations, but the possession and frequent exercise of control in Montana politics affords excuse for suspicion when it may not be deserved. It has been announced from time to time that the Amalgamated is "out of politics," but its lobby and other legislative agencies have not yet disappeared from public view, he wrote.[59]

Nor, as events would show, had the company relinquished its control over strategic portions of Montana's press.

In the years before World War I, Montana's copper giant emerged as a modern industrial powerhouse. The company controlled Butte's mineral riches and ruled vast swaths of Montana forest, while its relationship with the Montana Power Company assured a steady supply of cheap power for the mining and smelting operations, including the Anaconda smelter, shown here in 1903.

CHAPTER FIVE

T HE YEARS BETWEEN THE COP-
per wars and World War I saw
Montana's copper giant emerge
as a modern industrial powerhouse.
Under guiding geniuses John D. Ryan
and Cornelius F. "Con" Kelley, the company earned Wall Street's admiration
for efficiency, innovation, and ruthlessness. Augustus Heinze's political demise
and William A. Clark's decision to sell

A "Community
of Interests"

COMPANY ALLIES
IN THE
DAILY PRESS

most of his Silver Bow mining and smelting properties in 1910 gave the
corporation all but complete dominion over Butte's mineral riches. Its
timber division ruled vast swaths of Montana forest, and Ryan's pivotal
role in the creation of the Montana Power Company assured the mining and smelting operations a steady supply of cheap power.

Yet Montana was only part of the company's story. By 1915,
Amalgamated's metals empire stretched from Montana to Mexico, from
Arizona and Utah to Indiana and New Jersey—and it was just a start.
The company underwent a legal metamorphosis as well, shedding the
sixteen-year-old shell of its holding company, Amalgamated, to emerge
as a stronger, leaner entity, the Anaconda Copper Mining Company.

As it grew, the company's corporate culture changed too. Gone was
much of the paternalism that once colored Marcus Daly's relationship
with his workers, his enterprises, and his adopted state. From the vantage point of its New York offices at 25 Broadway, the new Anaconda
Company was more inclined to view labor as a commodity, politics as
a necessary evil, and its press as a tool to protect the company's image,
prerogatives, and profits.[1]

The period marked a time of rapid change for Montana as whole.
Fresh waves of farmers staked out homesteads on the state's central and
eastern benchlands, while other newcomers, many of them immigrants,

Under guiding geniuses John D. Ryan (center left) and Cornelius F. "Con" Kelley (far left), Amalgamated earned Wall Street's admiration for efficiency, innovation, and ruthlessness. The two men are pictured here circa 1920 with William A. Clark (far right) and company ally J. Bruce Kremer (second from right). The company also continued to protect and promote itself through the daily newspapers it owned outright and those controlled by conservative allies.

C. Owen Smithers, photographer, courtesy C. O. Smithers

made their way to western Montana's mines, smelters, and timber camps. As they struggled for footholds, the newcomers contributed to the push for Progressive reforms, and Anaconda faced continued opposition from workers, farmers, and politicians imbued with the era's anti-corporate spirit. Yet the company continued to press its agenda through allies in both major parties, its fabled corps of legislative lobbyists, a stable of attorneys, and its vast network of business and financial ties—its "community of interests," as one eastern Montana editor described it.

Most visibly, the company continued to protect and promote its health through the handful of daily newspapers it owned outright and those controlled by conservative friends.

Heinze's sellout in 1906 and the company's specious promise to stay out of politics ended Montana's copper wars, but the company's war-horse newspapers rumbled on. The *Anaconda Standard* could still rise to any threat against the company's profits and prestige, but peace sapped its editorials of much of their erstwhile fire. Their focus began to shift—"unduly" editor Durston would later confess—to national matters over which Montanans had little control.[2]

But as rival editors and critics well knew, readers didn't buy newspapers for editorials alone. After nearly twenty years in the field, Montana's premier daily was in its prime, its popularity resting on its muscular news and feature sections, if not the "editorial pabulum" that went with them. A circulation of 14,500 households on Sunday put the *Standard* well ahead of the competition, and a diligent reader could spend hours absorbing the paper's multi-section issue, which sampled the nation's best popular writing, including the gentle muckraking of Finley Peter Dunne's "Mr. Dooley" and fiction by Rudyard Kipling.

The *Standard* fussed over its appearance too, offering readers new typefaces and more photographs (made possible by leaps in engraving technology), and it maintained its reputation as a nursery for talented if temperamental newspaper illustrators. Its fabled Christmas issues, crammed with illustrations, photographs, and original and syndicated articles reviewing the state's and nation's progress, still rank among the most ambitious editions ever published in Montana.[3]

In both the Sunday and daily editions, readers still enjoyed the best statewide news report along with heavy doses of national and international news; the *Standard's* rural subscribers were as connected to the outside world as any urban newspaper reader in the United States. The *Standard's* excellence also conveyed the notion that what mattered in Montana mattered to the nation, even the world. According to the *Standard's* aggressive circulation office, customers could buy copies on the newsstands of New York, Chicago, and Los Angeles; one apocryphal *Standard* yarn recounted a Montanan's delight in finding the paper on the streets of Singapore.[4]

On local matters, the paper still gave readers good value. Though Durston's editorials reflected less on the state and local issues, his staff compensated by introducing their own humor and wit, poking clever fun at prevailing pomposities under such guises as "Mr. Dooley's Bartender," Charles Eggleston's homage to muckraker Dunne, and "Reverend Jerry Rounder," whose mock-serious Sunday sermons were actually written by Wally Walsworth, chief of the *Standard's* Butte news operations. Though old *Standard* veterans such as Arthur Stone and Edward Cooney had moved on—Cooney to edit the *Great Falls Leader* and Stone to edit the *Missoulian*—the *Standard's* senior staff remained remarkably constant through its first two decades.[5]

Despite the grumblings of some subeditors that the boss seemed less involved the paper's day-to-day routine, Durston continued to enjoy the relatively free hand he had enjoyed in Marcus Daly's day. After Daly's death, his widow shared the paper's ownership with the company, an arrangement that gave Durston full responsibility for determining how the paper could best serve the interests of both its owners and its readers. Durston could be prickly about his authority, but he gave every impression of being the complete company man. Unlike other *Standard* editors who complained privately about company policies and politics, Durston offered no hint that the company's views were not his own, and in return for such fealty, he thrived along with his paper. Besides the beautiful home he built for his wife and daughters in Anaconda and the farm he purchased near Bozeman for weekend getaways and vacations, Durston owned investment properties in Anaconda, including a three-story commercial building facing Daly's Montana Hotel.[6]

For all its prestige and technical modernity, the *Standard* shared little of the Progressive ardor that ran through the editorial columns of Montana's small dailies and weeklies. Though it sometimes joined the howl against the trusts and evils such as tainted food and the exploitation of child labor, it squinted at many popular political reforms, especially those that threatened the company's influence. The paper's grudging endorsement of the initiative and referendum in 1906 included mention of Durston's hope that lawmakers would curb the legislation's scope at the earliest opportunity. It opposed the direct primary, arguing that the supposed undue influence of party bosses or corporation lobbyists at party conventions could be rectified if ordinary citizens would only "tend to their political duties." The *Standard* stood virtually alone in its unsuccessful opposition to the era's most significant attempt to reign in corporate power: the creation of a state railroad commission empowered to improve rail service and safety and control freight rates. Such regulation, the *Standard* argued, could only hurt the railroads' chances of attracting the investment necessary to make such improvements on their own. The *Standard*'s empathy for the corporate viewpoint remained consistent, despite the tenor of the times.[7]

As for the day-to-day jousting of Montana's political aspirants, the *Standard* now contented itself with editorials endorsing a straight Democratic ticket, accompanied by fairly straightforward news coverage of both major parties' activities. Though company officials and lobbyists were clearly active in state political campaigns, Durston argued throughout the period that the company played no part in them; the *Standard*'s reluctance to wade into the major parties' internal battles seemed to confirm his claim.[8]

Yet the paper's treatment of Montana's Socialist Party offered a dramatic exception. The *Standard* roared its approval as Amalgamated weeded Socialists from it company payroll following the party's minor success in Anaconda's local government elections in 1903. Nine years later, the paper joined Clark's *Butte Miner* in a scorching campaign to drive Socialists from Butte's city government. Increasingly, it joined other Montana conservatives in denouncing the growing influence of radical unionists who threatened the company's smooth if patronizing relationship with Butte's conservative trade unions.

In those and other respects, the *Standard* performed all the functions of a modern corporate public-relations department: promoting the company's strengths, touting its leaders, and stressing its importance to the communal well-being while downplaying bad news and the company's persistent critics. When Amalgamated closed its mining and smelter operations in the winter of 1907–8, throwing as many as ten thousand men out of work, the *Standard* carefully explained that the shutdown was the company's only rational recourse to the worldwide economic crisis posed by the Panic of 1907. When the company's general manager, John D. Ryan, traveled to Anaconda in the spring

When Amalgamated closed its mining and smeltering operations in winter 1907–08, throwing ten thousand men out of work, the Anaconda Standard *explained that it was the company's only option given the ongoing economic crisis. When company general manager John Ryan (center, pulling string) reopened the smelter in spring 1908, the* Standard *greeted him as the mining industry's savior.*

ANACONDA STANDARD, MARCH 8, 1908

of 1908 to reopen the smelter, the *Standard* greeted him as the mining industry's savior. Along with the Butte *Inter Mountain,* it broke the news on February 29 with a special issue dispatched across the state by train. For two consecutive Sundays, Ryan's image and gushing articles detailing his benevolence stretched across the front pages of both papers. A *Standard* artist celebrated the occasion with a front-page cartoon featuring a tiny, happy figure set atop the Washoe smelter's main stack, drawing in the newly resurgent smoke and saying "Gee, that smells good." Durston joined the handful of Amalgamated lieutenants selected to advise and dine with Ryan, whose ascension to the company's presidency a year later would rate another eruption of front-page adulation.[9]

No controversy better illustrated the *Standard*'s public-relations function than its campaign against a group of Deer Lodge Valley farmers who sued the company for widespread crop and livestock losses caused by the massive smoke pollution that billowed from the stacks of

Anaconda's giant smelter complex. Durston had tackled smoke pollution before, back in the early 1890s, when he fought to end the open-air roasting of ores. In the end, the smeltermen had acquiesced, and the *Standard* declared victory, though it merely drove the practice indoors.[10]

But the *Standard's* environmental consciousness dissipated quickly when the focus turned to Amalgamated's own smoke. The problem arose in 1902 with the completion of the company's massive Washoe works at the mouth of Warm Springs Canyon. Smoke—heavily laced with arsenic, sulfur, copper, lead, antimony, zinc, and other toxins—gushed from the stacks of the world's largest smelter, only to settle on the surrounding pastures, croplands, and forests. By the fall of that year, carcasses of poisoned livestock dotted the countryside, and farmers reported heavy crop losses. The company spent three hundred thirty thousand dollars to settle farmers' individual claims that year, but an enormous flue system and taller stack, built at considerable expense in 1903 to capture minute amounts of copper from the smoke, only spread the pollution farther. When independent scientists verified the continuing crop and livestock losses in 1904, the company abandoned its strategy of buying off complainers and decided to fight. In response, more than one hundred farmers joined a federal lawsuit in 1905, and for the next six years their high-stakes legal battle echoed throughout the mining West.[11]

As company lawyers disputed the farmers' claims about the land's previous productivity, the *Anaconda Standard* and the Butte *Inter Mountain* attacked the "smoke farmers" on a variety of fronts, with Durston's paper describing them as "too lazy to work, preferring instead to coerce money out of the smelter through the threat of litigation" and comparing their strategy to Heinze's legal schemes during the copper wars. The papers discounted the farmers' damage claims by touting the Deer Lodge Valley as an agricultural paradise and publicizing the company's hastily created showcase ranch stocked with healthy imported livestock. Articles on the county fair described company-sponsored exhibits of the region's amazing fertility, including turnips "as big as a bucket." As the case wore on and farmers carefully documented the truth of their claims, the *Standard* switched tactics, praising the smelter's technological improvements and increased productivity, all in

Farmers in the Deer Lodge Valley sued the company in 1905, claiming smoke pollution from the Anaconda smelter killed their stock and crops. The company disputed the farmers' claims, promoting the valley's agriculture through exhibits like the one at the Montana State Fair in September 1905 that displayed turnips "as big as a bucket."

MONTANA HISTORICAL SOCIETY PHOTOGRAPH ARCHIVES, HELENA

support of its overarching contention that the farmers' interests simply paled when compared with the smelter's contribution to the state and local economy.[12]

The controversy peaked late in 1908 when President Theodore Roosevelt, upset over the damage to neighboring and newly na-tionalized forests, threatened an injunction to close the smelter un-less Amalgamated agreed to remedial measures. The reaction from Montana was swift and sharp. Montana's Republican senators Joseph Dixon and Thomas Carter pressed the administration to drop its suit, while Montana's newspapers, led by the *Standard*, howled in protest that the complaints from a "handful of citizens" over a "few square miles of forest" should be allowed to "turn back progress." Durston personally telegrammed Dixon, asking him to persuade Roosevelt to drop his threat, and the *Standard* duly reported Dixon's response that "one week's wages at the Anaconda smelter and in the Butte mines is of more value than all the lodge pole pine affected by smelter smoke."[13]

In fairness, the threatened shutdown frightened non-company editors too. Miles Romney, no friend of Amalgamated's, sent his own telegram to Dixon, warning that a shutdown would be "detrimental and disastrous to our citizens." In Great Falls, where prevailing winds blew its smelter smoke to the eastern prairies, the independent *Great Falls Tribune* offered little on the smoke controversy until early December, when it suddenly reported that it had been "asked to explain" the problem, which it did by repeating the company's contention that no practical technological solution to the problem existed. As loyal Democratic papers in an election year, both the *Tribune* and the *Anaconda Standard* also questioned Roosevelt's sanity, implying that the shutdown threat had its roots in Roosevelt's penchant for irrational trust busting.[14]

The "smoke farmers" complained bitterly about the slanted coverage, which in turn influenced editorial opinions across the state. "No newspaper in the state seemed to have any information about the farmers' side of the case," one farmer wrote a friend. Few editors came to the farmers' defense, a testament to the company's economic importance, the prevailing belief in the promise of technology, and the vigor and reach of the *Standard*'s editorial campaign, which successfully framed the issue as a nonpartisan defense of Montana's mining economy. The farmers' complaints clashed with the boosterism so deeply ingrained in frontier journalism. For Deer Lodge's *Powell County Call,* a weekly published in the epicenter of the farmers' protest, the issue was whether the county should "receive its rightful share in this coming era of prosperity" or "meet the incoming tide of investors and home seekers with the red flag of warnings, and crying out: Enter not! Within, death and desolation stalk the valley." The community's interests, it argued, should not be jeopardized "over unfavorable conditions in a certain section, regrettable as those conditions are."[15]

In late April of 1909, a federal judge in Helena dismissed the farmers' suit on the grounds that the company had taken suitable preventative

measures. The Butte *Inter Mountain* greeted the ruling with relief, arguing that the smoke case "has acted as a drag on the prosperity of the Deer
Lodge Valley." In Anaconda, news of the court's decision was celebrated in
style. "Exultant blasts from the whistle on the hill heralded to Anacondans
yesterday's news of the decision," the *Anaconda Standard* reported the
next morning. "Brass bands, trailed by hundreds of boys, marched in the
streets and roman candles and rockets made the air brilliant." After four
years of legal wrangling, the smoke case was "ancient history," the paper
predicted. "With the restoration of confidence in the cities of Butte and
Anaconda, there is no reason why both should not hum with enterprise
and activity."[16]

Three years later, when a federal appellate court rejected the farmers'
final appeal, the *Standard* celebrated with a cartoon that depicted a farmer tumbling to the ground as his rope thrown around Anaconda's giant
smokestack snapped in two. In the background, miners, citizens, and businessmen cheered as clouds of smoke labeled "Prosperity" billowed overhead. Inside, the paper ran portraits of "Con" Kelley and L. O. Evans, the
company's victorious attorneys, while Charles Eggleston marked the
occasion with a poetic parody of the "Star Spangled Banner," its point
made in the song's rousing finish:

> And the furnaces' glare, the whistles' keen blare,
> Gave proof though the night that our smoke was still there.
> The smoke of the smelter,
> Long may it flow,
> In the heavens above,
> O'er the earth here below.[17]

As Amalgamated grew, its promise not to meddle in Montana's politics vanished like smoke in the breeze. Under the aggressive leadership of
John D. Ryan and "Con" Kelley, the company served both as a bastion for
conservatives and a lightning rod for Progressives and radicals campaigning for reform among the fresh waves of newly arrived farmers and laborers. Company officials clearly saw the crucial importance of a sympathetic
press, which it worked secretly, and sometimes clumsily, to ensure.

When the company won in court, the Anaconda Standard *lampooned the farmers with this cartoon accompanied by a poem patterned after the "Star-Spangled Banner." Two lines read: "And the furnaces' glare, the whistles' keen blare, Gave proof through the night that our smoke was still there!"*

ANACONDA STANDARD, MARCH 7, 1911

The election of 1912—the first in which Montana's voters effectively elected a U.S. senator—reflected the company's impossible efforts to influence the press and yet somehow appear above the fray in a campaign where the company's political meddling itself was a central issue. The campaign and its outcome would reverberate throughout Montana newspapers, forcing changes in ownership and bolstering both the fact and myth of the company's influence over the state's daily press. By the year's end, Jerre Murphy, a former Amalgamated edi- tor turned muckraker, would charge that all but one of the state's major dailies "was sub- ject in policy to the control and influence of copper com- bine management."[18]

The sole exception, in Murphy's view, was the *Missoulian,* owned by Senator Joseph Dixon. The bright and handsome son of North Carolina Quakers, Dixon ar- rived in western Montana fresh from college and found it brimming with opportuni- ties to match his ambitions as a young lawyer and business- man with a taste for politics.

In 1907, rising young Republican star Joseph M. Dixon (pictured above in 1904) gained both a seat in the U.S. Senate and a con- trolling interest in the Missoulian.

Parker, photographer, Montana Historical Society Photograph Archives, Helena

By 1902, the young Republican star had held local office, served a legislative term, and bought shares in the dowdy Republican daily that would boost his election that year to the first of two congressional terms. Gradually increasing his investment in the *Missoulian,* Dixon gained control of the paper with his election to the U.S. Senate in 1907 and improved it considerably by hiring Arthur Stone, the former *Anaconda Standard* reporter and managing editor and one-time Democratic state legislator, as his editor.[19]

Under Stone, the *Missoulian* spruced up, modernized, and expand- ed its reach. It reflected its owner's brand of moderate, Main Street Progressivism, opposing Socialists and IWW radicals on the left while walking a wary line with the company, which controlled major tim- ber interests throughout the paper's circulation area. At least tacitly, the company backed Dixon in his congressional races and probably subsidized his newspaper during the fight with Heinze, though Dixon worked diligently to maintain an image of amiable independence. The

With Arthur L. Stone (above) at the helm, the Missoulian spruced up, modernized, and expanded its reach. It reflected its owner Dixon's brand of moderate, Main Street Progressivism while walking a wary line with the company.

SCHOOL OF JOURNALISM,
UNIVERSITY OF MONTANA, MISSOULA

relationship began to change with Dixon's election to the Senate. Dixon's friendship with President Roosevelt, his growing Progressivism, and feuds over patronage with his fellow Republican and Senate colleague Thomas Carter led inevitably to a clash with the company's conservative Republican allies. Besides Carter, Dixon's principal rivals within his own party included *Montana Daily Record* publisher "Doc" Lanstrum in Helena and state senator Jonathan E. Edwards, a prominent eastern Montana banker, cattleman, former Indian agent, and power broker with newspapers of his own. Both maintained close ties to Amalgamated, and both were committed to Roosevelt's successor, William Howard Taft, for president in 1912.

Roosevelt's decision to run a third-party campaign against Taft in 1912 divided Republicans nationally, and Senator Dixon's selection as the Progressive Bull Moose Party's national campaign manager ensured a similar split over his own reelection in Montana. When conservatives and Amalgamated lobbyists blocked Dixon's re-nomination at the state Republican convention, Dixon bolted from the party and launched his own Bull Moose crusade, determined, as his campaign slogan indicated, to "Put the Amalgamated Out of State Politics." Predictably, the Republicans' internal squabbling handed Democrats sweeping victories on nearly every level. Dixon finished ahead of his Republican rival but still lost to Democrat Thomas J. Walsh, a brilliant Helena attorney and Progressive whose 1910 U.S. Senate campaign the company had blocked.[20]

Acutely aware of the role Montana's press played in politics, Dixon understood the newspaper business too. Throughout his time in Washington, he carefully cultivated the friendship of Montana editors, especially those who edited Progressive Republican weeklies. As the owner of a financially struggling newspaper himself, he understood their keen interest in the appointments of local postmasters, who oversaw their papers' distribution through the mails, and of federal lands commissioners empowered to decide which newspapers would harvest the lucrative advertising homesteaders were required to publish to "prove" their claims. When Fort Benton's *River Press* suddenly lost its land-claims advertising to an upstart competitor in 1911, Dixon fired a brisk letter of protest, citing the paper's history as one of Montana's "strongest and most consistent" Republican sheets. "I know of no other republican editor in the state who has made more modest claims on the party . . . and who at the same time, has always supported the republican party, in season and out," Dixon wrote.[21]

But the support of a few weekly editors meant little against the opposition of every Democratic daily and weekly and the conservative Republican press, led by "Doc" Lanstrum's *Montana Daily Record* in Helena, Amalgamated's *Inter Mountain* in Butte, and a string of conservative pro-Taft editors in eastern Montana communities such as Livingston, Big Timber, and Forsyth—many of them under the influence of Dixon's fiercest Republican rival, state senator Jonathan Edwards of Forsyth.

Though Dixon ran well among Republicans generally, conservatives peeled off more than enough votes to ensure his defeat by Walsh, whose own newspaper support included the company's *Anaconda Standard,* the *Butte Miner,* and the Democratic dailies of Helena, Great Falls, Lewistown, and Missoula, where a new daily, the *Missoula Sentinel,* suddenly offered Dixon's *Missoulian* a feisty challenge. Established in 1911, the *Sentinel* changed hands in the spring of 1912, just in time for the fall campaign. If the sale's timing made Dixon suspicious, so did the paper's new proprietors: an obscure Idaho mine owner and Richard Kilroy, the caustic former editor of Heinze's *Butte Evening News.*

Even in a state stocked with colorful ink slingers, Kilroy's vituperative skills and exotic background were matchless. Born in Ireland and educated at the University of Dublin where he had been a rugby star, Kilroy's American journey began with a stint at Harvard followed by a succession of adventures that included "selling crayon portraits, teaching school,

punching cattle, tending bar, dealing faro, and playing politics." He dabbled as a prospector, served as principal of Anaconda High School, and
even coached the town's football club before signing on as a writer for
the Butte *Reveille,* under the tutelage of Patrick O'Farrell, a master ink
slinger himself. So successful was Kilroy's apprenticeship, and so keen his
interest in hardboiled politics, that when Heinze sought an editor for his
daily *Evening News,* he gave the job to Kilroy. The poet Berton Braley,
whose early career included a stint under Kilroy, described him as "the
most unreasonable, unfair and intolerant tyrant I've ever known, and
the most amenable, just and liberal boss." Although Heinze's daily was
seriously outmanned by the two Amalgamated dailies and Clark's *Butte
Miner,* any *Butte Evening News* reporter scooped by the competition
could expect to be fired, rehired, and toasted at Kilroy's expense—all
before the next edition hit the streets.[22]

A natty dresser who thrived in the barely controlled chaos of the
newsroom, Kilroy relished political intrigue. E. G. Leipheimer, a former *Evening News* man and later a top editor for the company press,
considered Kilroy little more than a political operative who could
write. In the thick of the copper wars, while others labored to produce
a daily newspaper, Kilroy spent his days huddled with Heinze, plot-
ting Amalgamated's demise, only to race into the newsroom long past
deadline and order the presses held while he banged out a new editorial. Like other journalists of the day, Kilroy tried to build a political
career of his own, running unsuccessfully for the state legislature in
1904 with Heinze's Anti-Trust Party, a hapless effort to continue the
Clark-Heinze "fusion" of 1900. In the wake of Heinze's sellout and the
collapse of his political machine, Kilroy tried to keep the *Evening News*
alive, but without Heinze's money, the paper sank within months.[23]

A man of malleable politics, Kilroy resurfaced in Missoula shortly thereafter, this time as a Democrat. He immediately trained the
Sentinel's guns on Dixon, accusing the senator who sought to "Put
the Amalgamated Out of State Politics" of being a company stooge
himself, a "polecat," "imposter," and "corporation messenger boy,"
whose anti-company stance was all "sham." Kilroy's claims were
pure hokum—and more politically astute Missoulians saw through
them—but such an audacious and cynical strategy reflected the

widespread confusion about the company's actual influence over Montana's press. Kilroy wasn't the only Montanan who exploited the public's bewilderment. So potent was the charge of company affiliation that by the end of the 1912 campaign, all three Senate candidates stood accused in the daily press of being in the company's pocket. Similar suspicions would reverberate through nearly every statewide election for years.[24]

Dixon fought back through Arthur Stone's editorials in the *Missoulian* and open letters to readers, in which he accused Amalgamated of concocting the *Sentinel's* assault to divert attention from Dixon's attacks on the company. It was true, Dixon wrote, that he had received company support earlier in his career, but so had anyone opposed to Heinze's corruption. The Missoula campaign struck its lowest note when Kilroy charged that Dixon accepted rents from a notorious Missoula madam. In response, the *Missoulian* reported that Kilroy had abandoned a wife and "two innocent babies" in Chouteau County in 1904 and had callously dodged court orders to pay for their support. Kilroy published a rabid but vague denial, but the *Missoulian* stood by its story. Election Day finally brought the scandalous exchanges to a halt, and though Dixon was buried in the statewide Democratic sweep, he took consolation in winning Missoula and neighboring Ravalli counties, despite Kilroy's best efforts.[25]

Unseated, Dixon returned to Missoula in the winter of 1913, determined to remake himself as an active newspaper publisher in a business he hoped would allow him to shore up his family's finances and retain some political influence should new opportunities arise. He rejected an offer of ninety thousand dollars to sell the *Missoulian* to a man he suspected of being an Amalgamated agent and set about improving the paper's dreary financial performance. The *Sentinel,* however, remained in his way, siphoning away just enough advertising revenue to keep the *Missoulian* perpetually on the edge of ruin. Too small to support but one decent daily, Missoula was a boneyard for failed newspapers, especially Democratic ones, and Dixon aimed to add the *Sentinel* to the pile. Though he had little day-to-day experience in newspapering, he threw himself into the effort. Gradually and with Stone's help, Dixon also assumed the paper's chief editorial duties. His talent for oratory served him well on the *Missoulian*'s editorial page, and he boldly demanded an increase in the mining industry's taxes and regulation of rates charged by utilities—issues sure to attract the attention of Amalgamated and its corporate sibling, the Montana Power Company.[26]

Such blasts were routine in the context of elections, but Dixon's intent to beat the anti-company drum year-round posed a threat the company had not faced since Heinze's demise. In response, Kilroy stepped up the *Sentinel*'s own attacks, but the fight only focused more attention on Amalgamated's political and journalistic influence. In the end, the company must have viewed Missoula's newspaper war as a losing proposition. Amalgamated sent more emissaries to sound Dixon out on the prospect of selling, but like a poker player running a strong bluff, Dixon raised the pressure and made it personal with editorial attacks on "Con" Kelley and other company officials, men whom Dixon had come to know during his decade in Washington.[27]

Dixon's battle brought the *Missoulian* close to collapse, but a former senator was no ordinary opponent. In late May of 1913, Amalgamated sent Roy S. Alley, a Butte attorney whose duties for the company included overseeing its publicity efforts, to negotiate a truce. Dixon made it clear that what he really wanted was the *Sentinel*. Without its financial competition, he was certain he could make the *Missoulian* pay. After a further visit from John G. Morony, the Great Falls banker who acted as the company's chief political agent in Montana, Dixon and the company struck a deal. The company agreed to halt publication of the *Sentinel* and grant Dixon the paper's name, its subscription list, and its afternoon Associated Press franchise—free of charge. A local bank was designated to sell off the *Sentinel*'s equipment, ensuring that it would not immediately fall into a new rival's hands. What the company received for the seventy thousand dollars it reportedly lost on the *Sentinel* is not clear—perhaps only a reduction in the frequency and venom of Dixon's attacks. Dixon biographer Jules Karlin maintained that Alley and Morony sought commitments from Dixon, but the former senator would agree only to treat the company fairly. On June 10, the *Sentinel* announced tersely that Richard Kilroy had sold his stock in the *Sentinel* and was leaving town. The company would employ his special talents at another time, another paper.[28]

THE YEAR 1913 BROUGHT crucial changes for other Montana dailies and none was more significant than the sale of John Neill's *Helena Independent* to a group of Democratic investors led by Lewis Penwell, a prominent attorney, rancher, and Progressive activist. When the paper became available following Neill's death, Penwell and freshly elected senator Thomas Walsh grasped the opportunity to build a platform for Progressive Democrats eager to press the advantage won in 1912. Banking on state printing contracts to help make their investment pay—contracts that had routinely landed at "Doc" Lanstrum's *Montana Daily Record* when Republicans ruled—Penwell and Walsh peddled the paper's shares to party faithful. Besides Penwell, the *Independent's* board of directors featured a who's who of prominent Democrats, including Walsh's law partner, former attorney general C. B. Nolan; T. M. Swindlehurst, chairman of the state Democratic central committee; and Bozeman judge W. R. C. Stewart. Stockholders included Walsh and an up-and-coming Burton K. Wheeler, a young, hard-charging Butte attorney with a radical bent. Penwell also offered ten thousand dollars worth of stock to the public.[29]

The lists of the *Independent's* directors and stockholders also included William A. Campbell, a young but well-traveled Nebraskan whom Penwell and Walsh had enticed to be the paper's editor and publisher. Campbell had cut his journalistic teeth at the *Omaha Bee,* followed by stints at the *Chicago Chronicle* and the *Sioux City Tribune.* His apprenticeship also included time on one of the West's great dailies, the crusading *Denver Post,* whose owners, Fred Bonfils and Harold Tammen, wielded the paper like a club. With blood-red headlines spanning its front pages, the *Post* acquired a reputation as "the yellowest of yellow journals," and Campbell clearly admired its swaggering style. From newspapering, Campbell had jumped to corporate relations, working as a traveling promoter for the Great Northern Railway, enticing would-be homesteaders to the prairies along the railroad's track through the Dakotas, Montana, and Idaho.[30]

But Penwell's offer of an editor's chair and Campbell's eventual ownership of the *Helena Independent* ended his wanderings forever, though it meant exchanging his Republican loyalties for the "principles of the Democratic party as formulated by Thomas Jefferson."[31] Despite the paper's obvious political connections, Campbell told readers that his *Independent* would serve as no politician's organ. "This is the understanding among those who control the stock of the Independent," Campbell wrote. "If they cannot be paid in cash dividends, they will not be paid in editorial favors nor undeserved political support. The stockholders understand that what the people want is news rather than their views."[32]

To allay suspicions that Amalgamated money lay behind the *Independent*'s new management, Campbell offered to open the paper's books to "anyone desiring to honestly know who holds the stock."[33]

A gifted writer with a slashing style, Campbell lost no time aligning his paper with Democratic conservatives with strong ties to the company, much to the chagrin of the Progressives who hired him. He drew close to Montana's new governor, Samuel V. Stewart, the conservative Virginia City lawyer who rode Woodrow Wilson's coattails to victory. Stewart would come quickly to the company's defense in its intensifying struggle with Butte's Socialists and labor radicals, especially its noisy if tiny contingent of "Wobblies," members of the revolutionary Industrial Workers of the World. The radicals drew Campbell's wrath from the start, and his flaying of dissenters, labor militants, and foreign "undesirables" mirrored the editorial sentiments of the company dailies and Clark's *Butte Miner,* though few editors could match Campbell's flaming prose.

The year brought major changes at the company papers too. In the summer of 1912, Marcus Daly's widow sold her majority share of the *Anaconda Standard* to the company, a move followed immediately by John Durston's sudden and unexplained resignation after twenty-three years as editor. The *Standard*'s curious silence about its founding editor's departure suggested personal motives, perhaps a shattered dream of sharing in the paper's ownership. The only informed speculation centers on a former assistant's claim that Durston quit amid a newsroom coup instigated by one of the paper's Butte editors, Charles Copenharve, and other younger staffers frustrated with the editor-in-chief's apparent withdrawal from the paper's day-to-day operations. Whatever the truth,

Durston retired to his Bozeman ranch, apparently through with journalism. In a reflective letter to senator-elect Thomas Walsh, he found himself "without settled plans" yet "lonesome" for active newspaper work. "It is not easy to get away from the habit of talking to others, through the editorial page, concerning current topics," he wrote.[34]

Durston's hiatus was short, however, and on January 1, 1913, he returned to Butte as editor of the city's new Republican sheet, the *Butte Daily Post,* a remake of the city's *Inter Mountain,* which Amalgamated had wrested from Lee Mantle in 1901 and now officially retired. The reasons for Durston's reappearance are as murky as his departure from the *Anaconda Standard,* though the editor's biographer, John Fought, suggests Margaret Daly intervened with company officials, urging them to give the war-horse a fresh start in recognition of faithful service. As for the paper's name change—an allusion to the pioneering *Montana Post*—Durston's gravitas surely precluded his return to an unreconstructed *Inter Mountain,* which had long been the weaker of the company's two dailies and Durston's old-time nemesis. Of the *Inter Mountain's* reincarnation, the *Standard* would only say that Durston himself had purchased the paper's "plant, circulation and good will," and it wished him success. Regardless of what caused the shakeup, Durston threw himself into the project, rebuilding the paper's staff, making technological improvements, and adjusting to his part as a Republican spokesman, a role he hadn't played since leaving the *Syracuse Standard* nearly a quarter-century before.[35]

Back at the *Anaconda Standard,* Durston's longtime deputy, Charles Eggleston, took the reins for an uneasy six-year run distinguished by the company's increasing dictation of the paper's editorial policy. Less stoic than his predecessor, Eggleston found himself an "editor in a straightjacket," confiding to friends and family that he frequently disagreed with the views he espoused in the *Standard's* editorials. The only way to write such editorials, he confessed to his son, was to set down his own convictions and then "rewrite to oppose himself, or in the negative, so to speak."[36]

Eggleston's elevation altered the paper's tone as well. For years, Eggleston's light "paragraphs" and comical touch offered a leavening contrast to the seriousness of Durston's editorials. But now, with

Eggleston weighed down with the duties of management and the chore of delivering the paper's daily sermons, the *Standard* seemed colder, heavier, more aloof, perhaps a reflection of the company's more business-like demeanor and its stern reaction to the rising political and economic ferment in Butte, where it faced an explosion of discontent.

Under pressures that included deteriorating wages and unsafe living and working conditions, Butte's once-solid miners' union fractured into conservative and radical factions, and reformers began to find receptive audiences. Promising to clean up the city's filth and political corruption—problems Butte politicians had long ignored—Socialists captured municipal government in 1911, despite the harangues of the Amalgamated dailies, which portrayed them as foreign-influenced enemies of "the American way, American ideals and American customs." The *Butte Miner*—still under Clark's control along with the Elm Orlu Mine, some valuable zinc mines, and assorted real estate he declined to sell the company in 1910—joined in on and often led the attack on behalf of the conservative mining industry. Under Socialist mayor Lewis Duncan, the city government improved public health and sanitation, reined in municipal graft, and upgraded Butte's streets, but its support for workers' rights and higher taxes on mining operations brought down the predictable wrath of the company and its editors.[37]

The Socialists fought back in the pages of the *Butte Socialist,* a biweekly newspaper established in 1910, and later in a Butte-based statewide weekly, the *Montana Socialist,* begun in the fall of 1912. Though neither publication could match the conservative dailies' pages, frequency, or reach, they campaigned with energy and nerve. On the eve of the Socialists' first municipal victories in Butte in 1911, volunteers went door-to-door to deliver twelve thousand free copies of the *Butte Socialist,* which bemoaned "the poisonous ordure and efflivia [*sic*]" that poured from the "subsidized political sewers" of the copper press.[38]

Beyond its attacks on the Amalgamated papers, the Socialist press found a favorite target in *Butte Miner* editor Larry Dobell, the lawyer-turned-newspaperman who had been a fixture in William A. Clark's newspapers for most of two decades. Dobell, like his counterparts at the *Anaconda Standard* and the *Butte Daily Post,* consistently painted the Socialists as un-American, un-Democratic, and un-Christian, little more than parasites on the public purse, eager to siphon taxpayers' dollars into party members' pockets. When Socialists campaigned in 1914 for a study of the fairness of Butte's property-tax valuations, Dobell sidestepped the argument and labeled the effort a scheme to increase the Socialists' share of city patronage jobs. In his reply to "Comrade Larry," the editor of the *Montana Socialist* could only shake his head. "We are almost never disappointed in anticipating that the editor of the Miner will make a consummate political arse of himself in his editorial attacks on the Socialist Party in Butte."[39]

The company matched its newspapers' rhetoric with action, including mass firings of workers suspected of having Socialist sympathies, but the Socialists' relatively tame political agenda paled compared with that of the IWW, which proposed nothing less than overthrow of the capitalist system. Though few in number, highly transient, and barely organized, the Wobblies struck fear across the political spectrum, even among Socialists, with their disdain for political solutions and the fiery rhetoric of leaders such as "Big Bill" Haywood, whose "free-speech fights" and calls for industry-wide strikes and other "direct action" appealed to the most marginalized workers, especially new immigrants and others shunned by established and more conservative trade unions. The Wobblies' rhetoric also made them useful foil for industrialists eager to discredit the demands of unionized workers for higher wages and safer working conditions.

By 1914, Wobblies—real and imagined—emerged as prime targets of the copper press and would remain so for years to come. IWW sympathizers, or company detectives posing as such, played a pivotal role as conservative and radical factions fought for control of Butte's disgruntled miners' unions. When tensions finally erupted in gunfire and the bombing of the Butte Miners Union Hall in June of 1914, Will Campbell's *Helena Independent* quickly blamed the IWW, castigated Butte's Socialist leaders for failing to keep the peace, and suggested that Campbell's friend, Governor Sam Stewart, send in militia to bring the radicals "to their senses and send them scurrying from Butte."[40]

In an attempt to calm their city's nerves, Butte's copper dailies at first shunned Campbell's heated calls for military intervention, but when Campbell scooped them with news of Governor Stewart's decision to send

The company and its newspapers opposed unions, especially the radical IWW. In June 1914, labor unrest erupted in gunfire and the bombing of the Butte Miners Union Hall, after which Amalgamated effectively locked out unions for the next twenty years.

MONTANA HISTORICAL SOCIETY PHOTOGRAPH ARCHIVES, HELENA

in the National Guard, they embraced the call for martial law, including its provision that any "publication, either in newspaper, pamphlet, handbill or otherwise, in any way reflecting upon the United States, the state of Montana or their officers, civil or military, or tending to influence the public mind against them, will not be tolerated."[41]

Soon after the troops' arrival, the officer in charge of censorship, one Lieutenant Baker, called a meeting of the city's editors to explain that all news published in Butte would first have to pass review. Of those in attendance—the *Butte Miner*'s Larry Dobell; John Durston, Charles Cohen, and Charles Shearer of the *Butte Daily Post*; Wally Walsworth and Charles Copenharve of the *Anaconda Standard*; an Associated Press reporter from Spokane; and Mayor Lewis Duncan representing the *Montana Socialist*—only Duncan questioned the scope of the censorship. Would it apply to newspapers bundled and shipped outside the city? Yes, the lieutenant replied. According to the *Standard*'s account of the meeting, which ran under a headline lauding the censor's "liberal" interpretation of his mission: "Editor Duncan attempted to argue the point, but the censor's reply was merely a repetition of what he had briefly said before. The socialist editor then wanted to know if he could run blank or black spaces in place of the matter censored and explain in the space that matter had been cut out by the censor. He was informed that that wouldn't do either."[42]

Gatling guns on the city's streets and a military court under Major Jesse B. Roote, a Butte attorney closely associated with William A. Clark, gave Amalgamated the muscle to lock out its troublesome unions, which it refused to recognize for the next twenty years.[43] Meanwhile, company newspapers and sympathetic editors such as Campbell and Dobell continued to hound Wobblies and the Socialists. Under such pressure, coupled with factional infighting and economic hardships, Butte's Socialists tumbled from power in the civic elections of 1915. Their newspaper, the *Butte Socialist*, suffered a similarly dire fate. In June, a dynamite explosion wrecked its presses, and though it was quickly reestablished, the paper stopped publication by year's end. Its editors blamed its demise on real and threatened violence, blacklists and boycotts of its subscribers and advertisers, and the incessant attacks of the "subsidized capitalist press," which it charged had "stopped at no misrepresentation, vilification, innuendo and downright falsehood with which to affect [*sic*] our destruction."[44]

As THE NATION INCHED CLOSER to World War I, the company reasserted its dominance over Butte with help from a sympathetic governor, the state militia, and the copper press. In its fight with reformers, the company could count on the support of all three Butte dailies as well as the Republican and Democratic dailies in Helena and Great Falls. Dixon's *Missoulian* remained something of a wild card, though it too opposed the Socialists who made brief inroads in local government and IWW organizers who found fertile ground in the hazards and poverty of western Montana's timber camps. In eastern Montana, a struggle for control of the region's most influential voice, the *Billings Gazette*, would eventually bring that newspaper into the company's orbit as well.

The *Gazette* remains the most mysterious of all the company's journalistic acquisitions. The evidence suggests the company's ownership evolved gradually through Anaconda's varied business and political ties to prominent ranchers and bankers who held sway over the vast and thinly populated range east of Livingston. Far from the company's mining, smelting, lumber, and hydropower operations, Billings and its Republican newspaper had enjoyed an unusual measure of journalistic independence during the copper wars, when the paper had argued that Montana would "never have any decent politics" until both Marcus Daly and William A. Clark "were shorn of power."[45]

Built from the bones of three pioneer papers—the *Billings Post,* the *Billings Herald,* and the *Rustler*—the *Gazette* barely survived its debut on May 2, 1885. As editors composed its inaugural edition, a fire broke out, and while the building smoldered, printers somehow salvaged a small job press and enough type to produce a three-column, single-sheet issue.[46] Such determination no doubt helped the paper survive the volatile environment that claimed Billings's other early newspapers, including the short-lived *Vociferator,* whose motto—"We did not come here for our health"—doubled as a fitting epitaph.[47]

In politics, the *Gazette* tilted toward the company in the war with Heinze and in its endorsement of the company's chief Republican ally, Senator Thomas Carter. Support for protective tariffs on wool and beef made Carter a favorite of eastern Montana's ranchers, but his death in 1911 left a vacuum in Montana's Republican hierarchy, which only intensified the party's internal struggle between conservatives loyal to Carter's patron, President Taft, and Bull Moose Progressives loyal to Taft's predecessor, Theodore Roosevelt, and Senator Joseph Dixon. The resulting Republican tug-of-war pitted Dixon against a quartet of conservatives led by Thomas Marlow, a Helena banker with strong ties to both the company and the Montana Power Company; "Doc" Lanstrum, an old Carter man and publisher of Helena's *Montana Daily Record*; Charles M. Bair, a wealthy eastern Montana sheepman; and state senator John Edwards, a Forsyth banker and rancher. Of the four, Edwards nursed the most virulent animosity toward Dixon, stemming from his attempt to block Dixon's election to the U.S. Senate in 1907. Like Lanstrum, Edwards also desired higher office, but such ambition required a supportive daily newspaper and so far Edwards's journalistic influence was limited to a string of weeklies in Forsyth, Big Timber, and Columbus.[48]

With Miles City's two small Republican dailies—the established *Yellowstone Journal* and the newly hatched *Miles City Star*—split along the Progressive-conservative lines, Edwards focused on the *Billings Gazette* and the *Billings Evening Journal*, both published by the Gazette Printing Company. Since 1907, the papers had been in the hands of Preston B. Moss, a Missouri-born banker, developer, and civic promoter. Moss's businesses centered on his ownership of the city's First Trust and Savings Bank, and it may have been through a defaulted loan that he acquired the newspapers. In any case, when Moss's own financial troubles forced his bank into receivership in 1910, the newspapers were put on the auction block to satisfy creditors. Moss planned to buy them back, but before he could raise the money, a judge sold them to Helena businessman Odell W. McConnell for $6,001—almost $70,000 less than what Moss figured they were worth. Moss sued, and in early 1912 the Montana Supreme Court negated the newspapers' sale but returned them to the receiver for more than a year of legal wrangling.[49]

Moss's interest in journalism had been largely financial. The papers held no obvious grudge against Amalgamated, but they had backed their owner in a fight with some company associates over control of the local power utility. Moss suspected Amalgamated's hand in McConnell's bid for the papers, and by the time Moss turned to Senator Dixon for help, the *Gazette*'s fate was thoroughly entangled in the Republican feud of 1912. Dixon shared Moss's hopefulness when the Supreme Court voided the papers' sale to the "Helena-Butte combine," but the action merely delayed a change in ownership. For more than a year, the papers suffered through a schizophrenic limbo that clearly reflected a behind-the-scenes struggle for control. *Gazette* readers could only scratch their heads during the 1912 campaign as the paper endorsed Robert M. LaFollete for president while warning voters against the hopelessness of third-party campaigns.[50]

Change finally came in January of 1914, when the *Gazette* abruptly informed readers that it was under a new but unnamed management, which vowed to make the *Gazette* "a truly metropolitan paper" by investing twenty-five thousand dollars in a plant and aggressively seeking new subscribers. To boost circulation, the *Gazette* sprinkled its pages with photos of silent movie starlets and debutantes and even hired a biplane to buzz the city as a man working a small hand press in the rear cockpit printed and tossed handbills to onlookers below. Politically, the paper was unabashedly conservative. It criticized the state railroad commission for ordering rate cuts for shippers, for fear that such cuts would bankrupt the railways. Other indicators included its frequent calls for the return of Bull Moosers to the Republican fold and its opposition to the enactment of a state workers' compensation law. By 1916, incorporation papers listed John Edwards as the Gazette Printing Company's principal director and largest stockholder in an ownership group that included an assortment of merchants and railroad officials and sheep rancher Charles Bair, whose ten-thousand-dollar investment would be worth millions one day.[51]

Edwards's hiring of veteran Helena newsman Leon Shaw as the *Gazette*'s editor solidified the paper's conservative credentials. A Kansan by birth, Shaw had been a railroad and commercial telegrapher in various states before landing in Helena in 1892. He eventually left Western

With Leon Shaw as editor during the turbulent years of World War I, the Billings Gazette *emerged as the leading conservative voice for eastern Montana and a solid friend of the newly renamed Anaconda Copper Mining Company. As the* Billings Gazette *swung the company's way, Dixon's* Missoulian *maintained its independence as best it could. Shaw is pictured here in 1907.*

J. M. MORIARTY, PHOTOGRAPHER,
MONTANA HISTORICAL SOCIETY PHOTOGRAPH
ARCHIVES, HELENA

Union to work as a wire editor for the *Montana Daily Record* in Helena and later for the *Butte Miner* before eventually returning to the *Record,* where he rose to associate editor. Like so many of Montana's editors, Shaw had political experience, having served a term in the legislature, where he worked closely with John Edwards and other conservatives in the Republican Party's Carter-Edwards-Lanstrum wing. For his service, Carter selected Shaw as eastern Montana's census supervisor in 1909, a controversial appointment that marked just one of many bitter skirmishes between Carter and Dixon over patronage.[52]

Politics also played a role in Shaw's decision to abandon Helena for Billings in 1916, the year of Edwards's unsuccessful run for the Republican U.S. Senate nomination. The campaign proved so acrimonious that it shattered Edwards's alliance with Helena newspaperman "Doc" Lanstrum, who had begun to fear that without the Progressives' support, Republicans might never win another election. In a bold break with conservatives and the company, Lanstrum bought enough additional stock to gain control of the *Montana Daily Record* and renamed it the *Montana Record-Herald,* which he proceeded to steer on a more Progressive course. Shaw saw his future with Edwards and moved to Billings.[53]

Under Edwards and Shaw, the *Billings Gazette* emerged as the leading conservative voice for eastern Montana and solid friend of the newly renamed Anaconda Copper Mining Company during the turbulence that rocked Montana during World War I and the years that followed. If Anaconda held stock in the *Gazette,* it was well hidden in the holdings of individual investors, yet there were plenty of opportunities for its financial involvement. Between 1916 and 1923, the Gazette Printing Company raised nearly three hundred thousand dollars through expanded stock offerings and the sale of bonds to unnamed investors. As late as 1935, *Gazette* officials still claimed the paper was free of Anaconda's control, a blatant lie that fooled almost no one.[54]

As the *Billings Gazette* swung the company's way, Dixon's *Missoulian* and Lanstrum's *Montana Record-Herald* in Helena maintained their independence from the company as best they could. Satisfied that he had "never been tempted to surrender to this bunch of pirates," Dixon took his job as publisher seriously, though running Missoula's Republican and Democratic papers posed a conflict of interest in which the *Sentinel* was bound to suffer. The company itself had pioneered such bipartisan arrangements with its ownership of the *Anaconda Standard* and the Butte *Inter Mountain* and a similar arrangement had existed in Billings with Preston Moss's ownership of both the Republican *Gazette* and the ostensibly Democratic *Evening Journal.* In Great Falls, *Tribune* publisher Oliver Warden figured prominently in the state's Democratic leadership and yet owned the city's Republican daily too. The phenomenon, hardly unknown in American journalism, was strictly business, a concession to commercial realities that were slowly eroding decades of partisan newspaper ownership.

Yet despite the lack of daily competition, Dixon still struggled to make his properties pay. To economize, he cut the *Sentinel*'s staff and installed an office-supply business, but he also borrowed to make mechanical improvements in the *Missoulian.* Dixon's dailies lost an estimated twenty-five thousand dollars in 1913 and 1914, and at one point he considered closing the *Sentinel.* He pressed his printers for wage concessions and haggled with feature services and the Associated Press for low assessments, yet still Dixon worried that his papers would suffer that fate that had befallen so many Missoula newspapers. "This town has so many tombstones erected in memory of bad judgment in the newspaper business that it is sad to contemplate," he wrote one colleague. To another, he bemoaned the logic of "publishing a twelve page paper in an eight page town."[55]

Journalistically, the Missoula papers compared favorably with small-town dailies of the time. They offered readers concise, timely, and balanced summaries of national and international news, an attentive local news report, a mix of entertaining features and columns, attractive advertising—all of it bound in clean, dignified design that reflected the craftsmanship of their production staffs and Dixon's sense of style. The effort did not go unnoticed by Dixon's Montana peers, including Congressman Tom Stout, a political rival but also a brother publisher who churned out Lewistown's *Democrat-News*. "I read the Missoulian with interest but somehow wonder how you can get by with a paper of that character in a town no larger than Missoula," Stout wrote.[56]

Dixon had capable help from managing editor French Ferguson, who replaced Arthur Stone in 1914 when Stone resigned to build a school of journalism at the State University of Montana (as Missoula's campus was then known), but the *Missoulian*'s editorial pages reflected Dixon's own talents. His voluminous state and national correspondence ensured that his editorials rang with first-rate political intelligence, and he waded into local, state, and national controversies with relish. Predictably, Dixon hammered away at Progressive issues, arguing for women's suffrage and low-interest loans to farmers. He demanded that Anaconda and Montana Power Company pay a larger share of the state's property taxes, and he also challenged both Anaconda and its creature, the Montana Development Association, with his spirited support for a comprehensive workers' compensation initiative in 1914. Although it failed due to fears that it would include farm and ranch labor, the measure won nearly two-thirds of Missoula County's vote.[57]

A general economic revival in 1915 and 1916 put the *Missoulian* and *Sentinel* back in the black, but their success was threatened almost immediately by the appearance of a new and hostile Democratic weekly,

the *New Northwest,* whose name reminded old-timers of the now defunct Deer Lodge weekly and whose publisher, Edwin B. Craighead,
nursed both political and personal grudges against Dixon and his papers. The feud began in 1914 with Dixon's opposition to a statewide
initiative to consolidate the far-flung units of Montana's university
system, the brainchild of Craighead, the Missoula campus's energetic
president. Craighead's proposal to eliminate the duplication inherent
in maintaining multiple colleges in a state with so few taxpayers infuriated business leaders who feared it could lead to the closure of local campuses. Missoula banker J. H. T. Ryman, Dixon's close friend
and confidant, led a fierce opposition, and when the initiative failed,
Ryman launched a successful, if nasty, back-channel campaign to have
Craighead fired. The *Missoulian's* support for the college president's dismissal sparked a running feud with Craighead, who had previously ir-
ritated the publisher by seeking competitive bids on lucrative university
printing contracts that had traditionally come the *Missoulian's* way.[58]

Craighead might have abandoned Missoula had it not been for
the personal attacks of his critics, Dixon included, who claimed the
campus president had bullied faculty members, squandered taxpayers'
money, and worse, drank to excess, a serious charge against a molder of
young minds on the eve of Prohibition. The accusations were specious,
and Craighead, a respected former president of Tulane University and
a friend of President Woodrow Wilson, mounted a noisy campaign
to clear his name and keep his job. Students lit bonfires and marched
in protest, while faculty members circulated petitions denouncing the
bald political interference in their school's management. Missoula's
clamor on Craighead's behalf encouraged him and his sons Edwin
and Barclay to remain and start their own weekly newspaper, the *New
Northwest,* a publication devoted to Progressive politics and the excoriation of Joseph Dixon.[59]

A veteran of grander battles on the national stage, Dixon treated
the fight with Craighead as a minor annoyance and claimed he paid
no attention to the new weekly's "vicious personal abuse"—which
at one point included a revival of the old story that Dixon had once
been a landlord to prostitutes. But Dixon could not ignore the slice
the Craigheads' "spite sheet" took from his papers' advertising revenues

nor its plans to open a competing commercial printing plant. Having just nursed his papers back to profitability, Dixon made it known by the fall of 1916 that they were for sale. Time, however, was precious. By early 1917, the Craigheads were considering converting their weekly to daily publication, and the potential backers reportedly included the Anaconda Company itself. According to Barclay Craighead, the company's pitch came from Anaconda attorney Roy Alley during a chance meeting in a Helena bar. Alley suggested the company might subsidize a daily, provided the Craigheads agree to "wear the copper collar." Informed of the offer, the elder Craighead reportedly said he would sooner "cut sassafras roots and peddle tea for a living."[60]

Regardless of whether Anaconda intended to finance a competing daily, Dixon knew the possibility existed at any time—and there were clues the company's patience was running thin. Anaconda's timber business abruptly canceled its advertising in both the *Missoulian* and the *Sentinel,* and the Chicago, Milwaukee, St. Paul and Pacific Railroad, better known as the Milwaukee Road, whose directors included Anaconda president John D. Ryan, stopped providing its local passengers with free copies of the *Missoulian.* Dixon quietly stepped up his efforts to unload the papers, but a prospective sale to Chicago investors fell through near the end of 1916.[61]

A new hope appeared in late April of 1917 when Dixon was approached with news that two more Chicago newspapermen, Martin J. Hutchens and Lester L. Jones, the respective managers of the *Chicago Journal's* editorial and business operations, were in the market for a Montana daily. The *Great Falls Tribune* and Helena's *Independent* had reportedly topped the pair's list of prospects, but when those papers appeared unavailable, they approached Dixon about the *Missoulian* and *Sentinel.* No record of ensuing talks ever surfaced, but Dixon eventually negotiated a deal, allowing the new owners to take control on May 1. In return for a fat down payment, Dixon agreed to carry a mortgage on the building and transferred the papers to Jones and George C. Rice, another *Chicago Journal* staffer. Hutchens, who had no apparent financial stake in the deal, would serve as the *Missoulian's* editor. Incorporation papers placed all but two of the paper's two hundred shares in Jones's control.[62]

Dixon would later maintain that he was duped into selling his papers to journalists fronting for Anaconda. His eagerness to unload the papers may have blinded him to obvious clues: the ease with which the buyers obtained local financing; their fraternization with Dixon's rivals and known Anaconda allies; and the willingness of Hutchens, an editor of national repute and metropolitan experience, to take the reins of two small-town dailies with limited financial potential. The most detailed, if anecdotal, account of the sale holds that the deal was an Anaconda operation from the start, hatched by Roy Alley in the Placer Hotel bar, with T. J. Hocking, a traveling typewriter salesman and owner of the *Glasgow Courier*, acting as a go-between. Hocking reportedly laundered a one-hundred-thousand-dollar company check through a Spokane bank and gave the money to Missoula attorney William L. Murphy, whose corporate clients included the Anaconda Company, the Milwaukee Road, and the Montana Power Company. Indeed, Murphy, who oversaw the transaction, would serve as an officer of the Missoulian Publishing Company until his death in 1954. It was only after a congratulatory drink at Missoula's Florence Hotel, when Dixon reportedly saw a political rival warmly greet the new owners, that he suspected the company's involvement in the deal.[63]

Given Dixon's savvy, his presumed familiarity with Murphy, and his nose for sniffing out earlier company-backed offers for his papers, it is difficult to believe he was so easily hoodwinked. It is at least conceivable that the sale was constructed to give both Anaconda and Dixon the political cover they required. In any case, Dixon wrote friends that the Chicago group proposed to run "an independent paper along the Missoulian's line," ostensibly Republican in politics but beholden to no candidate or faction. "I believed it," he added. To a fellow Republican editor, Dixon confirmed the papers' sale and gave his appraisal of the buyers' chances of success. "Of course, I hated to part with them but I was worn out with the eternal demand on every minute of my time to the exclusion of everything else," he wrote. "The new men are here and took charge today. They look like they know their business and I believe they are going to make good." But in his farewell editorial, as he introduced Rice, Jones, and Hutchens to his readers, Dixon also conceded his readers' suspicions. "Notwithstanding rumors to the contrary, I believe that no other interests are connected with the transaction."[64]

The papers' new owners were clearly aware of the suspicions too, though perhaps they too failed to understand the nature of Anaconda's grip. In the early stages of his nine-year editorship, Hutchens took extraordinary pains to protest the *Missoulian*'s independence and occasionally took positions contrary to the company's interests. After his death, Hutchens's widow insisted that her husband had been shocked to learn that the company held the notes that bankrolled the sale. In time, Hutchens would come to rue Anaconda's ownership of Montana's most influential dailies. So would Dixon, now a gentleman farmer pondering his political future on the spectacular south shore of Montana's Flathead Lake.[65]

By the spring of 1917, as America mobilized for the war in Europe, the Anaconda Copper Mining Company could count on editorial support across Montana, from every daily in Butte, and from sympathetic editors in Missoula, Helena, Billings, and Great Falls. "Doc" Lanstrum's *Montana Record-Herald,* a wistful reminder of the Fisks' independent *Helena Herald,* played the joker, but not even Lanstrum dared to oppose the company as war suddenly made copper a strategic industry.

As American troops arrived in France, and in the streets of Butte, the company counted friends in the editor's chairs of almost every major newspaper in the state. It would need them.

LISTENING TO MISS RANKIN

A crowd of more than eight thousand people gathered to listen to Congresswoman Jeannette Rankin in Butte on August 18, 1917. Addressing the crowd regarding the ongoing miners' strike, Rankin said, "I am convinced that the demands of labor in this trouble are just and should be granted."

BUTTE MINER, AUGUST 19, 1917

The Copper Press at War

HYSTERIA
ON THE
HOME FRONT

THE ASSIGNMENT CAME FROM Charles Copenharve, a veteran editor of the *Anaconda Standard* with a reputation for occasionally allowing his passions to outrun his judgment. Normally, questions concerning sensitive political coverage fell to Wally Walsworth, chief of the paper's Butte bureau, whose duties sometimes included weeding extraneous opinion from his assistant's news copy. But Saturday, August 18, 1917, found Walsworth on vacation and Copenharve pondering how to cover the visit of a congresswoman who had recently demanded a federal takeover of Butte's copper mines.[1]

Years later, reporter Charles L. Stevens, a ten-year *Standard* man, recalled both the day and Copenharve's open admiration for Jeannette Rankin, the first woman elected to Congress and one of its few members to vote against the United States' entry into World War I that spring. Having obtained an advance copy of the speech Rankin was to deliver that afternoon to thousands of striking miners at a baseball field on the edge of town, the editor summoned Stevens to his desk. "Go out and report the meeting, and report it just as it is." Copenharve told his reporter. "Give the whole truth."[2]

Stevens caught a ride to Butte's Columbia Gardens in the car carrying Rankin, U.S. Attorney Burton K. Wheeler, and Socialist labor lawyer H. Lowndes Maury—all known for their support of the strikers' cause. Upon arrival, they were greeted by a crowd of more than eight thousand, most of them miners. Packed around the speakers' platform erected near home plate, the crowd jammed the bleachers and fanned out over the field, as deep as the outfield fences. Reports would describe the throng as attentive and well mannered, despite the shocks Butte had suffered over the past ten weeks.[3]

On the fourth of June, police and national guardsmen had used clubs to break up demonstrations against the draft, arresting dozens in the first of many "slacker raids" to come. Four days later an accidental fire swept through the Speculator Mine, killing 162 in one of the deadliest disasters in the history of American mining. Many of the dead were found heaped against illegal concrete barriers that blocked their escape through the shafts of adjoining mines. On June 11, thousands of grieving, seething miners walked off the job to protest hazardous working conditions and wages devalued by wartime inflation. On August 1, as the strike seemed to be flagging, masked gunmen abducted and murdered an IWW agitator named Frank Little and hung his mangled corpse from a railroad trestle. Pinned to the tatters of Little's clothing was a cryptic warning to other radicals.[4]

Remarkably, Butte kept its head. Little's funeral drew enormous crowds, but they were orderly, like the one now gathered around Stevens at the baseball park. The last speaker of the day, Rankin told miners that while she despised the IWW's revolutionary aims and rhetoric, Little's brutal murder was inexcusable. So was the company's refusal to acknowledge miners' complaints, its blacklisting of union miners, and its portrayal of strikers as unpatriotic. "I am convinced that the demands of labor in this trouble are just and should be granted," she said. The applause seemed interminable.[5]

Later, back at the *Standard*'s Butte office, Stevens wrote a lengthy story, "without exaggeration or coloring," and sent it over the wire to Anaconda, where other editors would prepare it for the morning edition. But Stevens's story never ran. "Sunday morning we looked for the report," Stevens recalled. "It wasn't there. Another, shorter, and very different report appeared." On Monday, Charles Eggleston, the *Standard*'s editor-in-chief, arrived at the paper's East Broadway offices and summoned both Copenharve and Stevens, who was struck by Eggleston's obvious struggle to keep his composure.[6]

"Boys," he said, "I have the most unpleasant task to perform that I have ever had to do. Cope, you have been with us 26 years and I never knew a better companion or better man than you have been."

Turning to Stevens, he said, "Charlie, since that day 10 years ago when you landed out here and we had you over for dinner I watched your work and I want you to know that I was never disappointed in you."

But then the editor added, "It is with deepest regret that I have to tell you two that the directors of the Standard Publishing Company have decided to dispense with your services. I was instructed to notify you and to say that you will each be paid a month's salary in advance. I have also been instructed not to discuss the matter with you."[7]

IN MOST RESPECTS, the copper press's coverage of World War I differed little from that of thousands of American newspapers. News columns bulged with reports of recruiting drives, the training and deployment of local military units, and the countless ways in which ordinary Americans were enlisted to support the fight, from the purchase of war bonds to the donation of food, scrap metal, and bandages. News of faraway battles suddenly received more prominence, and newspapers willingly carried thousands of press releases cranked out by Woodrow Wilson's propaganda machine. Editorially, the copper press pushed a spirited but vague "Americanism," defined mostly by what it was not; and it was decidedly not foreign, nor did it tolerate criticism of American government or capitalism.[8]

The wartime campaign waged by Montana's "copper chorus" against Socialists, labor unions, and radicals mirrored those of conservative newspapers across the nation, but in Montana, the copper production's strategic importance raised the tone to a hysterical pitch. In their crusade for the sympathies of frightened readers, and to protect company profits, Anaconda's newspapers and those of its allies routinely exaggerated the threat posed by domestic dissenters, encouraging acts of repression and violence that would echo though Montana politics for generations.

At the war's beginning in 1914, Montana's major dailies followed the conflict with editorial detachment, a reflection of the nation's intense neutrality and in some deference to the anti-British sentiments of its German- and Irish-American readers. Yet wire service reports from the front lines featured a distinctly pro-British cast, marked by a tendency to exaggerate German atrocities while either downplaying or emphasizing German military prowess as the political situation required. The destruction of Germany's trans-Atlantic cable early in the war gave British censors effective control of American war news, and the one-sided coverage drew loud protests from anti-British publishers ranging from William Randolph Hearst to Dr. Karl Weiss, the editor of Montana's leading German-language weekly, Helena's *Montana Staats-Zeitung,* who bemoaned what he saw as either the gullibility or prejudice of the editors of the state's dailies. Company editors sometimes grumbled too but saved their most spirited wrath for Britain's interference in the exportation of American copper, a principal ingredient in the manufacture of brass cartridges and shell casings.[9]

But such concerns evaporated with the escalation of Germany's unrestricted submarine warfare, epitomized by the June 1915 sinking of the British liner *Lusitania* with hundreds of Americans aboard. Montana editors fell in line with Wilson's growing support for Britain and France, democracies after all. Still, there were limits. A proposed federal tax on copper production to aid the United States' pre-war military buildup drew the *Anaconda Standard*'s editorial fire as nothing short of "confiscation." Even so, by the time the country entered the war most Montana editors were spoiling for the fight.[10]

Montana's daily press embraced the war effort, including the restrictions on what they could and could not publish. The *Standard*'s Eggleston, who began the war opposing press censorship as unnecessary, reversed himself quickly when Wilson asked Congress for the power to edit or suppress the reporting of American war correspondents. "Freedom of the press is all right under ordinary conditions and ordinary times," he wrote. "But these are extra-ordinary times." On the prowl for "slackers," the *Standard* and others papers rode herd on local draft compliance by identifying suitable men and publicizing their eligibility for service, including requests for exemptions and results of physical exams. Similar scrutiny would soon fall on ordinary citizens who failed to buy war bonds or work in crucial war industries.[11]

War touched the newspapers directly as reporters, printers, and advertising men left for military service. Of the *Helena Independent*'s fifty-four employees, eleven either volunteered or registered for the draft, including the paper's managing editor. In Hamilton, Miles Romney, the forty-four-year-old editor of the *Western News* and a veteran of the Spanish-American War, enlisted as a captain in late August 1917 and was soon overseeing the stateside distribution of army supplies and inspecting training camps.[12]

The intensity of Montana's patriotism was most clearly reflected in the heavy percentage of Montanans who served. Volunteer enlistments ran high, but an error in estimating the state's population also led to the conscription of a disproportionately heavy share of Montana's youth. Nearly one in every ten Montanans saw service—a greater percentage than any other state—and they died in record percentages too. Montana editors highlighted the state's extraordinary contribution at every opportunity. As American troops poured off the troop ships in France, the *Missoulian* proudly informed its readers that Montana led the nation in the percentage of conscripts who claimed no exemption from the draft.[13]

Like newspapers nationwide, Montana's press saw its duty as mobilizing support for the war and filled its pages with war news that often featured exaggerated accounts of German atrocities overseas and the villainy of German agents at home. No Montana editor saw more evidence of Hunnish skullduggery at home than Will Campbell, whose *Helena Independent* seethed with anti-German paranoia reflected in such headlines as "YOUR NEIGHBOR, YOUR MAID, YOUR LAWYER, YOUR WAITER MAY BE A GERMAN SPY." Campbell's paper reported phantom flights over the Flathead Indian Reservation and Bitterroot Mountains by German military aircraft, encouraged the state's bumbling hunt for German agents, and hounded Montana's largest ethnic minority, its German-Americans, into abandoning most visible manifestations of its culture, including its language, which Campbell described as "the most despised language in history, a tongue which will be damned as the world spins down the corridors of time." Through his newspaper and leadership in the state's Council of Defense, Campbell led a successful effort to ban the German language from schools, libraries, and churches, the latter despite the pleas of German-speaking congregations.[14]

Campbell's xenophobia was largely responsible for hounding Montana's German-language press out of existence. Between 1886 and 1917, Montana counted as many as nine German-language newspapers, the most prominent of which, the *Montana Staats-Zeitung*, served approximately two thousand households. The Helena-based weekly proved to be the most resilient member of Montana's "sauerkraut press," but it withered under Campbell's scorn, despite repeated demonstrations of its loyalty. Before the country's declaration of war, the *Staats-Zeitung* had argued for strict neutrality. Yet once U.S. troops were involved, it lent its support. To ease suspicions, the weekly published major stories in both English and German, but the attempt at bilingual transparency failed to blunt Campbell's attack. Karl Weiss, the otherwise temperate editor of *Staats-Zeitung*, fumed when the *Independent* quoted an unnamed source to report that Helena's German-American citizenry had secretly collected twenty thousand dollars to support the kaiser's war. "If the Helena Independent spoke the truth, it would not hold back this person's name; anyway, that would be the duty of a newspaper which stands for truth and justice." Weiss's protests only brought his paper more scrutiny, fueling Campbell's demand that the German-language press be denied the right "to spread their un-American, treasonable propaganda" through the U.S. mail. When the *Staats-Zeitung* urged the U.S. military to avoid sending German-American draftees into combat against German units, and perhaps their kin, Campbell called the paper's editor a "radical Kaiser booster" and accused him of discouraging German-Americans from doing their patriotic duty.[15]

Complaints about the *Independent*'s unfairness only egged Campbell on, and in his crusade to crush the *Staats-Zeitung* he shrewdly targeted advertisers. How any "100 percent American business" could support "an instrument of the German ambassador and the German spy system in the United States" was a mystery, he wrote. Campbell's pressure took such a toll that Fred Naegele, a prominent member of Helena's German-American community whose company printed the *Staats-Zeitung*, felt compelled to protest that neither he nor the paper had anything "in common with the Kaiser or the German government." The protest, however mild, merely gave Campbell another chance to goad the German press and insist that "Herr von Naegele" had been "done no injustice by assertions that he had been disloyal to the United States by his disagreeably pro-German utterances of past months."[16]

Furious, Naegele replied that his family's credentials as loyal Americans were as solid as anyone's—certainly stronger than Campbell's. Naegele's father had fought for the Union in the Civil War, and Naegele himself had served in the Spanish-American War. In contrast, he noted, Campbell and his two "husky brothers" had somehow escaped military service. In response, Campbell sputtered that his brothers were past the age for conscription and he himself had registered for the draft but had not been called. In lieu of military service, he touted his family's purchase of war bonds, its donations to the Red Cross, and its efforts to keep vital businesses—especially his newspaper—running in difficult times. The Campbells, he added, had "volunteered their credit" to buy a thousand-acre wheat farm "to feed the hungry world." They also volunteered to "whack a German sympathizer over the head whenever they get a chance whether he means what he is saying or not."[17]

In the end, Naegele's stand proved fruitless. By September 1917, the *Staats-Zeitung,* a fixture in the homes of Montana's German-Americans for more than thirty years, was reeling under Campbell's bullying. When once-loyal advertisers withdrew their support, Weiss had little choice but to abandon his weekly. Within three weeks of Naegele's protest, Montana's last German-language newspaper quietly expired.[18]

Caught in the prevailing hysteria, other German-speaking Americans would suffer more personal humiliations. Henry Grubisch, a worker at East Helena's smelter, made the *Independent*'s front page when co-workers wielding iron rods forced him to his knees for allegedly criticizing the war. Before allowing authorities to haul Grubisch to jail, the mob, which included several Austrians, made him kiss an American flag. Campbell's cheering approval shone through all three stanzas of the story's headline, especially its first and second decks, which read:

> AUSTRIANS FORCE DISPARGER OF THE STARRY
> BANNER TO KNEEL IN THE MUD AND KISS EMBLEM
> GRUBISCH IS GIVEN LESSON IN
> PATRIOTISM BY HIS FELLOW
> WORKERS IN THE SMELTERS
> THAT HE WILL NE'ER FORGET[19]

WITH ENCOURAGEMENT FROM federal officials, Montana's newspaper campaigns to suppress German "kultur" and root out disloyal German-Americans were hardly unique, but a casual visitor would have been struck by the intensity of the copper press's effort to portray labor radicals and Socialists as traitors too. It could hardly have created a better foil for the purpose than the Industrial Workers of the World.

A radical beacon to many marginalized and desperate workers, the IWW preached the overthrow of capitalism by any means possible. Loosely organized, prone to internal squabbling, their ranks riddled with government agents and corporate spies, the Wobblies never attracted a following to justify the immense attention they received in Montana's press. Formed in 1905 with deep roots in the labor struggles of western miners, lumberjacks, and migratory farm workers, the union forged its early reputation in "free speech fights" and calls for general strikes in which workers would cripple then seize key industries and operate them in the workers' interests. With fearless and charismatic leaders such as "Big Bill" Haywood, Elizabeth Gurley Flynn, and Frank Little, the IWW struck real terror in the heart of American business, though its deeds rarely matched the violence of its revolutionary rhetoric. Portrayed in the conservative press as labor's misfit fringe, a collection of wild-eyed tramps, "red" foreigners, anarchists, and dynamiters, the Wobblies rarely gained more than attention for their efforts.[20]

Montana miners who helped create the IWW and its "free speech" protests in Missoula and Spokane made local headlines in the union's early years, but Wobbly involvement in Butte's labor unrest of 1914 sparked a preoccupation that would last most of a decade. Though evidence clearly suggests the disastrous 1914 strike was a grassroots protest by thousands of miners against the company and the co-opted leadership of the Butte Miners Union, the copper dailies placed most of the blame on the city's few hundred card-carrying Wobblies. It was a formula they would follow well into the next decade.[21]

By Butte's disastrous summer of 1917, the IWW's wooly reputation had grown through its role in high-profile strikes in Massachusetts and New Jersey, the Utah murder trial and execution of Wobbly songsmith Joe Hill, and the "Everett Massacre," a bloody confrontation between Washington state Wobblies and vigilantes in which seven people were killed and more than fifty wounded in a dockside gun battle. Wobblies led a series of wildcat strikes to protest truly dismal working conditions in the Northwest's timber camps, beginning in Eureka, Montana, in the spring of 1917. Though a presidential commission and U.S. Forest Service officials described the strikers as orderly, hardworking men with real grievances, the secretary of war ordered federal troops to Eureka to ensure a steady supply of lumber for the war. Elsewhere, mobs took matters into their own hands. On July 12, in Bisbee, Arizona, a vigilante force of townspeople and miners loyal to the Phelps Dodge Company, with help from local law enforcement and encouragement from the Bisbee *Daily Review,* broke an IWW-led strike of mostly Mexican and foreign-born copper miners by herding them at gunpoint into railway cattle cars and dumping them without water or food in the New Mexican desert.[22]

The Arizona deportations made front-page news in Butte and other Montana cities. In Helena, the *Montana Record-Herald* applauded Bisbee's strikebreakers, absolving them of any blame in the face of official reluctance to crush the Wobblies. "There is nothing left to do but suppress their crazy or criminal leaders, to scatter their deluded rank and file and intern the alien enemies among them," the paper editorialized. In Butte, which remained in the grips of the massive walkout that had followed the Speculator Mine disaster, the *Anaconda Standard* suggested local IWW members "should learn something" from Bisbee. It warned local and state officials that the Wobblies "will have to go," and urged them to begin by deporting aliens within the union's ranks.[23]

Throughout July and early August, the IWW popped up repeatedly in the headlines of Montana dailies. Along with news of IWW activities in Washington state and "Big Bill" Haywood's call for a general strike of western mine, farm, and timber workers, Montana editors focused on the perceived Wobbly threat at home. A *Billings Gazette* story, based on the report of an anonymous "traveling man," warned of IWW plans to burn the state's hay crop, and in grass-rich Beaverhead County, two drifters were reportedly arrested and jailed for allegedly urging area farmhands to do just that. A plea from Eureka's business leaders for federal troops to prevent Wobbly depredations on the railways made the *Anaconda Standard*'s front page, alongside week-old photos of Bisbee's vigilantes at work. Up north on the High Line, the *Havre Promoter* applauded Congress's passage of the federal Espionage Act, which authorized prison terms for speech that threatened military recruitment and operations. "Free speech is now only for patriots," the paper wrote.[24]

Campbell's *Helena Independent* led the way. With obvious glee, it featured the perhaps apocryphal story of a nameless farmer who had throttled a Wobbly orator for "treasonable talk" at Harlowton's rail depot. The story failed to make either of Harlowton's weekly papers, but the *Independent* reported the town's business leaders were collecting cash to present the man a "hero medal." A minor scuffle near Toston between a train crew and a dozen "rough looking strangers" who began "cussing the government, the railroads and the capitalist class" prompted page-one headlines about a "battle" in which "a gang of I.W.W.'s" reportedly threatened to blow up a railcar full of dynamite. Of the five arrested, "[a]ll but one had I.W.W. cards," the paper reported. "They were sullen and refused to talk." From its sources within the governor's office, the *Independent* reported gangs of Wobblies encamped near bridges in Mineral County and near the company's lumber mill on the Blackfoot River near Bonner and rumors that spikes were being hammered into logs headed for the sawmill. Otherwise, it reported, these young men—"just the kind which could help put in crops in the state or handle a rifle in the army"—appeared to be "'watchfully waiting' for an opportune time to start something."[25]

Overheated coverage and the IWW's own radical rhetoric obscured any real assessment of the threat the Wobblies actually posed to Montana's key industries. In Butte, where their numbers were greatest and mine owners still refused miners' demands for higher wages and safer working conditions, they offered the company press an easy target. The *Anaconda Standard*'s "paragraphers" engaged in a joyous competition to tell readers what the initials IWW really stood for, with entries that ranged from "Infernal Wretches of the World" to "I Work for Wilhelm." From the beginning of the strike on June 13, 1917, the paper waved off miners' real grievances, preferring to portray the walkout as a conspiracy to aid Germany. "The attempt to close the mines, whatever the pretext may be, is a decidedly unpatriotic action and in the interests of the company's enemies," it wrote. The *Standard* blamed the miners' frustration on "the rabid leadership" of Wobbly agitators, reputedly financed by the kaiser. "If there is German money being used in Butte to stir up trouble in this camp and close up the mines, then the miners who have been induced to play into the hands of the German agents and quit work should get their proper share of that money," it suggested.[26]

Butte's other company organ, the *Daily Post,* reacted similarly, stating flatly that the strike was part of a general IWW effort of behalf of Germany. In its front-page account of the walkout, the paper dismissed miners' genuine complaints of inadequate pay and workplace hazards.

> The attack upon Butte's industries is engineered in the main by the same element which was responsible for Butte's serious trouble in 1914. It is well known that recently there has been a large influx into Butte of I.W.W.s and other unpatriotic and seditious persons, whose aim is to paralyze our industries, and particularly those upon which government is depending for its arms and ammunition. . . .
>
> Neither this element nor any organization made or controlled by it will receive any consideration or recognition by the mine operators of Butte. No grievance of the workers in the Butte mines has been brought to the attention of the operators, and we believe none exists. The wages paid in Butte are on the average the highest paid anywhere in the world. The working conditions in Butte are better than average and compare favorably with those of any other camp. The same may be said of living conditions, which are very much superior to those of many camps for which the extravagant claims are made.[27]

As specious as the *Daily Post's* claims were, both company papers were correct in reporting the IWW's wider role in the current strike than the one in 1914, though their estimates of the number of Wobblies in town ran higher than those offered by federal authorities who pegged the number at seven hundred or so. Such estimates made no mention of the more than two hundred private detectives mine owners had hired to infiltrate the aspiring Metal Mine Workers Union, even when federal officials revealed that some of the union's most radical leaders were, in fact, company spies.[28]

The editorial attacks of the *Anaconda Standard* and *Butte Daily Post* dovetailed with those of the city's third major daily, William A. Clark's *Butte Miner,* under editor Larry Dobell. By 1917, Dobell had been a Montana journalist for more than twenty-five years. Born in Britain, he studied political economy, language, and law before discovering a flair for journalism and politics in Montana. His letters to the *Bozeman Chronicle* supporting the city's 1892 bid to become Montana's capital led to a job as the paper's city editor, followed by stints at the *Anaconda Standard* and the *Livingston Post* and a short-lived attempt at running his own Republican daily, the *Evening Recorder*, in Anaconda.[29] Dobell's politics proved sufficiently flexible, however, and in 1898 he landed at Clark's Democratic *Butte Miner*. A faithful soldier in the copper wars, he rose from city editor to associate editor, then edited the pro-Clark *Helena Independent* for two years before returning to the *Miner* as managing editor. Dobell acted as Clark's loyal voice in the conservative wing of the state's Democratic Party and served in the 1911 legislature. Dobell's critics accused him of writing first and thinking later, but no one disputed his influence.[30]

The *Miner*'s aggressive coverage of the 1917 strike illustrated the extent to which Clark's and the company's interests coincided. Though Clark had sold most of his Montana mining holdings to Anaconda by 1910, he and his youngest son, William A. Clark Jr., retained ownership of Butte's valuable Elm Orlu Mine—whose miners had been the

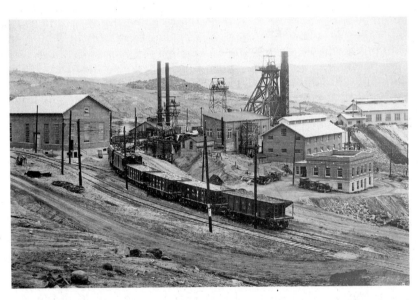

Although copper king William A. Clark had sold most of his mining properties to Anaconda by 1910, he and his son retained ownership of Butte's valuable Elm Orlu Mine (above). The aggressive coverage of the 1917 strike in Clark's Butte Miner *illustrated how his and the Anaconda Company's interests coincided.*

MONTANA HISTORICAL SOCIETY PHOTOGRAPH ARCHIVES, HELENA

first to walk off the job after the Speculator Mine fire. In response, Clark threatened to flood his mine shafts rather than recognize the "anarchist leaders" of the new Metal Mine Workers Union. Like the *Anaconda Standard* and the *Butte Daily Post,* Clark's *Miner* saw treason and IWW conspiracy behind the strikers' demands. "The time for half measures with these people has gone by," Dobell wrote, "and the government must deal with them in the future with a firm instead of [a] weak hand, otherwise they may impair the successful outcome of the war."[31]

Through newspaper exchanges and wire service stories based on the reporting of Butte's copper dailies, the IWW emerged as the principal instigator of Butte's labor troubles in the state's other major dailies. In Billings, the *Gazette* viewed the strike as an "I.W.W. scheme" that was "little short of criminal" in its attempt to smother wartime industry. Most miners, it suggested, would happily settle with mine owners were it not for the threats of Wobbly agitators, whose education about Montana's vigilante past was apparently lacking. "It might not be a bad idea to read some of the earlier Virginia City and Helena history to these trouble fomenters," it wrote.[32]

Such was the atmosphere in mid-July as a one-eyed Wobbly named Frank Little limped into Butte on a broken leg. A member of the IWW executive board and hard-boiled veteran of numerous strikes and "free speech fights," Little arrived from the Wobblies' disaster in Bisbee, Arizona, to find the Butte strike unraveling fast. Craft unions, which had initially supported the miners, had already returned to work, and though owners still refused to recognize Metal Mine Workers, miners were trickling back to work on the promise of raises and adjustments to the hated "rustling card" system by which only those miners who passed a company background check were allowed to work. With the copper dailies reporting the strike all but over, Little tried to stem the retreat with a mixture of persuasion and strong-arm tactics. The *Anaconda Standard* noticed Little's presence on June 29, reporting that the IWW leader had recruited Finnish women to physically attack and shame miners crossing the picket lines.[33]

More incendiary were the *Butte Daily Post* and the *Butte Miner*'s reports of Little's anti-war speeches. According to the *Miner,* the Wobbly leader, full of "maniacal fury," had scorned the "capitalist's" war and urged the crowds "to make it so damned hot for the government that they won't be able to send any man to France." In remarks the *Miner* described as just "short of treason," Little had "practically threatened the United States Government with revolution" and "expressed his view that the U.S. Constitution was but "a mere scrap of paper which can be torn up." Worse, Little had referred to American soldiers as "Uncle Sam's uniformed scabs."[34]

As Little's words rippled through Montana's leading dailies, the editorial reaction was swift and predictable. The *Butte Daily Post* labeled Little's July 27 speech to miners gathered at Butte's Finlander Hall "a treasonable tirade" and asked how long authorities would "stand for the seditious talk of the I.W.W. agitator?" The *Anaconda Standard,* in an editorial republished in the *Billings Gazette,* ominously predicted Little's words would eventually provoke a response, official or otherwise. "It is a good guess that in American communities treasonable and lawless utterances will not much longer be tolerated." Quoting extensively from the *Butte Miner*'s accounts, the new *Missoulian* editor, Martin Hutchens, urged U.S. Attorney Burton K. Wheeler to arrest Little under the terms of the federal Espionage Act and thus avoid an outbreak of violence that was sure to follow such seditious talk. "Does anyone doubt what Germany would do with Little under like circumstances?" Hutchens asked his readers. "Does anyone doubt what England would do? Does any reasonable man doubt what should be done?"[35]

Given such rhetoric, only the facts of Little's assassination came as a surprise. In the early hours of August 1, masked gunmen hauled him from bed in a Butte rooming house and stuffed him in a waiting car. Authorities would later speculate from the condition of Little's shredded kneecaps and bruised head that he had been dragged behind a car and then beaten before he was hanged from the trestle of a railroad bridge near town. A note, bearing the numbers 3-7-77—the mark of Montana territorial vigilantes—was pinned to the tatters of Little's summer underwear. The news flew through the wires, with most accounts emphasizing Little's quote about "uniformed scabs" in the lead, though few repeated the *Anaconda Standard*'s prominent speculation that Little might have been killed over rumors that he was a company detective. Most guessed at the difficulty of ever finding those responsible. In

Helena, all two thousand copies of the *Independent*'s special edition on Little's lynching sold out in less than an hour.[36] Editorially, most daily editors bemoaned the lawless act, but few offered any sympathy for Little's death or pressed the hapless investigation to find the killers. Many followed the lead of the copper dailies in blaming the incident on U.S. Attorney Wheeler for failing to put Little safely behind bars at the first utterances of the Wobbly leader's seditious talk. Such action, the *Butte Miner* supposed, might have spared the city of the stigma of murder. "As far as the man himself is concerned," the *Miner* reported, "his death is no loss to the world."[37] The *Anaconda Standard,* in an editorial headlined simply "3-7-77," called for the "detection, conviction and punishment" of those responsible for the "infamous" act, but it too blamed federal officers for failing to detain Little. The headline over its front-page story on Little's murder—"Butte's Name Tarnished by the Stain of Lynch Law"—seemed less chagrined by murder than the consequences for Butte's reputation.[38]

Editors at the *Standard,* like editors elsewhere, found the hangmen's use of the vigilante code too fascinating to ignore, and it appeared for days in the editorial page "paragraphs" that offered such insights as "No luck at all in any such odd numbers as 3-7-77." In Billings, where the *Gazette* had raised the specter of vigilante action weeks earlier, Little's death was "inevitable." "By their temerity in defying the government and state through their anarchistic utterances, these I.W.W. have served to bring upon their heads the wrath of a people that has been more than patient and tolerant."[39]

Will Campbell cloaked his own views on Little's death in what he assumed to be prevailing public opinion: "Good work. Let them continue to hang every I.W.W. in the state." If citizens took the law into their own hands, he argued, it was only because federal authorities had failed to do their job. "It is beyond the comprehension of the average citizen why the War Department has not ordered certain leaders arrested and shot," Campbell wrote. Like the *Anaconda Standard*'s editors, Campbell found the hangmen's use of the vigilante sign worthy of prominent mention. "It sort of quickens the blood in the veins of some of the old pioneers of Helena to see once more the fatal figures in print—'3-7-77,'" he wrote.[40]

The *Missoulian* blamed the lynching on the political ambitions of U.S. Attorney Wheeler and Congresswoman Jeannette Rankin. Their strategy of cultivating "all the discontented elements of Montana" had led to bloody results in Butte, it wrote. Kicking off a campaign that would echo through Montana's major dailies for months, it demanded that Montana's Senator Thomas Walsh, up for reelection in 1918, immediately replace his friend Wheeler with a "federal prosecuting attorney equipped with a hard spine, a brain that will function properly, and a sense of conscience that places duty to the people above politics." As for Little, "History tells of many men who have talked themselves into early graves." The *Great Falls Tribune* condemned the lynching and hoped Little's killers would be caught, but it too blamed the federal government's "mild and dilatory" handling of "disloyal elements." Yet in the end, it wrote, Little "fell a victim of his preachings and theories on direct action."[41]

Of those Montana weeklies that cared to comment on Little's murder, many echoed the dailies' sentiments, agreeing with Lewistown's *Fergus County Argus* editor J. A. Gilluly that the vast majority of Montanans were well rid of a "pest" that had threatened the state's very existence. A few, however, questioned the company's role in the affair. Editors of the *Cut Bank Pioneer Press,* Hamilton's *Western News,* and Missoula's *New Northwest* settled some of the blame on the mine owners' reluctance to deal fairly with their workers. In Virginia City, the *Madisonian Times* castigated the "company-controlled press" for focusing its "hue and cry" on the IWW. "Now the truth," it wrote, "is that but a very small percentage of the miners of Butte are in sympathy with the I.W.W. and by recognizing their union and meeting them halfway, the corporation managers could resume operations with 24 hours."[42]

Such comments, however, were rare. In fact, the copper press's success in focusing attention on the supposed disloyalty of Butte's strikers and away from the miners' grievances was nearly absolute in the wake of Little's murder. One by one, Montana's top political leaders pressed the case against the radicals, dissenters, and their sympathizers. U.S. Senator Henry Myers called Little's lynching "the logical result of the incendiary and seditious action and talk that has been going on for some time, apparently without any interference in Butte." His counterpart, Senator

Thomas Walsh, a Progressive under growing pressure in the copper press to distance himself from liberals such as Wheeler and Rankin, expressed his "regret that disloyal if not treasonable attempts of the I.W.W. to tie up industries of the country should have exasperated any of our people as to incite them to deeds of criminal violence." But Walsh also predicted the lynching would make Little a martyr in the strikers' cause. "It is worse than a crime, it is a mistake," he said.[43]

Few blamed Butte's volatility on the mine owners, and those who did paid a price. Before Little's murder, Congresswoman Rankin had criticized the company's hostility to miners' demands and warned of violence. On August 7, a week after the lynching, Rankin introduced a resolution calling for a federal takeover of the mines to protect both the nation's wartime supply of copper and Butte's miners. In her speech on the House floor, she blamed the city's turmoil on Anaconda president John D. Ryan's refusal to recognize the miners' union, and she also accused the company of profiteering in the manipulation of federal contracts for copper. In an interview later that day with Washington reporters, Rankin predicted her criticism would expose her to the wrath of the company, which, she added, owned not only Montana's government but also its press. "First I'll be roasted from one end of the state to the other," she said. "Every newspaper will print my shortcomings real or fancied, in the largest type."[44]

Already a target for her vote against the war, Rankin came home to face the storm. By mid-August, she was in Butte, hoping to mediate the dispute, though by now she was hardly a disinterested observer. The highlight of her trip came on August 18, when she offered strikers her continued support in a speech to more than eight thousand gathered in the city's Columbia Gardens baseball park. Newsworthy by any standard, the event was all but ignored by Butte's company-owned papers. The *Butte Daily Post* ignored it entirely, and the *Anaconda Standard*'s thin account, buried inside the paper, acknowledged Rankin's support for the miners' demands but claimed the crowd was composed largely of "curious women" and miners compelled to attend by union bosses. A more complete story and a full text of Rankin's speech had been spiked by the paper's editors, who fired its authors the following day. Surprisingly, Rankin fared better in Clark's *Butte Miner*, which carried not only a detailed account of the speech, but ran a dramatic front-page photo of Rankin surrounded by the crowd. Outside Butte, the *Billings Gazette* ignored the event completely, while Helena's *Montana Record-Herald,* arguably the state's leading Republican daily but owned by one of Rankin's intra-party rivals, carried no details of the congresswoman's speech, though it criticized her for making it.[45]

Of all the leading dailies, the *Missoulian,* Rankin's hometown Republican paper, offered the fullest and fairest account of her challenge to the mine owners, proof perhaps that the paper had yet to come under the company's full control. Its new editor, Martin Hutchens, though critical of Rankin's pacifism and her support for Butte's strikers, treated her with the respect due Missoula's "favorite daughter," one whose candidacy the paper under Joseph Dixon had endorsed the previous fall. Regardless of his editorial views, Hutchens understood that Rankin's challenge to the company was news and that its suppression would signal the company's control over his paper. Whatever the exact nature of the *Missoulian*'s relationship with the company, Hutchens operated with a measure of autonomy, at least at the outset of his nine-year tenure as editor. Years later, Hutchens's son, himself a journalist and author, maintained that while the *Missoulian* was unquestionably a "Company paper," his father ran it free of day-to-day direction from Anaconda officials and occasionally ran stories or took local editorial stands contrary to the company's interests.[46]

Hutchens's authority—and perhaps his relative autonomy—sprang from a journalistic résumé no other Montana editor could match. A native of upstate New York, he landed in Montana shortly after graduating from Hamilton College in 1888 and a brief stint as a reporter for the *Rome Sentinel* in New York. From 1889 to 1893, he worked as city editor for the *Helena Independent* but left to join the editorial staff of Charles Dana's *New York Sun,* a "newspaperman's newspaper," respected nationwide for its journalistic independence and clever, literate, and distinctly sensational style that emphasized news over partisan views. After three years at the *Sun,* he joined an even more influential paper, Joseph Pulitzer's groundbreaking New York *World,* then at the height of its fame and its sensational circulation battle with Hearst's *New York Journal.* Like so many of Pulitzer's top men, Hutchens was lured to the

Journal in 1898, during Hearst's outrageous bidding war for talent. He worked as an editor at the font of "yellow journalism" until 1902, when Hearst sent him to Chicago as city editor of the *American*. Amid the frenetic competition of the city's competing dailies, Hutchens jumped ship to become managing editor of Chicago's *Inter Ocean* and later the city's *Evening Journal*, where he earned a reputation as a mentor for aspiring writers, including a young Ben Hecht, whose screenplay for the movie *The Front Page* gave the world an enduring image of the cynical, wise-cracking American reporter. Hutchens's nostalgia and eagerness to run his own newspaper led him back to Montana.[47]

Hutchens left no doubt where the *Missoulian* stood on the IWW's "treason" and the failure of federal officials to prosecute the Wobblies, whom he regarded as common thugs. The sentiment was apparently mutual, according to Hutchens's son, who worked briefly for his father's paper. When Missoula's IWW contingent occupied a second-floor office directly across the street from the *Missoulian,* its leaders reportedly sent Hutchens a note saying that with the shade of his office window up, the editor offered an easy target. Hutchens reportedly put a Smith and Wesson revolver in his desk and left the shade up.[48]

Yet despite such tension, even a Wobbly could be a source of information for the paper's news columns. After Frank Little's murder, Hutchens published reactions from a wide array of Montanans, including Missoula's IWW chief Arthur W. Smith, who blamed Little's slaying on the "hired gunmen of the A.C.M." Others contacted included the even-handed Arthur Stone, dean of the state's journalism school and former *Missoulian* editor who considered Little a demagogue whose ilk had taken over a legitimate union protesting "the injustice which many of our present economic conditions have brought." Yet Stone deplored the lynching and warned Montanans not to overreact, for "there is sometimes as much wrong committed in the name of loyalty as there is by those who criticize—not the ideal democracy, but the controlled and misdirected machinery of government."[49]

Hutchens gave Congresswoman Rankin's criticism of the Anaconda Company front-page treatment with a detailed story that quoted extensively from her August 18 speech in Butte, but when Rankin traveled on to Missoula for an extended visit, Hutchens laced the *Missoulian*'s editorial "welcome" with criticism of her "sympathetic relations" with IWW leaders whom he labeled "vicious enemies of this republic." Hutchens particularly resented Rankin's "loose talk in her indictment of the State of Montana as a corporation-owned commonwealth," especially her published contention that Montana's newspapers were controlled by the Anaconda Company. "We do not believe that charge can be sustained, and we will be glad to know that it was withdrawn, unless full proof was offered as to its truth." Though Rankin claimed to have been misquoted, Hutchens noted the *Washington Times*'s insistence that its account of her comments earlier that month had been accurate.[50]

Hutchens refused to let the matter go at that. In an inspired bit of journalistic gamesmanship, he asked editors across the state to respond to Rankin's broad charge, and as the congresswoman made the rounds of Missoula's society the paper published the editors' replies for three straight days under the headline "HAS MONTANA A KEPT PRESS?" Though hardly an objective investigation of the facts, the series offered readers a rare debate on the controversy that had dogged Montana journalism since the copper wars. Hutchens himself argued that such claims had been made for years by "hare-brained demagogues, political castoffs and incendiaries of a particularly vicious type," adding that responsible editors had long ignored "the howls of these vermin-ridden coyotes; they are too small to notice." But such talk demanded a reply, he wrote. Without specifically denying the company's investment in his or other papers, he argued that Rankin had gone too far. He hoped the series would make her more cautious in her comments. "Our own view is that Miss Rankin talked rather loosely, and if she stated the things she is quoted as saying, she did not mean them," Hutchens wrote. "Certainly the charge that the copper company, or any other company, controls the press of this state is both absurd and without the fabric of truth."[51]

Others drew more subtle distinctions. As a one-time editor at both the *Anaconda Standard* and Joseph Dixon's anti-company *Missoulian*, Arthur Stone said he had always been told "to adhere to the fundamental newswriting policy of accuracy in the reporting and printing of the news." As for Rankin's charge of complete domination of Montana's press, Stone added: "There are a few newspapers in the state that are owned by the Anaconda interests; there are, I believe, some others whose ownership is in hands which are friendly, politically and in a business way, with these interests; but to say that the press of Montana is controlled by these interests is an injustice to a lot of earnest, loyal men and women who are engaged in the production of newspapers of the state."[52]

The *Butte Miner*'s Dobell acknowledged his paper's allegiance to William A. Clark but denied any corporation influence on his paper's editorial policy. Rankin's claim, he argued, was sheer demagoguery. The *Miner*, he said, had always fought the company "whenever it believed that the corporation's actions were detrimental to the interests of the people of this commonwealth." That was true of most Montana papers, he wrote. However, he added: "It is true that demagogues, who have acquired, or who endeavor to gain some passing notoriety, have occasionally slandered the press of Montana by asserting, without any justification, that it was under domination of the big copper company. That has been rather a favorite accusation for agitators, political or otherwise, to make from time to time."[53]

The *Helena Independent*'s Will Campbell also considered the charge "absurd." "I know who owns the paper you edit," he wrote Hutchens, "because you offered to buy my stock in the Independent with your own money." As for his paper, Campbell said he and his partners had gradually purchased all of the paper's stock from "one hundred good Democrats." The *Independent*'s only debt was a fifty-thousand-dollar note held by the estate of the late John S. M. Neill. "All of these things are a matter of public record and Miss Rankin could be proved a deliberate prevaricator if it was not so useless to try to tell her that she owes the newspapers of Montana an apology," Campbell wrote.[54]

Ignoring the company's *Anaconda Standard* and the *Butte Daily Post*, Campbell claimed that the company "does not care to own the press and has little or nothing to give the newspapers or publishers of the state. The company had certainly exercised its influence through the press in the "old Amalgamated" days, he wrote, but no longer. "John D. Ryan, Con Kelley and others now in control are not asking to control the political destinies of the state—they only want to be left alone and protected alike from grafting labor agitators and grafting politicians," he added. As for himself, Campbell wrote that Anaconda officials "have never asked for a single thing or suggested a single favor." Nor did they threaten or bully editors who opposed company policies, he added. "If a newspaper wants to fight them and stir up trouble for them, they simply let the paper alone until it gets tired." Yet Campbell conceded there were benefits to being open-minded with regard to its coverage of the company. "If a newspaper is fair and shows a disposition to give the big interests a square deal, the company will likely talk over a business matter with the publishers, the same as our banks or railways, sugar industries or other industries," he wrote. Such business relationships hardly reflected control, he argued.[55]

From Billings, *Gazette* editor Leon Shaw labeled the charge "unquestionably without foundation" as far as his paper was concerned—a stance echoed by most editors who responded, especially editors of Republican papers that had supported Rankin's election in 1916. Of those, Joseph D. Scanlan, publisher of the *Miles City Star,* lectured Rankin on the folly of making foes of her friends as well as her enemies. "Answering personally for ourselves we will say that Miss Rankin misstates the facts," he wrote. "Speaking offhand, I would venture that more than 95 per cent of the newspapers of Montana are individually owned."[56]

Though most editors denounced Rankin's blanket accusation, several argued that the claim was partially true, at least in regard to the state's major dailies. H. L. Knight, Republican publisher of the *Kalispell Times,* wrote that "no one conversant with the past political history of this state may doubt that the A.C.M. absolutely controls the dailies of Butte, Helena and Great Falls, perhaps a few scattered weeklies and dailies elsewhere of lesser importance.

> The Missoulian we are glad to have on our side, but it was generally supposed that Joe Dixon was bought out because of his recent antagonism to the company and also probable that the new management would be in line with the kept press. Having been in the newspaper business since territorial days, I do not hesitate to guess that the company owns all the papers necessary to its salvation.[57]

Alex Rhone, editor of the *Sanders County Signal* in Plains, stated flatly that since the fight with Heinze, the company had controlled

Montana's legislature and its daily press, though he had hoped "the condition would disappear with the settlement of eastern Montana." W. W. Holmes, of Musselshell's *Advocate,* believed Rankin's "unqualified statement" had unfairly tarnished the reputations of the state's independent papers though he admitted the extent of the company's influence—especially in political campaigns—remained a subject of much conjecture among editors themselves. "Many of them have discovered when too late that they have been influenced in the wrong direction, though they have been unable to say, exactly, where the influence came from."[58]

Tom Stout, the former congressman and publisher of the *Lewistown Democrat-News,* insisted that Rankin had libeled editors who had fought the company's pernicious influence over the decades. The state, he wrote, was "filled with newspapers, daily and weekly," that had no connection with the company:

> To assert the contrary is to impugn the honesty of scores of men . . . who stand ready at all times to combat any effort of the Amalgamated to fasten its corporate tentacles about the state, its industries or political institutions. Many of these men were fighting the insidious efforts of the Amalgamated to control Montana while Miss Rankin's golden hair was yet hanging down her back . . . which we hasten to say, was not so very long ago.[59]

Perhaps the most cogent analysis came from "Colonel" Sam Gordon, former editor of Miles City's *Yellowstone Journal.* A longtime critic of the company press, Gordon nevertheless blasted Rankin for tarring all of Montana's papers with her charge, especially Republican papers like his that had bucked Anaconda's political line a year earlier by endorsing Rankin for Congress. The state's papers were not, Gordon charged, "a lot of phonographs playing only the records distributed by the Anaconda management." The company's bipartisan political connections gave it enormous influence in state government, especially with the legislature, Gordon conceded, but Anaconda's hold over the state's newspapers was not what it had been in the time of the copper kings. Nowadays, he argued, the company and its allies, including certain newspaper publishers, formed an "undeniable community of interests" that exerted its influence in subtle ways:

Generous patrons in a business way, the year round, can often persuade the editor to use the soft pedal on some certain issue. These men working for their own interests which happen at the time to run current with those of the Anaconda ask favors that they think they have a right to ask of the local newspaper, but that does not argue either ownership or control of the newspaper.[60]

In the end, the debate over Anaconda's control over Montana's newspapers remained inconclusive at best. Given the secrecy surrounding the company's newspaper investments, it could hardly have been otherwise. If anything, Hutchens's attempt to dismiss the idea of a kept press only revealed its deep roots in the public's mind. The similarity of the major dailies' views during the war and over the tumultuous years that followed would do little to dispel the notion.

THE PRESENCE OF FEDERAL TROOPS and the company's eventual offer to increase wages effectively ended the strike of 1917, though anger over Anaconda's refusal to recognize the new miners' union persisted. By year's end, that anger found a voice in a new radical weekly, the *Butte Bulletin.* Organized by Butte union leaders and a group of young anti-company attorneys that included Burton K. Wheeler, the paper found a backer in James A. Murray, an independent mine owner and banker whose nephew James. E. Murray would one day represent Montana in the U.S. Senate. With William F. Dunne, an electrical worker turned militant unionist, supplying the editorial vitriol and R. Bruce Smith, the president of Butte Typographical Union, at the helm, the *Bulletin* hit the streets in December 1917 as Butte's most serious alternative to the copper press since Heinze's Butte *Reveille.* Unabashedly radical— the walls of its newsroom were plastered with portraits of Karl Marx and Vladimir Lenin—the *Bulletin* sent Montana conservatives into spasms with its attacks on the "insane system of capitalist production" and its open admiration for the Bolshevik revolution, which it followed by publishing journalist John Reed's breathless reporting from Russia. Though it took care not to criticize the war directly, the weekly's mere existence infuriated conservatives bent on suppressing even the mildest criticism of "the American idea."[61]

In their fight against seditious talk and publication, conservatives found ready allies in Montana's major dailies, nearly all of which backed passage of a draconian sedition law and the state's official and systematic prosecution of wartime dissent. Both efforts coincided in February 1918, when Governor Sam Stewart, encouraged by Will Campbell's editorials and those of daily editors across the state, called a special legislative session to request, among other things, new powers to "curb the pernicious activities of individuals and organizations guilty of sabotage, criminal syndicalism and industrial and political anarchy." With little debate, lawmakers quickly passed a criminal syndicalism law, effectively outlawing the IWW and any other organizations

Established to boost agricultural production, the Montana Council of Defense (pictured above) quickly gained sweeping powers to ferret out "slackers" and persecute those suspected of disloyalty to the United States. Will Campbell (top row, second from right), editor of the Helena Independent, *became the council's most active member and used his paper to promote its efforts and control publicity about its activities.*

MONTANA HISTORICAL SOCIETY PHOTOGRAPH ARCHIVES, HELENA

that advocated the violent overthrow of the political or industrial system. It also granted the state's Council of Defense, previously established to boost agricultural production, sweeping powers to ferret out "slackers" and persecute dissenters. In its final act, the legislature impeached a German-American district judge for the sin of serving as a character witness for an eastern Montana rancher accused of suggesting that the United States had entered the war to protect the fortunes of Wall Street.[62]

With an eye on the *Butte Bulletin* and with widespread support from the daily press,

Federal judge George M. Bourquin was a favorite target of conservative newspapers after he refused to convict several anti-war protesters under the federal Espionage Act.

Zubick Studio, photographer,
Montana Historical Society Photograph
Archives, Helena

the legislature also enacted a sedition law, making it a crime to speak, write, or publish "any disloyal, profane, violent, scurrilous, contemptuous, slurring or abusive language" critical of the nation, its government, its soldiers, and its symbols or "calculated to incite or inflame" resistance to those prosecuting the war. In its support for "a drastic law to punish the defamer of the country and the flag," the *Missoulian* trusted state officials to know the line between traitorous and constructive criticism when they saw it. In any case, it argued, the law should have teeth and be phrased to circumvent "such fine-spun interpretations as we have seen," an obvious jab at Wheeler, Montana's federal prosecutor, and federal judge George M. Bourquin, who had refused to convict several anti-war protesters under the federal Espionage Act. "We hope the iron heel will be set upon any political lawyer who attempts to juggle with this bill," Hutchens wrote. In Helena, the *Montana Record-Herald* also trusted state prosecutors to target those "pro-German propagandists and unpatriotic individuals who by act or word try to impede this country's successful prosecution of the war" while avoiding any interference with the expression of free speech, "the greatest heritage of the liberty loving people."[63]

Other Montana dailies joined the chorus. The *Great Falls Tribune* hailed the legislature's promise of "effective means for the punishment of loud-mouthed traitors," as did the *Lewistown Democrat-News,* which called for either new laws regarding espionage and sedition or new judges willing to enforce the old laws more forcefully. *Billings Gazette* editor Leon Shaw opposed "political censorship of the news," but applauded the sedition bill, saying "there is no room in Montana for any organization which is not patriotic." The *Butte Miner* praised the passage "of good strong measures to suppress sabotage and sedition," as did weeklies such as the *Fergus County Argus* in Lewistown, which had stressed the urgency of "an effective muzzle" on the state's "seditious spouters." Anaconda dailies nodded their terse approval. The *Butte Daily Post* simply urged lawmakers to "get on with it." [64]

Weeklies such as the Fergus County Argus *in Lewistown backed the state's prosecution of war dissenters and stressed the urgency of "an effective muzzle" on the state's "seditious spouters." The* Argus *office is pictured here circa 1915.*

Armed with tough laws and the means to enforce them, Montana conservatives began a statewide roundup of disloyal elements. Scores of Montanans would eventually stand convicted of sedition or criminal syndicalism, most on the thinnest pretexts and shreds of evidence. Led by the state Council of Defense, with the aid of county defense councils and local patriotic associations such as the Montana Loyalty League, the inquisition touched most communities in the state. No act or utterance seemed too insignificant, as the manager of Lewistown's railway station learned when he was hauled before a local loyalty board to explain why he had removed Red Cross posters from the walls of the depot's waiting room.[65]

The campaign drew vital support from Montana's press, and its most vigorous prosecutor—both journalistically and officially—was Will Campbell of the *Helena Independent*. Through his association with Governor Stewart, Campbell won appointment to the Montana Council of Defense in 1917. Campbell quickly became the council's most active member and used his paper to promote its efforts and control publicity about its activities.[66]

Though Campbell was the only newspaper editor on the state council, its loyalty campaign attracted the services of conservative journalists statewide, many with connections to the copper press. Among them was the council's secretary, Charles Greenfield, former editor of the pro-company *Montana Daily Record* in Helena, who also doubled as Montana's commissioner of agriculture and publicity. The council's first board also included state senator John Edwards, publisher of the *Billings Gazette*. Newspapermen also sat on numerous county councils of defense. The list included *Billings Gazette* editor Leon Shaw; Edward Cooney, editor of the *Great Falls Leader*; *Miles City Star* publisher Joseph Scanlan; *Anaconda Standard* editor Charles Eggleston; and Jerome Williams of Big Timber's *Pioneer*. Others contributed through the Loyalty League, whose leadership included Campbell, who served as its secretary, and vice president J. A. Gilluly of the *Fergus County Argus* in Lewistown.[67]

With advice from Anaconda lawyer L. O. Evans and company ally J. Bruce Kremer, the Montana Council of Defense granted itself investigative and judicial powers and went to work in the spring of

1918. Over the next few months, it issued seventeen orders, including bans on unauthorized public demonstrations, the use of German in schools and churches, and library books containing favorable depictions of German culture. Orders aimed specifically at IWW organizers and members included bans on vagrancy and stealing rides on railroad trains. The council also forbade the establishment of any new newspapers or the upgrading of any existing weekly or monthly to daily publication, a measure designed to conserve scarce paper supplies, though Campbell immediately grasped its potential to squelch the upstart *Butte Bulletin*.[68]

With little in truth to fear from German spies and speakers, Campbell, the council, and the copper press focused their crusade on labor radicals, Socialists, and leftist agrarian reformers. The result was Montana's own "Red scare," which would later sweep the nation. Butte's labor movement, radical and unrepentant, drew the crusaders' most withering fire. In late spring of 1918, Governor Stewart and his Council of Defense, working closely with company officials and military intelligence, ramped up efforts to silence the *Bulletin* and discredit its editors: R. Bruce Smith, a leader of the Butte Typographical Union, and William F. Dunne, the crew-cut unionist who had risen to prominence in the 1917 miners' strike. The campaign coincided with the *Bulletin's* impending conversion from weekly to daily publication, an aim the paper's backers had held from its debut in late December 1917.[69]

In an effort clearly aimed at quashing the *Bulletin*, Governor Stewart even asked publisher-members of the Montana State Press Association's legislative committee for their reaction to a possible newspaper licensing law, a notion sure to raise First Amendment hackles under ordinary circumstances. But these were hardly ordinary times, and most of the journalists who responded supported suppression of "disloyal" papers by one means or another. Arthur Stone, dean of the state's four-year-old School of Journalism, blanched at the thought of all newspapers being licensed by an appointed state board—especially when federal censors could do the job more selectively. "I am heartily in favor of the suppression of any publication which wobbles in its support of the government of this country and of this state in a time of war," he wrote. Lyle Cowan, editor and publisher of the weekly *Judith*

Editor of the radical Butte Bulletin, *William F. Dunne (above) attacked the Montana Council of Defense's "star-chambered sessions" and "putrid tactics" as well as its members, all of whom, he wrote, "have grown lean and gray, or fat and bald in the service of big business."*

GEORGE R. TOMPKINS, *THE TRUTH ABOUT BUTTE: THROUGH THE EYES OF A RADICAL UNIONIST* (BUTTE, MONT. 1917).

Gap Journal joined the *Butte Miner's* Larry Dobell in favor of a licensing law. "Decent newspapers can have no objection to having the disloyal ones checked up," Dobell wrote. J. A. Gilluly, publisher of Lewistown's *Fergus County Argus*, concurred, suggesting that the state's Council of Defense also be empowered to suppress the mailing of any newspaper "containing anything that tends to create discord and discontent in the minds of the American people at this time or which seeks to array one class against another." The publishers of the *Bozeman Daily Chronicle* and the *Miles City Star* feared a licensing law but urged postal officials to refuse mail service to disloyal editors. Seditious journalists could be punished under the state's new sedition law as well, they said. Charles Reifenrath, general manager of Doc Lanstrum's *Montana Record-Herald*, believed it better to leave the matter to federal officials. "I believe if the United States Government, through the Post Office Department is not big enough to handle the situation, the state Council of Defense are [*sic*] going to have a hard time to do anything with it." The licensing proposal fizzled, but the council duly forwarded the publishers' suggestions to the postmaster general.[70]

As it awaited federal action, the council engaged in a raucous interrogation of Dunne and Smith, prompted by the *Bulletin's* fearless assaults on the council's legitimacy. In an editorial in late May, Dunne attacked the council's "star-chambered sessions" and "putrid tactics" as well as its members, all of which, he wrote "have grown lean and gray, or fat and bald in the service of big business." Furious at the paper's insolence, the council ordered Dunne and Smith to Helena for a tense but ultimately inconclusive round of questioning, which the *Independent* heralded with the headline "I.W.W. CHIEFS MUST APPEAR AND EXPLAIN POLICY AND STATUS OF PAPER THEY PUBLISH." Though they denied IWW membership, the *Bulletin* editors gave as good as they got in the tense exchanges that followed, repeatedly questioning the council's own authority to question them.[71]

Buoyed by the performance, the *Bulletin* prepared for daily publication, though difficulties in obtaining a building, printing equipment, and an adequate paper supply—all of which it blamed on the company's intimidation—pushed its proposed June 1 start-up date to August 1. Four days after its debut, the federal War Industries Board banned the startup of any new newspapers, giving the Montana Council of Defense an excuse to resume the offensive. On August 12, the council issued Order Number Twelve, which not only reinforced the federal ban on new newspapers, but also forbade the conversion of weeklies and monthlies to dailies—a direct challenge to the *Bulletin*. Castigating the council's members as "the willing, cringing tools of the autocratic forces of the state," the *Bulletin* defied the council's order, and on August 20 the *Butte Daily Bulletin* hit the streets.[72]

Immediately notified by the War Industries Board of its violation, the paper's editors claimed they were never officially told of the ban and requested a hearing, which the board promptly delegated to the Montana Council of Defense. As its editors braced for further interrogation, the *Bulletin* fought a backdoor effort by Campbell and others to prevent it from obtaining the necessary newsprint. A shipment of paper ordered from Spokane on August 13 arrived mysteriously via Chicago on August 29, prompting charges that the order had been tampered with. With letters of protest pouring in from conservative Montana editors, the War Industries Board further crimped the *Bulletin's* future by ordering distributors to withhold additional newsprint.[73]

Forced to cut down the size of its editions, the *Bulletin* continued daily publication, though its prospects for survival seemed shaky. After a second and even more contentious showdown with Campbell and the council, during which Dunne charged that "practically every paper in the state" was "under the thumb of the corporation," another blow fell. On September 13, in response to the IWW's call for a national strike to protest the conviction of its leaders on federal charges of sedition in Chicago, a contingent of citizens, deputies, and soldiers led by a young Major Omar Bradley raided the *Bulletin*'s offices on a tip that the paper had printed posters endorsing the strike. None were found, though the paper's subscriber list mysteriously disappeared amid the ruckus. Jailed and quickly released on bail, Dunne, Smith, and the paper's circulation manager were arrested again two days later on state charges of sedition.[74]

Though Dunne and Smith's subsequent convictions would be overturned, the fireworks between the *Bulletin* and the copper press would rage on over the next two years as Butte suffered through the economic dislocations brought on by the war's end and the diminished demand for copper. Meanwhile, the company and its allies faced a growing political backlash from the prairies, where drought and the postwar collapse of crop and land prices threatened the survival of tens of thousands of dryland homesteaders. The impending showdown between the company and Progressives would shape Montana's politics for generations and forge a more formal union between the Anaconda Copper Mining Company and Montana's daily press.[75]

When Charles "Red Flag" Taylor arrived in northeast Montana in 1918 to promote the agrarian socialism of the Nonpartisan League, he found the area's beleaguered farmers ripe for political change and hungry for a newspaper to champion their fight against bankers, industrialists, and their subservient press.

Plentywood *Producers News*, August 29, 1919

CHAPTER SEVEN

C HARLES "RED FLAG" TAYLOR,
all three hundred pounds of
him, arrived in Plentywood,
Montana, in the spring of 1918, and
found the town a "God forsaken hole,"
a smattering of wood-frame buildings
huddled around a trio of tin-roofed
grain elevators set in an endless, un-
dulating prairie. Sent to spread the
gospel of agrarian socialism by the

The "Anvil Chorus"

JOSEPH DIXON
VERSUS THE
COPPER PRESS

Nonpartisan League (NPL), Taylor found town leaders hostile to the
NPL's vision of regulated rail rates and state-run banks and grain elevators, a platform of promises that had swept neighboring North Dakota
like a grassfire two years before. But enemies were useful in the struggle
to organize Sheridan County's beleaguered dryland farmers, those hapless "hayseeds" who had been hammered by drought, volatile grain
prices, confiscatory freight rates, and crushing mortgages that bankers
and government officials had urged them to assume in the patriotic
cause of boosting wartime food supplies. The pages of Taylor's upstart
weekly, the *Producers News,* were peppered with allusions to "small
town Kaisers," "crop grabbers," and "paytriotic [*sic*]" profiteers whom it
gleefully and regularly skewered.[1]

In two short years, the *Producers News* would claim a circulation of
2,500 households, impressive for a county of 12,000 souls and a testament to Taylor's charisma, wit, and energy as well as the NPL's vision
and strong support for the organization across northeast Montana. The
NPL also fostered weeklies in Richland, Roosevelt, and Valley counties,
but the *Producers News* outshined them all. By 1926, the paper would
absorb six neighboring weeklies, including its Plentywood rival, the
Pioneer Press, or as Taylor called it, the "Pie Near" Press, that "nauseous
rag that emits itself once a week from its stye down the street."[2]

As editor of Plentywood's Producers News *for most of its nineteen years, Charles Taylor skewered his foes with wit and distain. The "Kept Press" in this cartoon is smearing on paint from a can that says "Fake Patriotism. Apply externally. It is impossible to distinguish a profiteer from a real patriot if directions are followed."*

Plentywood *Producers News*, July 5, 1918

Taylor, an off-and-on Communist until his expulsion from the party in the early 1930s, used his newspaper as both pulpit and a blunt club to build a political machine that briefly captured Sheridan County's government and sent him to the state senate for two terms. As it boosted farmers' hopes, the newspaper's anti-establishment rhetoric also provided cover for bootleggers and thieves, including the masked men who stole more than one hundred five thousand dollars in tax payments from the county treasury in the fall of 1926, a crime many suspected of being an inside job. Taylor's combat with conservative editors of rival weeklies burned bright earlier that year when arsonists torched the offices of *Daniels County Leader* in Scobey, destroying its presses in a blaze so hot that it fused keys on the paper's Linotype. Authorities traced the firebugs to Plentywood before the trail went cold, but *Leader* editor Burley Bowler, who had once worked for Taylor, saw the attack as retribution for the *Leader*'s "exposure" of the "thugs" hiding behind the protection of the "Producers Noose." "Farmers, regardless of their political allegiance, do not try to burn newspaper offices," Bowler wrote. In response, Taylor suggested Bowler had set the fire to collect insurance.[3]

Controversy dogged the *Producers News* throughout its rocky nineteen-year run as the most radical of Montana's rural weeklies, an ideological ally of Bill Dunne's *Butte Daily Bulletin,* whose editorials Taylor frequently republished. During the war, NPL leaders trailed only "Huns" and Wobblies as targets for the scorn of conservative editors such as Will Campbell and organizations such as the Montana Loyalty League, or the "Lunacy League," as Taylor called it. Though NPL leaders avoided opposing the war directly, their clear ambivalence infuriated Campbell, who lumped them with "kaiser lovers" and other "slink-eyed skulkers" and cheered when conservatives took matters into their own hands. In the spring of 1918, a mob forced NPL organizer Mickey McGlynn to swear loyalty oaths before speaking in eastern Montana towns. He suffered worse in Miles City for questioning the credibility of a rumor that a trainload of Belgian children, their arms supposedly hacked off by German soldiers, was headed for Montana. A mob beat McGlynn senseless before local authorities could arrest him on sedition charges. Attorney General Sam C. Ford tried in vain to prosecute the vigilantes and warned the state's Council of Defense against encouraging such

Will Campbell is the director in Montana

During the war, Nonpartisan League leaders trailed only "Huns" and Wobblies as targets for the scorn of conservative editors, including the Helena Independent's *Will Campbell. Montana's official Nonpartisan League publication parodied Campbell as the leader of the "Patriots Chorus."*

GREAT FALLS *MONTANA NONPARTISAN*, SEPTEMBER 20, 1919

bare-knuckled suppression of free speech, but Campbell, the council's chief publicist, refused to print his remarks.[4]

Despite such vilification, thousands of Montana farmers followed the progress of the NPL's experiment in North Dakota, where a charismatic former farmer named Arthur C. Townley had grabbed power in the fall of 1916 by flooding the state's open Republican primary with NPL candidates. The party's Montana admirers included Congresswoman Jeannette Rankin, Miles Romney of the *Western News,* and former Montana university president Edwin Craighead, who witnessed the NPL's rise as North Dakota's education commissioner for two years before resuming the editorship of his Missoula weekly, the *New Northwest.* Craighead's paper became the party's unofficial voice and defender in western Montana, joining a smattering of NPL weeklies east of the mountains. As early as 1918, Butte's Bill Dunne and Plentywood's Charles Taylor had envisioned a labor-NPL alliance, but their best shot came in 1920, when embattled miners and the NPL's twenty thousand Montana members invaded the Democratic primary and snatched the gubernatorial nomination for Burton K. Wheeler, the ambitious former federal prosecutor who had defended Butte's radicals during wartime hysteria and who now vowed to toss Anaconda out of politics for good.[5]

In 1920, labor and Nonpartisan League leaders snatched the Democratic gubernatorial nomination for Burton K. Wheeler (above, circa 1910s), the ambitious former federal prosecutor who had defended Butte's radicals during wartime hysteria and who now vowed to toss Anaconda out of politics for good.

MONTANA HISTORICAL SOCIETY PHOTOGRAPH ARCHIVES, HELENA

The excitement that summer was palpable in the headlines of the *Producers News*, which urged northeast Montana farmers to attend campaign rallies and political encampments like the big Fourth of July picnic planned at Medicine Lake. Predicting "gigantic crowds," Taylor enticed readers with the promise of "fireworks, games and sports," and good music in the "dancing pavilion." A special train would bring Wheeler to deliver the keynote address, but NPL President Arthur Townley, a man "so cursed and so admired," would arrive instead from the sky, in a two-seater aircraft, a wonder worthy of its own front-page headline. "Hey Rube!" the *Producers News* called, "Townley Is Coming in His Big Aeroplane!"[6]

FOR ALL THEIR SUPPOSED SOPHISTICATION, the company and its conservative allies were caught flat-footed by the campaign of 1920. As Wheeler grabbed the Democratic gubernatorial nomination, Democratic dailies in Butte, Helena, and Great Falls moaned and implored Montanans to junk the open primary system exploited so skillfully by the NPL and the Butte-based Labor League. Progressive Republicans, meanwhile, rescued former U.S. senator Joseph Dixon from exile on his Flathead Lake farm, despite frantic lobbying by Anaconda officials and the editorial opposition of the Republican copper dailies in Butte, Missoula, and Billings. Company officials could only watch in horror as Montanans prepared to choose between two candidates vowing to drive the Anaconda Company from politics.

The copper editors howled their displeasure, and none did it better than Richard Kilroy. The former Heinze editor and Dixon's onetime Missoula nemesis at the *Missoula Sentinel* resurfaced in 1919 as editor of the *Anaconda Standard,* replacing an ailing Charles Eggleston. Demoted and assigned to write the paper's national and international editorials and "little essays" on historical or cultural topics, Eggleston watched as Kilroy ladled his special vitriol over Wheeler and his train of "red radicals," "professional agitators," "sedition-mongers," and "criminals" intent on wrecking private enterprise.[7]

Sensitive to the anti-Anaconda strain that ran hottest through Wheeler's primary campaign, Kilroy insisted the company had little interest in the state's political affairs, other than "protecting itself of course, when necessary, against the crooks and grafters, who whether they operate by bomb or ballot, are trying to get something for nothing." Regarded in industrial circles as "a paragon" in its relations with employees and communities, the Anaconda Company, Kilroy insisted, had long operated in peace and amity—"before the bolshevki came to Montana." "Make no mistake," he wrote, "when you vote for these scurvy destroyers of your community you vote for hard times, for idleness, for strife, for disaster."[8]

The *Standard* all but ignored Wheeler's primary campaign in its news columns, but it could not duck the editorial haymakers from the *Butte Daily Bulletin,* which gloated over the primary's results. "Never in the history of Montana has there been a more blatant repudiation of the sinister policies of the copper interests and their prostitute press," the *Bulletin* wrote. The coming general election, it predicted, would bring a final repudiation of the "the great industrial autocracy that has been throttling the state and the people for so many years."[9]

Anaconda's press and political strategists fared no better in the three-way Republican primary, where Joseph Dixon shrewdly positioned himself as a moderate alternative to Attorney General Sam Ford, who had dueled with the state Council of Defense and defended NPL organizers from wartime hysteria, and the conservatives' Harry Wilson, an attorney for the Montana Power Company. Though Dixon drew little support from the daily press, the attacks by newspapers ranging from the *Billings Gazette* to the *New Northwest* only solidified his stance as a friend of neither the company nor the radicals.[10]

The strategy served Dixon perfectly. With no conservative opposition, Dixon stressed his recent agricultural background and happily joined the copper press in its excoriation of Wheeler's "red" backers. Though it grieved them, Dixon foes such as John Edwards and *Billings Gazette* editor Leon Shaw had little choice but to endorse the Republican ticket. "There is only one issue," Shaw wrote, "the present system of government or that of the Russian soviet, and there is no doubt where Wheeler stands—his associates and his talks stamp him indelibly."[11]

The company's dilemma was not lost on Montana's veteran weekly editors, Democrats and Republicans alike, many of whom agreed with

Hamilton's *Western News* that there was "no use in dodging that issue by trying to make it a question between the two national parties on national lines." The conservative *Big Timber Pioneer* urged its readers to think of the state. "It matters little what your former opinion of Dixon may have been. . . . Dixon represents the Americanism of Montana right now and is pledged to support it." For the *Fergus County Argus* in Lewistown, which had once labeled Arthur Townley as "the most dangerous man in the United States today," it was Dixon or the "red tide."[12]

For the first time since the copper wars, Montanans watched as the state's leading Democratic dailies hammered their party's candidate. The *Butte Miner,* the state's oldest Democratic daily, moaned in mid-September that it saw no "lesser evil" between Dixon and Wheeler, but the paper's vision cleared considerably over the next three weeks. During the campaign's final month, its front page carried a standing headline exhorting readers to back Dixon: "DON'T LET THE RED HAND STRANGLE BUTTE/VOTE THE REPUBLICAN TICKET." In Helena, Will Campbell's *Independent* renewed the anti-Wheeler crusade it had begun years earlier when it hounded the young U.S. attorney from office for allegedly coddling Butte's Wobblies. Campbell gloated over reports that a hostile crowd in Dillon had caused the Democratic nominee to flee and spend a night hiding in an empty railcar.[13]

Nicknamed "Boxcar Burt" or "Bolshevik Burt" by his rivals, Wheeler suffered similar treatment from the *Anaconda Standard,* which promoted Dixon's platform as a matter of "sane government versus half-baked socialism." In Great Falls, the *Tribune* waffled, torn between its sympathies for farmers and its fears of what NPL-style socialism would mean for Montana's chief industrial citizen. But as the election drew nearer the paper made its choice clear. "This newspaper will not join with any candidate to drive the Anaconda Company, or any other industrial enterprise . . . out of Montana," it wrote. Likewise, the weekly *Hill County Democrat* warned Havre readers that a vote for Dixon was "for the religion of your mother," for "purity in the home," and "against the confiscation of your property." Wheeler even faced allegations that his NPL followers believed in "free love," a charge the candidate turned against *Anaconda Standard* editor Richard Kilroy. "You all know Dick Kilroy," Wheeler told a Butte audience. "You know the kind of life he has led. If there was free love in North Dakota, do you think he'd still be in Butte?" The company's Republican dailies swung round to Dixon as well, though their endorsements were lukewarm. Like the *Billings Gazette,* the *Missoulian* confessed its ambivalence. "Joe Dixon or B. K. Wheeler—yes, we are between the devil and the deep, deep blue sea—and we do not know which is which," it wrote. By late October, however, the *Missoulian's* choice was "Dixon or the Deluge."[14]

Dixon's strongest support came from a string of non-company dailies, led by "Doc" Lanstrum's *Montana Record-Herald* in Helena, whose day-to-day news coverage of Dixon's campaign was channeled to the wire services for consumption statewide. The *Miles City Star,* published by Dixon's campaign manager, Joseph Scanlan, proved especially helpful in Republican eastern Montana where memories of Dixon's Bull Moose defection still lingered. Scanlan's knack for publicity also kept Dixon's image before voters through posters and buttons and in newspaper and movie-house advertising, Smaller GOP dailies such as the *Havre Promoter* and the Kalispell *Daily Inter Lake* offered crucial support as well.[15]

With such backing, Dixon swept to victory, and the copper press took a share of the credit. Wheeler's press support had been limited to a handful of weeklies and two smallish dailies. The Craigheads' *New Northwest,* which challenged the *Missoulian* by publishing a daily edition throughout 1920, helped Wheeler embarrass Dixon on the former senator's home turf in Missoula County; Wheeler also won in Silver Bow County, where the *Daily Bulletin* battled the *Daily Post,* the *Anaconda Standard,* and the *Miner* for the hearts and minds of Butte's voters. Wheeler also won in Montana's "red corner," in Daniels and Sheridan counties, where Charles Taylor's NPL-backed weeklies, the *Producers News* and *Scobey Sentinel,* wielded their influence. But Wheeler lost heavily in Billings, where the *Gazette's* hostility had been palpable, and in Helena and Great Falls, whose Democratic and Republican dailies all opposed him.[16]

Dixon's newspaper support stretched beyond the big copper dailies to include a broad array of farm-country weeklies, most of them Republican but whose numbers also included Democratic papers that resented the NPL's "takeover" of their party's primary. The sheer number of Montana's rural weeklies, which peaked that year at nearly 160 papers, attested to their influence, and the voices of particularly influential weekly editors reverberated statewide through the grapevine of exchanges. The fiery pro-Dixon editorials of *Chinook Opinion* editor Harry Brooks were widely reprinted, while the *Dawson County Review* in Glendive and the *Terry Tribune* gave Dixon critical support in Republican ranch country. Dan Whetstone's *Pioneer Press* in Cut Bank joined T. J. Hocking's Glasgow *Courier* and other Republican farm weeklies in touting Dixon's credentials to thousands of farmers wary of the NPL's radical politics and frightened by news reports, though often exaggerated, of the party's practices in North Dakota.[17]

However, newspaper support told only part of the story. A far more experienced campaigner, Dixon outperformed Wheeler on the stump and in his own writings published in the press. Unlike Wheeler, whom the copper press enjoyed portraying as "Butte's favorite farmer," Dixon spoke the farmers' language in an election where the rural voters mattered more than ever. An enthusiastic proponent of reclamation, Dixon contributed articles on experimental agricultural practices to the state's leading farm journals. He also appealed to Main Street business owners, drawing support from the Montana Development Association, which financed an ambitious statewide advertising campaign on his behalf, placing feature articles and photographs touting Dixon's accomplishments and family life in scores of newspapers, including many that had endorsed Wheeler. Dixon also won endorsements from leading Montana Democrats, especially U.S. Senator Henry Myers, who accused radicals of "stealing" the party.[18]

Dixon clearly profited from the "Red scare" that echoed through most Montana's dailies. The year began with headlines announcing the notorious "Palmer Raids," a federal roundup of suspected radicals on the orders of U.S. Attorney General A. Mitchell Palmer. In September, just weeks before the election, the papers reported a terrorist bombing outside a Wall Street bank, prompting renewed fears of wild-eyed anarchists and revolutionaries. Montana's leftist press counterpunched with epithets of its own, though it could hardly match the reach of the copper press. When the *Anaconda Standard*'s Kilroy predicted Montana's enslavement by "red radicals" led by that "hissing serpent of sedition," Bill Dunne, the *Butte Daily Bulletin* editor, responded with cartoons variously depicting the state caught in the coils of a giant Anaconda or ensnared in the tentacles of a corporate octopus. In some of the most animated language of the campaign, Dunne described Kilroy as "the editorial leper who manages the Anaconda Standard," but that was just for starters. "The cuttle-fish of privilege has been spreading its dirty black ink upon the political seas," the *Bulletin* wrote. "The Anaconda Standard with its prostitute editor has become utterly discredited."[19]

The Republicans' victory brought relief to conservatives like John Durston at the *Butte Daily Post*. "The farmers are not such d—d fools as we were afraid they were," he wrote after the election. Yet the company could not claim total victory. Though voters rejected the creation of a special tax commission with the power to readjust property valuations—a fearful prospect for mine owners—they also rejected a conservative attempt to abolish or otherwise restrict the state's open primary.

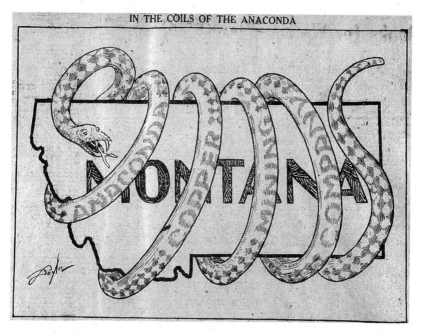

In 1920, Upton Sinclair wrote that the "gigantic Anaconda" had "swallowed" most of the state's dailies, leaving "only two newspapers in Montana not owned or controlled by 'copper'." The Butte Daily Bulletin's *cartoon, "In the coils of the Anaconda," echoed his sentiments.*

BUTTE DAILY BULLETIN, OCTOBER 2, 1920

Most worrisome, however, was the man voters had elected governor: Joseph Dixon. Miles Romney, whose *Western News* had backed Wheeler and disdained Dixon's demagogic appeals to "Americanism" during the campaign, was still happy to note that "at last Montana has a governor who is not responsive to the strings of the invisible powers lurking in the background."[20]

Commenting on Republican Joseph Dixon's win in the 1920 gubernatorial election, Miles Romney Sr. (above), whose Western News *had disdained Dixon's demagogic appeals to "Americanism" during the campaign, was still happy to note that "at last Montana has a governor who is not responsive to the strings of the invisible powers lurking in the background."*

SCHOOL OF JOURNALISM,
UNIVERSITY OF MONTANA, MISSOULA

FOR JOSEPH DIXON, winning the election proved to be the easy part. He took office during one of the bleakest periods of Montana's history. Drought that first appeared along the High Line in 1917 had spread inexorably across the state. By 1921, few areas had escaped it. Combined with poor postwar prices and tumbling land values, the disaster led to a collapse of the dryland homestead boom. The "proof" ads that had filled the pages of farm-country weeklies gave way to notices of farm auctions and sheriffs' sales, and by the decade's midpoint half of Montana's farmers had lost their land. Banks that had so eagerly financed the boom collapsed by the score. The toll was horrific; upwards of sixty thousand homesteaders would eventually quit the state, leaving broken homes and hopes rusting on the prairie. State government, its coffers nearly empty, seemed powerless to help. To replenish the treasury and ease the tax burden on farmers, Dixon immediately proposed a sweeping legislative program centered on proposals

Governor Joseph Dixon took office during one of the bleakest periods of Montana's history. Drought had spread inexorably across the state, and lush fields of dryland wheat like this one photographed near Glendive in 1911 were only a dim memory. The drought, combined with low crop prices and tumbling land values, led to the collapse of the homestead boom.

L. A. FOSTER, PHOTOGRAPHER, MONTANA HISTORICAL SOCIETY
PHOTOGRAPH ARCHIVES, HELENA

for a stiff inheritance tax—aimed largely at the enormous private estate of William A. Clark—a graduated income tax, taxes on oil production, auto licenses, and gasoline. Not least of all, the governor proposed an increased tax on the production of metal mines.[21]

The conservative-Progressive coalition that swept Dixon to power crumbled almost immediately, and over the next four years Dixon faced an unrelenting attack from conservatives, led by the Anaconda Company and channeled largely through what Dixon began to call its "interlocking press." As company lobbyists and political allies worked to block Dixon's legislative agenda, the copper press commenced a four-year anti-Dixon campaign that featured incessant editorial criticism and one-sided news coverage along with fabricated stories, deliberate distortion, and a gleeful focus on a string of distracting "scandals" within the administration. The copper chorus that had been powerless to prevent Dixon's election would play a decisive role in his administration's demise.

To replenish the state treasury and ease the tax burden on farmers such as these pictured outside the Nonpartisan League Office in Wibaux, Dixon proposed a sweeping legislative program centered on several tax proposals—not least of which was an increased levy on the production of metal mines.

MONTANA HISTORICAL SOCIETY PHOTOGRAPH ARCHIVES, HELENA

The campaign began within hours of Dixon's inaugural legislative message, which called not only for higher taxes on industry and the wealthy, but a state tax commission to ensure fairness. He also recommended reforming the state's anemic workers' compensation law to require that mining companies finally pay for the treatment of miners suffering from silicosis at the state's tuberculosis hospital. According to Dixon, the state's cost of treating silicosis victims from 1917 to 1920 was twice what the state received in taxes from the mines. It was an agenda aimed straight at the heart of "the interests." In response, the company cranked up its legislative lobby, invoked the power of its statewide business connections, and unleashed its newspapers.[22]

The editors arrayed against the governor were a seasoned bunch. All but Will Campbell had been battle tested in the copper wars, and all had more than political motives to back the company's fight with Dixon. Campbell, who bought out the Democratic investors who had helped him purchase the paper in 1913, was under severe financial pressure by the early 1920s. As businesses, newspapers were not immune to the economic depression that racked the state, and the Republican victory also meant the loss of state printing business that had been his due under the previous Democratic administration. With the spoils now going to "Doc" Lanstrum's *Montana Record-Herald,* Campbell needed a patron, and the company eagerly stepped in. Years later, Campbell would acknowledge accepting more than two hundred thousand dollars in loans from Anaconda during the Dixon years—loans he could never repay.

With its publisher and principal stockholder, state senator John Edwards, leading the opposition to Dixon's legislative agenda, the *Billings Gazette*'s loyalties were clear as well. But it too struggled against the disastrous economy and the cost of maintaining an almost constant campaign. Between 1921 and 1923, the paper raised two hundred thousand dollars through stock offerings and bond sales to manage its debt and finance operations, amounts almost certainly provided by the Anaconda Company with editor Leon Shaw acting as trustee. Of course, the most direct links between the daily press and the company were in Butte, where John Durston and Richard Kilroy represented the company-owned *Butte Daily Post* and *Anaconda Standard,* while the *Butte Miner*'s Larry Dobell continued to function as William A. Clark's agent in a fight with keen implications for Clark's remaining mine holdings and the millionaire's heirs.[23]

In every significant aspect, the *Miner* operated as if it were a unit of the Anaconda press. Dobell's close relationship with the *Missoulian*'s Martin Hutchens would lead Dixon to speculate that the two coordinated their editorial attacks against him. Dixon was so struck by similarities in the two papers' editorial language he mentioned it in his address to the special legislative session of 1921 and compared the papers' unnamed editors to tyrants George III and Louis XIV. In a private letter to *Western News* editor Miles Romney, Dixon said capitol aides had later observed "our friends Larry and Hutch, in walking back to the hotel, were having quite an argument as to which one was Louis and which one was George."[24]

The company's most complex relationship appears to have been with the *Missoulian*'s high-strung Hutchens, the most experienced of the state's daily editors. Hutchens's assertion of the *Missoulian*'s independence and

his relatively open discussion of the Anaconda Company's press ownership in 1917 supports his family's contention that he had been initially un-
aware of the company's financial stake in his paper. Such ignorance—or
naiveté—would also explain the *Missoulian's* fairly even-handed reporting
on the 1919 controversy over the firing and later reinstatement of university
economics professor Louis Levine, who published an authoritative study
showing that the mining industry paid a disproportionately small share of
the state's taxes. Hutchens's tenuous grip on the *Missoulian* and *Missoula
Sentinel* might also explain his furious campaign two years later to fire
another university professor, Arthur Fisher, whose leftist politics may have
had less to do with Hutchens's ire than Fisher's editorial work for the rival
New Northwest and plans for converting the paper to daily publication.
Fisher, the brash son of a former secretary of the Interior who had been an
old Chicago acquaintance of the Hutchens, had the bad manners to solicit investors and threaten to put "the *Missoulian* out of business" during
Thanksgiving dinner at the Hutchenses' home. The *Missoulian's* aggressive interest in local controversies further complicated Hutchens's relationship with well-connected company officials, who reportedly considered his dismissal as early as 1922. His fierce criticism of Governor Dixon,
frequently reprinted around the state, may have saved his job.[25]

The copper chorus, in language so similar that it seemed scripted,
immediately denounced Dixon's tax proposals, which had so incensed
Senator John Edwards that his *Billings Gazette* refused to carry so
much as a summary of Dixon's state of the state message to the legislature. Focusing largely on the mine tax, papers echoed the *Anaconda
Standard's* fears of what such a tax would do to the state's "poor struggling, [*sic*] industries." The *Missoulian* pronounced Dixon's tax proposals "confiscating and prohibitory." The mine tax alone, Hutchens wrote,
would be the "worst thing that could happen to Montana." In their
news columns, the papers largely ignored the progress of tax bills and
the attempts by company lobbyists to derail them, preferring to focus
instead on efforts to censor movies, require that teachers take loyalty
oaths, and regulate the state's young oil industry. But editorial opposition to increased taxation never flagged. Neither Will Campbell nor
Larry Dobell saw a need for additional state revenues, arguing instead
for more frugal government. "It is not more taxes that the people want,

but less," the *Butte Miner* warned. In the end, Dixon's income tax bill was killed, and his other tax proposals reduced to almost token gestures. His idea for a tax commission was dismissed as a needless expense.[26]

Frustrated, Dixon immediately called lawmakers back for a special session and browbeat them into passing a slightly improved inheritance-tax bill. Despite hot fire from the copper dailies, he also shamed legislators into taking his tax commission idea to voters as a referendum. Dixon's success prompted further howls from the company press, which accused him of being wasteful, dictatorial, and intent on driving industry from the state.[27]

For all its froth, the controversy over Dixon's tax policies paled compared to journalistic fireworks generated by the governor's decision to fire the warden of the state prison, the genial Frank Conley. A former prison guard, Conley amassed a fortune despite his meager salary by awarding himself and his business associates contracts to supply the prison's real and imaginary needs. In the two years after Conley's firing, the prison's coal bill would drop by more than half without any reduction in supply, but Conley's gregarious nature and widespread connections had earned him an array of powerful friends, including the Anaconda Company, for which Conley occasionally provided convict strikebreakers.[28]

The Conley case gave the copper press an opportunity to harass Dixon throughout the usual lull between legislative sessions and elections. Regardless of their political affiliations, the papers rose as a unit to Conley's defense. Making no pretense of objectivity, they engaged in a campaign of distortion and fabrication, led by Will Campbell's *Helena Independent,* which depicted Conley as the melodramatic victim of Dixon's ungrateful and dictatorial whims. The paper's most outrageous act was the publication of an anonymous yarn that recounted a soft-hearted Conley's generosity in helping a young convict find the upright path by sparing him additional prison time. The "kid," an unnamed but now successful Denver businessman, was supposedly a relative of the ungrateful governor—or so the *Independent* claimed. Editors at the *Missoulian* and *Butte Miner* immediately spread the tale but refused to carry a substantiated refutation of the story, including categorical denials from most of the story's purported players that appeared days later in Helena's *Montana Record-Herald.*[29]

The uproar over Conley's firing forced Dixon to launch a formal investigation of the former warden's alleged misuse of state funds, guaranteeing months of headlines and anti-Dixon editorials. As the investigation proceeded, Campbell struck with another hoax, funneling a report to Spokane's regional Associated Press bureau that a Montana ex-con named John C. Margelin had been killed there in a robbery. The story claimed that before his death, Margelin told friends that he been paroled prematurely in Montana in return for helping Dixon's investigators find dirt on Conley. The article arrived by wire in Spokane and was erroneously retransmitted back to Montana as a special dispatch under a Spokane dateline. The copper dailies jumped on the story, and once again Dixon and prison officials denied it explicitly. In the face of such hammering from what Dixon's friends called the "anvil chorus," only "Doc" Lanstrum's *Montana Record-Herald* in Helena and Joseph Scanlan's *Miles City Star* deigned to print the governor's responses.[30]

Amid a blizzard of publicity, the Conley investigation proceeded by fits and starts, complicated by an intra-party battle between Dixon's men and Conley's Republican defenders, which included Montana's attorney general Wellington Rankin. Throughout the Conley case, Dixon accused the copper press of printing "damnable lies," while opposition editors argued hotly that Dixon had purchased the *Montana Record-Herald*'s favorable coverage through the award of state printing contracts. When Conley's attorney repeated the charge to Dixon's face, the governor lamely implied that a difference existed between "patronage and subsidy and ownership by the big.interests."[31]

When the Conley matter finally went to trial, it generated such distorted partisan coverage from both the *Independent* and the *Montana Record-Herald* that the trial judge threatened both papers with contempt.[32] The admonition worked for a while, but the newspapers were again slugging away by the trial's end. Typical of the *Independent*'s bias were the headlines that followed Dixon's own testimony, which Conley's lawyers chose not to contest:

COUNSEL FOR DEFENSE DECLINE TO DIGNIFY TESTIMONY
Cross Examination is Their Theory
After Governor Makes an Unsupported Charge[33]

In the end, the court found Conley not guilty of all but one technical charge. The judge ruled that although the ex-warden had badly mismanaged state funds and property, his activities had enjoyed the full connivance and sanction of previous administrations.[34]

The copper press reveled in Conley's "vindication." Not only had the controversy diverted attention from Dixon's campaign for fairer taxation, but it also encouraged such an intense rivalry between Campbell's *Independent* and Lanstrum's *Montana Record-Herald* that Montanans statewide found it difficult to obtain timely and objective reporting on matters of crucial statewide importance. As respective morning and afternoon agents of the Associated Press, both papers fed the wires such blatantly partisan coverage that the *Billings Gazette* hired a special correspondent to cover the 1921 legislative session rather than have to explain differences between the reports that would otherwise appear in the morning *Gazette* and *Evening Journal*.[35]

Smaller dailies such as the *Miles City Star* and *Lewistown Democrat-News* could hardly afford their own statehouse bureaus and reportedly agitated for the creation of an independent Associated Press bureau. In late 1921, the Associated Press, which had long covered the state from Spokane or Denver, finally established a correspondency in Helena and placed it under the direction of its Denver bureau. It was an important step in the professionalization of Montana's press. Serving papers of all partisan hues, the Associated Press's credibility rested on the timeliness and fairness of its twice-daily news report, which it had previously gleaned almost entirely from member papers, a practice that long magnified the copper dailies' influence. An independent Associated Press Montana bureau charged with sifting fact from fiction was long overdue, though it would depend heavily on member papers for news beyond the capital.[36]

Despite the Associated Press's presence, the Anaconda Company could still marshal formidable resources for statewide publicity. As Dixon headed into the mid-term elections of 1922, he faced what he perceived as almost total opposition in the press, a condition he noted in a letter to an ally in Scobey in early 1922:

> The extent of their [the Anaconda Company's] control of practically all of the daily papers, except the Helena *Montana Record*, and their undercover control of the weekly newspapers is overwhelming.

During the last four months four special cases of newspaper control have been presented to me, each one of which was an appeal to save their paper from the hands of the "invisible government."

The danger to Montana at this time is that we either have to read the Butte Miner and the Helena Independent or turn to the equally impossible propaganda of the Butte Bulletin.[37]

Beyond its direct control of some newspapers, Anaconda and its creation, the Montana Power Company, had an enormous advantage in commercial advertising. As the fall campaign heated up, Anaconda launched a major ad campaign, which featured a ten-week series of slick ads titled "Taxation Talks" that laid out the company case against taxation in dizzying detail, arguing that, if anything, its existing tax burden was too heavy. As copper editors praised the ads for their clarity and candor, the series ran in almost every small daily and weekly in the state, skipping only the most virulent anti-company papers. Set against the fearful deterioration of the state's economy, the advertising bonanza—which also included an eighteen-week series of promotional ads from the Montana Power Company—must have appeared like manna to the rural weekly editors, though many saw the series for exactly what it was. Miles Romney ran them cheerfully and then noted editorially how the company had distorted its tax figures to avoid any side-by-side comparison with the taxes paid by farmers, whose crops were taxed at their full value, not the partial valuations afforded the proceeds of mines.[38]

Occasionally, the company reportedly used other means to impress its views on the editors of opposition weeklies. In 1920, the Republican *Virginia City Times* had supported both Dixon and his chief legislative ally, Madison County's senator, O. H. Junod. But just before the 1922 primary, the paper's publisher and editor, C. H. Browne, found himself summoned to Butte on business. Upon his return, the *Times* underwent a mysterious change of heart and suddenly turned its editorial guns against Junod and the governor.[39]

Dixon campaigned hard despite the odds, taking his message directly to the people in regions where the copper press held sway. A priority was his constitutional referendum that, if approved, would allow Dixon to appoint a three-member "board of equalization" authorized to balance the state's tax system. His chief concern, however, was retaining Republican control of the legislature. When the ballots were finally counted, the legislative assembly was still in Republican hands, despite the efforts of the copper press. *Billings Gazette* publisher John Edwards, Dixon's longtime rival, lost his bid for a fifth state senate term, and voters approved Dixon's tax equalization board. But there were signs of trouble too. Burton K. Wheeler won his race for the U.S. Senate amid the curious neutrality of a copper press that had vilified him just two years earlier, and liberal Democrats made gains in the legislature. As he headed into his second legislative session, Dixon faced not only a stronger Democratic faction, but also greater infighting among Republicans over future offices and patronage.[40]

It was a situation ripe for exploiting, and conservatives pounced when Dixon laid out another ambitious program of tax increases and budget cuts to halt the state's slide into debt. The copper dailies, led by the *Missoulian, Butte Miner,* and *Helena Independent,* labeled the governor "tax mad" and "extravagant" and argued for further frugality and "economy" in government. So harsh and one-sided was their criticism that Lewistown editor Tom Stout of the *Democrat-News,* a political rival, worried that it would create sympathy for Dixon's reelection. Meanwhile, Anaconda and Montana Power lobbyists and their political allies deftly outmaneuvered Dixon in the 1923 legislature, installing conservatives at the head of key committees with predictable results. Dixon's plans to increase taxes on the mines, hydropower, and the oil and gas industry and to enact progressive corporate and personal income taxes quickly withered. The hypocrisy of the attack on Dixon's reputed lack of frugality reached its zenith when the copper dailies ignored his successful efforts to cut nearly six hundred thousand dollars from the legislature's budget. Instead, it focused on a series of investigations launched by Dixon's rivals into various state agencies and institutions.[41]

Dixon limped into the 1924 elections against a backdrop of continued economic depression, an increasing number of bank failures, a mounting state deficit, political infighting, and a largely hostile daily press. One hopeful spot, however, had been the ease with which Dixon loyalists had placed on the November ballot an initiative asking voters to approve a 1 percent tax on the gross value of metal-mine production, with the money split between the state's general fund and schools. Meanwhile, a companion effort to make Anaconda shoulder greater workers' compensation costs failed to draw enough signatures amid rumors that Anaconda and Montana Power Company managers had threatened the jobs of workers whose names appeared on the petitions.[42]

Under such pressure, Dixon's political organization was badly frayed. Arrayed against him now were company-backed conservatives in both parties and a new Farmer-Labor Party composed of disaffected unionists led by former *Butte Bulletin* editor Bill Dunne, now a Communist Party organizer, and farm radicals led by the *Producers News* editor and state senator Charles Taylor. Their third party could hardly hope to win an election, but it could divert votes from Dixon, whose suspicions of the effort were roused by the fact that the party's campaign newspaper, the *Farmer-Labor Advocate,* was printed on *Missoulian* presses.[43]

Elsewhere, the company focused on recapturing the Democratic Party. In the company's hunt for a gubernatorial candidate, *Butte Miner* editor Larry Dobell privately suggested former Kalispell district judge John E. "Honest John" Erickson, a moderate of no particular distinction who would appeal to Montana's significant Scandinavian population and moderates weary of controversy. Damaged by depression and outflanked politically and in the press, Dixon's campaign for reelection was probably over before it started.[44]

The campaign's newspaper wars featured an overwhelming bias for Erickson, while Dixon's defense went unnoticed in dailies beyond "Doc" Lanstrum's *Montana Record-Herald* in Helena and the *Miles City Star.* Among Republican weeklies, only a handful that backed Dixon in 1920 dared to support him now. Cut Bank's *Pioneer Press,* the *Harlowton Times,* and the *Chinook Opinion* continued to defend Dixon, as did Fort Benton's *River Press,* whose editor tried to refute rumors of Dixon's spendthrift ways. "Never before in Montana has a governor made the fight Dixon has made for the people of the state," he wrote. "He has fought for two great ideas, to get them a square deal in taxes, and to reduce the expense of state government." More typical, however, were the editorial jibes from small papers such as the *Livingston Enterprise,* the *Big Timber Pioneer,* and the *Ryegate Reporter.* The editor of the *Whitefish News* accused Dixon of "taxing the people to death, and at the same time throwing Montana . . . in the red over three million dollars." Worse, he wrote, Dixon's continuing emphasis on Montana's poor economy was hurting the state's real-estate market.[45]

The press campaign sank to its lowest point in early October when the copper dailies published the story of a Wisconsin woman who had sued the director of the state mental hospital, a Dixon appointee, for false imprisonment and for "mutilating her body" in surgeries performed "despite her struggles and cries." According to the "special report" carried in both the *Helena Independent* and *Billings Gazette,* the woman had been transferred by her husband from an expensive Milwaukee sanitarium to Montana's cheaper Warm Springs state hospital with the help of "men prominent in political circles." The Helena and Billings dailies made the implications explicit in boldfaced, front-page headlines. "BRUTAL MUTILATION OF SANE WOMAN LAID TO DIXON'S POLITICS," the *Gazette* announced. The *Missoulian* showed more restraint, choosing instead to run an Associated Press version of the story, which reported the facts of the lawsuit without the manufactured political context. The damage done, the story faded quickly without follow-up, much less a response from Dixon.[46]

While its editors blazed away, the company pressed its case by other means. Anaconda officials distributed thousands of free copies of a pamphlet, titled *The Copper Target,* designed to counter Dixon's favorite stump trick of pulling out a one-dollar bill, the amount, he told listeners, that William A. Clark's Elm Orlu Mine had paid in state taxes the previous year. Though it claimed to have lost more than $13 million from its Montana operations over the previous four years, Anaconda reported contributions of $187,000 to the state's general fund in 1923. Statewide, the company argued, it had paid more than $1 million to city, county, and school districts. The pamphlet, with its blizzard of statistics, also appeared in multi-week installments as paid advertising in dozens of Montana weeklies. The copper dailies publicized the pamphlet in single-sourced news stories and highlighted its most salient features in their editorials. The company reinforced the pamphlet's message further with a series of speeches made by Anaconda attorney Dan M. Kelly, who used it as his text in town after town during the campaign's final weeks.[47]

State newspapers bombarded Dixon, claiming the metal-mines tax initiative would kill the "Goose that Lays the Golden Eggs" and cost the state jobs in an already depressed economy.

Red Lodge *Carbon County Chronicle*, October 29, 1924

The company brought other pressures to bear too. In mid-October, the pro-Dixon *Carbon County Chronicle* in Red Lodge suddenly changed owners as well as its tune. Over the next three weeks, it featured not only the company's "Copper Target" advertising and uncritical coverage of Kelly's speech in Red Lodge, but a front-page cartoon depicting an ax-wielding Joseph Dixon about to slay the Anaconda Copper Mining Company, portrayed as Montana's golden goose.[48]

The lopsided newspaper campaign foreshadowed the November vote. The copper dailies fed readers a steady diet of tributes to Erickson's honesty, modesty, and frugality, qualities Dixon by implication obviously lacked. They generally ignored Dixon's speeches and campaign appearances. The *Billings Gazette* refused to run a story on the governor's reelection announcement, and when Dixon partisans inquired about its reasons, editor Leon Shaw politely invited them to buy an ad. The Associated Press carried news of both campaigns from Helena, but because its coverage beyond the capital depended on the kindness of local papers, Dixon suffered disproportionately when his campaign chugged through swaths of Montana served by the copper press. Dixon's campaign managers fumed, but there was little they could do. When the *Billings Gazette* refused to cover a big Dixon campaign rally in nearby Huntley, Dixon campaign manager Joseph Scanlan complained bitterly to Associated Press's western supervisor in San Francisco, who in turn asked Shaw to play as fair "as your political conscience will allow." He instructed reporters in Helena and Denver to do likewise.[49]

A front-page Missoulian *article accused Dixon of proposing a tax that was tantamount to the confiscation of mining property.*

DAILY MISSOULIAN, OCTOBER 19, 1924

Beyond its daily bombardment of Dixon, the copper press hammered the metal-mines tax initiative in an attack whose elements were clearly orchestrated. Day after day on their editorial pages, copper editors replayed the argument that higher taxes would ruin Montana's mining industries, costing the state precious jobs in an already depressed economy. Typical of the copper press, the *Missoulian* jabbed incessantly at both Dixon and the mines tax and delighted in running occasional letters from readers who agreed.[50]

Local political cartoons pilloried Dixon too. One memorable *Missoulian* example portrayed Montana's mining industry as an overburdened camel, staggering under higher operating costs and local taxes, while Joseph Dixon, dressed in Bedouin garb, ordered a doubtful voter to toss on another tax. A front-page box on Election Day reported that the company's Missoula-area headquarters in Bonner had issued nearly $2.4 million in local checks for salaries, services, and supplies in 1923. "Now what does Governor Dixon propose to give to Missoula county in place of that?" In Billings, the *Gazette*'s attack featured political cartoons, customized for the sensibilities of eastern Montana's ranch country by the same artist who had pilloried Dixon for the *Missoulian*. The *Gazette*'s version featured a cowboy labeled "Mining Industries"' fighting to control a bronco labeled "Montana" and headed for a barbed wire fence described as the "Metal Mines Tax." "He's been treatin [*sic*] me pretty rough," the broncbuster says, "but if he keeps out of that entanglement I'll stay with him." Both papers also featured the same photo illustration of canceled tax checks paid by mine owners to various county treasurers.[51]

Besides their attacks on the tax initiative, the copper papers lambasted the Dixon administration as dictatorial and wasteful, blaming the governor and not the drought-deepened depression for Montana's evaporating treasury. Will Campbell made continued sport of Dixon's supposed "extravagant tastes" with reference to an apparently concocted story that Dixon had ordered, at state expense, a $12.50 gravy boat to serve his guests and family at the executive mansion. Helena's *Montana Record-Herald* countered that Dixon's predecessor, Governor Sam Stewart, Campbell's old friend, had actually ordered the offending tableware, but Campbell kept that story spinning for months, along

BREAKING THE CAMEL'S BACK

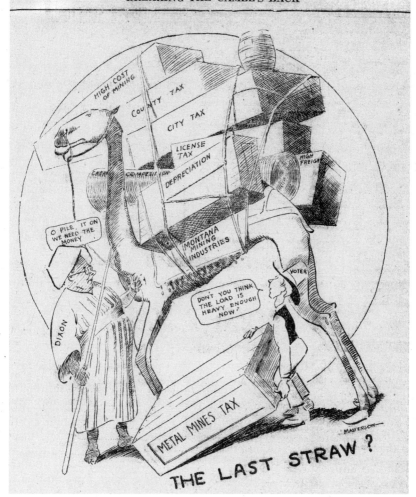

The Missoulian *portrayed Montana's mining industry as an overburdened camel, staggering under higher operating costs and local taxes, while Joseph Dixon, dressed in Bedouin garb, orders a doubtful voter to toss on another tax.*

DAILY MISSOULIAN, NOVEMBER 1, 1924

with other specious examples of Dixon's selfish stewardship of the public's money. In an editorial headlined "More Paint for the Lady," the *Missoulian* offered its own proof of Dixon's wastefulness and cronyism when it angrily accused the administration of illegally awarding state printing contracts to the *Montana Record-Herald,* Dixon's "subsidized,

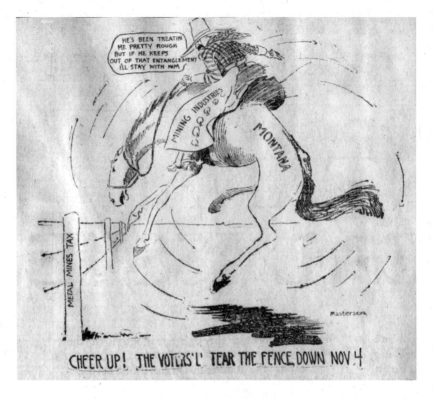

In Billings, the Gazette *featured a cowboy labeled "Mining Industries" atop a bronco called "Montana" headed for a barbed wire fence described as the "Metal Mines Tax." "He's been treatin me pretty rough," the broncobuster says, "but if he keeps out of that entanglement I'll stay with him." The bad press had mixed results: Dixon lost the next election, but his metal-mine tax initiative passed.*

BILLINGS GAZETTE, NOVEMBER 2, 1924

dishonest newspaper," a "journalistic street walker" whose only mission was to defend "the most incompetent and wasteful administration" since Montana's admission to the union.[52]

Despite his vigorous campaign, Dixon suffered a stinging defeat in November. He carried twenty-eight counties to Erickson's twenty-six but polled less than 43 percent of the vote. Given the incessant hammering of the copper press and the brutal depression that had whipsawed Montanans for nearly four years, Dixon's showing seems remarkable. He carried Yellowstone County, home turf of Senator John Edwards and the *Billings Gazette,* though he lost every other county served by the copper dailies.

In consolation, however, Dixon enjoyed the passage of his mine-tax initiative, which, despite the company's press and expensive advertising, carried every county but those most dependent on working mines and smelters. Over the harangues of the *Missoulian's* Martin Hutchens and Leon Shaw of the *Billings Gazette,* the measure sailed to easy victories in Missoula and Yellowstone counties, a fact that could not have escaped Anaconda's political operatives. With its four-year barrage against Dixon, the copper press surely contributed to his defeat, yet passage of the metal-mines tax once again demonstrated the limits of corporate propaganda and the company's supposed hold over the state. As political scientists would later suggest, most voters considered what the metal-mines tax would mean to their wallets and voted accordingly.[53]

The paradox was not lost on Dixon, who acknowledged the company's press campaign and advertising expenditures in a wistful post-election note to North Dakota's Republican governor. "It is a rather amusing circumstance," he added, "that the same voting population would pass the one big measure for which I made the fight during the past four years and then turn around and defeat the man who was alone responsible for the measure."[54]

While the copper press crowed at Dixon's defeat, Anaconda officials must have viewed the mixed results with some alarm. The future would demand more subtle methods of persuasion.

FOR THIRTY-FIVE YEARS, John Hurst Durston had been the company's ink-stained warrior, but in the campaign of 1924 the seventy-seven-year-old editor was only in the way.

The drawling professor with the double chins and walrus mustache, the man who once built a metropolitan newspaper in Anaconda, who had fought Marcus Daly's epic political battles and those of Daly's successors, now spent his days instructing cub reporters on the obscure origins of words and striking match after match in vain attempts to light his wheezing briar pipe. His clothes, impeccably tailored, often displayed the debris of his latest meal, earning him the newsroom nick-name "Dusty Dick"—but never to his face. He was still "the Maestro," but now, eleven years into his tenure as editor of the *Butte Daily Post* and more than thirty years since his move to Montana, Durston ruled his newsroom mostly by reputation. He found it easier to delegate the details of management that had once absorbed him, and his editori-als had long since lost their thunder, though flashes of his infamous temper still came through. Ed Hamner, a *Post* newsman in the 1920s, would never forget the old man's reaction to one angry reader's extend-ed harangue. When it was over, Durston strolled calmly to Hamner, who had witnessed the scene. "Blow some smoke up him, Ed," Durston instructed. "And misspell his name."[55]

Durston remained an imposing figure, not only in the newsroom, but also among former employees and politicians whose careers he had fos-tered. Senators still wrote him doting letters, and, Arthur Stone, once a cub reporter under Durston's tutelage and now dean of the state universi-ty's journalism school, secured an honorary doctorate for his old mentor. Montana's system of higher education remained a particular interest for Durston, and over the years the former professor used his clout to shape it. In 1914, when voters considered consolidating the state's scattered college campuses, Durston led the successful counterattack, much to the relief of business leaders in Butte, Dillon, Missoula, and especially Bozeman, where Durston maintained his vacation ranch. In response to criticism about the lack of administrative coordination among the campuses, Durston helped persuade lawmakers to create the office of chancellor.[56]

But the war-horse had mellowed considerably since the copper wars. During the brief hiatus between his departure from the *Anaconda Standard* and his reinstatement at the *Butte Daily Post,* Durston had wistfully confessed the sins of Montana journalism to newly elected U.S. Senator Thomas Walsh, whose candidacy the *Standard* had initial-ly opposed. Montana politics, Durston wrote, contained an "uncom-monly large amount" of vitriol, and he freely acknowledged his own contribution. On too many occasions, he had "indulged impulsively in comment which was needlessly personal or ill-natured and which I wish now I had never written." More important, Durston lamented the Montana press's obsession with national politics, which often obscured

During the campaign of 1924, eleven years into his tenure as editor of the Butte Daily Post, *John H. Durston still served the company press, but the fiery editor of old had mellowed considerably since the "copper wars." By the decade's end, Durston and others schooled in the bombastic rhetoric of nineteenth-century journalism would be replaced with less colorful men.*

SCHOOL OF JOURNALISM,
UNIVERSITY OF MONTANA, MISSOULA

issues of more importance to readers.[57]

If Durston felt constrained by tailoring his journalism to the company's needs, he was not alone. Charles Eggleston, Durston's longtime deputy at the *Anaconda Standard,* privately confessed similar frustrations. Yet that was the deal both men had knowingly struck, and though they occasionally chaffed at the consequences, they remained loyal, perhaps out of habit, philosophy, or the realization that no other owner could support newspapers in the style to which both had become accustomed—and for which they sacrificed a measure of credibility. In 1913, Durston had pretended that the *Inter Mountain*'s reincarnation as the *Butte Daily Post,* under his personal ownership, signaled a restoration of the paper's journalistic independence. In the *Post*'s inaugural issue, Durston told his new readers that the paper had once been "the property of a copper company that reached the sane conclusion that, for its purposes, a newspaper is not a valuable possession." He brushed away the mystery of his reemergence as a Republican by saying that there were enough Democratic papers already; and he assured his readers that the *Post* would be an independent herald "of Butte's industrial greatness." It is hard to believe anyone was fooled.[58]

In return for such loyalty and compromises of dignity, Durston demanded a degree of professional respect from his corporate patrons.

The *Post* was no mere organ, nor was he a mere figurehead. As a trusted lieutenant who owed the company his allegiance and his pen, Durston maintained his prerogative to determine how his newspaper would best serve its readers and fight the company's battles. A semblance of editorial control was crucial to both his pride and credibility.

The blow came from a dapper thirty-five-year-old company executive born in the same year that Durston had launched the *Anaconda Standard*. As a youth, James H. Dickey Jr. had delivered the company's newspapers, but by 1910 he was clerking for Anaconda's coal mining and merchandising operation in Belt. From there, Dickey joined the company's auditing department in Butte, where he mastered the intricacies of Anaconda's non-mining operations. By 1923, he was business manager of the Post Publishing Company, responsible for the paper's finances, if not its editorial policy.[59]

That was about to change as Dickey entered the *Butte Daily Post's* upstairs city room one summer morning in 1924, on the eve of the company's campaign to unseat Governor Dixon. As a young college student and summer staffer named Fred Martin would later tell it, Dickey skipped his usual morning consultation with Durston and headed straight for city editor James Cummins. "This is to run on page one as is without change," Dickey said, tossing news copy and artwork on the editor's desk. When Dickey was gone, Durston approached Cummins and asked what Dickey had wanted. The city editor handed over the story and art, and Durston took it to his office.[60]

The story—the company's opening salvo against Dixon's metalmines initiative—could hardly have caught Durston by surprise. But the fact that such material had been produced outside his newsroom and ordered into news columns without his consent struck Durston like a wet slap. Summoned to Durston's office, Dickey politely informed the editor that the package would run regardless of Durston's approval. Furious, Durston phoned the company's western vice president on the sixth floor of Butte's Hennessy Building only to be told that Dickey's authority was final. Durston then ordered Martin to reach Anaconda president "Con" Kelley at the company's New York headquarters. When Kelley proved unreachable, Durston told Martin to book passage on the first train to New York, but before the young intern could comply, Durston stormed from the newsroom. A year later, after his graduation from college, Martin returned to the *Post* newsroom for another summer's work and found the atmosphere changed. Durston, the dean of Montana's daily editors, was clearly "a whipped man." In the Butte speakeasies where Martin and other *Post* reporters gathered after work, "the talk was not about the stories we wrote but what we couldn't or didn't write."[61]

Anaconda's campaign against Dixon marked the transformation of Montana's copper press from a loose alliance of company-owned or -supported dailies to a formal subsidiary under Anaconda's direct supervision. By the decade's end, most of its editors schooled in the bombastic partisanship of nineteenth-century journalism would be replaced with less colorful men. It was more than just a change in the rhetorical fashion; journalism in general became more businesslike, more professional, as it shed its sensationalism and partisanship for a more complex future, one dependent on meeting the varied and often contradictory needs of both readers and advertisers. Yet with only the company's interest to ultimately serve, the Anaconda dailies would fall into step as dull links in a copper chain. Until its dissolution in 1959, only one man would truly challenge its existence.

A few months after his father's death in 1925, William A. Clark Jr. assumed management of the Butte Miner, *precipitating the resignation of its longtime editor Larry Dobell. An unfailing supporter of Clark Sr. and a power in the conservative wing of the state Democratic Party, Dobell's influence was confirmed by the vitriol he inspired from the* Butte Daily Bulletin, *which lampooned his rhetorical style and his tubby physique.*

BUTTE DAILY BULLETIN, SEPTEMBER 21, 1918

CHAPTER EIGHT

The Last Newspaper War

ANOTHER CLARK
CHALLENGES
THE COMPANY

THE FACT THAT WILLIAM A. Clark outlived his fellow copper kings was typical of the man. By the time he died of pneumonia on March 2, 1925, Senator Clark had made more money and attained higher office than either of his rivals. His multistate business empire ranged from mines and smelters to railroads, banks, and real estate, and he alone—not some corporate cabal of moneymen—held the reins. Montanans flocked to memorial services to pay their respects to an entrepreneurial giant, a self-made man whose success illuminated the American dream and whose story embodied the history of their state.[1]

But he was a difficult man to admire. To Mark Twain, Clark was "as rotten a human being as can be found anywhere under the flag," a "shame to the American nation," and "the most disgusting creature that the Republic has produced since Tweed's time." When it came to industrial titans, Twain much preferred his own benefactor, Henry H. Rogers, the cultured Standard Oil magnate and creator of the Amalgamated Copper Company. By contrast, Clark was aloof and self-absorbed. He valued flattery over friendship. His tastes in art and architecture favored the crass and gaudy. His politics were reactionary, rooted in prejudice, and always subservient to his business or his vanity, which was eclipsed only by his capacity for hard work and audacity. In a time of legendary graft, "Boodler" Clark's corruption stood out. Yet as other barons of capital sought redemption in philanthropy, the man who had bribed his way in the U.S. Senate saw little point in giving away what he had worked so hard to acquire. For all his money, Clark left his adopted state relatively little that would endure beyond his industrial and political legacy. There were no universities and no great foundations for the betterment of future generations. The future, he once told an acquaintance, could fend for itself.[2]

For Clark, the present had always been what mattered, and he had learned that a business and political career could be enhanced through ownership of the press. Clark was the first of Montana's copper kings to own a newspaper, and the first to see the added value in owning many. Through the tumult of the copper wars, no lie and no embarrassment of fact had gone unchallenged by Clark's editors, and none were as loyal or as useful as Larry Dobell of the *Butte Miner*. Late in Clark's career, when news threatened to leak that the senator had conceived a child by a pretty young ward in France, the *Miner* preempted a scandal by reporting that Clark and his companion had secretly married three years earlier. Few believed it, but the *Miner* created a sliver of doubt, and for Clark, that had always been enough. If the company learned the ways of media manipulation from anyone, it learned them from Clark, whose newspapers included Utah's *Salt Lake Herald,* which promoted his railroad connecting Salt Lake City to the ports of southern California.[3]

Clark's interest in newspapers was practical, and he generally sold them when they no longer served a purpose, but the *Butte Miner* proved the exception. From the end of Clark's undistinguished Senate term in 1907 and the sale of his major Butte mining properties to the company in 1910, the paper seemed to exist as an accessory to the old man's vanity. Clark's home and interests had long since shifted from Montana, and yet the *Miner* still chronicled his occasional visits and buffed his image with fawning items in the social columns. It also served the publicity needs of his most significant remaining Butte property, the Elm Orlu Mine, which Clark maintained for the benefit of its co-owner, his son and namesake William A. Clark Jr. Otherwise, the *Miner* seemed redundant. Its politics had long since meshed with those of the company's *Butte Daily Post* and *Anaconda Standard,* though its claim of independent ownership often made it a more useful public-relations tool than the company's own dailies.

Other beneficiaries of the *Miner*'s continued existence were the readers of Butte, who enjoyed the varied news and features supplied by three metropolitan-style dailies in a city whose commercial base could barely justify one. With its garish red headlines and comprehensive local reporting, the *Miner* often seemed the most vital of Butte's dailies during the war years and beyond. And when it came to editorial fireworks, Dobell held his own with the likes of Will Campbell and Richard Kilroy. *Missoulian* editor Martin Hutchens, the most experienced of Montana's daily editors and no milquetoast himself, considered Dobell the state's finest editor. A power in the conservative wing of the state Democratic Party, Dobell's influence was further confirmed by the vitriol he inspired from the *Butte Daily Bulletin,* which lampooned his rhetorical style and his tubby physique—abuse that only raised his stock with conservatives. But now Clark was gone, and no one lamented the fact more than Dobell. On the day after its owner's death, the *Miner* devoted five pages to Clark's memory, its column rules inverted to the thick, black lines of mourning. "No more democratic or sympathetic man ever lived," Dobell wrote.[4]

Dobell's sense of loss undoubtedly reflected some anxiety over the *Miner*'s future, now in the hands of the late senator's squabbling heirs. For the moment, control passed to Clark's second son, whose politics had rarely veered from those of his father. Born in Deer Lodge but raised primarily in France, William Jr., "Willie," was bright but had so far shown little of his father's aptitude for business. A star graduate of the University of Virginia's law school, he eventually joined the firm of one of his father's Butte lawyers, Jesse Roote, whose duties had included overseeing Clark's Helena and Great Falls newspapers during the copper wars. William Jr. himself served briefly as an officer of the *Great Falls Tribune,* though the title, like most he carried in association with his father's businesses, was largely ceremonial. By most accounts, he and his older brother Charles spent more time in Butte's taverns, theaters, and gambling halls than in the office, though both figured in the intrigues that surrounded their father's political adventures. Charlie's notoriety was enhanced considerably in 1902 when he fled the state rather than face charges of trying to blackmail a district judge presiding over a lawsuit between Heinze and the company over the control of a copper mine.[5]

With his father's retirement from the Senate, young Clark traded Butte for Los Angeles, where he supposedly oversaw various businesses he co-owned with his father but mostly engaged in various philanthropies to mask a life of genteel dissipation. Among the beneficiaries of his largesse was the Los Angeles Philharmonic Orchestra, and he would eventually donate his sprawling Los Angeles home to serve as the University of California's William Andrews Clark Memorial Library. His ties to Montana were reduced to summer vacations at a family lodge near Swan Lake and occasional business trips to ride herd on the family wealth. His politics were simple and self-serving; he abhorred such Progressive notions as inheritance taxes and eagerly joined the company's campaigns against higher mine taxes in Montana. He had little use for Governor Joseph Dixon, who enacted both reforms and also fired Frank Conley, a Clark family friend. The pile of telegrams Dixon received after his 1924 defeat included one gloating message from Los Angeles. "Providence has rid [Montanans] of a political incubus," young Clark wired the governor. "Barnum was wrong. Lincoln was right. You can't fool all the people all the time."[6]

Despite such episodes, few expected the late senator's son to assume active command of the family's Montana enterprises, much less its newspaper, but they soon learned otherwise. Dobell, whose loyalty and discretion had earned him a relatively free hand in the *Miner*'s management and in politics, now found himself increasingly second-guessed on both fronts. Within seventeen months of the senator's death, Dobell resigned. In a vague and terse farewell editorial, he allowed that he and the paper's new publisher were "not accord in relation to some administrative details connected with the *Miner* nor upon some questions of policy." The resignation raised eyebrows from Montana to Washington, D.C., including those of *Missoulian* editor Martin Hutchens, who praised Dobell's "long and valuable and faithful services and fine character" and questioned the wisdom of Charles and William Jr. in letting him go. "We will be surprised if the two young men who have come into the inheritance of that excellent property easily find a worthy successor," Hutchens wrote.[7]

If Dobell's departure was surprising, so was Hutchens's dismissal two months later. Schooled under Dana, Hearst, and Pulitzer, the high-strung Hutchens was easily Montana's most accomplished—and complicated—editor. He brought a bristling energy to the *Missoulian*'s news coverage, and his militant editorials were widely quoted. In his nine years at the paper's helm, he boosted local support for the war, fenced with Wobblies and Socialists, and led journalistic campaigns that

In his nine years at the Missoulian's *helm, Martin J. Hutchens supported the Anaconda Company, though its secret financial grip on the paper had reportedly come as a shock. Dismissed under murky circumstances and replaced by a company editor in 1926, Hutchens eventually became editor of the anti-company* Montana Free Press.

SCHOOL OF JOURNALISM,
UNIVERSITY OF MONTANA, MISSOULA

helped drive such company foes as Jeannette Rankin and Joseph Dixon from power. When required, Hutchens dutifully promoted Anaconda's interests and "puffed" company executives, including Anaconda's president, John D. Ryan, whom Hutchens once described as Montana's "most loyal and helpful friend."[8]

On balance, the enigmatic Hutchens served the company well, but he was no lapdog. Though his views generally meshed with the company's, he understood that his paper's credibility rested on at least some perception of fairness. In 1919, Hutchens granted university economist Louis Levine a fair hearing in the *Missoulian's* news columns when Levine was sacked for demonstrating that the mining industry paid a disproportionately small share of the state's taxes. Though he was careful to distance the paper editorially, Hutchins occasionally published critics' views of the company's newspaper ownership and labor policies, and he generally refrained from employing the blatant fabrications and outrageous distortions other company editors found useful in the heat of political campaigns. Editorially, Hutchens contributed to wartime excoriation of the IWW and other radicals, but his paper also offered IWW leaders' a chance to comment after Frank Little's lynching, and when striking Wobbly lumberjacks proved instrumental in fighting wildfires that raged across western Montana that summer, the *Missoulian* reported that too.[9]

Hutchens also demonstrated a willingness to plunge into community controversies, and it was that trait that probably cost him his job. A tireless booster of commercial interests, the *Missoulian* also kept a wary eye on municipal government, yet it was an early advocate of city planning and citywide drives to ban riverside dumping and spruce up neighborhoods, streets, and alleys. Hutchens's final campaign featured a protracted effort to recall a popular mayor who had tried to acquire the city's private water system from the heirs of William A. Clark. Anaconda and Montana Power operatives reportedly warned Hutchens off the story, lest it threaten their own quiet efforts to acquire various Clark properties, but the editor apparently ignored them. In the end, Hutchens may have resigned in frustration and exhaustion, but his ensuing anger at the company suggests he was fired.[10]

Whatever its cause, Hutchens's departure in the fall of 1926 was sudden and complete. An anonymous editorial told readers that Hutchens had sold his stock in the Missoulian Publishing Company and retired as a result of illness. "The effort proved too great a nervous strain to be continued for any length of time," the paper wrote. "Having an opportunity to dispose of his interests advantageously, Mr. Hutchens decided to accept relief from the task of directing two daily newspapers in addition to the publishing plant." Readers were also told that one Warren B. Davis had assumed the stock held by Hutchens and a partner, James A. Sage, and that Davis would personally oversee the management of both the *Missoulian* and the *Missoula Sentinel.* Davis's previous employment as an editor for the *Anaconda Standard* was not mentioned, nor was it deemed prudent to explain how someone in his position could suddenly afford two daily newspapers.[11]

The personnel changes in Butte and Missoula followed news of even greater importance to the future of Montana's copper press: the company's absorption of "Doc" Lanstrum's *Montana Record-Herald* in Helena. A company organ in the early stages of Lanstrum's management, the Republican sheet had changed its name and its loyalties in 1916, and by 1918 it emerged as Montana's leading Progressive Republican daily. As such, it enjoyed the spoils of state printing contracts throughout the Dixon administration, but with Dixon's defeat in 1924 that crucial patronage reverted to Will Campbell's *Helena Independent.* Sick, weary, and certain that no Helena daily could survive without some form of subsidy, Lanstrum finally surrendered the paper in the spring of 1926, selling out to a clique of conservative Republicans headed by Thomas Marlow, a Helena banker with impeccable connections to both Anaconda and the Montana Power Company.[12]

Those seeking clues to the paper's change of philosophy had only to read Will Campbell's praise for the *Montana Record-Herald*'s return to "sane Republicanism." A clearer signal came with an announcement that the paper would be printed on the *Helena Independent*'s press. Montana's independent publishers grasped the implications immediately. Joseph Scanlan of the *Miles City Daily Star* lamented that his paper was now the "lone orphan" among Montana's Republican dailies, while Tom Stout, editor of Lewistown's *Democrat-News,* noted glumly that Lanstrum's sale gave the company "practical control of the entire daily

Tom Stout (above right in 1906, with David Trepp), editor of Lewistown's Democrat-News *lamented the company's "practical control of the entire daily press." From the vantage point of his uneasy retirement, Dobell was beginning to see a problem, too. "This really is a damnable and un-American situation, when all the papers of a state become organs instead of really newspapers," he wrote.*

MONTANA HISTORICAL SOCIETY PHOTOGRAPH ARCHIVES, HELENA

press." From the vantage point of his uneasy retirement, Dobell was beginning to see a problem too. "This really is a damnable and un-American situation, when all the papers of a state become organs instead of really newspapers," he wrote Senator Thomas Walsh. Dobell's old paper remained beyond the company's direct control, but few expected the *Butte Miner* to wander far from the copper chorus. Fewer still would have predicted an attack on the company and its copper press from the playboy son of a copper king.[13]

The opening salvos came in the summer of 1927. After a generation of peaceful coexistence with the company, the *Butte Miner* suddenly declared its independence. "We are tired of being the tail to the A.C.M. dog and from this time on—we are against everything the company is for and for everything the company is against," the paper told readers. The phrase "An Independent Newspaper" suddenly appeared above each day's red banner headline, and by July 1 the masthead overlooking the papers' daily editorials featured the name of the *Miner's* new editor: Martin J. Hutchens. In an astonishing turnabout, the editor who began his *Missoulian* tenure by denouncing reports of Montana's "kept press" now charged that the state was "ruled by a floor in Butte that names the rubber-stamp appointees, that writes platforms, dictates vetoes, gags public opinion through its muzzled press and assumes a paternalistic guardianship over all the affairs of the people." Hutchens's about-face baffled most observers, and those who weren't surprised were suspicious. Behind the scenes and most certainly with his new employer's concurrence, Hutchens even reached out to his old nemesis, Joseph Dixon, asking him to "be the Moses" of a Clark-backed campaign to drive the company out of politics and recapture the statehouse. Hutchens backed the *Miner's* promise of journalistic support with ten thousand dollars in cash. Dixon promptly returned the money.[14]

William Clark Jr.'s assault had all the hallmarks of a personal crusade. As company editors in Butte quickly suggested, the *Miner's* sudden campaign had less to do with its owners' newfound concern for the purity of Montana politics than with the impending division of his late father's substantial Montana estate, which included not only the *Miner* and the Elm Orlu Mine, but real estate and utilities stretching across the state. After nearly two years of wrangling, William Jr. stood alone against his siblings' desire for a quick sale to the company. Some suspected him of merely trying to drive up the price, but the reasons were probably more complex. Whatever they were—ambition, greed, wounded pride, or some combination of the three—Hutchens downplayed them with all the imagery he could muster. Young Clark's frustrations with the Anaconda Company, he wrote, were no different from those of the ordinary Montanans who sought to rid their state of "this Octopus-like control that stretches its tentacles to every nook and corner of the state and fastens its coils to whatever it can, upon governors, courts, county attorneys, and tax-fixing bodies."[15]

As if on cue, the *Miner*'s attacks increased through the spring of 1928 as negotiations over the Clark estate approached a climax, but the most serious indication of William Clark Jr.'s resolve came in Missoula, where he fought to retain control of family-owned utility and lumber businesses. On the afternoon of May 19, thousands of copies of a new daily newspaper—the *Daily Northwest*—blanketed the city. Its front page dominated by circulation come-ons, the paper declared its intent to free Montana from the coils of Anaconda, whose "fangs" struck at every community in the state. Built on the bones of the Craigheads' *New Northwest,* the new daily's theme was hardly novel. The *New Northwest* had been a consistent critic of the company since its creation, struggling for most of its existence as a weekly, though it converted briefly to daily publication in 1920 to support Burton K. Wheeler's hapless gubernatorial campaign. With Wheeler's defeat and the death of its founder, Edwin Craighead, the paper lapsed into weekly publication. Craighead's sons sold out in 1922, and the paper limped along until 1927, when it was purchased by Hutchens's former *Missoulian* partner, James Sage, with money apparently provided by Clark.[16]

The *Daily Northwest* created an immediate sensation on the streets of Missoula and took its journalistic obligations seriously. Staffed with a mix of old hands and enthusiastic recruits from the university's School of Journalism, the paper labored to prove that it was no millionaire's passing whim. Though its looks were often garish and its editing sometimes sloppy, Missoula's newest daily waded into local and state issues with obvious relish. Unable to obtain an Associated Press franchise due to the company papers' exclusive agreements, the *Daily Northwest* acquired the national and international services of the United Press. Under editor Ernest Immel, it made sports coverage a specialty and delighted in scooping the company dailies with "extras" on major local athletic events. It boosted noisy campaigns to expand local air service, replace the county's dilapidated jail, and cover the open irrigation ditches in which so many of Missoula's children had drowned. Beyond its support for Clark and his political favorites, the *Northwest's* editors were free to engage readers on a host of topics. Immel routinely ignored the "canned" editorials sent over from Butte and wrote his own.[17]

By comparison, the company dailies seemed almost torpid. They fought back with circulation contests of their own, but otherwise ignored their new rivals in Missoula and Butte by focusing on national or international subjects and refusing to be drawn into editorial combat on most local or statewide issues. Of all the copper editors, only the *Helena Independent's* Will Campbell rose to the Clark press's bait with any regularity or flair, responding to its anti-corporate diatribes on one occasion by simply listing the dozens of companies the Clark family controlled in Montana and elsewhere.[18]

The fate of the Clark financial empire was indeed at the heart of the matter. In late July 1928, after three years of haggling, the Clark family feud finally came to a head when directors of several of William A. Clark's companies, including those of its Missoula utility, ousted William Jr. as president in a succession of deft legal coups. The logjam broken, his siblings quickly accepted Anaconda's offer for the family's Montana holdings, sending William Jr. into spasms of front-page rage in the *Butte Miner*. Under red, uppercase headlines that blared, "W. A. CLARK, JR. REFUSES TO YIELD TO THE OCTOPUS," he accused the company of orchestrating his defeats, attributing its animosity to the independence and anti-corporate campaigns of his newspapers. He even claimed the company had offered to allow him to remain in control of his late father's Montana businesses in return for muzzling the *Butte Miner* and the *Daily Northwest*. "I refused," he told readers. "My manhood is not for sale at any price. . . . They sought to gag the Miner and me by conveying threats of reprisal to the other heirs of the W. A. Clark Estate, who live in New York and have long been out of touch and sympathy."[19]

Outmaneuvered, William Clark Jr. could only howl as he was booted from one family company after another. The *Daily Northwest*, which wasn't a part of his father's contested estate, remained under William Jr.'s control, but the venerable *Butte Miner*'s days were numbered. The end came on August 23, 1928. Overnight and without explanation, the virulent rhetoric of its editorial page was replaced by a distant focus on faraway events. For the third time in as many decades, the Anaconda Company had bought out a competing daily newspaper in Butte. Only the *Butte Daily Post* offered the city's readers an explanation for the *Miner*'s sudden change in tone, suggesting that its recent anti-company campaign was only a ruse to boost the price of Clark's paper and other properties.[20]

At midnight on the day of the *Miner*'s demise, *Anaconda Standard* editor E. B. Leipheimer walked into the *Miner*'s newsroom to announce the takeover. A former Heinze newsman, Leipheimer had made his own peace with the company years before, but the *Miner*'s pride had deep roots. Though their paper had long been a member of the company's "community of interests," *Miner* staffers cherished William A. Clark's nominal independence and personal patronage. Many had won their spurs in the copper wars, besting the company's extravagant dailies in the capital fight and the epic struggle to send the old man to the Senate. Now, here was the editor of the *Anaconda Standard*, come to claim a victory in an old but not forgotten war.

For *Miner* business manager Adelphus Keith, who had fled to William A. Clark's paper when the company swallowed up the old Butte *Inter Mountain* in 1901, it was simply too much. As Leipheimer broke the news, Keith walked out, but not before telling co-workers they were welcome at the new Butte daily William Jr. hoped to publish soon. Within a month, most of the *Miner*'s crew followed Keith out the door. Archie Clark, a young *Miner* telegraph editor, lasted less than two days as "one of the Standard's top flunkies" watched over his shoulder, telling him which stories to run and how to play them. "I couldn't take much of this, having enjoyed a free hand on the Miner's telegraph desk," Clark later recalled. "The second day I told him, in effect, that he and the copy boy could do this kind of thing better than I could."[21]

Within weeks, Butte's newspaper field changed dramatically. The *Anaconda Standard* merged with the *Butte Miner,* and on September 11, 1928, readers of both papers awoke to the first issue of the company's new morning daily, the *Montana Standard.* A special section would continue to serve readers in Anaconda, but Marcus Daly's newspaper had finally moved to Butte, in fact as well as spirit. Loyal *Miner*

In 1928, William A. Clark Jr. lost control of the Butte Miner, *and, for the third time in as many decades, the Anaconda Company seized the chance to acquire a competing daily newspaper in Butte. Six days later, Clark Jr. and former* Miner *staff started the* Montana Free Press: *"An Independent Newspaper for the People" that "Prints All the News without Fear or Favor."*

Montana Free Press, November 3, 1928

readers, their subscriptions shifted to the *Montana Standard,* saw the changing sensibilities reflected in the paper's first editorial, which featured not a spirited sermonette on state politics but a stilted tribute to the recently deceased Norwegian explorer Roald Ammundsen. If they felt cheated, they did not have to wait long for an alternative. Six days later, seventy thousand copies of the *Montana Free Press* slid off the presses of William Clark Jr.'s hastily furnished plant on Butte's North Main Street, one for every adult in Butte and the rest to be distributed statewide. Billing itself as "An Independent Newspaper for the People" that "Prints All the News Without Fear or Favor," the upstart proudly explained that it was "Edited and Managed by Former Staff of the Butte Miner."[22]

In the fight for readers, *Montana Free Press* and *Daily Northwest* editors aimed squarely for the affections of working-class Montanans with a news formula reminiscent of Heinze's *Butte Evening News,* a salty mix of scandal, sports, and lurid crime, accompanied by incessant circulation contests and the relentless drumbeat of its anti-company editorials. Forced to rely on the United Press for national and international news, the papers nonetheless enriched the overall diversity of Montana's news report. Likewise, the rivalry that sprang up between the company press and the Clark papers delighted sports fanatics in Butte and Missoula, who enjoyed the papers' efforts to win them over. The papers stretched front-page deadlines to include half-time scores of local football games or published "extras" on the results of high school track meets. Clark's journalists also tried gamely to scoop their company rivals on local crimes, disasters, and politics. Based on enthusiasm alone, Clark's newspapers seemed destined for a lengthy run.

Of course, politics dominated Clark's crusading dailies as Montana headed into the fall elections. In the summer primaries, the *Daily Northwest* and *Butte Miner* had endorsed those candidates they considered most likely to take the company on, regardless of party affiliation. Democratic incumbent Burton K. Wheeler and Republican Joseph Dixon won Clark's endorsement in their respective Senate primaries, while Democrat Roy Ayers and Republican W. J. Paul earned his blessings to unseat Governor John Erickson, whom Clark editors hounded mercilessly. Echoing themes that worked so well against Dixon in 1924,

Hutchens pounded Erickson with charges of financial mismanagement and held him accountable for supposed abuses at the state mental hospital. In the subsequent voting, Clark's papers could—and did—claim responsibility as their candidates ran well in Missoula and Butte. The most serious demonstration of their clout came in Silver Bow County, where Erickson suffered a solid thumping, but still managed to squeak out a narrow victory statewide.[23]

With the company's takeover of the *Butte Miner* just after the primaries, Clark's dailies, led by the new *Montana Free Press,* dropped all pretenses of bipartisanship in the general election, endorsing a slate of anti-company Republicans, headed by Dixon for U.S. Senate and gubernatorial hopeful Wellington Rankin, the ambitious and enigmatic

The Montana Free Press *supported the 1928 campaigns of Joseph Dixon and Wellington Rankin, the ambitious and enigmatic former attorney general. A gifted trial lawyer who had earned his reputation representing union miners and Butte's radicals, Rankin made the company's "muzzled press" a central campaign theme. He is pictured here (center) in 1911 with Thomas J. Walsh (right) in Walsh's law office in Helena.*

former attorney general who had managed his sister Jeannette's successful congressional campaign a decade earlier. A gifted trial lawyer who had earned his reputation representing union miners and Butte radicals, Rankin had also helped launch the old *Butte Bulletin,* and like any Montana politician with serious political aspirations he owned shares in a daily newspaper—the *Havre Daily News-Promoter.*[24]

Though Rankin and Dixon had fought bitterly during Dixon's stormy administration, they now shared the front-page adulation of Clark's new dailies, with Rankin receiving the greatest attention. More than just an opportune marriage of convenience, the Clark-Rankin relationship had a history. When Dixon tried to raise William A. Clark's tax assessments along with those of other industrialists, it was Attorney General Rankin who had blocked the move as a member of the state's powerful Board of Equalization. Rankin had also fought to reinstate Clark family friend Frank Conley, the congenial prison warden whom Dixon had fired for corruption.[25]

Dixon and Rankin took full advantage of Clark's newspapers, and both made the company's "muzzled press" a central campaign theme. Dixon charged the copper press with ignoring his campaign appearances and distorting what little mention they did make of his record and positions on the issues. Rankin made similar charges, accusing the company of controlling nine of the state's sixteen daily papers and pressuring the *Great Falls Tribune* to refuse, at least initially, to carry his paid advertising.[26]

The Clark press also reviewed the company's history of attacks on academic freedom at the state's university in Missoula—a story Hutchens knew intimately.[27] During the primaries, Hutchens had even mocked a young Montana journalism professor's attempt to write a history of the state's press, a copper-colored story that journalism school dean Arthur Stone presumably knew better than anyone.

> Dean Stone isn't looking for the ax, which, assuredly, would be swung on his neck if he ventured to write a truthful history of Montana journalism. Hence, the job is taken over by [Robert L.] Housman, who tackles it with the reckless bravado of youth. If he writes all that wise Dean Stone knows he will be hiking out of Missoula before the first snow melts.[28]

The Clark papers' assaults on the company and its allies usually contained nuggets of truth, but they were occasionally reckless and inaccurate as well. A charge that *Great Falls Tribune* publisher Oliver Warden had used his position on the state highway commission to pave the road to his summer cabin was easily refuted. Claims that company-connected bankers had threatened Rankin supporters with foreclosure cost Clark a libel judgment, though the plaintiff, Helena banker Thomas Marlow, was awarded only two dollars in damages. And though the *Montana Free Press* and *Daily Northwest* routinely echoed Rankin and Dixon's complaints that their campaigns were being ignored in the copper press, the Clark papers were equally guilty of ignoring the speeches and appearances of Governor Erickson and Senator Wheeler.[29]

Despite the loss of such firebrands as Hutchens and Dobell, the Anaconda papers fought back as best they could, casting Rankin as an unpredictable hothead and chronic office-seeker who played loose with his facts. His attacks on the Anaconda and Montana Power companies, housed officially on the Sixth Floor of Butte's Hennessy Building, were motivated less by principle, they charged, than by Rankin's overweening ambition, a point the company press drove home late in the campaign with headlines such as "Wailing Wellington Gnashes Ivories at Wicked Montana Corporation" and "Rankin at his Rankest." Even so, copper editors such as Warren Davis, E. G. Leipheimer, and a fading John Durston were hardly the same howling chorus that had led crusades against wartime radicals and Dixon. Only Will Campbell still mustered the old vitriol, replying swiftly and in detail to nearly every rumor and allegation raised by Clark's papers. His rejoinders were often reprinted in the company's papers statewide. Otherwise, the copper dailies seemed dull, obvious, and heavy-handed. In Butte, a *Montana Standard* cartoon, running late in the campaign, portrayed a copper miner pushing a loaded handcart, its burden labeled "Pay roll $33,000,000 and taxes $1,500,000 annually." The miner, representing the company, put the question bluntly to readers. "If I dropped this, I wonder what would happen to you?"[30]

The campaign's most imaginative rhetoric came from the upstart *Montana Free Press,* where Hutchens described Erickson—the same man he had called "Honest John" just four years earlier—as the "jellyfish," a "truculent, subservient governor who salaams like a Turkish slave before the throne on the Sixth Floor." Hutchens also accused Wheeler of endorsing Erickson in return for the company's support in his tough race against Joseph Dixon, and he warned that the "Anaconda-Montana Power combine," through its agents and newspapers, threatened to extend the "one-man town idea in Butte to the one-man state." The conspiracy was far vaster than most Montanans knew, he claimed. "Sprinkled all over the state are combine newspapers, combine whisperers, agents and representatives busily engaged in peddling the dope that has its origins in the Butte headquarters of the combine: belittling, minimizing, detracting, scandalizing citizens and candidates for public office who do not bend the knee to the swollen, vainglorious, blatant crowd that assumes to rule the destinies of the commonwealth of Montana."[31]

The *Free Press* also warned of the "combine's" designs on the water in Montana's major rivers and offered a heated critique of the company's still hated "rustling card" system by which it weeded out dissident miners and unionists. In attacking the rustling card, Clark editors also played to Butte's latent racism. The system not only discouraged the exercise of free speech, they wrote, but also reduced the supply of "self-respecting, independent" miners. In their place, the paper warned, would come "hordes of Mexicans and floaters gathered from the scum of the earth." "With the camp populated by Filipinos and Mexicans Butte would soon become black as any convict colony in the southern states."[32]

For all their passion, Clark's newspapers failed to prevent Erickson's reelection. Wheeler faced a tough fight against Dixon, losing twenty-one counties, including Missoula and Yellowstone, but prevailed by more than twelve thousand votes in what was otherwise a banner year for Republicans. Factors surely included memories of Dixon's stormy term as governor, Rankin's association with his sister's pacifism, and a general suspicion of Clark's motives. The role played by either Clark's papers or the company press is hard to measure. Beyond the endorsements of Clark's dailies, support for Rankin and Dixon came from smaller Republican dailies in Havre and Miles City, plus a smattering of weeklies ranging across the spectrum from Dan Whetstone's Cut Bank *Pioneer Press* to Charles Taylor's *Producers News*. Whetstone's portrayal of Wheeler as a company

In the 1930s, Oswald Garrison Villard, editor of the Nation, *castigated Anaconda for hiding its newspaper ownership and acknowledged the efforts of anti-company editors such as Dan Whetstone of Cut Bank's* Pioneer Press *(above), Sam Teagarden of the* Denton Recorder, *and Harry Brooks of the* Chinook Opinion, *along with the "courageous and consistent attacks" of the "tremendously radical"* Producers News *in Plentywood.*

SCHOOL OF JOURNALISM,
UNIVERSITY OF MONTANA, MISSOULA

tool drew blood, reminding readers that in 1922 the senator had said voters would know that he had "sold out" if they saw the copper dailies in his corner. Yet with their higher circulations and broader geographic reach, the company newspapers surely gave their candidates some advantage. With support from the copper dailies in Butte, Helena, Missoula, and Billings, plus the *Great Falls Tribune,* Wheeler and Erickson also drew endorsements from Senator Thomas Walsh, then at the height of his fame as the investigator of the Teapot Dome Scandal, and Tom Stout, the former congressman and Lewistown publisher.[33]

For Clark, the only bright spot was the Republicans' capture of heavy majorities in Montana's legislature. As for its defeats, the *Montana Free Press* blamed them on "the mass efforts of the Anaconda Company" and promised to continue the fight in the upcoming legislative session, "confident that the day will come when the stigma borne by Montana as a corporation state will be removed." The paper also denied the pervasive rumors that it was planning to fold. "The Free Press was planted as an independent newspaper and it will continue and thrive as such," its editors wrote. "The response to it from the public surpassed all expectations."[34]

In truth, omens for the papers' survival were decidedly mixed. Public response, measured in circulation, seemed encouraging. The *Free Press* boasted a Sunday circulation of seventeen thousand within four months of its start, and the *Daily Northwest* posted respectable numbers too. However, advertising revenues—the lifeblood of an independent commercial press—lagged substantially, a condition Clark's editors blamed with some justification on company pressure on local businesses. Clark's newspapers continued to require heavy infusions of cash as they headed into the new year with plans to provide readers with extensive coverage of the 1929 legislative session and to launch a third Clark daily in Billings.[35]

Leadership proved to be a particular problem, and organization suffered a serious setback with the death of Martin Hutchens at age sixty-two. Citing exhaustion and an undisclosed illness, he resigned the eve of the November elections and checked into a Salt Lake City sanitarium, where he died on January 12. The *Free Press* reported Hutchens's death with two front-page stories, including a tribute from former *Butte Miner* editor Larry Dobell, a friend and ally from the days when both had edited papers for the "anvil chorus." In his recitation of his friend's career, Dobell reminded readers of Hutchens's time with the fabled *New York Sun*, Pulitzer's *New York World*, and Hearst's *New York Journal* and his editorial stints in Chicago, but he skipped conveniently over Hutchens's years in Missoula to focus instead on his militant editorials for the *Butte Miner* and the *Montana Free Press*, which "stood out among the stereotyped policy pages of the corporate press like a beacon in the fog."[36]

The irony of Hutchens's final years as an anti-company editor could hardly have been lost on Dobell, who found himself in a similar spot. After leaving the *Butte Miner*, Dobell became secretary-treasurer of the state Democratic Party and angled for appointment to the state's powerful tax commission. When Governor John Erickson refused to give him the job, Dobell blamed the company's lobbying and its lingering suspicions about his ties to William A. Clark. When Erickson won the Democratic nomination for a second term, Dobell quit in disgust. Prompted by Hutchens's illness and moved by Dobell's political misfortune, William Clark Jr. rehired his father's old war-horse to lead his papers' coverage of the 1929 legislative session.[37]

Dobell's insider's knowledge gave newspaper readers a rare peek behind the curtain of the company's legendary legislative lobby. From its headquarters on the mezzanine of Helena's Placer Hotel, where law-makers and lobbyists congregated in the company's notorious "watering holes," Clark's three-man capitol bureau tracked the progress of legislation and monitored the movements of lobbyists Dan Kelly, Will Rae, Frank Bird, George Scott, Al Wilkinson, and others whom Dobell suggested should wear bright copper uniforms so new lawmakers could recognize them.[38] In addition to Dobell's daily front-page column, "On the Sidelines in Helena," the Clark press's legislative team included Senate correspondent Walter Shay and House specialist Kenneth Hammaker. Both had signed on despite warnings from the copper press corps that they would never work for another Montana newspaper.[39]

It was Dobell's column, however, that best captured the session's tenor. He hammered away at Governor Erickson's alleged fiscal mismanagement but also demanded that the company solve the state's seemingly endless budget crisis by paying additional taxes "instead of squealing like a pig trapped in a gate every time a suggestion is made by this legislature that this corporation that is so wonderfully prosperous should contribute a fair proportion of the new revenue required at this time." He castigated the company's "be-diamonded lobby" for its incessant fight against an adequate workers' compensation system and strong workplace safety laws. The Montana Power Company drew Dobell's wrath for defeating a proposed tax on hydropower, which he considered a small price to pay for the hospitality Montanans had shown the company in allowing it to tap the state's mighty rivers "without exacting any royalty, rent, or other favors."[40]

The copper press consistently rated the *Montana Free Press*'s most virulent criticism. By February, the paper's front pages featured a daily list of company-controlled newspapers, running under the standing headline "Why the Ownership?" Its editors wasted few opportunities to sell the paper as Montana's independent choice and its principal purveyor of objective news to readers "weary of the hand-picked news stories and editorials in the nine newspapers—so-called—of the big copper company, papers the company owns and operates for its political prestige and its economic aggrandizement at the expense of the people of Montana." In contrast, the *Free Press* offered "a fresh point of view, an opposition history of the times, a free exposition of all the news and editorial comment to match."[41]

Though its coverage had little practical effect, the Clark press emerged from its first legislative session eager for expansion. Since October, a Clark team had maintained an office in Billings to solicit advertising, gather news, and serve as the city's distribution center for copies of the *Montana Free Press* sent by train from Butte. Since February, Billings-bound issues of the paper had sported a special section of Billings-area news and advertising. Finally, in March, Clark's editors launched the *Billings Free Press* from a headquarters in the Midland Empire office building on First Avenue North and Twenty-ninth Street. With its initial editions stuffed with news, editorials, and features supplied from Butte, the new morning daily boldly announced its intention to trounce the *Billings Gazette,* a paper so complacent that it rarely published editorials for fear of stirring the public's emotions.[42]

Clark's third and final daily struggled to get off the ground. As in Butte and Missoula, Clark's Billings editors hoped to circumvent the Gazette Printing Company's stranglehold over the morning and afternoon Associated Press franchises by using the United Press wire service. But when they inquired about a United Press license, they were shocked to find that the *Gazette* had already snatched it up. Outfoxed, the new daily was forced to suffer along with the cut-rate International News Service, a report so meager that it barely covered the national headlines and offered no vital services such as stock listings. When a full stock report appeared in the *Billings Free Press* anyway, *Gazette* editors immediately smelled a rat and set out to prove it by inserting in their report a stock listing for a company named "Nelots," the word "stolen" spelled backwards. When the fake stock appeared in the next day's *Free Press,* the *Gazette* gleefully reported the theft to its readers and advertisers.[43]

Clark's Billings daily never had a chance. On Saturday May 18, barely two months after its launch, Clark suddenly stopped publication of all three dailies. If subscribers were puzzled, Clark's employees were stunned. Only the day before Missoula's *Daily Northwest* had celebrated its first birthday by predicting "healthy growth and progress." Now it carried Clark's eight-paragraph announcement that his effort to foster "free and unhampered expression concerning the manner and conduct of our state government [had] not met with the response that

I anticipated." To continue publishing money-losing papers would expose him to charges that his aim all along had been personal power, he wrote. "Rather than have it said that I personally sought any political aggrandizement or personal progress, I am content to withdraw." Clark failed to add that he had sold his papers to the Anaconda Company, the only Montana entity that could afford to buy them just to shut them down. As duly noted in the copper press, Clark earned just enough in the deal to cover his losses.[44]

In the end, it came down to money, and estimates of Clark's losses ran high. His initial investment in Missoula and Butte was reckoned at four hundred thousand dollars, with monthly operating losses ranging from thirty thousand dollars and twenty-two thousand dollars with no real hope that the papers would ever turn a profit. They made respectable progress in circulation but failed to attract adequate advertising in the face of the company's none-too-subtle pressure. Confusion among the papers' managers also contributed to the waste and inefficiencies that had dogged the dailies from the start. Beyond the fundamental problem of an absentee owner whose attentions often wandered, the papers suffered an inordinate turnover in the management of both its news and business operations, which led to inconsistencies in substance and form.[45]

Beyond Hutchens's death, the most serious administrative blow had been the defection of the *Montana Free Press* general manager Bryan Woolston in an apparent dispute with Clark over pay. Woolston, who joined Clark after a stint as advertising director for the *Anaconda Standard,* was instrumental in shaping both the *Free Press* and its fledgling counterpart in Billings, but his resignation shortly after the Billings paper's launch, coupled with his almost immediate reemergence as national advertising director of the *Butte Daily Post,* sent the organization into a tailspin. With his intimate knowledge of Clark's struggling operations, Woolston's departure posed more than just a blow to morale. When Clark's Butte daily publicly accused its former top executive of sabotaging its national advertising accounts and trying to steal the *Free Press*'s subscriber list, Woolston sued for libel, and though his case was eventually dismissed, it surely contributed to Clark's disenchantment with the newspaper business.[46]

Former *Montana Free Press* employees and others would later claim that Clark simply lost interest in his newspapers, which might have survived had he given them the same support he lavished on his beloved Los Angeles Philharmonic. The blunt reality, however, was that given the paucity of Montana's population and advertising base, no purely commercial daily press with metropolitan intentions could have competed with papers subsidized by one of the country's biggest industrial corporations. In its eulogy for the Clark press, the *Great Falls Tribune* ascribed its demise to the raw fact that the three cities involved had no business supporting competing metropolitan-style dailies.[47]

Although Clark's papers were hyperbolic and sometimes garish and sensational, and though Clark's own motives were highly suspect, the papers offered thousands of Montanans a vigorous if brief alternative to the copper chorus. Even the *Great Falls Tribune,* which rarely strayed from the company line in matters of politics and policy, praised the papers for their progressive politics and use of the United Press service. Beyond their statewide political function, the papers had waded eagerly into local controversies, exposing such problems as Missoula's dilapidated jails and deadly irrigation ditches as well as Butte's "unofficial licensing" of illegal bootleg joints and the outrageous rents callous landlords were charging the city's poor and indigent.[48]

By contrast, the company papers, in their increasing fear of entangling their masters in local disputes, made a virtue of their indifference to all but the safest local news. In its self-damning commentary on the death of the *Daily Northwest,* the *Missoulian* attributed its continued existence and that of the *Missoula Sentinel* to the fact that the papers had "pursued a calm and even tenor," contenting themselves with "unostentatious though devoted service" to the up-building of western Montana, a cause in which "animosity and dissention" could have no place. "No newspaper can harbor such sentiments and serve its constituents," it wrote.[49]

In the wake of Clark's challenge, the copper papers stood again like forts against threats to the company's power and profits. Disdainful of debate and smug in their paternal support, they dominated strategic ground so no one else could have it. For as long as the company owned its newspapers, no one would ever again launch a daily to challenge them.

THE 1920S WERE CRUCIAL to the evolution of the copper press. By the decade's end, the militant partisanship that had long defined Montana journalism—a relic of nineteenth-century newspapering—was rapidly fading. If anything, Montana's fierce industrial politics had kept such journalism fashionable long past its surrender elsewhere to a modern commercial press, which valued objectivity and independence as the best means of attracting the readers and advertisers. Combative, colorful editors such as Hutchens, Dobell, Durston, and Kilroy—their careers forged early in Montana's copper wars—were gradually replaced by milder, quieter men. In their silence, the company's grip had only grown stronger.[50]

The copper press was clearly changing tactics, and the gradual process stemmed as much from the fading of Anaconda's old warriors as the company's efforts to forge a more formal relationship with the papers in which it held controlling interests. Changes in the political landscape and lessons learned from the campaigns of the 1920s surely played roles as well. With little organized opposition in the state's political parties or its press, the company editors increasingly saw their function not as spear-throwers, but as cogs in a smooth-running public-relations machine. Under such circumstances, selective censorship and subtle editorial indifference toward the company's enemies would prove far more effective than the heavy-handed campaigns that had met with such mixed results in the decade's major political campaigns. Overt partisanship, company editors had learned, could be a liability as well as an asset. In its conquest of Clark's newspapers, Anaconda dailies had fought largely behind the scenes, serving notice that such encroachments would require enormous sums of money—a daunting prospect as Montana sank into the Great Depression.

Meanwhile, the company moved aggressively to shore up its control of strategic newspapers. No longer willing to operate through temperamental allies such as Larry Dobell or semi-autonomous editors like Martin Hutchens, the company solidified its hold over the dailies in Butte and Missoula. Its absorption of Helena's *Montana Record-Herald* in 1926 and its growing financial stake in Will Campbell's *Helena*

Independent gave it sure control in Helena. With the death of the *Billings Gazette*'s publisher and principal stockholder John Edwards in 1925, principal control of the Gazette Printing Company passed to editor Leon Shaw, who held most of the paper's stock, presumably as the Anaconda Company's trustee. Anaconda also controlled smaller papers such as Livingston's daily *Enterprise* and weeklies in Superior and Libby. The company's most rabid critics would wrongly argue that it now controlled every newspaper in the state, but with the company's penchant for secrecy how could they know otherwise?[51]

As befitted a modern, diversified corporation with operations scattered throughout the western hemisphere, the Anaconda Copper Mining Company, the world's largest supplier of nonferrous metals, insisted on an increasing level of accountability from its various holdings, including its newspapers. In the summer of 1930, Anaconda's attorneys quietly created the Fairmont Investment Company, a Delaware holding company capitalized at $1 million and charged with overseeing Anaconda's investment in Montana newspapers. Operational responsibility for the company's newspaper holdings fell to the efficient and capable James Dickey Jr., who would eventually trade his offices in the Butte Daily Post Building for one in the Hennessy Building. From there, Dickey would eventually manage all of Anaconda's non-mining-related businesses in Montana.[52]

Lost in the transition were voices of the company's old lions, once famous and feared across Montana. By 1930, most were either dead, discharged, or pushed aside. Martin Hutchens was gone and so was Richard Kilroy. Larry Dobell, a dependable ally for nearly a quarter century, would spend the remainder of his career tossing barbs at the company for a succession of small, leftist weeklies. Will Campbell could still launch the occasional rocket, but the old venom would soon lose its sting as age and illness took its toll. Of those who earned their stripes in the copper wars, *Billings Gazette* editor Leon Shaw would carry on the longest, insulated to some extent by distance and his paper's more diverse ownership.

An era surely ended on November 25, 1929, as the wires reported the death of John Durston, the eighty-one-year-old dean emeritus of the Anaconda press. Retired as editor of Butte's *Daily Post* only the year before, Durston died of brain cancer, but those who knew him blamed some measure of his demise on a series of emotional blows suffered over his final decade, not the least of which was the disappearance of the remarkable newspaper he had built for Marcus Daly forty years before.

At his death, the most eloquent tribute came from Durston's deputy, Charles Eggleston, who had followed his old professor to Montana. The two were nearly inseparable in the minds of the *Anaconda Standard*'s readers, and Eggleston would outlive his superior by only four years. In their heyday, Eggleston's wit and Durston's thunder had combined to make the *Standard*'s editorial page Montana's most provocative read, but it was a much different paper that now carried Eggleston's praise for his mentor's "vigorous diction, his Swift-like gift of withering invective, his scorn of cant and deception, his broad culture and scholarly attainment."[53]

Durston had understood that newspapers had to offer more than just their politics, and it was that understanding, backed by Daly's money, that set a standard for metropolitan-style newspapers in a remote state where readership and advertising alone could never entirely justify the costs. But such excellence carried a professional price, and that would be Durston's legacy too.

*While the ownership of many Montana newspapers remained a tightly held se-
cret, the papers themselves were readily available on the streets of Butte and other
Montana cities. By 1912, an estimated 250 boys belonged to Butte's "newsboys
club," which the* Anaconda Standard *praised as a means of curbing "shooting
nickels, smoking cigarettes, stealing and other evils the newsies fall for."*

CHAPTER NINE

The Copper Curtain

S MOKING OUT A NEWSPAPER'S secret owners was tricky business. Across the country, rumors of secret ownership of the press by "the interests" had swirled for decades. At one time or another, reformers suspected railroad barons Jay Gould, Henry Villard, and James J. Hill of promoting and protecting their investments by controlling newspapers. Similar suspicions fell on J. P. Morgan and John D. Rockefeller, whose secret ownerships of the press was assumed to be vast and systematic.[1]

Proving it was the problem, but with pressure from muckraking journalists—and over publishers' vigorous objections—Congress finally succeeded in requiring disclosure as a condition of obtaining cheaper second-class postal rates in 1912. Yet those who scanned the resulting "statements of ownership" were quickly disappointed. In many cases, they found the names of innocuous sounding companies or little-known individuals acting as trustees for real stockholders. Some publishers simply lied. Others didn't have to: the law's failure to require the disclosure of indebtedness effectively hid a more subtle means of control.[2] Critics could do little but complain. Enforcement was lax, prosecution rare and costly. Cases could languish in the courts for years. Tracking down a newspaper owner determined to hide his identity still boiled down to an educated guess.[3]

In the spring of 1930, Florence Sanden, a graduate student in journalism at Columbia University, offered her remarkably accurate guess that the Anaconda Company owned nine of fourteen daily newspapers in Montana, one of the first states, she wrote, "to fall under the pressure of the large monied powers in the news field."[4] For her thesis on the consolidation of Montana's newspapers—a timely topic as newspaper "chains" continued to gobble up individually owned papers across the nation—Sanden pored over the copper press's postal statements to little avail. Eventually, she resorted to sending questionnaires to Montana's daily editors, whose responses proved only slightly more illuminating. Most declined to answer the question, and of the six who did, half rejected the notion while the rest acknowledged the company's investment in papers other than their own. Of the copper dailies, only the *Billings Gazette* responded in detail, still insisting that individuals controlled all of the paper's stock. Sanden concluded that Anaconda controlled every major daily in Montana except the *Great Falls Tribune*, whose strong business ties to Anaconda rendered the distinction all but moot. "While there is absolutely no question of the paper being independently owned, there is a noticeable lack of any particular personal policy," she wrote. "It rather has a tendency to fit in with the opinions and views of the other large papers in the state."[5]

If Sanden's estimate of Anaconda's newspaper ownership struck home, so did her clear-eyed analysis of the uses to which the company put its papers. Sanden found the company clearly willing to use its press to protect its profits and prerogatives. Evidence included the duplication of editorials promoting certain interests and candidates. Only common ownership "would account for supposedly Republican and Democratic papers supporting the same men and the same measures, it accounts for concentrated actions for or against state propositions such as the metal mines tax, storage reservoirs, power dams, and governors," she wrote.[6]

But Sanden also concluded that corporate ownership provided Montana with newspapers "better than the population warrants." In comparing Butte's *Montana Standard* with the *Courier Express* of Buffalo, New York, a daily serving a population roughly ten times that of Silver Bow County, Sanden was impressed with how well the *Standard* fared. Both newspapers averaged twenty-eight pages per issue and devoted similar space to international and national news, sports, and features. Aesthetically, she found the *Standard* more modern and appealing in its design, but the Buffalo paper covered more local news, a trait Sanden attributed to its much larger circulation.[7]

In concluding, Sanden bemoaned Montana's lack of a large, independent daily offering more objective news and "opinion from more than one side of the fence." But given the state's scant population, she doubted the situation would change soon. Most Montanans seemed loath to complain, though they tended to be skeptical of the copper press at election time. "Some day there will probably be a . . . reckoning," she wrote. "Until that day comes and until there is some other means of visible support for papers of equally true work, Montana will continue to have good fortune if corporate interests furnish her citizens with timely news at cut rates."[8]

MONTANA WAS NOT THE ONLY western state whose press felt the grip of heavy industry. California's railroad and mining barons wielded political power for decades, aided in part by newspapers under their control. In Idaho and eastern Washington, editors of the region's largest dailies sided consistently with mine owners during the labor struggles of the 1890s. And in Utah and Arizona, silver and copper magnates shared their Montana counterparts' penchant for newspaper ownership. By 1905, Arizona's Phelps Dodge Company reportedly controlled nine of the territory's dailies, usually through subsidies to individual editors. When editors ran into financial or political trouble, which they invariably did, the company bought them out. Over the years, the shifting lineup of Arizona newspapers under industry control ranged from small weeklies to the William A. Clark-controlled *Jerome News* and the Phelps Dodge-dominated Bisbee *Daily Review,* Tucson's *Arizona Daily Star,* and the *Phoenix Gazette*. At one point, Arizona mine owners even considered establishing their own wire service.[9]

For all that, the company's dominance of Montana journalism still stood out, and the newspaper jugglery and flagrant corruption of the state's copper wars caught the flitting attention of the national press over the years. Montana's copper press rated a chapter in muckraker Jerre Murphy's odd and scathing polemic *The Comical History of Montana*, published in 1912. Congresswoman Jeannette Rankin attacked Anaconda's newspaper ownership in the national press during the tumultuous years of World War I. In 1920, Montana's copper press drew the scorn of muckraker Upton Sinclair. In *The Brass Check*, a scorching critique of corporate influence over the press, Sinclair targeted

California's railroads, the steel industry in Pennsylvania and Illinois, the Northwest's timber barons, mine owners in Colorado and West Virginia, and "the milling trust" in North Dakota and Minnesota—all of whom, he asserted, wielded enormous influence over local news and opinion. But the copper industry headed Sinclair's list of malefactors. Its sway over the press, he alleged, stretched from Michigan's Upper Peninsula to southern Arizona, but it exercised its most effective grip on Montana. There, he wrote, the "gigantic Anaconda" had "swallowed" most of the state's dailies, leaving "only two newspapers in Montana which are not owned or controlled by 'copper'." Of those "[o]ne . . . is owned by a politician who, I am assured, serves the interests without hire; and the other is the 'Butte Daily Bulletin,' Socialist, whose editor goes in hourly peril of his life." Sinclair exaggerated the company's newspaper holdings and overlooked Montana's vocal covey of anti-company editors in the weekly press. Yet there was truth enough in Sinclair's allegations, and Anaconda's silence only gave them additional credence.[10]

So too did the company's battles with Joseph Dixon and William A. Clark Jr. in the 1920s. That period's most trenchant criticism came from Oswald Garrison Villard, editor of the *Nation*. Throughout the 1930s, Villard examined the state of the American press, including the Anaconda Company's annexation of a "very considerable portion" of Montana's daily newspapers. It was only natural, he concluded sarcastically. "The people ought to get the truth; who could give it to them better than those whom chance and nature and good business enterprise have made controllers of the destiny of the Commonwealth?"[11]

Villard castigated the company for hiding its ownership behind separate publishing companies while publishing both the Republican and Democratic dailies in Montana's major cities. Citing the recent fate of William Clark Jr.'s papers, Villard argued that Anaconda's deep pockets and pressure on advertisers squelched any hope of establishing a competitive daily press sustained by commercial enterprise alone. Of Montana's smaller dailies, only Joseph Scanlan's *Miles City Star* could claim independence, wrote Villard, who added, "but even here there are those who declare that during the past three or four years it has made no attacks on the Company but has kept very quiet lest the Company come into this lively town of 7,000 and start a rival daily." The upshot, he concluded, was an absence of meaningful political debate, which fueled an almost overwhelming sense of political cynicism, "making it very hard indeed to get a reformer in the State of Montana not to suspect the worst of every man in public life."[12]

Unlike Sinclair, Villard acknowledged the efforts of anti-company editors such as Dan Whetstone of Cut Bank's *Pioneer Press,* Sam Teagarden of the Denton *Recorder,* and Harry Brooks of the *Chinook Opinion,* along with the "courageous and consistent attacks" of the "tremendously radical" *Producers News* in Plentywood. But the bulk of Montana's weeklies were co-opted in subtle ways, he charged. As many as eighty weeklies subscribed to a Great Falls service that printed "patent insides" featuring "first-class historical matter" in addition to "Company propaganda of the most insidious kind." Altogether, Anaconda's press strategy was effective in controlling or blunting debate on such issues as an adequate workers' compensation system, fair taxation, and reasonable prices for utilities and fuel. "Meanwhile," he concluded, "the Company goes ahead. Its newspapers continue to boost all their friends and ignore their enemies, and they are silent on the really vital issues. The good plain common people are plucked, and plucked, and plucked."[13]

MUCH OF THIS CRITIQUE of its press Montanans already knew, though details of Anaconda's newspaper ownership remained effectively hidden. Corporation records of individual papers offered no clue of the company's quiet consolidation of it newspaper stock under the Fairmont Investment Company, a wholly owned Delaware holding company created for just that purpose in 1930. By late 1931, Fairmont listed a controlling interest in the daily newspapers of Billings, Butte, Helena, Livingston, and Missoula as well as weeklies in Libby and Superior.[14]

Other changes were more apparent. Copper editors had always served their owners by fighting labor unions, higher taxes, and costly regulations, and their influence had been most obvious at election time, but by the 1930s observers noted a change in tactics. Gone were the crusades and hammering editorials; the modern copper editor offered a more distant, distracted tune. In his news columns, this editor served the company much as a modern public-relations department would, by buffing the images of its executives, by promoting the reasonableness of its policies, and by downplaying its mistakes, setbacks, and critics. Rarely did Anaconda's papers show the company or its associates in a bad light, and their sensitivity to controversy seemed heightened as the state entered the tumult of the Great Depression.

In Butte, the new sensitivity included a virtual blackout on news of workers killed in mining accidents. In the past, such stories had been routine, though editors almost always attributed the accidents to bad luck or the victims themselves. Typical was the *Anaconda Standard's* 1904 account of the death of one William Kiley, crushed 1,800 feet below the surface by a one-ton rock that fell as he placed an explosive charge beneath it. The story noted the coroner's finding "that all due precautions had been taken by the management," and offered the *Standard's* verdict as well: "It was a case of one of those unavoidable accidents so common to mining."[15]

Over time the papers gradually limited their coverage of mining accidents to those too spectacular to ignore or those involving the deaths of prominent men. Butte's copper dailies reported the disastrous Speculator Fire in June of 1917 in remarkable detail and with due regard for the disaster's 162 dead, but few of the 67 miners killed in individual accidents over the following year rated more than vague, one-paragraph death notices. However, the *Butte Daily Post* did find front-page space to report a company study touting Anaconda's "creditable" accident rate, which it ran beneath the headline "ACM Publication's Figures Indicate Few Fatalities in Butte's Mines."[16]

By the late 1920s, Butte's dailies routinely ignored mining's death toll. Donald McDougal, an eighteen-year-old son of Scottish immigrants, fared better than most when his name and the news that he had "died last night" were included in the *Butte Daily Post's* mortuary listings for November 23, 1929. The fact that he was hurled to his death from a runaway ore car was left to the coroner's report. More typical was the coverage given an incident twelve years later, in November 1941, when "bad air" caused the asphyxiation of four miners, among them a sixty-two-year-old Finnish widower and a thirty-nine-year-old Austrian immigrant married three weeks before.[17] Not a word of their deaths appeared in the local papers. Andrew Cogswell, a journalism professor at the State University of Montana (as Missoula's campus was then known) who spent a year on the *Montana Standard*'s city desk during the 1930s, observed that the paper played down mining-related deaths and injuries because they were so common. To "overplay" such stories only served "to heap fretfulness upon the miners and their families," he wrote, adding that the company worked hard to promote safety. "No good, but much harm, can come from featuring mine accident stories."[18]

The duty to protect both their papers' credibility and company's image often put Anaconda editors in impossible positions. A story's news value was often only part of a complex equation, especially if the issue was controversial. Editors also had to consider whether the article would be viewed as a reflection of company policy. Ignoring a story sent messages too. It was like being an editor at *Pravda,* one non-company journalist observed. Under such constraints, copper editors naturally steered news coverage toward "safe" subjects when they could, and resorted to thin reporting when they could not.

The results often left readers baffled. For Cogswell, the *Montana Standard*'s reporting on the Montana Power Company's controversial bid to build a major hydroelectric dam on the Flathead River at Polson exemplified the problem. Despite the story's importance, the *Standard*'s "bare" article on the Federal Power Commission's approval of the project failed to mention either the controversy or the commission's reasoning. Such incomplete reporting, Cogswell wrote, had everything to do with Anaconda's ties to Montana Power. "To give the story the prominence that it deserves might bring down the wrath of the anti-company element in the state and the *Standard* would be branded again as a propaganda organ of the company." Local disputes made increasingly poor subjects for the *Standard*'s editorial page as well, Cogswell noted. "Local controversies are avoided probably for the reason that the paper's peculiar position would cause even a most worthy effort to be looked upon as 'axe grinding'," he wrote. "There has been a tendency in the last few years to avoid mixing in state political squabbles."[19]

The rhetoric was toned down, but the papers' loyalty remained unquestioned, as illustrated in Butte by the *Montana Standard*'s lopsided news coverage of a pivotal 1934 strike that idled more that 4,200 miners, smeltermen, and engineers from May to late September. Encouraged by New Deal labor reforms, the mine workers demanded recognition for their union and reinstatement of a "closed shop" after twenty years of company refusals, but *Standard* news editors blamed the shutdown on the "excessive wage demands" of workers ungrateful for the company's maintaining its operations "month after month and year after year through the greatest depression known to history and in the face of the most unfavorable conditions ever known to industry." Editors supplemented the one-sided news with front-page reports of a copper glut, suggesting the company's ability to weather a long strike.[20]

Except in union newsletters, the miners' arguments went unreported while *Standard* editors gave Butte business leaders a front-page platform to lobby for an end to the strike that had "needlessly interrupted" company operations. Strikers were castigated for abandoning the pumps that prevented underground water from filling the mine shafts, and *Standard* reporters were there when "hoodlum gangs" of strikers allegedly attacked newsboys to prevent delivery of the company's *Butte Daily Post*. For all the early excitement, the *Standard*'s strike coverage all but disappeared over the following months save for short, terse updates on the status of mediation efforts. The union's landmark victory, though never described as such, made front-page news when it finally came in September, but the paper's editorial voice remained oddly silent, as it had throughout the strike.[21]

Such yawning disengagement would mark the copper press through the remainder of its existence. The unwritten policy emanated from *Montana Standard* editor E. G. Leipheimer, who served as liaison between Anaconda officials and top editors at the company's other dailies. Editors in doubt about how to play a particular story usually followed the *Standard*'s lead. Edwin Erlandson, who began his nearly four decades at the *Missoulian* as a copyboy in 1936, described the policy as fairly straightforward: Anaconda editors were expected to publish nothing harmful to the company's image; news favorable to the company—promotions, annual reports, and new projects—was to be played prominently; and, finally, editorials were to be "confined to noncontroversial items with the theory that a calm society was a satisfied and happy society." With such limits, copper editors required little additional direction, Erlandson said, adding:

When the Anaconda Company was particularly interested in a story, the Missoulian would receive a call from the Montana Standard news room telling us how the Standard was playing the story. Never do I recall any instructions to play a certain story a certain way, but it was another unwritten law that the way it appeared in the Standard was the way the company would like to have it appear in the Missoulian. These calls did not come often.[22]

Within such constraints and corporate penny-pinching, Erlandson and other company journalists maintained that copper editors were free "to publish the best newspapers possible," though critics questioned just how good they could be. Many, if not most, company journalists from the 1930s onward considered their papers to be competent and largely accurate in what they reported. The papers' principal weakness, as many saw it, was their editorial timidity. Years later, University of Montana political scientist Thomas Payne argued that the company's silence on local and state matters effectively sapped the papers of any vitality. "A variety of historical, exotic or otherwise irrelevant topics graced the editorial pages, constituting in all probability the blandest diet of editorial commentary ever served to any group of American newspaper readers," he wrote.[23]

Montana historian K. Ross Toole went further. The copper press had all but abandoned the "blasting editorials, the diatribes, the big black alliterative headlines" that had once given Montana journalism its spice. "If the vituperation was gone, so was aggressive reporting and imaginative writing," Toole wrote. "So was the thorough coverage of local and state news which did not affect the Company. Talent departed along with the invective. The Company simply dropped a great, gray blanket over Montana."[24]

As MONTANA SANK INTO the Great Depression, the company faced serious threats to its political clout. Franklin D. Roosevelt's New Deal reforms encouraged liberals and revived labor unions, whose members joined just enough disaffected farmers to send liberals to Congress and the state legislature, where they tested the power and prerogatives of the "Montana Twins," as critics now called Anaconda and the

Montana Power companies. Though the two corporations were hardly distinguishable in the public's mind and in terms of their interlocking directorships, Montana Power would draw an increasingly heavier share of liberals' fire as issues such as rural electrification, reclamation, and water rights came to the fore.

Though "the Twins" viewed the New Deal with alarm, the sweep of its programs and the public's early enthusiasm made it impossible for the copper press to ignore. News items featuring the urgent activities of various New Deal initiatives dotted the pages of company papers, making them resemble alphabet stew. Major projects, such as the construction of the massive Fort Peck Dam in eastern Montana, rated regular coverage, as did news of various relief and work programs. Editorially, the company's ostensibly Democratic dailies in Butte and Helena bit their tongues, leaving any criticism to the company's Republican papers. The news columns of the *Montana Record-Herald* in Helena served up copyrighted coverage from Washington, D.C., that routinely chastised the reformers' ruthless zeal, while the paper offered national editorials on the "hokum" contained in Roosevelt's National Recovery Act. More significantly, however, it allowed Montana Power officials direct access to its front page to combat the so-called Wheeler-Rayburn Bill, which sought closer regulation of utilities. In a "special" report from Butte, Montana Power executive Frank Kerr saw the specter of "nationalization" in the Senate's "unparalleled" assault on investors. The story also appeared in the *Missoulian*.[25]

The New Deal posed serious political challenges as well. In 1934, Montana's farm-labor coalition sent liberal Butte attorney James E. Murray to the U.S. Senate, where he would rank among the most ardent New Dealers and crusade for the federal development of public power in the Missouri River Valley, a stance that ensured conflict with "the Twins." Voters also elected company critic Jerry J. O'Connell to the state's crucial Railroad and Public Service Commission and two years later sent him to Congress. After a string of unsuccessful runs for governor and other state offices, the venerable Miles Romney finally left the *Western News* to son Miles Jr. and signed on for a stint as Montana's New Deal administrator. Liberals made other significant policy gains too, including the enactment of progressive individual and corporate

Alarmed by their losses, liberal Democrats— led by the AFL-CIO, the Farmers Union, and Senator James E. Murray (above)—regrouped under the Montana Council for Progressive Action and raised the money to establish a new statewide weekly, the People's Voice, *to crusade for the cause.*

MONTANA HISTORICAL SOCIETY
PHOTOGRAPH ARCHIVES, HELENA

income taxes to bolster a property-tax base eroded by plummeting land values. They also extended the eight-hour day to all non-agricultural occupations, despite charges by company officials that the effort had been backed by "labor agitators and communists."[26]

The copper press found itself on the defensive as well. Its usefulness as a political and a public-relations tool appeared doubtful, even as the company pumped in subsidies to offset the depression's disastrous effects on the papers' commercial revenues. Worse, Anaconda's press found itself under official scrutiny. On the evening of February 28, 1935, *Helena Independent* editor Will Campbell and two other men were ushered under subpoena to Room 4 of Helena's Placer Hotel to appear before a special legislative committee charged with investigating the lobbying activities of "certain public utilities and other corporations of the state."[27]

The extraordinary probe—all but unthinkable in previous sessions—sprang from the intense but ultimately unsuccessful campaign by the Montana Power Company and its Anaconda allies to block Jerry O'Connell's election that fall to the rate-setting Public Service Commission. That O'Connell had been the target of critical stories and editorials in the copper press was hardly a surprise, but Montana Power's "paid" newspaper advertising on behalf of O'Connell's opponents touched off a storm of protest from liberals who argued that the utilities' ratepayers had been forced to bear the expense of fighting those committed to lowering their power bills.

From the start, the panel sought to prove that the "Twins" and the copper press routinely flouted the state's Corrupt Practices Act. Approved by voter initiative in 1912, the law not only prohibited corporations from making undisclosed contributions to political campaigns, but also required publishers to note the names and addresses of those who bought political advertising, a practice the copper papers routinely ignored. Investigators also charged Montana Power with passing on the cost of its lobbying to energy customers. Given the rumored losses suffered by company newspapers, committee members wondered if utility ratepayers were in fact subsidizing the copper press. The committee also hoped to expose the companies' statewide lobbying practices, including the amount of gin and whiskey lobbyists bought to lubricate lawmakers at the Placer Hotel's already notorious "watering holes."[28]

In the end, the investigation proved to be an exercise in frustration as key witnesses either refused to cooperate or simply fled. Still, the probe gave Montanans a rare peek behind the copper curtain. Of the twenty-one witnesses who testified in three separate hearings, eight, including Campbell, were represented by Anaconda's chief legal counsel, Dan Kelly. Under questioning, Campbell denied that the *Independent*'s articles and editorials were inspired by outside influences, but when his interrogators asked about his paper's ownership, he conceded what his critics had long suspected. The bulk of the paper's stock, Campbell acknowledged, was held by James Dickey Jr., an Anaconda executive and manager of the Butte Post Publishing Company. Campbell also testified that Dickey's investments began in 1925 and that in the ten years since, Dickey had loaned him at least two hundred thousand dollars to cover the paper's losses. Campbell acknowledged that his paper had not paid a dividend since 1921. Where Dickey got such sums the committee could easily guess, and because he was conveniently out of state on business, guessing was all it could do. When Campbell was asked the source of Dickey's money, the editor grinned and said he did not know and would not say if he did.[29]

Other officials from the copper press offered the committee varying amounts of cooperation. Joseph Markham, business manager of the *Montana Standard* in Butte, admitted Anaconda's ownership of both the

Standard and Post publishing companies but contributed little else. Leon Shaw, the *Billings Gazette*'s publisher and principal stockholder, fled the state, but the paper's managing editor, Eugene MacKinnon, testified that the paper played no favorites in recent elections. MacKinnon also produced a sworn statement of the paper's stockholders, "many of them men and women or estates in Yellowstone County, but none connected with a holding company, mining company or public utility in Montana."[30]

Meanwhile, lobbyists for the "Twins" deftly parried investigators' demands for information. Al Wilkinson, a top Anaconda lobbyist and "advertising man" whose duties included delivering company ads to newspapers across Montana, refused to produce a record of his lobbying expenses. Nor would Wilkinson concede that his political discussions with Montana editors represented more than his personal views. Other lobbyists for the "Twins" followed suit, testifying to the legitimacy of their efforts—including their efforts to slake legislators' thirst—but refusing to provide legislators with any records of their spending.[31]

The investigation, with its budget of only five hundred dollars, faced constraints in time and staff as well as the company's shrewd blocking tactics. When the committee requested more time, money, and authority, Helena Representative Edmond G. Toomey led a successful push to expand its charge—and ensure its failure. Under the guise of fairness, Toomey's amendment obliged the panel to investigate not only the "Twins," but every lobbying organization in the state, including "the Labor unions, the Railroad Brotherhoods, Chinese Herb Doctors, and any other group or organization represented in the campaign or during the present session of the legislature." The list also included the *Western Progressive,* a liberal farm-labor weekly published in Helena that covered the probe in more detail than any other newspaper.[32]

Surprisingly, most of the copper dailies not only carried Associated Press stories on the investigation, but played them prominently, though ignoring them would have illustrated their critics' central charge. Even so, the Associated Press's reporting—at least what ran in the copper press— was largely sympathetic to those being investigated. It was careful to note the statements by Will Campbell and *Billings Gazette* editor McKinnon that neither Anaconda nor any other industry dictated their papers' editorials policies, yet overlooked Dickey's curious financial relationship with the *Helena Independent*. It recounted the lobbyists' refusals to submit evidence of their political activities and highlighted their outlandish assertions that their political activities were entirely personal, but the tone of the reporting seemed skeptical of the investigators' motives as well. *Great Falls Tribune* correspondent Ernest J. Immel dismissed the investigation as "so much grandstanding" by the company's rivals. A comprehensive investigation into legislative lobbying could have revealed "some surprising information," Immel hinted, but given scant time and the committee's own prejudices, he dismissed its findings as simply "old stuff."[33]

In its final report to the House, the investigative committee chaired by Billings Republican C. W. Fowler made the most of what evidence it found. The "Twins," he submitted, did "wield a controlling influence" over a number of the daily newspapers, and consumers, through their utility bills, did finance the company's political campaigns. Furthermore, the committee found that "a conspiracy exists, backed up by great financial resources and the influence of dominant publications and a powerful lobby to defeat the will of the people in the selection of officials for public office and in legislative assemblies."[34]

The panel suggested specific reforms, including a requirement that lobbyists register and report their expenses. They also sought laws prohibiting corporations from publishing campaign advertising or articles and from pressuring employees or stockholders into voting for or against any candidate or ballot measure. It also recommended the state prosecute the "Twins" for the breaches of the Corrupt Practices Act it believed the probe had exposed. But in final debate, critics portrayed the investigation as nothing more than a partisan effort to "roast the corporations" that had invested millions in Montana's progress. They also noted the committee's failure to investigate lobbies other than those financed by Anaconda and Montana Power. In the end, the House refused to adopt the committee's report.[35]

THE MOST SYMPATHETIC COVERAGE of Fowler's inquest came from Helena's three-year-old leftist weekly, the *Western Progressive,* which published verbatim excerpts of exchanges between investigators and

Will Campbell and publicized the heavy debts listed by the *Helena Independent* and other copper dailies on their annual corporation reports. Its partisan reporting on utility regulation and its incessant anti-corporate editorials made it the company's most annoying journalistic opponent since the demise of the *Butte Bulletin* eleven years before.[36]

Born with the New Deal in 1932, the semi-monthly publication became a weekly by 1935 and offered a small readership an unabashed liberal alternative to both the copper dailies and the parochial country weeklies. Originated by Lewis Penwell, a Helena-area attorney, businessman, rancher, and sometimes federal officeholder, the paper got its support from a loose alliance of labor and farm groups seeking tax reform, utility regulation, and an end to the corporate influence over Montana's government and daily press. It wasn't Penwell's first venture in journalism. A generation earlier, he and Senator Thomas Walsh had hired Will Campbell to make the *Helena Independent* a platform for Progressive Democrats.[37]

This time Penwell found an editor of markedly different stripe. H. S. "Cap" Bruce, a veteran newspaperman and old-time Socialist, had taken a meandering path to Montana. A former reporter for Chicago's daily *Inter Ocean,* the Nebraskan drifted to Montana, where he surveyed the future Glacier National Park, edited a weekly in Roundup, and joined the Montana militia. He chased Pancho Villa with John "Black Jack" Pershing's Mexican expedition in 1916, and when the United States entered World War I, Bruce shipped to France where exposure to artillery fire cost him the hearing in one ear. Discharged, he returned to publish a string of Texas weeklies in the 1920s, but by 1928 he was back in Montana, this time handling publicity for Senator Thomas Walsh's last reelection campaign.[38]

Under Bruce, the *Western Progressive* promoted the cause of ratepayers and consumers against monopolies in energy, telephone service, and railroad transportation, with the "Montana Twins" as its principal targets. In concert with the paper's reconstructed columnist, former *Butte Miner* editor Larry Dobell, Bruce denounced the companies' alleged failure to pay a fair share of Montana's taxes and their opposition to levies on corporate income and hydropower. His paper dug into their property assessments and spotlighted their ties to politicians and their opposition to the New Deal's labor reforms. It scrutinized the state's rate-setting Railroad and Public Service Commission and boosted Jerry O'Connell's successful campaign for it, over the objections of the "Twins" and the copper press.

From its start, the *Western Progressive* pounced on "the capitalistic press, tools of the great corporations," and it delighted in publishing the copper dailies' annual corporation reports, revealing their indebtedness and therefore their dependence on the company. As Montanans struggled through the depression, the *Progressive* argued that the money the "Twins" poured into their newspapers might be better spent on lower rates for consumers or higher wages for their employees.[39]

The paper's excoriation of the Anaconda press peaked in 1935, the year of the legislative investigation. By then, the paper's own debts had forced its sale to owners whose liberalism was mixed with an interest in the state's post-Prohibition liquor business. Bruce quit to edit the liberal Farmers Union newsletter, and his replacement, John W. Nelson, took the *Western Progressive* to new heights of partisanship. In 1934, the paper endorsed U.S. Senator Burton K. Wheeler for a third term and also backed James Murray's successful campaign to replace Senator Thomas Walsh, who had died the year before. In addition to Larry Dobell's column, the *Progressive* featured Drew Pearson's influential support of Roosevelt and the New Deal, and it flirted with the economic populism of Huey Long and Father Charles Coughlin.[40]

Under Nelson, the *Progressive* continued its anti-corporate themes, but its tone was harsher, and much more personal. Nelson's favorite target was the *Helena Independent*'s Will Campbell, "that little pot-bellied, ill-natured gink" who wrote "the poisonest [*sic*] editorials of any copper-collared editor in the state."[41] In parodies of Campbell's editorial style, peppered with parenthetical hiccups, Nelson also insinuated that the *Independent*'s editor was a drunkard. Ironically, Campbell had pioneered such tactics. In 1922, when U.S. Senate candidate and Lewistown publisher Tom Stout was cited for fishing without a license, Campbell's headline had shouted "Dry Senate Candidate Angles Near Lincoln with Empty Flask." Six years later, the *Independent* falsely reported that Burton K. Wheeler, a proponent of Prohibition, had rolled a car following a "gay party." But now, facing such abuse himself, Campbell had little to say. Nor did he rise to the bait when Nelson attacked the company and its "army of spies, stool pigeons, bribers, lobbyists, procurers, stumble bums and sleek, suave lobby-lawyers" who specialized in dodging taxes and exploiting workers toiling in "the death pits of the Butte mines." In truth, Campbell was a sick man. His death of heart disease in 1938 elicited tributes from fellow Montana editors, many of whom touted his patriotism, vigor, and expertise in state and national politics. Some also noted his slashing editorial militancy as if it were a quaint relic of a bygone era, which indeed it was.[42]

Even so, Anaconda's failure to respond to its radical critics baffled independent Lewistown publisher Tom Stout, who, despite his own run-ins with the company, preferred a vital copper press to one that snored. In their silence, Stout argued, copper editors not only deprived Montanans of an essential debate, but sacrificed their credibility. "A real newspaper has a function to perform which is above and beyond that of a mere colorless recital of happenings in its community, state and nation," Stout wrote. It had an obligation to discuss important matters with its readers. "As never before in its history, Montana needs today newspapers with a sense of decency and also with some intestinal stamina." Predictably, Stout's frustration drew no response from the copper press, but the *Western Progressive*'s Nelson rose to call him a corrupt company lackey and laughed at Stout's assertion that a controlled press could lead a frank and fair public discussion of Montana's problems. "If the papers serve their masters, they cannot serve the public at large," he wrote.[43]

In its anti-corporate rhetoric and excoriation of the copper press, the *Progressive* followed a well-trampled journalistic trail, blazed by such weeklies as Heinze's *Butte Reveille*, Montana's Socialist press, the *New Northwest* in Missoula, and the string of Nonpartisan League papers whose numbers had included the *Montana Nonpartisan* published first in Great Falls and later Billings, the Inverness *News*, Lambert's *Richland County Leader*, Glasgow's *Valley County News*, and the *Roosevelt County Independent* in Poplar. The sometimes-daily *Butte Bulletin*, dead since 1924, took the themes to new heights with the livid, revolutionary language of its editor-provocateur William F. Dunne, a future editor of the Communist Party's *Daily Worker*.[44]

The most durable of the period's radical papers continued to be the *Producers News,* edited through most of its nineteen-year run by Charles "Red Flag" Taylor, who skewered his foes with wit and disdain for proprieties. His tactics, however, made fierce enemies, whose numbers included Harry Polk, the conservative publisher of the competing *Plentywood Herald,* which joined Burley Bowler's *Daniels County Leader* in Scobey in its attacks on Taylor's "Soviet splatter-gun" and the alleged corruption of Taylor's political machine. Taylor's clout faded with the late 1920s, and he left for South Dakota in the early 1930s to work as an organizer for the Communist Party's United Farmers League. The *Producers News* would never be the same, its sprightly populism supplanted by the heavy dogma of the Communist Party U.S.A. But the Communists, never more than a blip on Montana's political radar, grossly underestimated the independence of American farmers, their resistance to party discipline, and the depth of their religious beliefs.[45]

Disillusioned, Taylor either quit the party or was expelled and returned to Plentywood in 1935, hoping to revive the now flagging *Producers News,* but it was too late. The old sparkle was gone, and the farm-labor movement now put its faith in more moderate vehicles such as the Farmers Union and the American Federation of Labor. Without outside financial support, the *Producers News* limped along before finally closing shop in 1937. Taylor left Montana for good, and eventually ended his career as copy editor for the Hearst's *Seattle Post-Intelligencer.*[46]

The *Western Progressive* died that same year as Montana's fragile New Deal coalition fractured over Senator Wheeler's opposition to Roosevelt's "court-packing" plan. A last-ditch effort to revive the paper as a daily collapsed after a month, and for the next two years, Montana's liberals offered the company and conservatives no significant, statewide opposition in the press. In 1938, Western District congressman Jerry O'Connell lost his reelection bid, opposed by Democratic conservatives led by Wheeler, his own radicalism now long behind him. Shaking off its torpor, the copper press joined in, portraying O'Connell as both a "Red" and an enemy of labor. Though they generally ignored other campaigns that season, the Anaconda papers showed they could still play a little politics. They almost certainly aided the election of

O'Connell's undistinguished opponent, Republican Jacob Thorkelson, a retired Navy doctor whose conservatism was eclipsed only by his anti-Semitic views.[47]

Alarmed by their losses, liberal Democrats—led by the AFL-CIO, the Farmers Union, and Senator James Murray—regrouped under the Montana Council for Progressive Action and raised the money to establish a new statewide weekly to crusade for the cause. On December 6, 1939, the first issue of the weekly *People's Voice* emerged from the presses of the paper's ramshackle plant located in the shadow of the capitol's copper dome in Helena. Edited by "Cap" Bruce, the *People's Voice* promised to pick up where the *Western Progressive* had left off. According to Harry Billings, Bruce's eventual successor, the idea for a

On December 6, 1939, the first issue of the weekly People's Voice *appeared in Helena. According to Harry Billings (above), who became the paper's editor in 1946, the idea for a "one voice, one vote" cooperative newspaper took shape in the wake of the state legislature's 1937 session, one liberals considered "a corporate controlled disaster for the people of Montana."*

SCHOOL OF JOURNALISM,
UNIVERSITY OF MONTANA, MISSOULA

"one voice, one vote" cooperative newspaper took shape in a Helena café almost immediately after the *Progressive's* death and in the wake of the state legislature's 1937 session, a session liberals considered "a corporate controlled disaster for the people of Montana." Attorney Lee Metcalf, a young state legislator from Ravalli County and future U.S. senator, drew up the *Voice's* incorporation papers, stipulating that it would accept no advertising except that of nonprofit, cooperatively owned organizations and that it would remain free of debt.[48]

The *Voice* made its intentions clear from the start. A box in the paper's left "ear" announced its commitment to "economic justice and equality," and during its first year of publication, the paper declared its support for a broad array of liberal objectives, including increased taxation for the state's major industrial corporations, public ownership of utilities and agricultural facilities such as stockyards and flour mills, a system of public health care, civil rights for minorities, workers' compensation coverage for miners afflicted with silicosis, labor's right to strike, prosecution of illegal gambling, a fairer and more competitive system of allotting public grazing lands, and the conservation of natural resources. The paper also condemned the nation's "ostrich neutrality" toward Nazi Germany, a posture it attributed to American industry's fear of losing valuable European markets.[49]

High on the *Voice*'s list of targets was the copper press, and from its first issue Bruce challenged Anaconda to divest itself of its papers whose only purpose, he wrote, was to publicize "news which favors Big Business" and editorials, which, "when not covering some inconsequential, trivial subject, are blatantly reactionary in tone." As he had in the early years of the *Western Progressive,* Bruce made a point of publishing the debts listed by individual Anaconda papers on their annual corporation reports, proof, he insisted, that their survival depended not upon public support, but the company's largesse. Though he confessed that Anaconda's newspaper ownership would be difficult to prove in a courtroom, Bruce added to the growing mass of circumstantial evidence. The *Voice* was first to report James Dickey Jr.'s official oversight not only of the *Butte Daily Post* and *Montana Standard* in Butte, but of the *Livingston Enterprise* and Helena's *Independent* and *Montana Record-Herald,* and when Dickey moved his office from the *Butte Daily Post* building to Anaconda's headquarters in Butte's Hennessy Building, Bruce noted that too. He was the first to reveal the existence of the News Publishing Company, headquartered in Helena's National Bank Building, and he correctly labeled the company a "blind" used by Anaconda to disguise its Montana newspaper holdings. "Another probable 'agent'," he wrote, "is the Fairmont Investment Company of 25 Broadway, New York City, which is reported to own one percent or more of the stock of the papers."[50]

Bruce also took a stab at assessing the company's influence among the state's weekly newspapers, most of which the *People's Voice* considered to be independently owned and largely responsible to the local interests of their communities and readers. However, when it came to state and national issues, Bruce complained that too many weekly editors were "influenced by the patronage or some other consideration of the great industrial or financial groups, and they forget, temporarily, the interest of the laborer or farmer in their respective communities." Other editors hitched their editorial views to the platforms of the two major parties and thus sacrificed their impartiality. Bound by no political party and immune from "having its freedom of expression curtailed by the interests of advertisers," the *People's Voice* was distinctly free to serve the educational needs of all Montanans, Bruce wrote.[51]

Of course, the *Voice* nursed its own political agenda, which it freely admitted and defended in the face of severe criticism and "red-baiting" that would intensify down the years. Bruce repeatedly asserted the paper's commitment to democracy and denied rumors that it was controlled by Communists, though he argued Americans had the right to associate themselves with any political movement. In the main, the *Voice* represented a fundamental liberalism, exemplified by its support for Montana's loose farm-labor coalition that wielded significant political strength from the mid-1930s to the late 1970s. As the coalition's nexus, the *People's Voice* provided Montanans with news and commentary they could find virtually nowhere else, and it rendered valuable support to liberals such as James Murray and future U.S. senators Mike Mansfield and Lee Metcalf. But though its influence within Montana's liberal community provided a vital check and a rallying point against the copper press, the paper's reach was severely limited by its noncommercial advertising policy, and infighting among the nonprofit groups that supported it often threatened its existence. Throughout the *Voice's* run, its paid circulation varied between five thousand and seven thousand copies, though its readership was arguably much higher.[52]

Other voices also chipped away at the political influence of the copper press. Radio, which debuted in Great Falls with station KDYS in 1922, was slow in developing its potential as an original source of state and local news, yet it remained substantially free of

Through radio, Joseph Dixon and other anti-company candidates appealed directly to voters in cities served exclusively by the copper newspapers. Senators Burton K. Wheeler and Thomas Walsh were instrumental in helping Montana broadcast pioneer Edmund Craney build his Z Bar Network, which served Butte, Helena, and Bozeman. Above, Craney (right) and Emmett Burke record "The Night Owl" program in the mid-1930s.

Al's Photo Shop, photographer,
Montana Historical Society Photograph Archives, Helena

the company's influence. Owners of pioneering stations in Butte and Billings brushed off attempts by local copper dailies to buy them out, and savvy Montana politicians immediately grasped the promise of independent broadcasting. The 1928 election featured paid radio addresses by the company-backed Governor John Erickson and his opponent Wellington Rankin. Through radio, Joseph Dixon and other anti-company candidates appealed directly to voters in cities served exclusively by the copper newspapers. Senators Burton K. Wheeler and Thomas Walsh were instrumental in helping Montana broadcast pioneer Edmund Craney build his Z Bar Network, which covered Butte, Helena, and Bozeman. By the late 1930s, radio broadcasts were common in statewide campaigns, and the example of FDR's "fireside chats" also encouraged politicians to use radio outside the confines of elections. Montana broadcasters eagerly rented their microphones and growing audience to the state's most prominent leaders and maintained their independence in the bargain.[53]

Radio also provided an avenue for attacks on Anaconda and its press. In August 1941, Senator Murray used the frequencies of Butte KGIR to castigate the copper dailies for refusing to announce, much less cover, his recent speech over a nationwide NBC hookup, in which he had endorsed Roosevelt's growing support for Britain and the Soviet Union on the eve of the United States' entry into World War II. Murray began by thanking the state's radio stations for allowing him to talk to his constituents. "Were it not for our independent radio stations, Montana would indeed be ranked as a benighted and backward state," he said. He then launched into a scathing critique of Anaconda's "prostituted press," which he accused of practicing "Hitlerian" techniques of censorship by trashing his press releases, deleting his name from Associated Press stories, ignoring his local public appearances, and failing to publicize his services to constituents.[54]

Murray's anger was somewhat self-serving, but it also illuminated the copper press's silent suppression of liberal perspectives in the general political debate. The company papers' tactics, he told listeners, were prompted "by no other motive than a desire to injure me because I have been independent, fair, and just to the people of my State and have not served in Washington as a mere tool of the Anaconda Copper Company." Anaconda's hostility, he insisted, was grounded in his support for Roosevelt and the New Deal and his work to make the company accountable for silicosis and other industrial diseases. "They are hostile to me because they desire to exploit the State and its people, and because I have supported just legislation designed to curb them," he said. He also accused the copper press of prejudicing labor's case for wages and working conditions. Though he claimed the copper press was "becoming more harmless every day" as more Montanans relied on radio for news, the senator betrayed his doubts by threatening the company with investigation, "unless their corrupt policy in conducting these papers is changed."[55]

Murray's harangue failed to make the papers.

ONE EXPLANATION FOR the apparent lethargy of the copper press may have been Montana's shrinking importance in Anaconda's global operations, which included mines and smelters in Chile and northern Mexico and wire and brass fabrication plants in the American Midwest and Northeast. "Con" Kelley's ascension to company chairman at the death of John D. Ryan in 1933 ensured that Montana would remain close to the corporation's heart—in fact, the state would continue to serve as a proving ground for Anaconda's top executives for another generation—yet the sheer expanse of its industrial holdings left its leaders less time to dwell on the politics of the company's birthplace. Through shrewd financial management and government assistance, the company weathered the worst of the Great Depression, and as Europe went to war in 1939, it stood poised for its greatest expansion since the early 1920s.[56]

The country's entry into World War II, and the enormous industrial and human mobilization that followed, dominated the editorial pages and news columns of the copper press, as it did most of the nation's newspapers. In Montana, war news competed for space on rationed newsprint with stories about the draft and enlistment drives, fears of enemy infiltration and sabotage, shortages of goods and services, and efforts to boost industrial and agricultural production as well as public morale. Political debate centered largely on the administration of federal wartime programs.

Throughout the 1940s, Senator Murray complained his work in Washington was specifically ignored in the company press, but in truth Anaconda's papers seemed less interested in Montana's scrambled politics in general. Occasionally, they could still speak with one voice against politicians bold enough to attack the company head-on.

Their successful red-baiting of liberal Democrat Leif Erickson in the 1944 governor's race and in Erickson's 1946 U.S. Senate race briefly recalled its "Red scare" campaigns in the wake of World War I, but such outbursts were rare and paled in magnitude. Things were different now. An analysis of the copper press's election coverage over the first half of the decade found that Anaconda dailies provided generally thin but reasonably balanced coverage to most candidates in 1942 and 1944, with the notable exception of Erickson's gubernatorial campaign against Republican Sam Ford. In 1942, readers of the company's Helena, Billings, and Missoula dailies even found their local papers favoring different candidates in key campaigns. The *Helena Independent*'s coverage of that year's Senate race favored Senator Murray over Republican Wellington Rankin, while the *Billings Gazette* tilted toward Rankin and the *Missoulian* simply waffled. Nor was there any evidence that endorsements in the copper press carried much weight with Montana voters.[57]

Its newspapers could still provide Anaconda with an important public-relations service, however, and that function continued to distinguish the copper press in its final two decades. During the war, the copper press promoted increased production at the company's mines and smelters as a patriotic duty, a practice encouraged by the federal government, but astute readers also noticed the papers' condemnation of price controls proposed in the federal government's pre-war buildup. In Butte, the company and its workers formed a joint committee to oversee increased production of copper, manganese, and zinc, all vital war materials. To publicize their efforts and boost morale, the committee published its own newspaper, the *Copper Commando,* with the help of an editor recommended by the U.S. War Department.[58]

The copper dailies also touted the company's awards for increased production, quality, or on-the-job safety. But in late 1943, when a federal grand jury indicted an Anaconda subsidiary for knowingly supplying the military with defective communications wire, it was the *People's Voice* that broke the story for Montanans. The news, though buried, eventually appeared in some of the company papers, but only after the indictment of a second Anaconda subsidiary on similar charges. The *Billings Gazette* and Helena's now merged

Independent Record ignored subsequent convictions in both cases—including the sentencing of four Anaconda officials to short prison terms for falsifying product quality tests.[59]

It wasn't the first time Anaconda papers had ignored or downplayed the company's occasional problems with the law. When federal prosecutors accused dozens of western lumber companies of price fixing in the fall of 1940, the *Missoulian* and the *Helena Independent* not only buried the stories, but failed to mention that Anaconda's own timber division stood among the accused. Again, the *People's Voice* broke the news of the scheme, for which the company was later found liable.[60]

The Anaconda papers carefully managed the company's image in its coverage of statewide issues as well, conveniently hiding or underplaying corporate campaigns to kill legislation to raise taxes on utilities and lower them for banks. Nor did the copper press provide its readers with insightful coverage of two of the decade's most controversial legal fights: Montana Power's unsuccessful bid to deny irrigators' access to flows of the Missouri River, and successful federal action that forced the utility to reduce the inflated value of its assets and therefore the rates it charged customers. What coverage the papers did provide on those issues focused almost exclusively on the power company's arguments and ignored the consequences for irrigators and ratepayers. Both stories received national attention when *Harper's* magazine published an analysis by Joseph Kinsey Howard, a former *Great Falls Leader* editor whose book, *Montana: High, Wide and Handsome*, published the year before, had portrayed the state as a province exploited by the company and its allies.[61]

As Montana settled into the post-war boom, with its expanded economy and a population more attuned to the world beyond the state's borders, Anaconda's newspaper ownership would seem increasingly anachronistic—blunt tools from a bygone time. The papers themselves, their usefulness eroded by public cynicism, inertia, and increasing public criticism, would seem hardly worth their cost.

Author John Gunther, who toured Montana after the war, rated Anaconda's newspaper ownership as the most puzzling of the state's unique characteristics. The copper press struggled to appear unslanted, even as it suppressed news unfavorable to the company, refused the political advertising of its foes, and mounted self-serving attacks against public power projects. Yet for all its efforts, Gunther wrote, nobody was fooled.

> Why the company thinks such an antediluvian tactic as ownership of its own newspapers is a good idea remains a mystery to most experts in public opinion; it derives from the Daly-Ryan tradition of holding close to the chest everything they could get; but Ryan himself once told an independent editor, "You know, it's a kind of advantage that you're not on our pay roll, after all, because if *you* print something good about us, people believe it."[62]

ANACONDA
from mine to consumer
REG.U.S. PAT OFF.

Anaconda's ownership of Montana newspapers ranked high among Montana's worst-kept secrets, yet the details remained obscure until 1951, when the company revealed the extent of its newspaper ownership in an application to the Federal Communications Commission for approval of the company's purchase of a controlling interest in Havre radio station KFBB.

ANACONDA COPPER MINING COMPANY, *1950 ANNUAL REPORT* (N.P, N.D), COVER

CHAPTER TEN

The Captive Press

MOUNTING
CRITICISM

I T RANKED HIGH AMONG MONTANA'S worst-kept secrets, yet the company guarded the truth of its newspaper ownership until it was forced to give it up. Over the decades, there had been few cracks in the silence. Butte's old *Inter Mountain* acknowledged in 1903 that "some corporations have made investments in newspapers" as a means to "protect the public as well as the corporate interests from misrepresentation," but that was as far as it went. Beyond the obvious ownership in Butte and Anaconda, the extent of the company's newspaper chain remained a guessing game.[1]

The Montana legislature's clumsy investigation in 1935 provided the first official admission that Butte's *Montana Standard* and *Daily Post* were indeed Anaconda organs, and Will Campbell's confessed indebtedness confirmed his Helena daily was independent in name only. The *Billings Gazette*'s claim that its stock remained in private hands was a technical truth but a practical lie, as the company's own records would show. Meanwhile, Anaconda continued to play an elaborate shell game, hiding its interest in vague corporate entities and individual proxies, a practice perfected in the copper wars. Statements of ownership, required by federal postal regulations since 1912, offered few clues beyond the name of the each paper's local publishing company. State corporation reports offered hints in the affiliations of individual stockholders and officers listed, but the evidence remained circumstantial. From the mid-1930s onward, James Dickey Jr.'s name appeared on the annual reports filed by each copper daily, but Anaconda's did not.[2]

The company's jugglery extended to corporate accounting as well. In 1930, Anaconda attorneys formed the curiously named Fairmont

Investment Corporation, a Delaware company created to hold Anaconda's newspaper stock. Within weeks of the Montana legislature's 1935 probe, the company switched its newspapers to yet another corporate shell, the News Publishing Company, only to move it back to Fairmont twelve years later. Helena's *Western Progressive* and *People's Voice* did their best to connect the dots, but it wasn't until October of 1947 that Fairmont's status as "a subsidiary of the Anaconda Copper Mining Company, 25 Broadway, New York, N.Y.," finally graced the copper dailies' annual ownership statements, though the notices ran in the papers' smallest type, near the legal ads.[3]

For most Montanans, the details of Anaconda's newspaper ownership remained obscure until the company raised both the curtain and the public's ire in an awkward attempt to expand into broadcasting.

THE TARGET WAS KFBB, a pioneer Montana radio station begun in Havre in 1922 by grocery magnate F. A. Buttrey, who joked that the call letters were short for "Keep Frank Buttrey Broke." By the early 1950s, the station had long since moved to Great Falls, where it became a staple on the dial, featuring the audible antics of Charlie McCarthy and Red Skelton and the news and commentary of Edward R. Murrow, Eric Sevareid, and Charles Collingswood. By then, the station's control had passed to Fred Birch, a Great Falls builder with plans to establish another radio station—and perhaps a television station—in Billings, Montana's fastest-growing market.[4]

Birch had friends who could make such things happen, among them attorney Roy H. Glover, who had represented Buttrey in KFBB's early years, long before Glover's rise to become chief western counsel for the Anaconda Company and president of its Fairmont subsidiary, which held nearly a quarter of the station's stock. Birch's friends also included William Hoover, another Montana lawyer who had risen through the company's ranks to its presidency, one rung below chairman "Con" Kelley. Beyond Fairmont's shares in KFBB, Glover and Hoover also owned personal stock in the station, and in the winter of 1949–50 they agreed to purchase a controlling interest.[5]

Pressed later to explain their motives, company officials insisted that they were in it only for the money, but there were other benefits as well. Great Falls served the heart of central Montana's rich wheat country, but it was also home to an Anaconda smelter complex and a strong tradition of unionism that extended even to the newsroom of the independently owned *Great Falls Tribune*. A broadcast outlet in Great Falls might turn a spare dollar, it might even lead to greater profits in television, but a radio station under Anaconda control could also give the company a voice in the only major Montana city without a company daily.[6]

The *Great Falls Tribune* maintained a long and respectful appreciation for the benefits afforded by Anaconda's smelter and Montana Power's hydroelectric dams on the Missouri River. To the consternation

By the mid-1950s, after the company's failure to expand into broadcasting, Anaconda changed its mining operations, expanding to open pit mining, shown here below Butte Hill operations. Even so, profits from Anaconda's Chilean mines continued to reduce Butte's importance to the company's bottom line.

Montana Historical Society Photograph Archives, Helena

of company critics, the paper rarely criticized the company head-on, and over the years its coverage of the company could only be considered sympathetic. But it was no company organ, and by the mid-1930s Montana journalists considered it the best paper in the state. *Tribune* newsmen like Fred Martin, who had worked for the company press too, considered it "Montana's newspaper heaven," not only for its superior working conditions and pay, but for the moderation of its politics and the intelligence of its staff. The paper's longtime owner and publisher, Oliver Warden, had served as the state's Democratic national committeeman since the New Deal's onset, and his newspaper promoted better roads, better schools, and reclamation projects such as the Canyon Ferry Dam. Warden, who also owned the city's afternoon daily, the *Great Falls Leader,* had also tolerated the efforts of *Leader* subeditor Joseph Kinsey Howard and other *Tribune-Leader* staffers in organizing a local chapter of the American Newspaper Guild, which set a pace for wages and working conditions at Montana's larger dailies for more than fifty years.[7]

But it was the paper's independence that impressed Martin and others most. "The Tribune was not anti-Company or anti-labor, but it operated as a newspaper, recognizing that news was a free-flowing commodity. . . . Staffers didn't have to worry about the business office policy on any reasonable news story," Martin wrote. The paper's reporters were free to cover labor troubles at the Anaconda smelters, lawsuits against the "Twins," or the activities of politicians regardless of whether the company favored or opposed them. A grateful Senator James Murray wrote frequent notes to *Tribune* editors, thanking them for running Associated Press stories on federal legislation important to Murray and the state, articles that company editors often spiked.[8]

Tribune newsman Terry Dwyer knew the difference between his paper and the copper press too. As a young reporter for the *Helena Independent Record,* Dwyer had once strolled by a picket line of striking laundry workers. He rushed to the newsroom with notes for a story but was told the copper press did not report strikes. Nor, he would eventually discover, was it likely to report on-the-job deaths of Anaconda workers, or the achievements of politicians the company opposed, or the embarrassments of those it favored. Shortly after jumping to the

Tribune for better pay, Dwyer encountered a different response when he learned of a worker's accidental death at Anaconda's Black Eagle smelter. When he called the plant's general manager for details, he was told the story would never see print. Concerned, Dwyer reported the exchange to his city editor, Bill Zadick. As Dwyer later recounted in his memoir, *Looking Back in Black and White*, Zadick told him to remind the smelter boss that the *Tribune* was not a company paper. "It was my first feeling of independence from the company," he wrote.[9]

Though it was rarely critical of the company, the *Tribune*'s news coverage occasionally pressured the copper dailies into publishing stories it could not ignore without making a flagrant show of censorship. When Montana governor John Bonner, a company favorite, was arrested for public drunkenness during a 1950 junket to Louisiana, the *Tribune* offered readers a short Associated Press story quoting the governor's claim that the arrest had been a case of mistaken identity. The copper dailies skipped the story for a full day, but as the rumors piqued by the *Tribune* story persisted, they ran brief Associated Press articles, which they buried next to their classified ad sections. No Montana daily got to the heart of the story—the New Orleans *Times-Picayune*, the *New York Times*, and Spokane's *Spokesman-Review* reported that Bonner had indeed been arrested—but the *Tribune* broke the ice. With its diverse base of readers and advertisers, its solid local news and statehouse reporting, and its contributions to the wire services that provided Montana broadcasters with much of their news, the *Tribune* posed the most serious obstacle to Anaconda's efforts at statewide news management—if news management was indeed a motive for the company's sudden stab at broadcasting, as critics clearly feared.[10]

Whatever its reasons for wanting a radio station, the company could not hide its leap into broadcast ownership as it had once hidden its stake in newspapers. Prompted by widespread confusion over the assignment of frequencies in the 1920s, the federal government regulated broadcasting. The Communications Act of 1934 required that broadcasters be licensed to use the public's airwaves and that major changes in station ownership required approval by the Federal Communications Commission (FCC) in an open process. Among the criteria FCC officials were bound to consider was that the station be operated "in the public interest."

The standard was vague and rarely enforced, but it opened the door to an investigation of the company's character and reputation, a prospect the company's critics eagerly awaited and one Anaconda tried to avoid. To shepherd its application and limit publicity, Anaconda hired the Washington law firm of former U.S. Senator Burton K. Wheeler. Politically, it could hardly have made a poorer choice. Wheeler's name alone was enough to attract the fire of organized labor and farm groups that had suffered his red-baiting after the war and who contributed to his humiliating primary defeat in 1946.[11]

On January 21, 1951, Fairmont Investment Corporation formally requested FCC approval for its purchase of a controlling interest in KFBB. From its application, Montanans learned that the mysterious Fairmont was indeed a wholly owned subsidiary of the Anaconda Company and that it owned 100 percent of the companies that published Butte's *Montana Standard,* the *Butte Daily Post,* the *Missoulian,* and the *Missoula Sentinel.* It owned nearly 73 percent of the *Helena Independent Record,* two-thirds of the *Billings Gazette,* all but 5 percent of the *Livingston Enterprise,* a third of Libby's weekly *Western News* (not to be confused with the Romneys' Hamilton weekly of the same name), and a defunct weekly in Superior. The documents also revealed that the company had invested heavily in its newspapers over the decades only to recoup meager returns in the years it had not actually lost money.[12]

The application also provided a rare glimpse into the interlocking corporate relationships that gave the company its clout. Fairmont's president, Roy Glover of Great Falls, was western general counsel for both the Anaconda and Montana Power companies, but he also served as director of banks in Great Falls, Butte, and Minneapolis. Beyond that, he was president of a wholesale grocery business, a director of a Great Falls brewery, and an officer in the company that operated the amusement park at Butte's Columbia Garden. The documents also revealed the operational responsibilities of Fairmont vice president James Dickey Jr., who served additionally as an assistant to Anaconda's vice president and directed the company's Interstate Lumber Company. Other Fairmont officers had similar connections. William L. Murphy, the Missoula lawyer who served as president of the Missoulian Publishing Company, was also a director of the

Montana Power Company and served on the boards of Missoula's largest bank, department store, and hotel.[13]

Montana's daily press ignored the story, but the news spread quickly through the state's labor unions and farm organizations. Within days of Fairmont's FCC filing, John Evanko Jr., secretary of the Cascade County Trades and Labor Assembly, fired a letter to the FCC chairman Paul Walker, protesting any expansion of Anaconda's control over the state's news media. "The Anaconda Copper Mining Company already owns or controls all except one of the daily newspapers in Montana," Evanko wrote. His numbers were off but his thrust would become the battle's central theme, and FCC officials quickly served Fairmont officials notice that Evanko's concern was theirs as well.[14]

Fairmont officials disputed the issue as best they could. In a letter, Glover argued that Fairmont's newspapers represented but a fraction of those serving Montanans. Anaconda had no interest, "either directly or indirectly," in the small dailies published in Miles City, Lewistown, Bozeman, Kalispell, and Havre. Nor, he added, did the company hold stock in any of the state's 102 weekly newspapers. "From the foregoing you will note that we have no interest, either directly or indirectly, in any newspaper in the Great Falls area," Glover added.[15]

The company's critics conceded Glover's numbers but countered that the copper press served more than half of the state's daily newspaper audience, and their area of geographic coverage stretched across two-thirds of Montana, including four of the five largest centers of population and industry. In letter after letter to FCC officials, protestors like Joliet drugstore owner John Jarussi urged commissioners to deny the company "this juicy plum it so ardently and greedily seeks." He hammered away at the company's "viselike grip" over state government and its "sabotaging" of schools and other public institutions by stifling taxation and state spending bills. Anaconda's newspapers specialized in "suppressing public news and viewpoints" and "smearing" independent public officials. "To give it control of another radio station would simply be tightening its stranglehold on us and entirely contrary to the public interest in Montana," Jarussi wrote. Similar letters poured into the FCC, but Saims Myllymaki, secretary of the Judith Basin County Farmers Union, went straight to the top, registering his organization's protest in a looping scrawl to President Harry S. Truman himself.[16]

Critics also feared the company's influence would extend to FCC officials themselves and made certain commissioners knew they were watching. In its letter to Washington, the Great Falls Mill and Smeltermen's Union No. 16 worried that Anaconda lawyers would try to win approval by some "Back Door Method," while *People's Voice* editor Harry Billings registered similar fears in a missive to Senator Murray, who sent it on to the FCC. Six-term congressman Mike Mansfield, a former Montana history professor and onetime mucker in Anaconda's mines, ducked a public stand on the controversy but quietly passed his constituents' protests on to the commission. Meanwhile, former congressman Jerry J. O'Connell, still smarting from election defeats in 1938 and 1940 that he blamed on the company, requested permission to testify at any public hearings the commission might hold. Despite the intensity of the lobbying, the story still failed to catch fire in the Montana press, except for the *People's Voice,* which speculated that the Anaconda radio deal was but a first step in Anaconda's scheme to build a statewide broadcast network.[17]

Finally, after nearly six months of letters and internal ruminations, the FCC ordered a public hearing on the KFBB sale, though not in faraway Washington, as Anaconda officials had hoped, but in Great Falls. The commission also warned Anaconda that it intended to investigate the company's "character qualifications" in view of the company's 1941 conviction for conspiring to illegally fix the price of western pine lumber. More important, the commission intended to fully explore what effect KFBB's acquisition "would have upon the diversification and competition in media for dissemination of news information." To that end, it requested a full report on Anaconda's control over Fairmont, including "the method of exercising such control" and its policies for operating the newspapers themselves. The hearing was scheduled for September 24, 1951, and the commission put Anaconda and Fairmont officials on notice that they would also seek a broad disclosure of both companies' holdings, including detailed information about all plants, properties, or other business interests controlled by Anaconda and any of its subsidiaries. Furthermore, it ordered Anaconda to provide the operational guidelines for all its companies, plus a tally of every Montana worker it employed.[18]

For Anaconda, once dubbed the "most secretive of the great American corporations," the prospect of such disclosures was appalling. For decades, it had carefully guarded its image to the point where even stockholders had difficulty obtaining anything beyond the minimal corporate documentation made public through the requirements of the Securities and Exchange Commission. Protected by its lawyers, lobbyists, and newspapers, the company rarely found itself under official scrutiny, and never the kind of free-for-all examination the FCC clearly had in mind. Worse, hearings in Montana would surely devolve into a litany of grievances in a city where the company had little control over news coverage. The resulting testimony, relayed by the wire services to independent newspapers and broadcast stations statewide or even nationally, would be difficult to refute.[19]

Anaconda's Washington lawyers went to work, haggling over the parameters of the FCC's disclosure requests and the ground rules for any hearing. As they waited for news, the company's critics feared the commissioners were wavering in their initial insistence on a public hearing. Their worries seemed valid when the *Great Falls Tribune* reported that the FCC had indefinitely—and without explanation—postponed the scheduled September 24 hearing. The news had taken days to reach Montana, fanning suspicions that some sort of deal had already been cut. In an anxious letter to Senator Murray, Harry Billings suspected everyone, the FCC included, of trying to squelch news about the case. Why, he asked, had Montanans received no news of the FCC's initial decision to conduct a Montana hearing? Billings suspected the KFBB story was "scotched" by the FCC's publicity branch or by the Associated Press. "If so, WHY?" he asked. "If so, Who done it? Was it Fairmont? Was it Wheeler & Wheeler (BK, I presume)." Meanwhile, commissioners sent the company's foes another alarming signal by rejecting former congressman O'Connell's request to testify on the KFBB case. As neither a buyer nor a seller in the transaction, O'Connell had no standing, the FCC ruled. Similar objections would presumably apply to most of those protesting the station's sale.[20]

In late January of 1952, Fairmont's lawyers formally asked the FCC to approve its purchase of KFBB without a hearing. They also sought to make the hearing superfluous by providing much of the material commissioners had said they wanted to see. The company spelled out its newspaper holdings, accounted for all 11,656 Anaconda employees in the state, and protested that neither Anaconda nor its individual officers held any additional interests in Montana newspapers or broadcast stations. Although Fairmont officials expected KFBB to play "an increasingly important role in the community's life," they reiterated that the company's interest lay not in the stations' value as a news or public-relations outlet but rather in "the cold and impersonal corporate approach that KFBB represents a good investment." They also brushed aside concerns about media monopoly, arguing that its ownership of one radio station would have little impact on the state's highly competitive broadcast market in which several individual stations boasted strong network affiliations. As for Anaconda's antitrust violation, company lawyers argued that the infraction was an isolated, minor, and technical violation of the law, adding that the company had since experienced no additional antitrust problems. The issue, they insisted, was a dodge. No owner of any Montana broadcasting company had as clean a record as the Anaconda Company.[21]

More significantly, the company also provided its first-ever statement concerning the editorial conditions it placed on its newspapers:

> The policy of each of Fairmont's newspapers is determined locally, subject only to the several general policy considerations established by Mr. Glover. Mr. Glover's directions are, in summary, to avoid "yellow journalism." His policy directions call for publications which do not embrace public scandals, misfortunes of local residents tending to bring them into disgrace or embarrassment, or local petty quarrels. The objective is to place in the homes and business places of the readers news and editorials that are fit to print and be consumed by the adults and children having access to their pages. Otherwise, the management of each such paper is autonomous, both as to the news and editorials. Further, in no instances are news slants or editorials pipelined from management of either Anaconda or Fairmont to such papers.
>
> As regards advertising, each newspaper controlled by Fairmont accepts copy from any source able and willing to pay its uniform rates, provided that the advertising matter proposed for insertion is not deemed libelous or inimical to the interests of the United States, Montana, or her people."[22]

As high-minded as the company's press policy sounded, it flouted all notions of journalistic objectivity and the idea that a free press was duty bound to act as the public's watchdog. Fairmont's "general policy considerations" made more sense for the conduct of a public-relations firm than a newspaper obliged to protect the public interest. As guidelines, they offered Anaconda editors a convenient excuse for avoiding any and every controversy. With such timid rules of engagement, the company hardly needed a "pipeline" to its editors.

As Fairmont made its case, its opponents pressed the FCC to drop the application. The American Civil Liberties Union (ACLU) entered the fray in May, arguing that the KFBB sale would violate "the civil liberties principle of diversification in the ownership and policies of the media of mass communication." In a letter to commissioners, the ACLU's executive director, Patrick Murphy Malin, also questioned the effect of the company's "general policy considerations" on the operation of its newspapers, adding, "What all these 'general policy considerations' are, we are not told; whether local management is hired with a view to implementing Fairmont's policies through sympathetic editorialization—not an unremote possibility—we are not told; we are given no statements whatsoever to the effect that there are any significant differences between the editorial policies of one Fairmont publication and another."23

Finally, on May 28, 1952, nearly seventeen months after Fairmont submitted its original application, the FCC rejected the company's motion that the sale be approved without a hearing. In its ruling, the commission restated its concern that KFBB would "add measurably to Anaconda's and Fairmont's already substantial influence" in Montana. Furthermore, the company's additional documentary disclosures did not fully answer the commission's questions regarding Anaconda's interests in Montana or the operations of its newspapers. Finally, the FCC's concern about Anaconda's character had only increased since it had first ordered a hearing in the case. Through its own investigators, commissioners discovered that Anaconda had run afoul of federal antitrust laws not once, but several times. In fact, one company subsidiary, the American Brass Company, had been convicted and fined for violating the act as recently as 1946, and over the years the federal government had sued three other Anaconda subsidiaries—the Greene Cananea Copper Company, the Anaconda Sales Company, and the

Butte, Anaconda and Pacific Railway Company—on similar grounds. Worse, FCC officials wrote, they had learned that several Anaconda employees had been convicted and fined in 1946 for a wartime conspiracy to ship defective wire to the U.S. and British militaries.[24]

Unwilling to submit to further indignities, Fairmont tersely withdrew its application. With the doors to broadcasting effectively closed, the company was stuck with its newspapers, with their leaking bottom lines, and their credibility groaning under decades of political baggage.[25]

FINANCIALLY, THE FAILURE of a global corporation to acquire a small Montana radio station hardly rated a second look, but the controversy clearly demonstrated the company's growing sensitivity to bad publicity, especially on the matter of federal antitrust policy. In 1951, as company lawyers battled to keep the KFFB sale from becoming a free-for-all for its Montana critics, Anaconda had won a high-stakes campaign to land a lucrative federal defense contract to produce aluminum with the cheap power generated by the federal government's new Hungry Horse Dam on Montana's Flathead River.

The company's bid to make aluminum—copper's chief rival as a conductor of electricity—raised serious antitrust questions. Those concerns, coupled with the irony of Anaconda's attempt to acquire the electrical output of a dam whose construction both the company and Montana Power had initially opposed, proved too rich for critics to ignore. Late in 1951, the *New Republic* published a scathing critique of the deal under the headline "Monopoly vs. Public." The *Nation*, writing a month later, described the affair as "Anaconda's Big Steal." The furor quickly subsided, but it served notice of the heightened scrutiny the company could expect as it juggled its diversified holdings. What's more, Anaconda's disclosure of its newspaper holdings in the KFBB case ensured that the oddity of its newspaper ownership would resurface repeatedly with every mention of the company in the popular press.[26]

Yet for outsiders, the effects of Anaconda's newspaper control proved remarkably elusive. A *Time Magazine* reporter sent to Montana in 1952 to investigate the sins of the modern copper press found little to report. When questioned, Anaconda editors denied any regular contact with company executives, much less any interference in the day-to-day operation of their papers. Despite their old reputation for vitriol, the papers now seemed inordinately passive. After several weeks of such yawning revelations, the *Time* reporter surrendered, telling his editors that researching a story on the copper press was like "trying to get in a solid blow against feathers."[27]

Denver Post reporter Thor Severson fared somewhat better. In a series of six articles, appearing weekly from early April through May 1952, Severson detailed Anaconda's influence over Montana's state government and the role played in that effort by the company's "captive press." Severson focused specifically on the press's blatant downplaying of legislation aimed at making the company shoulder more of the state's costs in treating thousands of miners suffering from silicosis. He found additional bias in the papers' one-sided coverage of critical court cases involving both the company and Montana Power and in its lopsided coverage of some statewide political campaigns. Severson also reported the company's venture into broadcasting, providing Colorado readers with more detailed coverage of the KFBB affair than Montanans had received from any homegrown newspaper beyond the *People's Voice*.[28]

In preparing his stories, Severson interviewed numerous Anaconda journalists and quoted their views concerning the company's influence over news coverage and editorial policy. In another first, the reporter asked Fairmont director T. B. Weir the question that had gone unanswered for decades: What business did a mining, smelting, and manufacturing company have in publishing newspapers? "We're in the business because it's a good investment," Weir said. "That's our only interest."[29]

Although Severson found the copper press much tamer in its modern incarnation, he also recounted episodes revealing Anaconda's subtle control of the news. Earlier in the year, a proposed voter initiative to increase Anaconda's financial support for silicosis victims merited a five-paragraph story in the *Helena Independent Record*. Buried on the financial page, the article made no mention of silicosis and its wooden headline—"Initiative Plans to Change Parts of Statute" offered readers no hint of the measure's purpose. However, it did offer the assessment of an anonymous industry spokesman who dubbed the legislation "patently socialistic." By contrast,

Severson wrote, the next day's *Great Falls Tribune* carried news of the proposal in a front-page story that included reaction from both the measure's critics and its supporters.[30]

Severson also recounted the *Helena Independent Record*'s decision to spike its coverage of a statewide conference on occupational safety, which eventually concluded that Montana suffered a far too heavy toll from workplace diseases. Dropping the story also meant the news would not appear in other Montana papers via the Associated Press, whose statewide service depended heavily on the contributions of its member papers. According to Severson, the Helena daily's lackadaisical attitude extended to its all-but-nonexistent coverage of recent legislative sessions. Rather than staff the session, Helena editors found it easier to rely on Associated Press reports, which they could carefully edit for news inimical to the company's welfare, especially items concerning labor issues, taxation, or workers' compensation reform. Severson quoted Leo Graybill, a Great Falls lawyer and legislator, who found the situation baffling. "They have one man at the press table with full credentials of a press man. But he doesn't write a word," Graybill said. "All he does is keep track of the roll call votes and telephone Butte the results." Though Severson didn't mention it, some company lobbyists also held press credentials, allowing them to roam the Senate and House during floor sessions. No other lobbyists enjoyed such a privilege.[31]

Severson offered other examples of the copper press's journalistic negligence, including its biased or nonexistent coverage of Leif Erickson's hapless campaigns for governor and the U.S. Senate, of Senator Murray's ill-fated dream of a Missouri Valley Authority, and of a landmark ruling denying Montana Power Company's claim to the flows of the Missouri River. The list also included the copper press's slanted coverage of federal hearings into charges that Montana Power customers had historically paid higher-than-necessary rates to cover the allegedly inflated costs incurred in the utility's creation. In the latter case, Severson reported, the copper dailies' news reports were so opinionated that an Associated Press man lost his job for transmitting one of the stories over the wires.[32]

Severson's own reporting included no point-by-point response from company editors to his specifics, but he did quote *Butte Daily Post* editor Law Risken, who bristled at the "absurd" charge that Anaconda maintained a "propaganda press." "There is no such thing as a policy as some say," Risken said. "For example, if the company used the papers for a propaganda tool, it would have its own reporters at the legislature, wouldn't it?" Risken's comment spoke volumes about the bind in which Anaconda's editors now found themselves, but it failed to alter Severson's conclusion that the copper press continued to serve the company's needs at the expense of its readers by omitting or underplaying unfavorable news. "The searching reader chafes under the scissor blades of a company press," he wrote.[33]

In the end, Severson wrote, Montana remained the nation's last outpost of a captive industrialist press, a relic of the days of gaslights and robber barons. "Nowhere in America today is there a parallel." Despite its "meatless" news menu and its "flowers-in-spring, havoc-in-China, life among the Eskimos" news judgment, the copper press still reflected the company's "latent backroom power." Its continued existence also bolstered the credibility of its critics, he added.[34]

In fairness, Severson also reported signs of the company's new eagerness to improve its image. In Butte, it had recently built a $4-million state-of-the-art hospital and an impressive employees club. It also launched an innovative project to provide its workers with new homes at cost, but as Severson also noted, the effort coincided with the beginnings of open-pit mining, which would ultimately swallow huge chunks of the city. Still, Severson suggested, such efforts reflected "a new and progressive era in public relations." Other signs of a "new order," he wrote, included the copper dailies recent willingness to air the U.S. Justice Department's concerns about Anaconda's suitability for federal help in entering the aluminum manufacturing business at Columbia Falls.[35]

Even so, it was questionable whether Anaconda could truly improve its image as long as it owned Montana's leading newspapers. Lee Metcalf, a liberal justice on Montana's Supreme Court and soon to become a U.S. senator, told Severson that while he found the copper press "deliberately dull," Montanans still feared it. "Everyone remembers the bad old days when the Montana press was openly a propaganda organ for Anaconda," Metcalf said. "In Montana, we feel there is always the threat this monopolistic power will be turned against some individual or organization. The result would be disastrously unjust."[36]

The *Denver Post* series won a recommendation from the *People's Voice* but no mention from the Montana dailies. Then again, its revelations were hardly news.

AT THE AGE OF EIGHTY, Cornelius Frances "Con" Kelley embodied both Anaconda's past and its modern industrial vision. He could still recall the sound of Marcus Daly's voice and the excitement and tension of Anaconda's legal and political battles with Clark, Heinze, Socialists, labor radicals, and the "smoke farmers" of the Deer Lodge Valley. Audacious, tough-minded, and ruthless, Kelley, with his mentor, John D. Ryan, had taken a raw Montana enterprise and forged it into one of the world's preeminent metals companies, a fabricator of brass, a manufacturer of cable and wire, and a producer of zinc, copper, aluminum, and even uranium. In 1955, he had changed the company's name from the Anaconda Copper Mining Company to the Anaconda Company; the identification with copper, most of which now came from its Chilean mines, was simply too confining. That same year, Kelley—the bright boy from Walkerville, a miner's son schooled in Butte's streets and the University of Michigan's school of law—stepped down as chairman of a multinational corporation with earnings that were as strong as they had been in the glory days on the brink of the Great Depression.[37]

Kelley's retirement ushered in a new generation of Anaconda executives, and though a remarkable number had ties to Montana, many had joined the company long after its formative battles, while others had advanced through the ranks of Anaconda properties outside the state. Roy H. Glover, Kelley's Oregon-born and -educated successor, was already a successful Montana railroad lawyer when he was asked to oversee legal affairs for both Anaconda and Montana Power in 1936. But other rising Anaconda stars had spent little time in Montana. Clyde E. Weed, Glover's second-in-command and successor by 1958, was a Michigan mining engineer who had spent his career in Michigan, Arizona, Mexico, Washington, and New York. Weed knew the company's

Montana operations intimately, but was hardly steeped in the state's lore and romance.[38]

To such pragmatic men, Anaconda's newspapers could only have seemed an embarrassment as the decade wore on and criticism of the copper press mounted. More attuned to the value of good press, Kelley's successors took immediate steps to polish the company's past by commissioning former muckraker Isaac F. Marcosson to write a fawning history. Published in the spring of 1957, *Anaconda* was a masterpiece of selective memory that overlooked much of the controversy that attended the company's development. Except for Marcus Daly's creation of the *Anaconda Standard* and a brief mention of Anaconda's absorption of Clark's properties, including the *Butte Miner,* Marcosson pointedly ignored the company's dominance of Montana's daily press. Nevertheless, three of the state's copper dailies gave the book sparkling front-page reviews, and editors at the *Billings Gazette* each received a free copy.[39]

Yet as Anaconda's interest in Montana seemed to wane, the controversy over its influence there continued to grow, fueled in part by the anachronism of its newspaper ownership. Following the *Denver Post*'s analysis in 1952, the most detailed attack on Anaconda journalism came in 1956, with the publication of a blistering critique by John M. Schiltz, a Billings attorney and former Republican state legislator who urged Anaconda's new managers to do themselves and the state a favor by selling the company's newspapers. Schiltz's article, "Montana's Captive Press," headlined the inaugural issue of *Montana Opinion,* a short-lived but influential journal devoted to discussion of the state's "political and economic ills" and published by an eclectic assortment of Montana academics, professionals, and clergymen that included historian K. Ross Toole, literary critic Leslie Fiedler, and novelist Walter Van Tilburg Clark. "We have no partisan axe to grind and no vendettas to launch," the journal's editors insisted at the outset, "but we are convinced that preceptive [sic] Montanan is sick and tired of living without a candid and intelligent press."[40] It was only fitting that the copper press served as the journal's first target.

The sin of Anaconda journalism, Schiltz argued, was not in trying to protect the company's interests, but in sacrificing the interests of more than half of Montana's daily newspaper subscribers in the process. The problem was not Anaconda's high pressure lobbying efforts, nor its conservatism, which many Montanans presumably shared, he wrote, but it had no business constraining the public debate. "In my opinion," Schiltz wrote, "the company has a perfect right to be as big as it wants to be; it has a right to lobby; it has a right to influence; it has a right to negotiate. It has the right to do everything legal of which I am aware, except it has no right to own, edit and publish bad newspapers, and this it does."[41]

Decades of company control, Schiltz charged, had produced newspapers so innately fearful of offending either their Anaconda owners or their readers that they had become "dull, colorless, devoted to the status quo." Such journalism stifled community and state interest in vital public issues. Rather than foster vigorous debate over the state's problems, editors simply ignored them and substituted "feel-good" palliatives that perpetuated the myth that Montana was "the best of all possible worlds." Anaconda journalism was simply bad journalism, though the average Montanan "never knows how bad until he sees other papers and survives the first shock of seeing controversy in print." It had not always been so, and Schiltz wistfully recounted the fiery journalism of the Clark-Daly feud, which had at least given Montanans vital and vibrant newspapers that expressed diverse points of view. Yet he also conceded that feud had sown the seeds of a company press that now served more than half of the state's daily newspaper subscribers and effectively precluded daily newspaper competition across more than two-thirds of the state.[42]

Schiltz also attacked the hypocrisy he saw in Anaconda's defense of its ongoing newspaper ownership. Citing Fairmont's own financial figures and statements, he punctured the assertion that the papers were held purely as an economic investment. According to Schiltz's calculations, the papers' return on investment for 1954 was a paltry .014 percent. "From an investment standpoint government bonds would be twice as good; patriotically, there is no comparison," he wrote. Nor did Schiltz find much consistency in the way Anaconda editors applied the company's "general policy considerations" that supposedly barred "yellow journalism" or reporting that emphasized public scandals or disgraced and embarrassed local residents. Schiltz argued that copper editors showed little compunction about embarrassing the poor or members of minority groups whose misfortunes routinely surfaced in the papers' crime news; nor were they queasy about muddying the reputations of company critics. As for Fairmont's claim that Anaconda officials never "pipelined" news to its supposedly autonomous editors, Schiltz could only point to the papers' unanimous failure to adequately cover strikes, Montana Power's controversial grab for the state's rivers, or a grassroots push to make Anaconda shoulder more of the state's costs in treating silicosis victims. Such coverage surely affected the public debate, he added, arguing that the company's most persistent political problems seemed to come from areas of the state with independent news outlets.[43]

In the end, Schiltz could only wonder why Anaconda continued to operate newspapers in the face of criticism that offset any public-relations benefit. Surely, he argued, in "an age of public and press relations" the money Anaconda spent publishing papers could be better invested in a crack public- and press-relations department devoted solely to defending the company's interests. Such a move would serve Montana's welfare too. "Freedom of the press means both freedom from the press and freedom for the press," he wrote; "in Montana we have the latter but not the former."[44]

Predictably, the copper press ignored Schiltz's criticism, though the piece prompted a few editorial replies from independent weekly editors, some of whom complained that its criticisms were nothing new. Charles Doherty, editor of the weekly *Missoula County Times* in Missoula, bristled at the *Montana Opinion*'s blanket assertion that Montana lacked a "candid and intelligent press" and characterized the journal's editors as "[a]nother group of high-domed, starry-eyed boys." As for Schiltz's article, its criticism of the company press "has been warmed over so many times it looks and smells like a dried up buffalo chip." Nor was it particularly edifying. "The smart boys have been unable to come up with a solution to change the company press to independents," Doherty wrote. "In the first place it would require millions of dollars and the guy that has that kind of money would not be interested in a flock of dailies in a sparsely settled state."[45]

But Dan Whetstone, the aging editor of Cut Bank's *Pioneer Press* and a longtime critic of the copper press, vouched for much of Schiltz's critique, especially its inference that the copper press had endured such a long period of captivity that its editors no longer required direction as to how best serve their industrial masters. "They well know what's required of them," Whetstone wrote. Schiltz's revelations, though nothing new, only reinforced Whetstone's belief that the company would be better liked "and probably treated just as fairly—perhaps more so" if it simply sold its newspapers.[46]

As long as such musings remained confined to Montana, the company could afford to ignore them, but echoes of Schiltz's article quickly found their way into an article written by an anonymous special correspondent for the *Economist,* the British weekly magazine of international business and politics. In a report headlined "Anaconda Country," the magazine found Montana "the outstanding example of a 'company' state" but predicted that Anaconda's dominance would wane as the state's economy slowly diversified. For now, it found the company more restrained and tactful in wielding its power. Instead of bribes, its "smoothly operating" Helena lobby now "achieved its effects by whiskey and bonhomie." Its workers were better treated, as were the company's foes. "Occasionally its newspapers even publish parts of speeches critical of the company," the correspondent reported. Yet while its techniques had surely been refined, Anaconda could still apply considerable pressure through its lobbyists, its web of business connections, and newspapers that avoid controversy, effectively leaving Montana's newspaper readers "worse informed about their own affairs than the inhabitants of almost any other state."[47]

Against a global backdrop of the Cold War and the company's increasing dependence on uneasy foreign concessions, Anaconda needed such publicity like a kick in the head.

DUANE "DOC" BOWLER's initial experience as a reporter for Anaconda's Helena dailies was pleasant enough. The son of a respected Montana weekly publisher and a recent graduate of the state's School of Journalism, Bowler was accustomed to the company's brand of journalism by the time he joined the staff of the *Montana Record-Herald* in 1941, just two years before the paper was merged with the *Helena Independent* to form the *Independent Record*. His stories—some of them daring for the times—ran much as he wrote them. The influence of the paper's "benefactor" seemed all but nonexistent until Bowler sniffed out a case of embezzlement at the Lewis and Clark County courthouse and presented his editors with the scoop. The article never saw the light of day, a victim of the company's reluctance to embarrass its friends. As Bowler would recall decades later, "The story was killed on orders from Butte because the malefactor . . . had performed a useful errand some years before and had been promised protection." The company saw to it that the embezzler lost his job, Bowler added, but his shame and his name never hit the papers.[48]

In Butte, the *Montana Standard*'s aversion to scandal extended to its coverage of the city's courts. In the mid-1950s, reporter Lewis Poole uncovered a bizarre and long-running system of negligence in which residents convicted of misdemeanors routinely escaped jail and fines by appealing their convictions to district court, which never heard the appeals. When Poole approached his editors about exposing the situation, he was warned off the story.[49]

Robert Miller, who covered Helena in the late 1920s and early 1930s as one of only two city desk reporters for the *Montana Record-Herald*, discovered the limits of Anaconda journalism in 1935. Asked to fill in for the paper's vacationing editorial writer, Lynn Young, Miller called readers' attention to a gold dredge digging unsightly craters at the lower end of Last Chance Gulch and asked if such activity was necessary. When Young returned, he was immediately summoned to Butte where Anaconda officials "gave him the devil." "I guess I was about to be fired," Miller later recalled. "At any rate, the message I got was that no Anaconda paper ever questioned any facet of the mining industry. It was just a little while after that that I was sent to Livingston and I never could figure out whether that was done as punishment to get me out of Helena." Miller, who survived to write editorials for the *Livingston Enterprise*, never forgot the lesson. "Every morning my first task was to read the Montana Standard very thoroughly and determine how many controversial matters had been handled," Miller recalled. "Thus I was able to follow company instructions without any day-to-day instruction."[50]

Gary Sorenson, freshly graduated from the state's School of Journalism in 1957, received his education in the realities of copper journalism soon after reporting for duty at the *Helena Independent Record*. Assigned to cover a luncheon speech by Democratic Attorney General Forrest Anderson, a sometime critic of the company, Sorenson took copious notes and filed a two-page story summarizing Anderson's themes. When the paper appeared later that afternoon, Sorenson found his article reduced to a single paragraph and buried on the back page. When Sorensen asked his city editor what he'd done wrong, the man grinned and sent him to see managing editor E. A. "Shorty" Dye, who told him that Anderson's name was listed in the editor's "little black book" of politicians who were to receive little or no publicity.[51]

The self-censorship practiced by the copper press was hardly the concoction of a few "high-domed, starry-eyed" critics, though the company's subtle communication with only a few top editors often conveyed the impression that it had little, if anything, to do with the operation of its papers. Remarkably few company journalists were ever approached directly by an Anaconda official and asked to drop a story or editorial or slant the news. Yet most agreed the boundaries were clear, and in cases where they weren't, the instinct toward self-preservation usually prevailed. The result was a bland, perfunctory sort of journalism in which reporters on the street were conceded a generally free hand, while editors upheld the taboos.

Sooner or later, copper editors learned what was out of bounds. At the *Montana Record-Herald*, "Doc" Bowler's list included union matters, mining accidents, consumerism and cost-of-living issues, and industrial diseases such as silicosis, which was allowed to be mentioned only in such general terms as "industrial hygiene" or "health hazard." The papers played legislative sessions straight, relying mainly on heavily edited Associated Press coverage, which featured a sort of stenographic accuracy that passed for objectivity but offered readers little insight into motives and consequences. Some politicians were given prominent treatment; "others didn't exist." Bowler also recalled that company officials, as businessmen primarily, were characteristically sensitive to complaints about coverage of their associates, vendors, subcontractors, and political allies. Editors gradually accumulated their own lists of people and issues to avoid. "To make it short, editors of the company papers found their life was easier when the Sixth Floor . . . received the fewest calls from politicians, lawyers, business [and just about anyone else] who didn't like something that was about to appear."[52]

Bowler and other Anaconda journalists occasionally tested the boundaries, only to repeatedly run afoul of "policy." In the late 1940s, Bowler and fellow *Independent Record* reporter John Willard wrote a tongue-in-cheek account of an alleged statewide crackdown on illegal slot machines. The story, which Bowler described as "one of those smart-ass stories reporters write, and you could almost hear the ice clinking in the glass," eventually landed on the desk of editor "Shorty" Dye, who laughed as he read it but refused to run it. When asked why, Dye replied that one of the Anaconda Company's lobbyists ran slot machines in Lake County. On another occasion, Bowler sniffed out a case of assault that police seemed reluctant to pursue until after it appeared in the paper's early mail edition. Dye brushed off a company-connected lawyer's attempt to spike the article in the paper's home edition, only to get a call from Dickey ordering him to kill it. Consequently, the report appeared in some papers but not others. "There were actually fist fights in Helena that night over whether we'd carried the story or not," Bowler recalled, "and both sides had proof."[53]

As far as commentary was concerned, the papers' editorial writers sidestepped the traps faced by local news reporters by focusing their attention almost exclusively beyond Montana, a practice *Denver Post's* Severson described as "a sort of editorial Afghanistanism." Tom Stout, the former congressman and Lewistown newspaper publisher who had once complained of such editorials himself, became a master of the art after selling his paper and hiring on as an editorial writer for the *Billings Gazette*. His specialty, he later acknowledged, was in writing informational backgrounders on national or international matters, subjects that skirted local topics and avoided hard expressions of opinion. It was safe strategy, sure to avoid contact, much less confrontation, with the paper's owners. "[T]here was never any suggestion about what I should write," Stout told a journalism student years later. "I felt as free to express my opinions as I did when I was publishing my own newspaper."[54]

Other company editorial writers agreed with Stout's claim, but also acknowledged that they understood the topical boundaries as clearly as their editors did. Local and state politics simply proved too hazardous to negotiate, but forays into national politics could boomerang too, according to *Missoulian* editorial writer Guy Mooney. For him, the problem hit home when Anaconda executive Roy Glover went to Washington, D.C., to consult with certain dignitaries. "One dignitary pulled out copies of the Anaconda newspapers which had denounced him and asked the Anaconda representative for an explanation," Mooney wrote. "After that incident, the word went out that the papers were to lay off political matters."[55]

Thus hobbled, the copper press's editorial targets ranged from "bad motherhood to cancer," as one Anaconda reporter put it. Hitler and communists were fair game too. Otherwise, copper editorial writers could safely tout Montana's natural glories and the resilience of her people, but the luster of such wonders dulled with repetition. "The bosses realized it was hard to keep writing about the bears in Yellowstone Park year after year," *Billings Gazette* night editor Tom Astle said, "but that was about all we were allowed to editorialize on." For those who recalled the slashing editorials of yesteryear, the turnabout was more than startling. "With their heavy artillery spiked, Anaconda papers became monuments of indifference," one critic wrote.[56]

A survey conducted on the copper press's editorial subjects in 1959 found that of all the editorials that year, state topics accounted for only 2.9 percent of the total. Local subjects received less than half a percent. Letters to the editor, long a standard feature in most American dailies and a principal means of encouraging debate on public issues, were nonexistent, except in the *Missoulian*, which occasionally published readers' submissions on safe topics, though it insisted on concealing most writers' identities.[57]

BERT GASKILL JOINED the *Montana Standard* as a night police reporter in 1949, against the advice of the university's journalism dean, who urged him to avoid the company press for the sake of his career. He earned "shoe clerk wages" in Butte, but the city's people were friendly and colorful, and it was close to good fishing. "We stayed on the job because we liked Montana, not the pay," he later recalled. He could have done better, but as young Gaskill figured it, five years' experience at the *Standard* would give him the requisite skills to move anywhere. He would remain at the paper for nearly thirty years.[58]

It was a calculation made by scores of young journalists who joined the copper press over the decades and not so unusual from the perspective of those accustomed to Montana and Anaconda's brand of newspapering. After all, most newspaper publishers had their sacred cows, and within Anaconda's unwritten boundaries an aspiring reporter could still find colleagues who valued a well-spun phrase, a punchy headline, a light touch with a feature, or the speed and nimbleness of cool-headed editors who could stitch the day's chaos into a coherent tapestry by deadline. Over the years, the copper press had its stars, men like Eggleston and Stone and the *Anaconda Standard*'s wonderful artists. Perhaps none were as bright as the *Missoulian* sportswriter Ray Rocene, the cigar-chewing, lightening-quick Swede with a librarian's memory who delighted readers in a column that ran regularly for a remarkable fifty-one years. Decades later, Rocene's readers could still recall his coverage of the 1923 heavyweight championship fight between Jack Dempsey and Tommy Gibbons in tiny Shelby. Although salaries shriveled in the wake of the copper wars, the benefits weren't bad, at least not by Montana standards. By the late 1950s, staffers cited unlimited sick leave, health coverage, a decent retirement plan, and a strong sense of job security. Anaconda journalists were rarely fired or transferred.[59]

Still, the papers suffered in the latter days of Anaconda ownership, and the damage went beyond their political impotence. The company's negative press policy, its professional detachment, and its odd frugalities engendered an ambivalence that even affected the papers' appearances. Once vibrant and sensational, they now appeared dull and uninviting, their layouts uninspired and remarkably devoid of illustrations and photos, especially local ones, which Anaconda's accountants considered luxuries. Although the company built new modern plants in Billings and Helena in the late 1950s, the newspapers as businesses were grossly out of step with industry trends, a condition some employees attributed to their stepchild status in a corporation devoted to mining, smelting, and metal fabrication.

With the exception of the *Billings Gazette* and *Missoulian*, the copper press struggled financially. As businesses, the papers were expected to cover their costs, but advertising and circulation staffers, like their colleagues in the newsrooms, received little if any professional training in the latest newspaper trends or efficiencies. Reporters felt little pressure to pursue difficult or complicated stories, a function of inadequate staffing and resources as much as their papers' ambiguity over what they considered news. In an environment that considered a long-distance phone call in pursuit of a hot story extravagant, company editors stuffed their news holes with wire service reports at the expense of locally produced news—which only added to the overall ambivalence. As some employees would later complain, the papers' vaunted job security, admirable as it might seem, also bred a lack of cohesion and laziness. In Butte, where it all began, managers of the *Anaconda Standard* and *Butte Daily Post* now suffered not only the constrictions of the company's news policy, but the restrictive work rules imposed by the papers' production unions, whose affiliation with Butte's increasingly powerful mining and trade unions gave them real clout.[60]

To newspaper professionals, the problems of the copper press were obvious. Few, however, expected a change, and so the rumors that began to swirl in late 1958 caught most by surprise. On a November trip to New England, Mel Ruder, the talented owner-editor of the weekly *Hungry Horse News* in Columbia Falls, confirmed them during a stopover in New York, where he met with an unnamed Anaconda executive. The company, Ruder was pleased to learn, had finally decided to sell its papers.[61]

MANY FLATS AND SHARPS, BUT MUCH OF ONE TUNE

John R. Toole Makes the Tunes the Amalgamated Copper Standard Oil Press of the State Plays and Tommy Carter Furnishes the Wind With Standard Oil Money.

By the 1950s, the Anaconda Company-owned newspapers had become out-moded and all but irrelevant. Company leaders finally questioned their value as political and public-relations tools and decided to sell them. Almost half a century earlier, this cartoon portrayed Montana politicians John R. Toole and Tom Carter "playing the company tune."

BUTTE REVEILLE, SEPTEMBER 13, 1902

CHAPTER ELEVEN

I N SEPTEMBER OF 1958, AN EMISSARY
of the Anaconda Company offered
Great Falls Tribune publisher Alex
Warden the opportunity of a lifetime:
a chance to own all of Montana's daily
newspapers. The moment was both historic and unsettling. Some sixty-three
years earlier, Marcus Daly had offered

Emancipation

ANACONDA
SHEDS ITS
NEWSPAPERS

Warden's father a chance to buy the *Great Falls Tribune.* The terms were
generous then and they were generous now: the company would finance
the sale on agreeable terms. Warden's father, Oliver, had grabbed his
chance, and the paper he left his sons at his death in 1955 was both profitable and respected. But Oliver had been a young man; Alex was not.
And as his visitor would later relate, Alex's polite refusal included another
reason, one rooted in the tangled history of Montana's politics and its
press. "[H]e did not believe it would be good for the state for all of the
principal newspapers to be in one package."[1]

Whatever they thought about the political or journalistic implications of selling the Fairmont papers, Anaconda's leaders had finally come
to the conclusion that newspapering was bad business. Financially, the
papers were hardly worth the bother, and company chieftains, including
John D. Ryan, had long questioned their actual value as political and
public-relations tools. As symbols of corporate power, the animosity they
generated increasingly undermined their credibility on subjects large and
small, on issues real and imagined. Hamstrung by orders to shun controversy and targets of mounting criticism at home and abroad, the papers
themselves were self-conscious and defensive—no way to run a newspaper. Political reforms, labor reforms, broadcasting, and the shrinking
importance of Montana to Anaconda's future had all combined to render
the papers outmoded and all but irrelevant. The company's ambivalence
reflected from their pages, and yet serious talk of selling the copper press

In 1958, Anaconda executives quietly offered Great Falls Tribune publisher Alex Warden the opportunity of a lifetime: a chance to buy most of Montana's major daily newspapers. Despite agreeable terms, he politely turned the company down, saying that it would be bad for the state to gather its principal dailies under a single owner.

GREAT FALLS TRIBUNE, GREAT FALLS, MONTANA

surfaced only in the wake of "Con" Kelley's death in 1957. Free of loyalties forged in forgotten battles, a new generation of company leaders saw the papers for the anachronisms they were. On a tour of Montana shortly after assuming Anaconda's helm in 1958, chairman Clyde Weed made a point of asking company executives and state leaders why the company should retain its newspapers. Their silence said it all.[2]

Weed and C. Jay Parkinson, Anaconda's vice president and general counsel, needed little convincing. Neither had roots in Montana. For them, the company's newspaper ownership was little more than a relic from Anaconda's brawling youth, an "antiquated situation" that no longer served the corporate interest. Julian Hayes, a company publicity manager, concluded that years of company ownership eventually stripped the papers of their credibility, and there was little Anaconda editors could do about it. Their motives were suspect no matter what they wrote, no matter how they played a given story. Weed's solution was simple, Hayes remembered: "Anaconda is in the metals producing business—not the newspaper business."[3]

That decided, the company moved quickly to find a suitable buyer. To limit unwanted offers, executives kept their decision quiet through the fall of 1958. Characteristically, the company kept its Montana newspapers ignorant as long possible. Richard Morrison, the *Missoulian's* veteran business manager, learned the news in mid-September from Alex Warden. For weeks, Morrison told no one, not even his boss. James Dickey Jr., Fairmont's chief executive for nearly thirty years, was notified on the day after Thanksgiving when he was told to prepare the papers for inspection by teams of prospective buyers. Six months later, with a deal all but signed, Weed notified Anaconda's stockholders. Profits from the sale, he told them, would be secondary to "what the Company thinks the purchasers can do for the State of Montana."[4]

IT WAS NEW YEAR'S DAY, 1959, and Don Anderson, publisher of the *Wisconsin State Journal* in Madison, was in his office, trying to catch up on paperwork, when the phone rang. On the line was Philip Adler, chief executive of the Lee syndicate, a small, loosely organized midwestern media chain that included Anderson's paper and nine other smallish dailies, plus a handful of radio and television stations. The group's national advertising representative had heard that Anaconda's Montana newspapers were on the block. Adler asked Anderson, born and reared in Montana's Gallatin Valley, to scout the possibility.[5]

Anderson jumped to the

Philip Adler, chief executive of Lee Enterprises, a small midwestern media chain, immediately responded to the opportunity to expand Lee's operation.

· LEE ENTERPRISES, INC.

task, quickly tracking down an address for Fairmont's Dickey. In a carefully composed letter, Anderson stressed his Montana upbringing and his brief stint as a cub reporter at the *Bozeman Chronicle* where he had worked alongside several ex-Anaconda newsmen. Dickey confirmed that the papers were indeed for sale and directed Anderson to the New York offices of Anaconda's vice president and general counsel C. Jay Parkinson.

Once contacted, Parkinson invited Anderson to Anaconda's Manhattan headquarters at 25 Broadway.[6]

Anderson's approach was cautious. If the papers were to be auctioned, Lee stood little chance of matching offers with the large newspaper chains rumored to be in the hunt. Parkinson relieved that anxiety immediately; the papers, he said, would not necessarily go to the highest bidder. But that raised a more delicate question: If money was not the company's chief demand, what was? Deeply aware of Montana's long history of feudal journalism, Anderson anticipated the question, and so had Adler. They agreed to break off talks at the first hint that Anaconda expected favorable editorial treatment as a condition of the sale. But Parkinson, a fellow westerner, had not been so crude in their first meeting, and Anderson tactfully dodged the issue for now, promising only that Lee would publish newspapers committed to the well-being of their communities and that it would retain the papers' "deserving employees." The unspoken question would hang over the negotiations for the next four and a half months as Lee examined the Montana properties—and while Anaconda studied Lee.[7]

Adler sent Gallatin Valley–born Don Anderson, publisher of the Wisconsin State Journal, *to New York to meet with Anaconda's vice president and general counsel C. Jay Parkinson to pursue the purchase. He approached the acquisition cautiously, fearing Anaconda might expect favorable editorial treatment as a condition of the sale.*

Lee Enterprises, Inc.

What Lee found was a gamble. Of Anaconda's papers, only the *Billings Gazette* and the *Missoulian* could be considered profitable enterprises in growing communities. Butte's copper dailies, once Anaconda's flagship papers, made little money, the result of mismanagement and inefficiency as well as the city's declining population and importance in the mining world. Helena's *Independent Record* struggled for profitability in a small, volatile market, as did the smallest of the copper dailies, the *Livingston Enterprise*. The challenge, Lee officials realized, would be in finding business managers capable of wringing efficiencies from each property and editors with the talent to make dull papers bright and credible.[8]

What Anaconda saw in Lee was a group of essentially conservative businessmen, linked by family and professional bonds and with a record of investing in their papers and their communities. Lee's story began in Iowa in the 1890s with modest acquisitions by the group's founder, Alfred W. Lee, who had moved west from a Quaker homestead near Philadelphia. By 1959, the chain owned dailies in Iowa, Nebraska, Missouri, Illinois, and Wisconsin as well as three television stations and four radio stations. Lee Loomis, the founder's aging nephew, served as the organization's titular head, but it was Phil Adler to whom Anderson and other Lee publishers reported. Within the newspaper industry, Lee ranked well down the list of newspaper chains, but it enjoyed a reputation for profitability, conservative business management, and the intensely local focus of its newspapers. Debt free, privately held, and with a relatively flexible corporate structure, the chain was ripe, even eager, for expansion.[9]

Politically, the papers offered a mix of Republican and Democratic affiliations, yet generally reflected the conservative, pro-development concerns of Main Street America at the height of the Cold War. Their suspicions of unions, leftists, and intrusive government scored points with Anaconda officials who quietly checked into the reputations and résumés of Lee's top officers. Anderson passed muster with the enthusiastic recommendation of a Madison banker named Jim Hobbins, the winner of the *Wisconsin State Journal*'s editorial endorsement in a recent mayoral race and the nephew of a former Anaconda president. As Anderson would later learn, Lee officials were also being scrutinized by the Montana Power Company, which had the right to approve or reject any prospective purchaser of Anaconda's papers. A Montana Power vice president traveled to Madison to confer with executives of Wisconsin Power and Light, who enjoyed the *Journal*'s support during a hot but unsuccessful campaign for publicly owned utilities. Once again, Anderson passed the test.[10]

Despite such hopeful omens, Anderson's anxiety only increased as

Anaconda's sister entity, the Montana Power Company, retained the right to reject any of the prospective newspaper buyers.

POLK'S GREAT FALLS CITY DIRECTORY (GREAT FALLS, MONT., 1953), AD SECTION P. 65

the months wore on. Lee's bid of approximately $5.7 million—too high, according to Lee accountants—was nevertheless certain to be lower than offers submitted by other suitors, including John Cowles, head of the ownership group behind *Look* magazine, the *Des Moines Register,* the *Minneapolis Star,* and other media properties. On his first visit to Anaconda's New York offices, Cowles reportedly offered Parkinson a $5-million check as a "down payment" for the company's Billings and Missoula papers alone. Other interested parties included the Ridder Corporation, soon to become part of the powerful Knight-Ridder newspaper chain, owners of New York's *Journal of Commerce,* St. Paul's *Pioneer Press,* the *San Jose Mercury News,* and other papers. The list also included the Scripps League chain of California, an offshoot of the Scripps-Howard empire and owner of numerous small western papers; the Shearman Newspaper Corporation, publishers of small dailies in

Louisiana and New Mexico; and Federated Newspapers, publishers of daily papers in Michigan and Indiana and the chain Anderson considered Lee's closest rival in the competition. Among interested individuals was U.S. Secretary of the Interior Fred Seaton, a Nebraska newspaper publisher and broadcaster, who prudently decided that a deal between the nation's chief public lands manager and one of its largest mining companies might be viewed as a conflict of interest.[11]

Yet Lee offered advantages. Unlike other suitors, Lee was willing to buy all of Anaconda's newspapers—and Lee had no partners with which it might split the properties. From the outset, Anaconda executives made clear their intention to sell the papers as a package, thus simplifying the transaction and their disengagement. In the end, few bidders promised honor Anaconda's condition, and Lee itself rebuffed offers from publishers interested in buying individual newspapers or acting as silent partners in order to divide the papers later on.[12]

Lee's primary edge, however, may well have been Don Anderson himself. Tall, distinguished looking, and impeccably groomed, Anderson was also articulate, engaging, persuasive, and unusually perceptive in his judgments of character and situations—in short, a natural diplomat. Raised in a barely settled West, steeled in the army during World War I, and polished at the University of Wisconsin, Anderson was as comfortable in the scotch-and-leather world of gentlemen's clubs as he was around a wilderness campfire. Those traits, enhanced by an easy wit, propelled him quickly through the ranks of the *Wisconsin State Journal,* which he joined in 1923 as a fifteen-dollar-a-week humor columnist. Within four years, he was promoted to managing editor. Impressed with his managerial talent, Anderson was shifted to the *Journal*'s business side, and by 1933 he was made the paper's associate publisher. By 1942, he was named publisher, a title he would hold until his retirement twenty-six years later.[13]

Anderson's personality and well-rounded understanding of the newspaper business obviously impressed Anaconda's executives, but his knowledge of Montana gave Lee a distinct edge. Anderson knew Montana's tangled history and politics; as a youth he had campaigned for Senator Thomas Walsh and circulated nominating petitions for Tom Stout, the former congressman and Lewistown publisher now hammering out editorials for the *Billings Gazette.* Anderson also understood the contempt many Montanans held for the Anaconda Company; his own father-in-law, former Big Timber *Weekly Express* publisher Walter Aitken, counted himself among Anaconda's early critics. He also understood their suspicions of the copper press and how that suspicion had eroded its usefulness to the company as well as the public.

In short, Anderson understood Anaconda's eagerness to sell its toothless, outdated newspapers. Compared with their fiery past, the copper dailies in recent years "have not been venal, only dull," Anderson confided to a friend. In their "splendid isolation," most Montana readers and advertisers had no idea of just how bland the papers had become. "It's a brand of journalism circa 1915," he added. "They even refused to take a stand on the weather. In fact it was so anemic that even the company which owned these newspapers suffered."[14] Then and later, Anderson blamed the papers' ills on their owners' principal identification as miners, lawyers, and accountants, a matter of fact and perception the papers' editors could never overcome. Anderson also speculated that the "time, attention and executive thought" required to run such a relatively small subsidiary had ultimately proved too great a distraction for the company.[15]

As the weeks wore on, Anderson and Adler remained hopeful, but there was still the question of a quid pro quo, and both expected that Anaconda would somehow link the sale to a guarantee of favorable press coverage. Yet to Anderson's continued surprise, the issue never surfaced in any of his conversations with Anaconda officials leading up to the company's decision in late May to accept Lee's bid. Summoned to New York to go over the details, Lee's team arrived in a state of high excitement. As the lawyers for both sides prepared a final draft of an agreement, Anderson asked Anaconda's C. Jay Parkinson to read the announcement Anderson intended to make if the sale went through. As Anderson would later recall, Parkinson read the announcement carefully, then asked if Anderson would mind a suggestion:

> "Why don't you put in there a line to the effect that there are no strings attached to the sale." I asked him if he really meant that, and he replied by asking me what I meant. I said, "Okay, three weeks from today a high executive of the Anaconda Company will be arrested for drunken driving on the streets of Butte. The next morning

the gentleman's picture and a story will be on the front page of the *Montana Standard*."

The vice president threw back his head and laughed and said, "Anybody who is fool enough to do that ought to have his picture on the front page."[16]

With that, Anderson knew the sale was above board. He confessed that he had expected otherwise. "No, there are no strings," Parkinson reiterated. "We only expect to be treated as fairly as you would treat any other business or industry."[17]

Beyond its cash and promissory notes, Lee offered Anaconda assurances that it would publish good papers, that it would treat the company as it treated Montana's other industries, and that it would not immediately sell any of the former Anaconda papers to recoup its costs in the sale. It also agreed to continue the company's employee benefit plans and cover the retirement costs of some employees caught in the transition. Lee's executives also agreed there would be no wholesale changes in the papers' staffs and that it would rebuild the papers from within, a strategy based as much on Lee's limited pool of managerial talent as its aim to minimize the disruption to the Montana newsrooms and communities they served.[18]

With that, only the formalities remained. Once Anaconda's bankers had received Lee's first installment on the purchase price, the new owners were free to take possession and announce that Montana's copper press was finally a relic of history. As lawyers and accountants prepared a final agreement for signatures, Anaconda executives invited Lee officials for lunch at Manhattan's exclusive India Club. Seated next to Anaconda chairman Clyde Weed, Anderson asked why the company had decided to sell. Writing years afterward, Anderson recalled Weed's answer explicitly:

> Coming from Montana you know the old stigma on the Company for owning the press of the state. We got blamed for a lot of things we didn't do, and it hurt our image. A lot of people who had no legitimate gripe against Anaconda nevertheless did not like the idea of a huge mining company owning its press.
>
> Last year I did a tour of the state and asked probably a hundred people what they thought of it. With only one exception, everybody said we should sell them. That's why you are here today.[19]

IN THE WANING DAYS of May, five teams of Lee officials traveled to Montana to meet with the staffs of each Anaconda newspaper and community leaders. To prevent its new employees from reading about the sale in other newspapers, Lee planned no announcement until June 2, though Anderson's instincts warned him the story would surely break before then. *Time Magazine* scored the beat as advance issues of its June 1 issue hit the streets in the last week of May. In Montana, the honors went to the *Montana Kaimin,* the student newspaper in Missoula, which confirmed the news with "official sources" on May 28. Associated Press carried the news a day later.[20]

Among the first to welcome Lee to Montana was the *People's Voice* in Helena. Co-editor Gretchen Billings applauded the sale in hopes that it would bring Montana a "new era," one in which Montanans "might dare dream that we can become an alert and argumentative public, in the interest of local democracy." The "great crime" of the copper press, she added, had not been its philosophy but its absence of one. "Their state Capitol press floated through crucial legislative sessions with editorial columns that kept the fact that the state was grappling with tremendous issues a well-guarded secret."[21]

In an exchange of letters, Anderson expressed his gratitude for the *Voice's* high hopes and goodwill, though he predicted the liberal weekly and Lee's more conservative dailies were bound to clash. Lee's politics did not matter, Billings replied. It was a relief, "to have newspapers in the hands of newspaper people." But she predicted that it would take time for the reality to sink in. When the *Helena Independent Record* published an excerpt from the *Voice's* "welcome" column a week later, Billings's home was flooded with calls from friends worried that she had "sold out" to the company press.[22]

Roughly half of Montana's daily newspaper subscribers got the news on June 2 when the front pages of each former Anaconda paper carried a "hello" from its new owners, who promised to produce the "best possible home town newspapers." Unlike the copper dailies, they wrote, Lee's papers would prosper only if their communities did, and the new owners promised "to do all we can to promote that prosperity." Readers were also told that Lee had a strong record in that regard and that no Lee paper, "once acquired," had ever been sold.[23]

Furthermore, Lee assured its readers, the Montana papers would be staffed largely with people readers already knew, "competent and devoted" editors and reporters already on staff. "We have met many of them," the new owners said, "and we plan to build with this team." Above all, the announcement stressed, each paper would set its own tone and make its own editorial decisions without influence from Lee. Lee's midwestern newspapers were variously Democratic and Republican but mostly independent. The only policy each paper followed was "to help improve its community." Local publishers and editors would call the tunes as they saw them; there would be no shared editorial policy. Moreover, Anderson added, "We serve only one interest—the public. There are no strings attached to the sale of these newspapers. Our only obligations are to our subscribers and our communities." In Butte, an acquaintance of Anderson's got the news not from his newspaper, but from a local radio announcer who was reading his while on the air. "Well, an editorial on the front page of the Standard this morning," the commentator said with surprise. "Somebody has bought the paper. Good! Now maybe we'll get some news."[24]

Had it not been for the novelty of Anaconda's ownership, the sale might have attracted little attention in the national press. As it was, *Editor & Publisher,* the chief journal of the newspaper industry, not only reported the sale, but also blessed the company's decision on its editorial page. Though the Anaconda Company had taken a "more enlightened attitude" toward its Montana papers in recent years, it could never have escaped "the appearance of evil" or the accusations of "a propaganda press" that persisted even though other Montana cities had independently owned papers. Such allegations, the journal added, tarred not only Anaconda's papers, but were "used many times by foreign propagandists as 'proof' that the U.S. is not free but the 'tool of Wall Street'." The sale to a group of "successful and reputable middle-Western newspapers" ensured an end to such talk. As for the company, "Anaconda is to be complimented for getting out of the newspaper business where it never belonged."[25]

Within the region, Portland's *Oregon Statesman* labeled the sale "a victory for good journalism," but it was *Time Magazine*'s June 1 issue that brought news of the papers' impending sale to millions of readers. Reporting that the likely buyer was Lee, the article described the company as "a tidy little empire that is generally pro-Republican but allows its members to play the news as staidly or sensationally as they like." Behind the sale, *Time*'s editors wrote, lay the story of how "iron-fisted" Anaconda had bought its newspapers "to consolidate its hold on Montana" but "came to discover that they were doing the company more harm than good." By the 1920s, the company had toned its papers down and "tried to shape the news more by selecting than slanting or denouncing," by ignoring and downplaying "events harmful" to the company, and by avoiding local controversy. "But Anaconda could not overcome its reputation," the editors wrote. "Suspicious Montana readers automatically looked for the 'copper collar' riveted around every story." As businesses, the magazine added, the copper press had "netted a paltry $183,411" for 1958.[26]

In Montana, the state's independent dailies reacted with a mixture of joy, suspicion, and detachment. The *Great Falls Tribune* acknowledged the sale's historical significance by playing the story on its front page but kept its editorial silence, as did the *Miles City Star*, the *Bozeman Daily Chronicle*, and Kalispell's *Daily Inter Lake*.[27] The exception was the *Lewistown Daily News,* which labeled the sale "historic" and congratulated Anaconda's "enlightened" move. "If anything, the removal of this tremendous club from Anaconda's hands will assure a much easier understanding and better public relations." The state would surely benefit by having its major newspapers in the hands of experienced and reputable newspaper executives such as Lee's, the paper wrote, but it also bemoaned the fact that the papers had been sold to out-of-state interests. "We believe that most Montanans, had they had their way about this decision so vital to them, would have preferred that the newspapers be owned and operated individually and locally." Conceding that higher costs and the trend toward consolidation had made individual ownership of dailies all but obsolete, the *Daily News* nevertheless hoped that Lee would sell some of its Montana papers "in order to permit a great variety and versatility in our State press."[28]

Characteristically, the most colorful comment came from the state's weeklies. Harold Stearns, publisher of the *Harlowton Times* and former president of the state press association, presumably spoke for most in welcoming the change:

> Many is the story of how the Copper Collar encircled the necks of all newspaper operators in Montana, but we can truthfully say that in our 25 years in the business we have never been approached with a bribe by the monied interests (doggone it!). Although we doubt the ACM ever controlled the minds of the people of the Treasure State as the story tellers have it, we are glad to see new ownership of the papers. The Gazette and the rest will be livelier and better competition for the Tribune. These new operators are money makers and won't maintain stodgy papers.[29]

The harshest assessment of Anaconda journalism came from Hamilton's *Western News,* whose editor, Miles Romney Jr., inherited all of his father's suspicions of the company and its press. Anaconda, he wrote, had long used its papers as political weapons to promote and defend its relatively light share of the state's taxes, to escape responsibility for its "silicotic victims," and to retain the "privilege of polluting the waters and air adjacent to its manufacturing works, et cetera." When such tactics became too transparent with time, the papers simply "turned their editorials into competent dissertations on irrelevant matters usually far afield from Montana." Even so, through skillful news editing and through their stable of conservative syndicated columnists, the papers continued to "wield an unholy influence" over public opinion. As for Lee, Romney withheld judgment, though he noted that the papers' personnel would undergo little change and speculated that Anaconda "would not sell its newspapers to an organization with which it could not get along." Still, he concluded, without Anaconda in the newspaper business, there was at least hope for improvement.[30]

Mel Ruder, publisher of the *Hungry Horse News* in Columbia Falls, told his readers that he had been suspicious when rumors of Anaconda's impending sale began circulating earlier in the year. According to the grapevine, Anaconda was insisting on favorable news coverage as a condition of the deal, but Ruder hoped that wasn't true. Enough was enough. For generations, the copper press had muffled public debate, and even cast a cloud over the state's press in general. "The papers became so timid that they didn't even champion issues of special interest to Anaconda," he wrote. Ruder assured Lee's editors that he would be

watching for signs of life and local independence, despite their common ownership. "The important thing is that newspapers take a stand,
and we hope the Lee papers won't all agree on all issues," he concluded.
He saw hope in the front-page editorials Anderson had written to announce the sale. "If such a clause was in the contract, we doubt that
it is now," he wrote. "The most politically conservative newspapermen
wouldn't favor that clause."[31]

While Anderson was generally pleased with the press's reaction to
the sale, he also noted the silence of many Montana newspapers. The
Associated Press's failure, months later, to include the sale among its
top Montana stories of 1959 left him dumbfounded. Yet the unsolicited
response from individual Montanans, he reported, had been "electric."
Congratulatory letters poured in, many from businesses eager to meet
the new owners' needs, but also from individuals eager for change.
Missoula merchant Walter H. McLeod professed to know little about
newspapers but knew enough to consider the *Missoulian* inferior to
regional dailies such as Spokane's *Spokesman-Review,* which did not
hesitate to publish "all of the news" and letters critical of the paper
itself. "I need not tell you how frustrated Montana citizens have been
because our Montana papers have had no policy and published little
information that was helpful, particularly when it came to politics and
issues," he wrote.[32]

Lee's post-sale correspondence also included unsolicited advice concerning the organization's future as Montana publishers. Frustrated
with his hometown paper, historian Merrill G. Burlingame suggested
that Lee buy the *Bozeman Daily Chronicle* too. Others offered to light-
en Lee's burden by buying individual papers. John Cowles, head of
Cowles Media, congratulated Lee Loomis, Lee's president, on the sale
but also expressed interest in purchasing the *Billings Gazette,* suggesting
that from a public-relations standpoint it "might not be wise for any single outfit to continue publishing in as many different cities as Anaconda
was." Despite Anaconda's insistence on selling its papers as a package,
Cowles claimed to have assurances from company executives that they
would not object to Lee selling "one or two of the papers to us." In
response, Loomis wrote that Lee had carefully considered the question
of owning multiple papers in Montana but politely declined Cowles's

offer, insisting that Lee remained "under some obligation to operate all of the papers for some time."[33]

The most vehement complaint against Lee's purchase came from Livingston, where *Park County News* publisher Fred Martin had tried to get Lee to sell him the *Livingston Enterprise* in the waning days before the sale was announced. A former *Butte Daily Post* and *Great Falls Tribune* newsman who had also served as Republican Governor J. Hugo Aronson's executive secretary, Martin wrote both Parkinson and Anderson about a possible deal for the *Enterprise,* a request Anderson considered presumptuous. When Parkinson politely brushed aside Martin's request for a meeting "at this time," Martin took it to mean a future deal was still possible.[34]

Throughout the final days of May, Martin peppered Anderson with letters and phone calls. Anderson finally promised that if Lee were to acquire the *Enterprise,* and if it decided someday to sell the paper, Martin would have first shot at making an offer. But when Martin finally learned the terms of the sale, and Lee's decision to keep the *Enterprise,* his anger boiled over. In a letter to Parkinson, Martin complained that he had been "conveniently dangled by you both as a sucker." The next day, Martin vented his frustration publicly in a front-page editorial. For more than half a century, he wrote, Montana journalists and others had "dreamed of a day when there would be a 'free daily press' in Montana, one without 'company' domination with local direction and management and dedicated to what was best for the state and local community." However, when the day finally arrived, Montanans had been all but excluded in the sale to an "out-of-state concern." Martin charged Anaconda with stacking the deck against Montana buyers. "We believe in a free press, but with equality for the little guys as well as the big chains and bigger corporations," he wrote. "In the present case, the only way a fellow could be considered was for him to own an out-of-state newspaper chain. Every effort by Montanans seemingly got no consideration."[35]

Lee's ownership of so many of Montana's major dailies would remain a sensitive issue. Writing for *Journalism Quarterly* ten months after the sale, University of Oregon historian Richard Ruetten cataloged the sins of the copper press and acknowledged the sale's significance, but also noted that Anaconda's dailies had effectively "substituted one form of absentee control for another." In a lengthy private response, Anderson agreed with Ruetten that local ownership of the press was preferable, but costs had long put daily journalism beyond the reach of most individuals. If there was an acceptable alternative to group ownership, Anderson confessed he didn't know what it was. "There was not in Montana enough available investment capital with a newspaper background to purchase the Anaconda properties," Anderson wrote. "Certain business and political groups made bids for individual papers, but I think you will agree that would have traded one undesirable type of ownership for another."[36]

Occasional complaints that Lee's "Iowa carpetbaggers" were interested only in milking the profits of their Montana papers—a criticism rooted in the state's experience with Anaconda—would continue to dog Lee. For Anderson, the answer could only come with time, talent, and a demonstrated commitment to community service. The key lay in the ability and willingness of longtime Anaconda employees to embrace the change, a concern of both Anderson's and Lee's skeptics. When the editor of Helena's *Independent Record* asked what Lee expected him to do now, Anderson had simply replied, "Start publishing a newspaper." At every opportunity, Anderson assured his Montana newsrooms that the copper collar was gone; they were free to follow the news wherever it might lead, free to shape their editorial judgments according to their perceptions of the community's needs. Lee's corporate officials would provide advice and expertise, but editorial decisions would be made locally.[37]

After years of Anaconda's unwritten strictures and professional indifference, some found the prospect daunting; others were simply suspicious. In Billings, the paper's editorial writer cautiously requested a list of topics Lee considered unsafe for public discussion. His frustration at being told there would be no such list spoke volumes; privately Anderson wrote that any editorial writer who needed such a list had no business writing editorials. In Butte, Anderson stopped at the desk of the *Montana Standard*'s veteran editorial writer, George McVey, for a get-acquainted chat. To Anderson's shock, the man immediately offered to quit. When asked why, McVey fought back tears and said: "I have been sitting in this office for more than 20 years doing my work. In all that time no one has ever come in to tell me it was good, bad, indifferent. I can't take it any longer." Anderson promised plenty of professional feedback and urged McVey to stay on.[38]

Anderson observed a more heartening response from rank-and-file reporters and subeditors who had chaffed at the papers' timidity and reputation. Many found Anderson's enthusiasm and talk of professionalism infectious. "It was just like freeing men from slavery," Anderson wrote a friend only days after the sale's announcement. He had witnessed the results, however modest, in Butte on Lee's first day as the *Montana Standard*'s new owner. Negotiators for Anaconda and the city's unionized metal workers were scheduled to meet that day to begin talks on a new contract, and Anderson watched as *Montana Standard* editors prepared to cover the story—a routine assignment almost anywhere but Butte. "It practically set the town on fire because it was the first time in recorded history that this event had ever been recorded," Anderson would later write a friend. "I was in the Montana Standard office that night, working out of sight in a dark corner, when the little reporter came dashing in from covering the event. He slapped a colleague on the back and said: "By God, Bill, at last we are newspapermen, not company whores.""[39]

WHAT DIFFERENCE DID the change of ownership make?

Ruth Towe, a Montana graduate student who compared the last year of Anaconda journalism to the first three years of Lee's ownership, found substantial changes. The papers seemed livelier, the result of editors' willingness to experiment with new typography and modern trends in layout. More and better photojournalism, another weakness of the Anaconda papers, contributed to the effect. Meanwhile, Lee executives pushed for fresher syndicated offerings, from comics to columnists, and urged editors to expand their sports and feature sections.[40]

The papers made immediate gains financially. Circulation and advertising grew quickly, and Lee soon had its new Montana properties operating in the black, the result of higher revenues and operational efficiencies. In Butte, Lee discontinued the afternoon *Butte Daily Post*, a Mining City mainstay since its creation from the bones of the old Butte *Inter Mountain* in 1913, and merged its operations with the morning *Montana Standard*, reducing the city to one daily newspaper for the first time in almost eighty years. Missoula's afternoon *Sentinel*, established in 1911 as a company-backed challenge to Joseph Dixon's *Missoulian*, would also soon get the axe, as would the *Billings Gazette*'s afternoon edition, victims of readers' and advertisers' growing preference for morning newspapers. Lee executives were keen to invest in new production technologies and, after a series of hard-fought battles, gained effective control of their presses and production shops from the powerful printers' unions, even in Butte.

In its newsrooms, Lee improved salaries, making it clear in the process and through promotions that merit mattered more than seniority. A few old Anaconda hands retired or were eased into it, but most of the papers' employees stayed on. Lee reshuffled management between the Montana papers to encourage innovation, yet with only one exception, in Missoula, the top jobs at Anaconda's former papers remained in the hands of former company journalists, men who exercised their new freedom cautiously, too cautiously at times for Anderson, who prodded them to make the papers more distinct and vital.[41]

Editorially, Towe found Lee's Montana papers surprisingly conservative, a disappointment to Montana's liberals though the Lee editors' views on national and international affairs tended to reflect the Cold War suspicions and mainstream conservatism of the Eisenhower years. Conservative syndicated columnists Westbrook Pegler and George Sokolsky dominated the op-ed spaces, though moderates such as Drew Pearson and Marquis Childs made inroads.[42]

One crucial difference on the editorial page was the increase in the number of local editorials devoted to state and local matters, and to the astonishment of many observers, the papers sometimes disagreed. The regular letters-to-the-editor columns that suddenly appeared in most of the papers marked perhaps the more important change of all. Letters, a staple of newspapers elsewhere, had no place in the Fairmont press policy that encouraged editors to avoid local and statewide controversies. Of Anaconda's papers, only the *Missoulian* had tolerated occasional letters but only those that skirted local squabbles and even then writers' identities were usually masked by pseudonyms or initials. The new letters columns were instant hits; local readers jumped at the chance to spout off on an array of topics that included criticism of the Lee papers themselves.[43]

The most significant change, however, was the freedom the former Anaconda journalists found to cover the news. Decades of self-censorship and the company's penny pinching made them hesitant at first, but gradually, and with the encouragement of Anderson and others, the papers found their news legs. For Lloyd Schermer, son-in-law of top Lee executive Phil Adler and the *Missoulian*'s new general manager, the change came two and half months after the sale, on August 17, 1959, when a major earthquake killed twenty-eight

For the most part, Lee retained the editors and reporters already on staff at the former Anaconda dailies. One exception occurred in Missoula, where Lloyd Schermer took over as the Missoulian's *publisher. Schermer quickly encouraged reporters to use their freedom to cover news, including the August 1959 earthquake. He is pictured here with his wife Betty Adler Schermer and, on the left, Don Anderson.*

WILBUR CROSS, *LEE'S LEGACY OF LEADERSHIP: THE HISTORY OF LEE ENTERPRISES, INC.* (N.P., 1990), P. 121

people near Yellowstone National Park. The story was national news, yet the *Missoulian* editors were content to wait for wire services reports. Flabbergasted, Schermer jump-started the coverage himself and immediately approved the use of a chartered plane to fly newsmen to the scene. More important, he let staffers know the *Missoulian's* late start on the story had been an embarrassment.[44]

Stories reflecting political controversies or criticism of public officials began seeping into the daily news coverage, and in 1960 Lee took a crucial leap in that effort by creating the Lee State Bureau, which it charged with providing its papers with competitive coverage of state government, coverage the copper press had for decades conceded to Associated Press reports, which its editors carefully vetted. Overall, state legislative coverage was so poor that a nationwide survey of state legislators, conducted in 1957 by *Quill* magazine, ranked Montana's legislative news coverage forty-seventh among the forty-eight states. Only Delaware fared worse. Anderson attacked the problem immediately, knowing that Lee's credibility in political coverage hinged on finding "a fast-moving reporter who knows how to dig out the news both in the halls of legislation and in the entertainment parlors of the Placer Hotel and who isn't afraid to spit in the eye of the labor crowd, the Farmers Union, or the Montana Power lobby." The upshot was more complete and livelier coverage. In comparing the *Missoulian's* coverage of the first fifteen days of the 1959 legislative session—the last it had covered as an Anaconda paper—with its coverage of the same period during the 1961 session, Towe counted almost twice as many stories, a large percentage of which had been staff produced or written by a special Lee correspondent.[45]

To Anderson's frustration, the papers were slower to improve local coverage, but with time, turnover, and Lee's commitment to outside professional training—something Anaconda's isolated journalists had never enjoyed—the work improved. Anderson and Strand Hilleboe, Lee's publisher in Billings, knew the paper's municipal reporting had arrived when the city's principal business leaders, long used to running the city with little comment from the press or public, began complaining that the *Gazette's* scrutiny was creating public controversies where none had previously existed. The fact that the complainers were also major advertisers was beside the point, Anderson wrote the paper's editor. Someday, he wrote, they would realize that open debate was a sign of healthy civic life. "I'd a lot rather live in a town where the city council or the chamber of commerce fights openly about important issues, than one where there are star chamber sessions where all matters are settled."[46]

Investigative reporting, nonexistent beyond the copper press's various one-sided campaigns against Anaconda's political enemies, made a cautious debut in the Lee papers as well. In Butte, the *Montana Standard* scored a coup on April 5, 1961, when it kicked off reporter Lewis Poole's four-day series on the systematic negligence of Butte's court system. Over the years, hundreds of Silver Bow County criminals had escaped jail and fines by simply appealing their misdemeanor convictions to higher court officials who eventually dropped them without consideration. Among the cases Poole carefully documented was that of a man convicted of sexually molesting a nine-year-old girl. By simply requesting an appeal, the suspect dodged a ninety-day jail sentence and three-hundred-dollar fine. In another example, Poole witnessed the conviction of a man on drunken driving charges. When the judge read his sentence, the man appeared confused and briefly despondent then brightened when he remembered the crumpled piece of paper in his pocket that carried the official ten-word request for an appeal.[47]

Poole's series, "Ten Magic Words," prompted an official investigation and reforms before its four-day run was over. Readers' filled the *Montana Standard*'s letters columns with their outrage, and the papers followed its reporting with a ringing editorial demanding additional reforms. Anderson monitored the coverage closely from Wisconsin and wrote the *Standard*'s publisher to offer his congratulations on a stellar job of community journalism. Butte was making the change to a modern city. "Seems to me the Standard has started to point the way and that's something we can be proud of," he wrote.[48]

Other papers made similar gains. The *Missoulian* broke important journalistic ground as it crusaded for a sewage treatment plant and an additional bridge over the Clark Fork River. In Billings, the *Gazette* campaigned for higher education and fences around the open irrigation ditches that claimed the lives of area children with horrible frequency. Meanwhile, academic studies of the political campaigns of 1960 and

1962 found the Lee papers' political coverage generally fair. Left-hand-ed testaments to the new vitality of the papers' local report came from readers who complained that local coverage was encroaching on space traditionally devoted to national and world news.[49]

Anderson's cheerleading had much to do with the changes. It en-gendered a sense of enterprise, professionalism, and commitment to readers that many of the papers' employees clearly found inspiring and perhaps redemptive. It was certainly infectious, *Billings Gazette* colum-nist Addison Bragg wrote years later: "All I can say is that once he came out here . . . a whole lot of fresh air started blowing through the city rooms in Helena, Livingston, Butte, Missoula, and Billings. . . . We grew in it, we moved in it—and we all, as a profession, profited by it."[50]

THE REAL TEST of the Lee papers' independence, of course, lay in their coverage of the Anaconda Company. The *Montana Standard* faced the question immediately after the sale as talks between company and met-al workers collapsed into a bitter six-month strike. The paper's straight-forward and balanced coverage, though hardly in-depth, betrayed no apparent bias, much to the disappointment of Butte union leaders who had clearly expected favorable treatment and who wondered whether the sale to Lee had truly been without strings. Among other things, they accused the paper's news editors of refusing to run the union's press releases verbatim, and they blanched when *Standard* editorials urged both the unions and the company to reach a quick settlement for the community's sake. However, such criticism lost much of its steam when the paper allowed its publication in the *Standard*'s new letters-to-the-editor column. Even the paper's harshest critics had to admit that after nearly four decades, in which strikes and shutdowns had received scant attention in the copper press, the coverage was as revolutionary as the sudden appearance of front-page articles on the deaths of workers killed in mine accidents.[51]

Anaconda officials seemed generally pleased with the coverage throughout the strike. Both Anderson and Lee president Phil Adler kept in regular touch with Anaconda officials in New York and Butte, and their private correspondence reflected a shared concern for the walkout's effect on both enterprises. Yet Lee officials carefully avoided any commentary on the relative merits of either Anaconda's or the unions' positions in the controversy. In the strike's final days, Ed Renouard, Anaconda's vice president for operations, wrote Adler to express his general appreciation for the paper's treatment. "I can't always agree with everything you do, but for the first time in history the public knows what's going on," he wrote, "and for the first time the public is beginning to understand the Company's view."[52] *Montana Standard* reporters echoed the sentiment. Long used to one-sided, anti-company diatribes in Butte bars and barbershops, they now reported an equally vigorous debate on the union's demands as well.[53]

In the end, the paper's evenhanded strike coverage earned the applause and respect of company officials and the union's chief negotiator, which led Anderson to believe the *Standard*'s news strategy had been nearly on target. "The only thing which would have convinced me more effectively would have been for both to tell us that we were lousy," he wrote managing editor Tom Mooney. When negotiators finally struck a deal, the *Standard* rustled up some green newsprint and a set of large, antique wooden type and hit the streets with an old-time "extra." Delighted with such enterprise, Anderson ordered Mooney to treat the news staff to a steak dinner at Butte's Finlen Hotel and send him the bill.[54]

Ironically, the strike's end also precipitated Lee's first head-on collision with the company when Anaconda officials prepared for the resumption of mining and smelting operations by flushing its neglected settling ponds, which contained millions of gallons of wastewater. The surge, laden with heavy metals including copper and arsenic, washed down the Clark Fork River's long valley, killing fish and other aquatic life for nearly 120 river miles before dumping much of its toxic sediment behind Montana Power Company's Milltown Dam near Missoula.[55]

Federal officials would eventually designate the corridor a federal Superfund site, but in 1960 it was the *Missoulian*'s Lloyd Schermer who first raised the environmental issue in the press with a fiery editorial holding Anaconda directly responsible for the pollution that had literally turned the river red. Throughout his tenure in Missoula, Schermer encouraged groundbreaking environmental investigations that covered

not only water pollution, but air quality and forestry practices. The coverage inevitably led to Anaconda's door or those of its subsidiaries. The *Missoulian's* reporting broke ground for other Lee papers as well. In Butte, the *Montana Standard* also turned its attention to water pollution, while in Billings the *Gazette* examined the environmental conse-

When they sold the newspapers, Anaconda officials asked for no special treatment for the company—only the same fair coverage that would be afforded any other business. Lee's first head-on collision with Anaconda came in 1960 when the Missoulian *fired off an editorial holding Anaconda directly responsible for the release of pollution that literally turned the Clark Fork River red. The water was too turbid to observe wild fish, so Montana Fish and Game fishery biologists (above) placed fish in live cages to observe their survival rate. All died within sixty-seven hours.*

ARTHUR N. WHITNEY, "A PRELIMINARY REPORT OF FISHERY INVESTIGATIONS ON THE CLARK FORK RIVER DURING MARCH, 1960," MONTANA FISH AND GAME, HELENA, APPENDIX 2

quences of eastern Montana's coal industry—namely the effects of strip mining and power plants on the region's landscape, water supply, and air quality—raising the ire of Montana Power Company officials, who complained bitterly about the press's sudden interest in "ecology" as well as the coverage afforded successful U.S. Senate hopeful Lee Metcalf, a vigorous critic of private utilities.[56]

Anderson and Adler, who continued to cultivate professional and personal relationships with Anaconda and Montana Power executives, deflected much of the criticism, offering their occasional sympathies but upholding their editors' right to cover the news as they saw fit. Schermer, who flew to Lee's Davenport, Iowa, headquarters on the day his paper first scolded Anaconda for pollution, arrived to find Adler curious about the uproar from Montana. "What in the world did you put in your paper before you left?" Adler asked. "Something about Anaconda?" Schermer replied that the company had polluted the river. "Were your facts right?"

Adler asked. "Hell, yes," Schermer said. Satisfied, Adler dropped the subject.[57]

By the 1970s, Anaconda and Montana Power were complaining regularly about their treatment at the hands of their former Montana dailies. C. Jay Parkinson, now chairman of Anaconda, politely registered his frustration to Lee's Adler, expressing his concern "about the fact that the papers are not always giving a balanced and fairhanded picture concerning ecological problems and their practical solutions, nor in the field of trying to improve the political and industrial climate to promote industrial enterprise."[58]

Anderson, who kept the lines to Montana's industrial leaders open with frequent letters, social invitations, and occasional gifts of Wisconsin cheese, bore the brunt of their increasing displeasure. Though he occasionally sympathized with their politics and their frustration with critics such as U.S. Senator Lee Metcalf, Hamilton's *Western News*, and the *People's Voice,* Anderson steadfastly rejected their demands that he exert his influence over the Montana papers' news columns or direct their political endorsements, which had already begun to vary from paper to paper. Montana Power Company President John E. Corette objected specifically to the ink Lee's papers were giving Metcalf and urged Anderson to do something about it. "I realize that you may not want to walk into a newspaper and give specific instructions of 'do this' and 'don't do that' but I thought if you had the background which this letter gives you that in your policy discussions with your editors and publishers you may be able to give them some basic philosophies."[59]

Instead, Anderson used the opportunity to instruct the utility's president that the press was no longer at his beck and call. Furthermore, if the company had complaints with Lee's Montana editors, it should make them directly. In Montana's new court of public opinion, the companies would have to make their case by persuasion and explanation.[60]

For industrialists long accustomed to using Montana's press as a public-relations department, such wholesome advice was bound to fall flat. As Lee's reporters and editors continued to stretch the boundaries of their newfound independence, Anaconda and Montana Power executives would increasingly echo the sentiments of a "gravely concerned" Corette, who wrote Anderson seven years later to complain

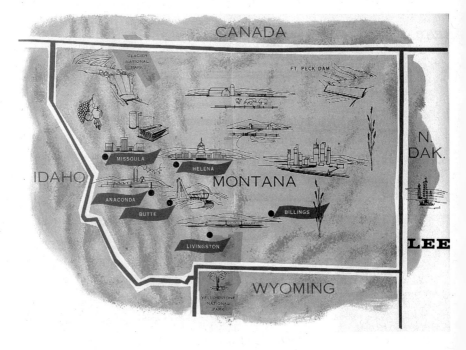

Lee's newspapers continued their professional transformation, spurred by infusions of new talent and technology. By the 1980s, Lee's Montana dailies enjoyed the industry's respect for quality and coverage. With the exception of its purchase of a small daily in Hamilton and its sale of the Livingston Enterprise, *Lee's Montana lineup today remains much the same as it did in 1960.*

THE LEE GROUP: MID-AMERICA TO THE MOUNTAINS (DAVENPORT, IOWA, 1960), P. 70

that the policies of "some of your newspapers" were "more detrimental to the future economic growth than anything that has appeared here in my lifetime."[61]

Whatever the truth of such charges, they were proof that Montana journalism had indeed entered a new era.

The lasting legacy of the copper press remains the concentrated ownership of Montana's major dailies that began in the era of the copper kings. Here editor Louis M. Thayer (left) and an unidentified man pose in the office of the Helena Independent, *which came under Anaconda's control in the 1930s.*

EPILOGUE

WHAT, ULTIMATELY, WERE the consequences of Anaconda journalism? For the company, the benefits were mixed at best. The copper press gave Anaconda a voice in the seminal political battles of early statehood, but its persuasive power proved limited. From a public-relations standpoint, it functioned most effectively as a means of news suppression, but such tactics only provoked suspicion and further fueled a long-running anti-corporate response that proved remarkably resilient. Unable to speak, and damned by its own silence, the copper press exhausted its usefulness long before Anaconda sold the papers.

The consequences for democracy, though hard to measure, seem particularly harsh, especially during World War I and throughout the 1920s, and the silences of the copper press's final thirty years surely stifled public debate across a broad array of political and economic issues. Still, the relative successes of early Progressives and of Montana's farm-labor alliance decades later illustrates that Montanans could and did find alterative views in the weekly press, in some small dailies, in radio broadcasts, in union and association newsletters, and in a string of boldly anti-corporate newspapers culminating in the *People's Voice.* Yet in terms of volume, reach, and frequency, such outlets could hardly compete with a daily press, and one can only wonder how a more vigorous debate would have colored the state's history.

More than anything, Anaconda's sale of its newspapers reflected Montana's dwindling importance in the company's grand scheme. Its venture into aluminum production solidified its stance as the world's largest nonferrous mining company, with operations stretching from Australia to New York and from Latin America to Butte, but the company's real strength lay in its Chilean mines, where labor was cheap and profits enormous. By the late 1960s, foreign operations accounted for roughly three of every four dollars in company revenues, but these operations also posed greater risks. Chile's nationalization of Anaconda's mines, begun in 1969 and completed under Salvador Allende's leftist government in 1971, sent the company into a fatal tailspin. Bankers and accountants toppled miners and lawyers from the company's leadership and struggled to cut costs and fend off the demands of labor and a growing environmental movement. It was all too much. By 1977, the company was all but dead, its carcass chopped up and picked clean.[1]

Montanans watched it all—strikes, shutdowns, layoffs—with a mixture of fascination and dread. The company unloaded its forest lands and its timber mills, closed its smelters, sold its mines, and cut its interlocking ties to the Montana Power Company, which filled a part of the economic void with its expansion into coal mining and power generation. As the state's heavy industry dwindled, so did the power of the "Montana Twins." The hired-gun editors were long gone, replaced by the softer sell of modern public relations and "feel good" advertising, and the company's critics found avenues for expression in a more sympathetic press.

The "Twins" simply didn't understand the depth of Montanans' feelings, especially about the environment, Lee publisher Don Anderson wrote after Anaconda officials protested Lee's coverage in 1971. "And it isn't just the oddballs who are raising hell," he said. "The real muscle in the movement to keep Montana clean comes from citizens as solid and as conservative as you or I." The push for reform applied to Montana's politics too, and that same year saw the closing of the company's notorious "watering holes" for state lawmakers in Helena's Placer Hotel. In 1972, by thin margin, Montanans adopted a progressive new state constitution that aimed to put the rights of individuals on a par with those of industry. The specter of Montana's experience with Anaconda hung over the debate.[2]

Lee's Montana newspapers, which recorded the changes, would slowly continue their professional transformation, guided by Anderson and spurred by the infusion of new talent. The creation of the Lee State Bureau in 1960 offered Montanans a broader view of state government and fostered a healthy competition for statehouse news with the *Great Falls Tribune*. Over their first two decades, the papers investigated corruption and mismanagement in government and demonstrated a heightened interest in the environmental costs of decades of mining, smelting, and timber cutting. Their editorial endorsements would prove crucial to passage of the new state constitution. Technologically, the papers continued to improve, prodded by managers who encouraged innovation and wrested control from production unions resistant to change. By the 1980s, Lee's Montana dailies enjoyed the industry's respect for quality despite their remoteness and relatively small circulations, and in that sense, they were true descendents of Marcus Daly's *Anaconda Standard* and William A. Clark's *Butte Miner*. What's more, Lee's talent for economy ensured that the papers made money.[3]

But Lee's ownership of so many newspapers in such a small state would also ensure occasional sightings of old ghosts. Lee's insistence on the autonomy of each paper kept fears of coordinated editorial campaigns at bay, but the temptation would always be there. The retirements of Don Anderson and Lee president Phil Adler, coupled with Lee's decision to take its stock public, brought more centralization of the chain's operation—and at least one attempt to marshal the papers' political endorsements—but Montana publishers such as the *Billings Gazette*'s Strand Hilleboe and the *Missoulian*'s Lloyd Schermer fought to keep the news operations free. Lee's executives were indeed the solid, conservative businessmen that Anaconda and Montana Power executives had hoped they would be, but they were hardly reactionaries. Lee's Montana papers would have their critics, from within and without, but they would be hard pressed to demonstrate a pattern of consistent favoritism to any specific political or commercial interests beyond their own.[4]

Yet the ghost took other shapes as well. Lee's papers would also be measured against those of the copper kings, who produced newspapers better in many respects than their communities could support, and also against the penury and neglect that marked the copper press's final decades. Today, Lee's Montana dailies represent only a fraction of the corporation's holdings. Their leaders keep their eye firmly on the bottom line, on industry trends, and on the stock price. The papers

Could Anaconda-style journalism rise again? Given modern Montana's lack of a dominant corporate entity and potential for competition for news from television, weeklies such as the Shelby Promoter, *and even the Internet, it seems unlikely. These agreeable-looking lads hawked the weekly* Shelby Promoter *in March 1966.*

MONTANA HISTORICAL SOCIETY PHOTOGRAPH ARCHIVES, HELENA

themselves, located mainly in small to mid-sized markets, retain their intensely local flavor. Their quality hinges largely on the talents and skills of their staffs, though critics worry that cost cutting has taken its toll on aggressive and comprehensive reporting. That's a common criticism throughout an industry struggling to meet the challenges posed by declining readership, an increasingly fragmented media market, and the growing power of the Internet. Even so, the ambivalence of the copper press's final years may offer fresh lessons.[5]

The lasting legacy of the copper press remains the concentrated ownership of Montana's major dailies. Lee would have owned them all had *Great Falls Tribune* publisher Alex Warden not brushed aside a Lee feeler in 1965, offering the same reason he had given six years earlier to an emissary from the Anaconda Company: Montana would be best served by diverse ownership. Warden's paper eventually sold to Lee's old rival, the Cowles chain, and then to the nation's largest newspaper group, Gannett. With the exception of its purchase of a small daily in Hamilton and its sale of the *Livingston Enterprise,* Lee's Montana lineup remains much the same as it did in 1960, though its regional prominence has grown with its acquisition of key dailies in Idaho, Wyoming, and the Dakotas.

Could Anaconda-style journalism rise again? Given modern Montana's lack of a dominant corporate entity and potential for competition for news from television, alternative weeklies, and the Internet, it seems unlikely. Yet the concentrated ownership of Montana's major news providers—in both newspapers and in broadcasting—and the national trend toward media consolidation does leave the state open to sudden changes that could bring sweeping changes to local and state news coverage over large swaths of the state. Montana's vast distances, Lee's policy of local editorial autonomy, and competition from local broadcast news outlets and alternative weeklies have muted complaints of concentrated ownership, but the sensitivity remains. So does the possibility of a sale to distant owners with a much different philosophy—and with commercial interests other than providing news. In 1959, Lee officials boasted that they had never sold a newspaper once they acquired it. They cannot make the claim today.

Whatever the future, the story of Anaconda journalism, with its harsh consequences for democracy, for the diversity of expression, and for credibility of both the news media and industry, still resonates today.

NOTES

PREFACE AND ACKNOWLEDGMENTS

1. Will Irwin, "The American Newspaper, Part XI: 'Our Kind of People,'" *Collier's*, June 17, 1911, 17.

2. Will Irwin, "The American Newspaper, Part XII: 'The Foe From Within,'" *Collier's*, July 1, 1911, 18.

3. Michael P. Malone, *The Battle for Butte: Mining and Politics on the Northern Frontier, 1864–1906* (Seattle: University of Washington Press, 1981), 213.

INTRODUCTION

1. For accounts of the convention, see *Anaconda (Mont.) Standard*, Sept. 2–7, 1899; *Butte (Mont.) Inter Mountain*, Sept. 4–7, 1899; and Sam Gilluly, *The Press Gang: A Century of Montana Newspapers, 1885–1985* (Helena, Mont.: Montana Press Association, 1985), 34–36.

2. Isaac F. Marcosson, *Anaconda* (New York: Dodd, Mead, 1957), 41–42; *Anaconda (Mont.) Standard*, Sept. 6, 1889; *Butte (Mont.) Inter Mountain*, Sept. 6, 1899; Malone, *Battle for Butte*, 81; Patrick F. Morris, *Anaconda, Montana: Copper Smelting Boom Town on the Western Frontier* (Bethesda, Md.: Swann, 1997), 45–46.

3. *Anaconda (Mont.) Standard*, Sept. 5, 1899.

4. *Butte (Mont.) Inter Mountain*, Sept. 5, 1899.

5. David Nasaw, *The Chief: The Life of William Randolph Hearst* (Boston: Houghton Mifflin, 2001), 96–97; *Anaconda (Mont.) Standard*, Sept. 6, 1899.

6. For an account of Durston's youth, academic career, and early newspaper experience, see John P. Fought, "John Hurst Durston, Editor: The *Anaconda Standard* and the Clark-Daly Feud" (master's thesis, Montana State University, 1959), 8–14.

7. *Butte (Mont.) Inter Mountain*, Sept. 6, 1899.

8. Ibid., Sept. 4, 1899.

9. For background and characterizations of Clark, see Malone, *Battle for Butte*, 13–14, 82–83, 200; *Anaconda (Mont.) Standard*, Sept. 6, 1899; *Butte (Mont.) Inter Mountain*, Sept. 6, 1899; and *Anaconda (Mont.) Standard*, Sept. 7, 1899.

10. *Butte (Mont.) Inter Mountain*, Sept. 7, 1899; *Anaconda (Mont.) Standard*, Sept. 6, 1899.

11. The paper did not last beyond an issue or two and was unnamed, according to Dorothy Johnson's "Montana's First Newspaper," in *A Century of Montana Journalism*, ed. Warren J. Brier and Nathan B. Blumberg (Missoula, Mont.: Mountain Press, 1971), 4–5.

12. *Anaconda (Mont.) Standard*, Sept. 6, 1899.

13. Ibid., Sept. 7, 1899.

14. Ibid.

15. For Daly's personal involvement in the *Standard,* see Charles H. Eggleston's account in the *Anaconda (Mont.) Standard's* fortieth-anniversary issue, Sept. 4, 1929; and the *Butte (Mont.) Inter Mountain,* Sept. 6, 1899.

16. *Anaconda (Mont.) Standard,* Sept. 7, 1899.

17. Gilluly, *Press Gang,* 36.

CHAPTER 1

1. Mills recorded his first meeting with Durston in an article celebrating the *Standard's* tenth anniversary. See *Anaconda (Mont.) Standard,* Sept. 5, 1889.

2. Robert J. Goligoski, "Montana's Pioneer Editor," in Brier and Blumberg, *A Century of Montana Journalism,* 7; Dorothy M. Johnson, "Montana's First Newspaper," ibid., 5–6. Mills's career is outlined in William G. Breitenstein, "A History of Early Journalism in Montana, 1863–1890" (master's thesis, Montana State University, 1915), 7–8; and in Gilluly, *Press Gang,* 27. See also "Montana Newspaper Hall of Fame: Capt. James Hamilton Mills," *Montana Journalism Review* 4 (1961): 34; and *Medicine Lake (Mont.) Wave* circa 1917 or 1918 clipping, copy in the author's possession.

3. Warren J. Brier, "A Newspaper for Montana's Miners," in Brier and Blumberg, *Century of Montana Journalism,* 38–40; Daniel Boorstin, *The Americans: The National Experience* (New York: Random House, 1966), 124.

4. *Virginia City (Mont.) Madisonian,* July 6, 1876.

5. Stanley R. Davison and Dale Tash, "Confederate Backwash in Montana Territory," in *The Montana Past; An Anthology,* ed. Michael P. Malone and Richard B. Roeder (Missoula: University of Montana Press, 1969), 115.

6. Breitenstein, "A History of Early Journalism," 11.

7. Davison and Tash, "Confederate Backwash in Montana Territory," 118, citing the *Helena (Mont.) Herald,* Feb. 28, 1867.

8. Ibid., 117, citing the *Helena (Mont.) Herald,* June 11, 1867.

9. Ibid., 120, citing the *Helena (Mont.) Rocky Mountain Gazette,* July 1, 1870.

10. Breitenstein, "A History of Early Journalism," 12.

11. Gilluly, *Press Gang,* 27.

12. Rex Myers, "Montana's Colorful Press: From Crazy Quilt to Great Gray Blanket," in *Montana and the West: Essays in Honor of K. Ross Toole,* by K. Ross Toole, Rex C. Myers, and Harry W. Fritz (Boulder, Colo.: Pruett, 1984), 76; Gilluly, *Press Gang,* 27.

13. Breitenstein, "A History of Early Journalism," 26, 32.

14. Chauncey Barbour to S. T. Hauser, March 4, 1878, in *Not in Precious Metals Alone: A Manuscript History of Montana* (Helena: Montana Historical Society Press, 1976), 123; Breitenstein, "A History of Early Journalism," 17.

15. *Anaconda (Mont.) Standard,* Sept. 5, 1889; Breitenstein, "A History of Early Journalism," 17.

16. Nasaw, *Chief,* 40; W. A. Swanberg, *Citizen Hearst: A Biography of William Randolph Hearst* (New York: Bantam, 1967), 26.

17. For Daly's acquaintance with Mark Twain, see Marcosson, *Anaconda,* 43. For Daly's newspaper reading habits, see David M. Emmons, *The Butte Irish: Class and Ethnicity in an American Mining Town, 1875–1925* (Urbana: University of Illinois Press, 1989), 21. Daly's relationship with his newspaper is outlined in the *Anaconda (Mont.) Standard,* Sept. 4, 1929.

18. For the beginnings of the Clark-Daly feud, see David M. Emmons, "The Orange and the Green in Montana: A Reconsideration of the Clark-Daly Feud," *Arizona and the West* 28 (Autumn 1986): 225–45; K. Ross Toole, "The Genesis of the Clark-Daly Feud," in *Montana's Past: Selected Essays,* ed. Michael P. Malone and Richard B. Roeder (Missoula: University of Montana, 1973), 284–99; and Malone, *Battle for Butte,* 80–158.

19. *Anaconda (Mont.) Standard,* Sept. 4, 1929; Fought, "John Hurst Durston," 13–16.

20. Carl B. Glasscock, *The War of the Copper Kings: Greed, Power and Politics, the Billion-Dollar Battle for Butte, Montana, the Richest Hill on Earth* (1935; repr., Helena, Mont.: Riverbend, 2002), 94–95; Marcosson, *Anaconda,* 63–64.

21. *Anaconda (Mont.) Standard,* Sept. 4, 1929.

22. Fought, "John Hurst Durston," 14.

23. Ibid., 8–12; Tom Stout, *Montana: Its Story and Biography . . . ,* 3 vols. (Chicago: American Historical Society, 1921), 2:471.

24. Fought, "John Hurst Durston," 12; *Anaconda (Mont.) Standard,* Sept. 4, 1929.

25. Fought, "John Hurst Durston," 13; *Anaconda (Mont.) Standard,* Sept. 4, Nov. 6, 1929.

26. *Anaconda (Mont.) Standard,* Sept. 4, 1889.

27. Ibid.

28. Ibid.

29. Ibid.

30. Ibid.

31. Ibid.

32. Ibid.

33. Fought, "John Hurst Durston," 22, citing the *Anaconda (Mont.) Weekly Review,* Sept. 5, 1889.

34. Ibid., 18, citing the *Butte (Mont.) Inter Mountain* progress edition, Jan. 1891.

35. *Butte (Mont.) Miner,* Sept. 5, 1889.

36. Fought, "John Hurst Durston," 17.

37. *Butte (Mont.) Inter Mountain* progress edition, Jan. 1891.

CHAPTER 2

1. Glasscock, *War of the Copper Kings,* 112; Christopher Powell Connolly, *The Devil Learns to Vote, the Story of Montana* (New York: Covici, Friede, 1938), 102–3; Malone, *Battle for Butte,* 104; H. Minar Shoebotham, *Anaconda: Life of Marcus Daly, the Copper King* (Harrisburg, Pa.: Stackpole, 1956), 138–39.

2. Connolly, *The Devil Learns to Vote,* 103.

3. Fought, "John Hurst Durston," 64, citing the *Anaconda (Mont.) Standard,* Nov. 11, 1894.

4. Ibid., 65, citing the *Anaconda (Mont.) Standard,* Nov. 13, 1894.

5. According to *Standard* lore, Daly originally planned to publish his news-paper in Butte, but Clark's *Butte Miner* and Lee Mantle's Republican *Inter Mountain* held the city's exclusive morning and afternoon Associated Press fran-chises, and no serious daily could afford to be without the nation's premier source of news. K. Ross Toole, "Marcus Daly: A Study of Business in Politics" (master's thesis, Montana State University, 1948), 119.

6. Fought, "John Hurst Durston," 37, citing the *Anaconda (Mont.) Standard,* March 18, 1890.

7. *Butte (Mont.) Inter Mountain* progress edition, Jan. 1891.

8. For Daly's early alliances with Mantle and Butte's Republicans, see Malone, *Battle for Butte,* 94.

9. Fought, "John Hurst Durston," 26–27, citing the *Anaconda (Mont.) Standard,* Sept. 17, 1889.

10. Shoebotham, *Anaconda,* 109; *Anaconda (Mont.) Standard,* Sept. 4, 1929.

11. Donald MacMillan, *Smoke Wars: Anaconda Copper, Montana Air Pollution, and the Courts, 1890–1924* (Helena: Montana Historical Society Press, 2000), 26–31. For the *Montana Standard* reporter's description of the city in the smoke, MacMillan cites *Anaconda (Mont.) Standard,* Nov. 16, 1891. For Butte's death rates from respiratory disease, see MacMillan, *Smoke Wars,* 34.

12. MacMillan, *Smoke Wars,* 38.

13. Ibid., 31–32.

14. Ibid., 32.

15. Ibid., 53–54, citing *Anaconda (Mont.) Standard,* Dec. 8, Feb. 2, 1891.

16. MacMillan, *Smoke Wars,* 79–81, citing the *Anaconda (Mont.) Standard,* Dec. 22, 1891.

17. *Anaconda (Mont.) Standard,* Jan. 1, 1892.

18. Ralph H. Wanamaker, "Eggleston of the *Anaconda Standard*" (master's thesis, University of Montana, 1978), 67; *Anaconda (Mont.) Standard,* Aug. 25, 1892.

19. *Anaconda (Mont.) Standard,* July 31, 1892; *Butte (Mont.) Miner,* Aug. 8, 1892; *Anaconda (Mont.) Standard,* Sept. 30, 1892.

20. Wanamaker, "Eggleston of the *Anaconda Standard,*" 77, citing the *Helena (Mont.) Daily Journal,* Oct. 11, 1892.

21. Ibid., 82, citing the *Anaconda (Mont.) Standard,* Nov. 2, Oct. 6, 1892; Fought, "John Hurst Durston," citing the *Anaconda (Mont.) Standard,* Nov. 4, 1892.

22. *Anaconda (Mont.) Standard,* Nov. 7, 1892; Ellis Waldron and Paul B. Wilson, *Atlas of Montana Elections, 1889–1976* (Missoula: University of Montana, 1978), 15.

23. Malone, *Battle for Butte,* 92–97. For Eggleston's legislative work, see Wanamaker, "Eggleston of the *Anaconda Standard,*" 86; and Forrest L. Foor, "The Senatorial Aspirations of William A. Clark, 1898–1901: A Study in Montana Politics" (PhD diss., University of California, Berkeley, 1941), 60.

24. *Anaconda (Mont.) Standard,* March 2, 1893.

25. Robert F. Karolevitz, *Newspapering in the Old West: A Pictorial History of Journalism and Printing on the Frontier* (Seattle: Superior Pub., 1965), 23; Ralph E. Dyar, *News for an Empire: The Story of the Spokesman-Review of Spokane, Washington, and of the Field It Serves* (Caldwell, Idaho: Caxton, 1952), 138.

26. *Anaconda (Mont.) Standard,* Nov. 9, 1894. The *Standard* reported a profit of $23,940.64 for 1895. Folder 7, box 474, Anaconda Copper Mining Company Records, 1876–1974 (hereafter Anaconda Company Records), MC 169, Montana Historical Society Research Center, Helena (hereafter MHS).

27. Jerry W. Calvert, *The Gibraltar: Socialism and Labor in Butte, Montana, 1895–1920* (Helena: Montana Historical Society Press, 1988), 16; Emmons, *Butte Irish,* 230–31; *Anaconda (Mont.) Standard,* Jan. 8, 1893.

28. *Anaconda (Mont.) Standard,* Sept. 5, 1899.

29. For overviews of the capital fight, see Michael P. Malone, Richard B. Roeder, and William L. Lang, *Montana: A History of Two Centuries,* rev. ed. (Seattle: University of Washington Press, 1991), 213–14; Malone, *Battle for Butte,* 99–105; Connolly, *Devil Learns to Vote,* 102–4; and Glasscock, *War of the Copper Kings,* 99–113.

30. Malone, *Battle for Butte,* 100.

31. Rex C. Myers, "Montana's Negro Newspapers, 1894–1911," *Montana Journalism Review* 16 (1973): 17–18; the *Independent* is quoted from the *Anaconda (Mont.) Standard,* July 1, 1895.

32. Malone, *Battle for Butte,* 100, citing the *Missoula (Mont.) Missoulian,* Oct. 17, 1894, and the *Billings (Mont.) Gazette,* Nov. 10, 1894.

33. *Butte (Mont.) Inter Mountain,* Oct. 6, 1894.

34. *Anaconda (Mont.) Standard,* Oct. 2, 1894.

35. Ibid., Oct. 23, 1894.

36. Charles H. Eggleston, *Helena's Social Supremacy,* pamphlet published during the capital fight, copy in the possession of the University of Montana School of Journalism, Missoula.

37. Ibid.

38. *Butte (Mont.) Miner,* Sept. 26, 1894.

39. Ibid.

40. Ibid., Sept. 26, Oct. 22, Nov. 5, 1894.

41. Malone, Roeder, and Lang, *Montana,* 214; Wanamaker, "Eggleston of the Anaconda Standard," 102, citing the *Anaconda (Mont.) Standard,* July 1, 1894.

42. *Butte (Mont.) Miner,* Oct. 22, 1894.

43. *Anaconda (Mont.) Standard,* Nov. 6, 1894.

44. *Butte (Mont.) Miner,* Nov. 8, 1894.

45. Waldron and Wilson, *Atlas of Montana Elections,* 19.

46. As quoted in the *Butte (Mont.) Miner,* Sept. 29, 1894.

47. Malone, *Battle for Butte,* 105; *Anaconda (Mont.) Standard,* Jan. 20, 1894, Sept. 19, Oct. 22, 24, 1896.

48. *Anaconda (Mont.) Standard,* Sept. 18, 1896, Sept. 5, 1929; Wanamaker, "Eggleston of the Anaconda Standard," 50–59, citing the *Anaconda (Mont.) Standard,* Sept. 18, 1896.

49. Malone, Roeder, and Lang, *Montana,* 217; *Anaconda (Mont.) Standard,* Nov. 2, 1896.

50. Malone, *Battle for Butte,* 108–9; Marcus Daly to M. Donohoe, May 12, 1896, folder 15, box 3, Marcus Daly Papers, 1873–1900, SC 63, MHS, Helena.

51. Wanamaker, "Eggleston of the *Anaconda Standard,*" 162, 166; *Anaconda (Mont.) Standard,* Aug. 13, 1897.

CHAPTER 3

1. *Great Falls (Mont.) Tribune,* May 12, 1985. See Bole's entry in *Progressive Men of the State of Montana,* 2 vols. (Chicago: A. W. Bowen, 1903), 1:55; and Warden's obituary, *Great Falls (Mont.) Tribune,* March 13, 1951.

2. *Great Falls (Mont.) Tribune,* May 12, 1900, as quoted in *Great Falls (Mont.) Tribune,* May 12, 1985.

3. *Great Falls (Mont.) Tribune,* May 12, 1985; Foor, "Senatorial Aspirations," 90–91.

4. "Montana Fourth Estate," Montana State Press Association newsletter, Dec. 1959, 1, 6. The paper frequently reminded its readers of its ownership. See Oliver S. Warden's obituary, *Great Falls (Mont.) Tribune,* March 13, 1951.

5. For overviews of Clark's climb to the Senate and the corruption accompanying it, see Malone, *Battle for Butte,* 105–30; Glasscock, *War of the Copper Kings,* 146–81; Connolly, *Devil Learns to Vote,* 121–219; Dorothy M. Johnson, "Three Hundred Grand!" *Montana The Magazine of Western History* 10 (Jan. 1960): 40–50; U.S. Congress, Senate Committee on Privileges and Elections, *Report of the Committee on Privileges and Elections of the United States Senate Relative to the Right and Title of William A. Clark to a Seat as Senator from the State of Montana,* 56th Cong., 1st sess., 1900, S. Rept. 1052, passim; and Foor, "Senatorial Aspirations," passim.

6. Malone, *Battle for Butte,* 111; Foor, "Senatorial Aspirations," 20–21, 39, citing the *Butte (Mont.) Times,* Nov. 12, Dec. 7, 1898.

7. Joining Eggleston in the legislature were Arthur L. Stone, the *Standard's* Missoula correspondent, and Edward H. Cooney, the paper's reporter in Great Falls. Both served as Democrats in the House. Foor, "Senatorial Aspirations," 47–48, citing the *Anaconda (Mont.) Standard,* Jan. 4, 5, 11, 1899. For details on the payment to Greenfield, see Foor, "Senatorial Aspirations," 91; and U.S. Congress, Senate Committee on Privileges and Elections, *Report of the Committee on Privileges and Elections,* vol. 2, 2260, 2270.

8. Foor, "Senatorial Aspirations," 62–63, citing the *Anaconda (Mont.) Standard,* and the *Butte (Mont.) Miner,* Jan. 11, 1899; Malone, *Battle for Butte,* 116.

9. Foor, "Senatorial Aspirations," 85; Johnson, "Three Hundred Grand!" 60; U.S. Congress, Senate Committee on Privileges and Elections, *Report of the Committee on Privileges and Elections,* vol. 2, 1552–53, 1593.

10. U.S. Congress, Senate Committee on Privileges and Elections, *Report of the Committee on Privileges and Elections,* vol. 3, 2548; *Hamilton (Mont.) Western News,* Jan. 14, 1899.

11. U.S. Congress, Senate Committee on Privileges and Elections, *Report of the Committee on Privileges and Elections,* vol. 2, 694; Connolly, *Devil Leans to Vote,* 156–58; Foor, "Senatorial Aspirations," 80, 84.

12. Foor, "Senatorial Aspirations," 90–91; U.S. Congress, Senate Committee on Privileges and Elections, *Report of the Committee on Privileges and Elections,* vol. 3, 2274–75, 2456–59.

13. *Big Timber (Mont.) Weekly Express,* Jan. 28, Nov. 18, 1899.

14. For a list of politicians attending the press association convention, see *Anaconda (Mont.) Standard,* Sept. 7, 1899.

15. For early examples of Trowbridge's work, see the *Anaconda (Mont.) Standard,* Sept. 5, 1899. For an overview of the early newspaper cartoons and illustrations, see Frank Luther Mott, *American Journalism, A History: 1690–1960* (New York: MacMillan, 1962), 587–88.

16. Malone, *Battle for Butte,* 129.

17. Foor, "Senatorial Aspirations," 152, citing the *Billings (Mont.) Gazette,* April 10, 1900; *Townsend (Mont.) Star,* April 1900; Malone, *Battle for Butte,* 129. For an example of the *Butte (Mont.) Miner*'s coverage, see the April 11, 1900, issue.

18. Malone, *Battle for Butte,* 126–28.

19. Ibid., 134.

20. For an overview of Amalgamated's formation and aim to control copper production, see Malone, *Battle for Butte,* 131–40.

21. Marcus Daly to John H. Durston, in *Not in Precious Metals Alone,* 147. For an overview of Heinze's lawsuits against other mining companies, see Malone, *Battle for Butte,* 140–48.

22. Malone, *Battle for Butte,* 149.

23. Foor, "Senatorial Aspirations," 232.

24. J. S. M. Neill to Charlie Clark, May 7, 1900, folder 1, box 2, Neill Family Papers, 1886–1964 (hereafter Neill Family Papers), MC 248, MHS, Helena.

25. J. S. M. Neill to W. G. Eggleston, May 10, 1900, ibid.

26. Foor, "Senatorial Aspirations," 239. Foor's estimate of Clark's newspaper spending was supplied by Clark's opponents and published in the U.S. Congress, *Congressional Record,* 56th Cong., 2d sess., 1901, p. 3428.

27. Malone, *Battle for Butte,* 153.

28. Ibid.; Foor, "Senatorial Aspirations," 231.

29. Sworn statement, *Newton R. Dexter v. The Record Publishing Co., District Court of Silver Bow,* published in *Butte (Mont.) Miner,* Oct. 26, 1900; Foor, "Senatorial Aspirations," 232.

30. Fought, "John Hurst Durston," 87–88; *Anaconda (Mont.) Standard,* Oct. 16, 1900.

31. *Anaconda (Mont.) Standard,* Oct. 11, 1900.

32. *Butte (Mont.) Inter Mountain,* Oct. 16, 1900; Wanamaker, "Eggleston of the *Anaconda Standard,*" 217, citing the *Anaconda (Mont.) Standard,* Aug. 6, 1900.

33. For examples of the paper's artistry, see *Anaconda (Mont.) Standard,* Oct. 28, Nov. 3, 4, 1900.

34. Malone, *Battle for Butte,* 154, citing the *Butte (Mont.) Miner,* Nov. 1900.

35. *Helena (Mont.) Independent,* Nov. 8, 1900; *Anaconda (Mont.) Standard,* Nov. 5, 1900; *Helena (Mont.) Independent,* Nov. 2, 1900.

36. Fought, "John Hurst Durston," 104–5, citing the *Anaconda (Mont.) Standard,* Nov. 8, 1900.

37. Ibid., citing the *Anaconda (Mont.) Standard,* Nov. 10, 1900.

38. Malone, *Battle for Butte,* 156–57; Fought, "John Hurst Durston," 106, citing the *Anaconda (Mont.) Standard,* Nov. 13, 1900.

39. Foor, "Senatorial Aspirations," 231n2.

40. *Hamilton (Mont.) Western News,* Jan. 10, Oct. 17, 1900.

41. Both papers were quoted in the *Butte (Mont.) Miner,* April 23, 14, 1900.

42. Foor, "Senatorial Aspirations," 21n6; J. S. M. Neill to W. G. Eggleston, May 10, 1900, folder 1, box 2, Neill Family Papers, MHS, Helena.

43. J. S. M. Neill to W. A. Clark, April 21, 1900, ibid.

44. Foor, "Senatorial Aspirations," 92.

45. Ibid., 92n24, 133.

46. Ibid., 111.

47. Ibid., 112.

48. Ibid. For Neill's fight with the railroads, see Richard B. Roeder, "Montana in the Early Years of the Progressive Period" (PhD diss, University of Pennsylvania, 1971), 95.

49. Foor, "Senatorial Aspirations," 233.

50. Ibid., 283–84n22.

51. J. S. M. Neill to General James T. Stanford, March 7, 1902, folder 1, box 2, Neill Family Papers, MHS, Helena; J. S. M. Neill to George Evans, Aug. 26, 1902, ibid.

52. J. S. M. Neill to W. K. Connor, Aug. 26, 1902, ibid. For examples of the paper's editorial views and its criticism of Clark, see *Helena (Mont.) Press,* Sept. 13, 1902, Jan. 3, 1903, April 23, 1904.

CHAPTER 4

1. *Great Falls (Mont.) Tribune,* Nov. 11, 1903.

2. Ibid.

3. *Missoula (Mont.) Missoulian,* Nov. 12, 1903.

4. *Spokane (Wash.) Spokesman-Review,* as reprinted in the *Fort Benton (Mont.) River Press,* Nov. 18, 1903.

5. *Fort Benton (Mont.) River Press,* Nov. 18, 1903.

6. *Great Falls (Mont.) Tribune,* Nov. 1, 1903.

7. *Missoula (Mont.) Missoulian,* Oct. 24, 1903.

8. *Butte (Mont.) Inter Mountain,* July 14, 1900. For details of Mantle's sale of the *Inter Mountain,* see Janet C. Thomson, "The Role of Lee Mantle in Montana Politics, 1889–1900, An Interpretation" (master's thesis, Montana State University, 1956), 152–58.

9. Neill to Evans, Aug. 26, 1902.

10. Daniel J. LaGrande, "Voice of a Copper King: A Study of the (Butte) *Reveille*, 1903–1906" (master's thesis, University of Montana, 1971), 27, citing the *Butte (Mont.) Reveille*, April 14, 1905.

11. Malone, *Battle for Butte*, 52, 141–56; Sarah McNelis, "The Life of F. Augustus Heinze"(master's thesis, Montana State University, 1947), 38.

12. Ibid.; LaGrande, "Voice of a Copper King," 31, citing the *Butte (Mont.) Reveille*, Sept. 11, 1900.

13. *Butte (Mont.) Reveille*, Nov. 4, 1904.

14. Federal Writers' Program, *Copper Camp: Stories of the World's Greatest Mining Town, Butte, Montana* (New York: Hastings House, 1943), 43.

15. *Butte (Mont.) Reveille*, July 31, 1903.

16. *Butte (Mont.) Inter Mountain*, Sept. 4, 1903.

17. *Fort Benton (Mont.) River Press*, Sept. 13, 1903.

18. *Butte (Mont.) Reveille*, Sept. 11, 1903.

19. Calvert, *Gibraltar*, 24–25.

20. LaGrande, "Voice of a Copper King," 49, 53, citing the *Butte (Mont.) Reveille*, Feb. 27, July 28, 1903.

21. Malone, *Battle for Butte*, 173.

22. *Fort Benton (Mont.) River Press*, Nov. 18, 1903.

23. *Hamilton (Mont.) Western News*, Nov. 4, 1903.

24. *Lewistown (Mont.) Democrat*, Nov. 4, 1903, as quoted in Myers, "From Crazy Quilt to Gray Blanket," 81.

25. LaGrande, "Voice of a Copper King," 63–64, citing the *Butte (Mont.) Reveille*, Oct. 23, 1903.

26. Ibid., 65, citing the *Butte (Mont.) Inter Mountain*, Oct. 27, 1903.

27. Malone, *Battle for Butte*, 176; LaGrande, "Voice of a Copper King," 69, 77, citing the *Butte (Mont.) Reveille*, Oct. 26, Nov. 6, 1903.

28. Calvert, *Gibraltar*, 25, citing the *Anaconda (Mont.) Standard*, April 5, 1904.

29. Calvert, *Gibraltar*, 30; Waldron and Wilson, *Atlas of Montana Elections*, 31.

30. LaGrande, "Voice of a Copper King," 173–74.

31. *Butte (Mont.) Reveille*, Nov. 10, 1902, Feb. 26, Oct. 7, Jan. 29, 1904.

32. For Leipheimer's coverage of the Haywood trial, see J. Anthony Lukas, *Big Trouble: A Murder in a Small Western Town Sets Off a Struggle for the Soul of America* (New York: Simon and Schuster, 1997), 724; Berton Braley, *Pegasus Pulls a Hack: Memoirs of a Modern Minstrel* (New York: Minton, Balch, 1934), 50–51.

33. Braley, *Pegasus Pulls a Hack*, 64–65; and Federal Writers' Program, *Copper Camp*, 96. For the beer story, see LaGrande, "Voice of a Copper King," 195, citing an interview with E. G. Leipheimer. Another version of the tale holds that the newspaper involved was the *Inter Mountain*. See Federal Writers' Program, *Copper Camp*, 96–97.

34. LaGrande, "Voice of a Copper King," 212.

35. *Helena (Mont.) Press*, Sept. 13, 1902.

36. Ibid., April 23, 1904.

37. Ibid., Jan. 17, 1903.

38. *Marysville (Mont.) Mountaineer,* reprinted in *Helena (Mont.) Press,* Sept. 13, 1902.

39. *Miles City (Mont.) Yellowstone Journal,* reprinted in *Helena (Mont.) Press,* June 20, 1903.

40. Ibid.

41. *Helena (Mont.) Press,* June 20, 1903.

42. Ibid., May 28, 1904.

43. J. S. M. Neill to John D. Ryan, Oct. 23, 1905, folder 3, box 2, Neill Family Papers, MHS, Helena; J. S. M. Neill to A. H. Melin, Nov. 3, 1905, ibid.

44. *Great Falls (Mont.) Tribune,* May 12, 1985.

45. Jerre C. Murphy, *The Comical History of Montana: A Serious Story for Free People* (San Diego: E. L. Scofield, 1912), 77–79, 81, 83, 86–87; *Helena (Mont.) Montana Daily Record,* Nov. 3, 1905. Murphy's account of the transaction is based on the court testimony of Helena's Republican mayor, Frank J. Edwards, who helped "launder" company funds to pay for the unsold stock. Murphy had worked as a senior editor for the *Inter Mountain* during the Heinze fight. Both Murphy and Edwards later became severe critics of the company.

46. For details of Heinze's sellout and downfall, see Malone, *Battle for Butte,* 190–95.

47. *Butte (Mont.) Evening News,* Feb. 3, 1911.

48. Roeder, "Montana in the Early Years," 86, citing the *Chinook (Mont.) Opinion,* Oct. 25, 1906.

49. Richard B. Roeder, "Montana Progressivism: Sound and Fury—and One Small Tax Reform," in Malone and Roeder, *Montana's Past,* 395–96, citing the *White Sulphur Springs (Mont.) Meagher County Republican,* Aug. 17, 1906, and the *Helena (Mont.) Montana Staats Zeitung,* Dec. 14, 1906; Roeder, "Montana in the Early Years," 74, citing the *Helena (Mont.) Montana Daily Record,* Oct. 20, 1906; Roeder, "Montana in the Early Years," 177.

50. For details on Romney's background and early career, see Stout, *Montana,* 2:538–39.

51. Roeder, "Montana in the Early Years," 92–93; and *Hamilton (Mont.) Western News,* Aug. 8, 1908.

52. Roeder, "Montana in the Early Years," 66.

53. Ibid., 95–105.

54. Stout, *Montana,* 2:538–39; Waldron and Wilson, *Atlas of Montana Elections,* 55.

55. Waldron and Wilson, Atlas of Montana Elections, 55; Emmons, *Butte Irish,* 248; *Hamilton (Mont.) Western News,* Feb. 7, 14, 1913, Sept. 17, 1914.

56. *Hamilton (Mont.) Western News,* Feb. 14, 1913; Roeder, "Montana in the Early Years," 213, 213nn6–7.

57. Roeder, "Montana in the Early Years," 108n39.

58. Ibid. For Harber's background, see "Montana Newspaper Hall of Fame: W. K. Harber," *Montana Journalism Review* 14 (1971): 1.

59. *Fort Benton (Mont.) River Press,* March 26, 1913.

Chapter 5

1. Malone, *Battle for Butte*, 206.

2. For background on the company's promise, see Jules A. Karlin, *Joseph M. Dixon of Montana*, 2 vols. (Missoula: University of Montana Press, 1974), 1:152. See also Roeder, "Montana in the Early Years," 173.

3. For an example of the paper's quality during this period, see *Anaconda Standard*, Dec. 16, 1900.

4. Wanamaker, "Eggleston of the *Anaconda Standard*," 231–32, Fought, "John Hurst Durston," 114–15.

5. Wanamaker, "Eggleston of the *Anaconda Standard*," 232; Federal Writers' Project, *The WPA Guide to 1930s Montana* (1939; repr., Tucson: University of Arizona Press, 1994), 71; Braley, *Pegasus Pulls a Hack*, 84. The paper also included Montana's finest commercial printing shop. The only threats to the paper's operations came from within. In 1907, unionized pressmen and typesetters shut down all of Butte's newspapers in a six-week strike over wages. Some reporters found temporary work in the mines.

6. Fought, "John Hurst Durston," 72; Wanamaker, "Eggleston of the *Anaconda Standard*," 229.

7. *Anaconda (Mont.) Standard*, Oct. 26, 1906, Oct. 9, 1912; Roeder, "Montana in the Early Years," 100–101, citing the *Anaconda (Mont.) Standard*, Nov. 11, 18, 1906.

8. *Anaconda (Mont.) Standard*, Oct. 13, 1912.

9. *Butte (Mont.) Inter Mountain*, Feb. 29, March 16, 1908; *Anaconda (Mont.) Standard*, March 1, 15, 1908.

10. MacMillan, *Smoke Wars*, 32–81 passim.

11. Ibid., 87–99.

12. Ibid., 132–33, citing the *Anaconda (Mont.) Standard*, Aug. 20, 1905; *Butte (Mont.) Inter Mountain*, Oct. 4, 1905.

13. *Anaconda (Mont.) Standard*, Dec. 4, 5, 1908.

14. Miles Romney Sr. to J. M. Dixon, Dec. 5, 1908, folder 3, box 10, Joseph M. Dixon Papers (hereafter Dixon Papers), MSS 55, K. Ross Toole Archives, University of Montana, Missoula (hereafter Toole Archives, UM); MacMillan, *Smoke Wars*, 192, citing the *Great Falls (Mont.) Tribune*, Dec. 9, 1908; *Anaconda (Mont.) Standard*, Dec. 10, 1908.

15. MacMillan, *Smoke Wars*, 132–33.

16. *Butte (Mont.) Inter Mountain*, April 26, 1909; *Anaconda (Mont.) Standard*, April 27, 1909.

17. *Anaconda (Mont.) Standard*, March 7, 1911.

18. Murphy, *Comical History of Montana*, 71.

19. For details on Dixon's acquisition of the *Missoulian*, see Karlin, *Joseph M. Dixon*, 1:50. At about the same time, Karlin writes, Dixon also purchased and quickly sold the money-losing *Missoula Democrat*, which became the *Missoula Times* and was published briefly as a daily in support of F. A. Heinze's political machine. Amalgamated reportedly offered the *Missoulian* financial support in response, though Dixon's correspondence indicated the company fell short in its

payments. Throughout 1903 and 1904, Dixon worried that readers would think the paper had "gone completely over to Amalgamated." For details, see Karlin, *Joseph M. Dixon*, 1:49–54.

20. Karlin, *Joseph M. Dixon*, 146.

21. Joseph M. Dixon to E. L. Barnes, Nov. 21, 1911, folder 5, box 14, Dixon Papers, Toole Archives, UM.

22. For Kilroy's background, see Braley, *Pegasus Pulls a Hack*, 55–56; and Morris, *Anaconda, Montana*, 93.

23. For Leipheimer's views on Kilroy, see LaGrande, "Voice of a Copper King," 196.

24. For an assessment of Kilroy's editorial tactics, see Karlin, *Joseph M. Dixon*, 1:147. The *Sentinel's* charge that Dixon had once been an Amalgamated partisan had also surfaced in the *Missoula Herald*, a Democratic daily that challenged Dixon's Senate bid in 1906. During the 1912 campaign, Lanstrum's *Montana Daily Record* accused Thomas Walsh of being Amalgamated's candidate, while the *Missoulian* and other progressives made a similar charge against the conservative Republican nominee, Henry C. Smith. *Helena (Mont.) Montana Daily Record*, Oct. 5, 7, 8, 1912; *Missoula (Mont.) Missoulian*, Oct. 9, 10, 1912.

25. Karlin, *Joseph M. Dixon*, 1:151.

26. Ibid., 1:192.

27. Ibid., 1:194–95.

28. Ibid., 1:196. Dixon cited the seventy-thousand-dollar figure two years later in a letter to the *Missoulian's* pressmen's union. Joseph M. Dixon to O. S. Warden, May 12, 1915, folder 7, box 17, Dixon Papers, Toole Archives, UM.

29. Charles S. Johnson, "An Editor and a War: Will A. Campbell and the *Helena Independent*, 1914–1921" (master's thesis, University of Montana, 1977), 10–12. Original articles of incorporation on file at the Montana Secretary of State's Office, Helena, show the venture capitalized at seventy-five thousand dollars at one hundred dollars a share.

30. Johnson, "An Editor and a War," 9–10.

31. *Helena (Mont.) Independent*, March 6, 1913.

32. Ibid., March 7, 1913; Johnson, "An Editor and a War," 13.

33. *Helena (Mont.) Independent*, March 7, 1913.

34. Fought, "John Hurst Durston," 115–17.

35. Ibid., 116–17; *Anaconda (Mont.) Standard*, Jan. 1, 1913.

36. Wanamaker, "Eggleston of the *Anaconda Standard*," 255.

37. *Anaconda (Mont.) Standard*, Nov. 7, 1912.

38. Calvert, *Gibraltar*, 35, 42.

39. *Butte (Mont.) Miner*, Feb. 14, 1914; Calvert, *Gibraltar*, 64.

40. Johnson, "An Editor and a War," 31.

41. For an account of the censorship order, see the *Anaconda (Mont.) Standard*, Sept. 2, 1914.

42. *Anaconda (Mont.) Standard*, Sept. 5, 1914.

43. During Clark's brief ownership of the *Great Falls Tribune*, Roote served as the paper's president. William A. Clark Jr., Roote's law partner, was its secretary.

44. Calvert, *Gibraltar,* 100, citing the *Butte (Mont.) Socialist,* Dec. 18, 1915.

45. Malone, *Battle for Butte,* 129, citing the *Billings (Mont.) Gazette,* April 10, 1900.

46. Gilluly, *Press Gang,* 77.

47. Federal Writers' Project, *WPA Guide to 1930s Montana,* 116.

48. Karlin, *Joseph M. Dixon,* 1:34.

49. For an overview and details on the lawsuit, see the February 1912 Montana Supreme Court ruling, "In the Matter of the Receivership of the First Trust & Savings of Billings, Montana. Gazette Printing Co. et al, Respondents, v. McConnell, Appellant," case no. 3075, copy in State Law Library, Helena, Montana. For Moss's background, see Stout, *Montana,* 2:218–19.

50. P. B. Moss to Joseph M. Dixon, Feb. 27, 1912, folder 6, box 15, Dixon Papers, Toole Archives, UM; Joseph M. Dixon to P. B. Moss, Feb. 28, 1912, ibid.. For details on the behind-the-scenes fight over the *Gazette,* see Murphy, *Comical History of Montana,* 87–88.

51. *Billings (Mont.) Gazette,* Jan. 2, 9, 18, May 29, June 19, Oct. 2, 1914; Gazette Printing Company articles of incorporation, 1916, on file at the Montana Secretary of State's Office, Helena. Edwards's thirty-five-thousand-dollar investment represented the largest individual share of the company's stock.

52. For background on Shaw, see Stout, *Montana,* 2:161–62.

53. For details of the Lanstrum-Edwards break, see Karlin, *Joseph M. Dixon,* 1:209, 213–14, 223.

54. For *Gazette* history, see *Billings (Mont.) Gazette,* Sept. 14, 1968. For an overview of the paper's financial development, see the Gazette Printing Company's annual corporation reports for 1916, 1921, and 1923, on file at the Montana Secretary of State's Office, Helena.

55. Joseph M. Dixon to A. W. Copp, Aug. 21, 1915, folder 1, box 18, Dixon Papers, Toole Archives, UM; Karlin, *Joseph M. Dixon,* 1:197–98.

56. Tom Stout to Joseph Dixon, Feb. 19, 1914, folder 3, box 17, Dixon Papers, Toole Archives, UM.

57. Waldron and Wilson, *Atlas of Montana Elections,* 59.

58. Lyle E. Harris, "Dr. E. B. Craighead's *New Northwest*: 1915–1920" (master's thesis, University of Montana, 1967), 7, 8, 8n13.

59. Ibid., 17–20.

60. Joseph M. Dixon to James Donovan, March 15, 1917, folder 9, box 20, Dixon Papers, Toole Archives, UM; Harris, "Dr. E. B. Craighead's *New Northwest,*" 38.

61. Karlin, *Joseph M. Dixon,* 1:232–33.

62. Ibid.; Missoulian Publishing Company article of incorporation, May 1917, on file at the Montana Secretary of State's Office, Helena.

63. Karlin, *Joseph M. Dixon,* 1:233. For the story of Hocking's involvement, see John H. Toole, *Red Ribbons: A Story of Missoula and its Newspaper* (Davenport, Iowa: Lee Enterprises, 1989), 76–78. For details on Murphy's corporate clients and his relationship with the *Missoulian,* see his obituary in the *Fourth Estate,* official publication of the Montana Press Association, July 1954, 2.

64. Karlin, *Joseph M. Dixon*, 1:222–33; Joseph Dixon to Jerre Locke, May 1, 1917, folder 2, box 21, Dixon Papers, Toole Archives, UM; Toole, *Red Ribbons*, 78.

65. For Mrs. Hutchens's claim, see Mary Lou Koessler, "The 1920 Gubernatorial Election in Montana" (master's thesis, University of Montana, 1971), 4–5n7.

CHAPTER 6

1. For Eggleston's assessment of Copenharve's talents, see Eggleston's history in the *Anaconda (Mont.) Standard*, Sept. 5, 1929.

2. Wanamaker, "Eggleston of the Anaconda Standard," 256–57, citing the *Great Falls (Mont.) News*, 1933.

3. Ibid., 256. For contemporary news accounts of the speech, see the *Butte (Mont.) Miner*, Aug. 19, 1917; *Billings (Mont.) Gazette*, Aug. 19, 1917; *Missoula (Mont.) Missoulian*, Aug. 19, 1917.

4. For an overview of Butte's summer of 1917, see Calvert, *Gibraltar*, 104–14; Malone, Roeder, and Lang, *Montana*, 274–76; and Arnon Gutfeld, *Montana's Agony: Years of War and Hysteria, 1917–1921* (Gainesville: University Presses of Florida, 1979), 18–36.

5. *Butte (Mont.) Miner*, Aug. 19, 1917.

6. Wanamaker, "Eggleston of the *Anaconda Standard*," 257.

7. Ibid.

8. For an overview of the American press's coverage of World War I, see Mott, *American Journalism*, 616–27.

9. For Hearst's view of the war, see Nasaw, *The Chief*, 243; Andrew C. Cogswell, "The Sources, Transmission and Handling of World War News in Representative Montana Newspapers from 1914–1917" (master's thesis, University of Minnesota, 1943), 249.

10. Cogswell, "The Sources, Transmission and Handling of World War News," 249; *Anaconda (Mont.) Standard*, Sept. 7, 1916;

11. Wanamaker, "Eggleston of the *Anaconda Standard*," 284–85, citing the *Anaconda (Mont.) Standard*, April 17, May 29, 1917.

12. *Helena (Mont.) Independent*, July 31, 1917; *Anaconda (Mont.) Standard*, Feb. 2, 1917; Stout, *Montana*, 2:538.

13. Malone, Roeder, and Lang, *Montana*, 268–70; *Missoula (Mont.) Missoulian*, Jan. 24, 1918.

14. Malone, Roeder, and Lang, *Montana*, 270, 278; Johnson, "An Editor and a War," 106–9, 136; *Helena (Mont.) Independent*, March 24, 1918.

15. Marian Holter Brod, "The *Montana Staats-Zeitung* 1914–1917: A German Newspaper in America during World War I" (master's thesis, University of Montana, 1979), 3–4, 82, 84, 88, 84.

16. Johnson, "An Editor and a War," 99–102, citing the *Helena (Mont.) Independent*, Sept. 1, 3, 1917; Brod, "*Montana Staats-Zeitung*," 88–89.

17. Johnson, "An Editor and a War," 100–102.

18. Brod, "*Montana Staats-Zeitung*," 88–89, citing the *Helena (Mont.) Independent*, Sept. 1, 1917.

19. *Helena (Mont.) Independent*, May 25, 1917.

20. For an overview of the IWW in America, see Patrick Renshaw, *The Wobblies: The Story of Syndicalism in the United States* (Garden City, N.Y.: Doubleday, 1967), 21–26.

21. For Montana's role in the IWW's founding and the IWW's role in Butte's 1914 labor disputes, see Malone, Roeder, and Lang, *Montana,* 266–67, 271–73; Calvert, *Gibraltar,* 83–85; and Gutfeld, *Montana's Agony,* 12–13.

22. For details on the timber strikes, see Gutfeld, *Montana's Agony,* 34–35. For details on the Bisbee deportation, see Renshaw, *Wobblies,* 234–35; and Calvert, *Gibraltar,* 108.

23. *Helena (Mont.) Montana Record-Herald,* July 12, 28, 1917; *Anaconda (Mont.) Standard,* July 12, 14, 17, 20, 1917.

24. The *Billings Gazette,* Beaverhead County, and *Havre Promoter* accounts were reprinted by the *Helena (Mont.) Montana Record-Herald,* July 13, 26, Aug. 3, 1917; *Anaconda (Mont.) Standard,* July 21, 1917.

25. *Helena (Mont.) Independent,* Aug. 2, May 25, April 26, 1917.

26. *Anaconda (Mont.) Standard,* June 14, 23, 1917.

27. *Butte (Mont.) Daily Post,* June 13, 1917.

28. Malone, Roeder, and Lang, *Montana,* 211.

29. For an outline of Dobell's career, see Stout, *Montana,* 3:1387–88.

30. Ibid.

31. Gutfeld, *Montana's Agony,* 19–20, citing the *Butte (Mont.) Miner,* July 1, 1917.

32. *Billings (Mont.) Gazette,* June 14, 1917.

33. *Anaconda (Mont.) Standard,* June 29, 1917.

34. *Butte (Mont.) Miner,* July 21, 23, 1917.

35. *Butte (Mont.) Post,* July 28, 1917; *Billings (Mont.) Gazette,* July 31, 1917; *Missoula (Mont.) Missoulian,* July 22, 1917.

36. Johnson, "An Editor and a War," 84; *Helena (Mont.) Independent,* Aug. 2, 1917.

37. *Butte (Mont.) Miner,* Aug. 2, 1917.

38. *Anaconda (Mont.) Standard,* Aug. 2, 1917.

39. Ibid., Aug. 5, 1917; *Billings (Mont.) Gazette,* Aug. 2, 1917.

40. *Helena (Mont.) Independent,* Aug. 2, 1917.

41. *Missoula (Mont.) Missoulian,* Aug. 2, 1917; *Great Falls (Mont.) Tribune,* Aug. 2, 1917.

42. For an overview of the weeklies' reaction, see Gutfeld, *Montana's Agony,* 32–33.

43. *Great Falls (Mont.) Tribune,* Aug. 4, 1917.

44. Gutfeld, *Montana's Agony,* 51.

45. *Anaconda (Mont.) Standard,* Aug. 19, 1917; *Butte (Mont.) Miner,* Aug. 19, 1917; *Helena (Mont.) Montana Record-Herald,* Aug. 19, 1917.

46. John K. Hutchens, *One Man's Montana; An Informal Portrait of a State* (Philadelphia: J. B Lippincott, 1964), 146.

47. For an assessment of the *New York Sun,* see Mott, *American Journalism,* 421–22.

48. Hutchens, *One Man's Montana,* 146–47.

49. *Missoula (Mont.) Missoulian,* Aug. 2, 1917.

50. Ibid., Aug. 22, 1917.

51. Ibid.

52. Ibid.

53. Ibid.

54. Ibid.

55. Ibid.

56. Ibid.

57. *Missoula (Mont.) Missoulian,* Aug. 26, 1917.

58. Ibid., Aug. 24, 25, 1917.

59. Stout's comments were published in the *Helena (Mont.) Independent,* Aug. 20, 1917.

60. Ibid, Aug. 25, 1917.

61. For details on the *Bulletin's* origins, see Kurt Wetzel, "The Making of an American Radical: Bill Dunne in Butte" (master's thesis, University of Montana, 1970), 23–26; and Calvert, *Gibraltar,* 111. For its political philosophy, see *Butte Daily (Mont.) Bulletin,* Dec. 18, 1918. For John Reed's articles, see *Butte (Mont.) Bulletin,* Sept. 3, 1918.

62. Gutfeld, *Montana's Agony,* 44–45; Malone, Roeder, and Lang, *Montana,* 276.

63. *Missoula (Mont.) Missoulian,* Jan. 25, Feb. 3, 5, 1918; *Helena (Mont.) Montana Record-Herald,* Feb. 11, 1918.

64. *Great Falls (Mont.) Tribune,* Feb. 3, 1918; *Lewistown (Mont.) Democrat-News,* Feb. 1, 1918; *Billings (Mont.) Gazette,* Jan. 11, Feb. 16, 1918; *Butte (Mont.) Miner,* Feb. 24, 1918; *Lewistown (Mont.) Fergus County Argus,* Feb. 8, 22, 1918; *Butte (Mont.) Daily Post,* Feb. 8, 1918.

65. *Lewistown (Mont.) Fergus County Argus,* Jan. 11, 1918.

66. Johnson, "An Editor and a War," 130–31.

67. For details on the state council's officers, see Montana Council of Defense Records, 1916–1921, RS 19, MHS, Helena; Nancy Rice Fritz, "The Montana Council of Defense" (master's thesis, University of Montana, 1966), 31–32, 77. For information on Montana Loyalty League officials, see Johnson, "An Editor and a War," 212n3. See also John H. Shober Family Papers, 1832–1952, MC 69, MHS, Helena.

68. For details on the Montana Council of Defense's newspaper order, see Johnson, "An Editor and a War," 269. For details on the council's beginnings, see K. Ross Toole, *Twentieth-Century Montana; A State of Extremes* (Norman: University of Oklahoma Press, 1972), 178–79.

69. For details of Dunne's early career and role in Butte's strike of 1917, see Wetzel, "Making of an American Radical," 4–28.

70. The letters, each addressed to Montana State Press Association President George H. Cade, can be found in folder 15, box 2, Montana Council of Defense Records, MHS, Helena. Specifically, see letters from Arthur Stone, March 22, 1918; Lyle A. Cowan, March 21, 1918; J. L. Dobell, March 22, 1918; J. A. Gilluly, March 22, 1918; H. H. Howard, March 25, 1918; J. D. Scanlan, March 23, 1918; and Charles Reifenrath, March 23, 1918. See aslo Johnson, "An Editor and a War," 163–64.

71. Johnson, "An Editor and a War,"164–72; Wetzel, "Making of an American Radical," 84–93.

72. Wetzel, "Making of an American Radical," 95.

73. Ibid., 96; Johnson, "An Editor and a War," 175–79.

74. *Butte (Mont.) Daily Bulletin,* Sept. 16, 1918; Wetzel, "Making of an American Radical," 104.

75. For details on Dunne's sedition case and its appeal, see Johnson, "An Editor and a War," 192–97, 204–6.

CHAPTER 7

1. For background on Taylor and the *Producers News,* see Charles Vindex, "Radical Rule in Montana: The Amazing Years," *Montana The Magazine of Western History* 18 (Winter 1968): 6; Verlaine Stoner McDonald, "'A Paper of, by, and for the People': The *Producers News* and the Farmers' Movement in Northwestern Montana, 1918–1937," *Montana The Magazine of Western History* 48 (Winter 1998): 20–22. See also William C. Pratt, "Rural Radicalism on the Northern Plains, 1912–1950," *Montana The Magazine of Western History* 42 (Winter 1992): 44–47; *Plentywood (Mont.) Producers News,* May 13, 1918.

2. McDonald, "'A Paper of, by, and for the People,'" 21n12. For details on Montana's NPL papers and those the *Producers News* absorbed, see "Montana Historical Newspaper Project: A Union List of Montana Newspapers in Montana Repositories," 1968, pp. 3, 178, copy in MHS, Helena. For Taylor's description of the *Pioneer Press,* see *Plentywood (Mont.) Producers News,* June 21, 1918; and Vindex, "Radical Rule in Montana," 7.

3. For details on the Sheridan County robbery, see Vindex, "Radical Rule in Montana," 12; and McDonald, "'A Paper of, by, and for the People,'" 26. For reporting on the *Leader* arson, see the *Scobey (Mont.) Daniels County Leader,* July 15, 1926; *Scobey (Mont.) Sentinel,* July 15, 1926; and *Plentywood (Mont.) Producers News,* July 16, 1926.

4. For editorial cooperation between the *Producers News* and the *Butte Daily Bulletin,* see *Plentywood (Mont.) Producers News,* April 25, 1919. For Campbell's attacks on the NPL and the McGlynn incident, see Johnson, "An Editor and a War," 138–39, 142.

5. For accounts of the labor-NPL campaign for Wheeler, see Malone, Roeder, and Lang, *Montana,* 285–86; Gutfeld, *Montana's Agony,* 132–33; and Calvert, *Gibraltar,* 135–44. For Craighead's views on the NPL, see Harris, "Dr. E. B. Craighead's *New Northwest,*" 48–73.

6. *Producers News,* June 18, 25, 1920.

7. Wanamaker, "Eggleston of the *Anaconda Standard,*" 290–91; *Anaconda (Mont.) Standard,* Aug. 20, 1920.

8. *Anaconda (Mont.) Standard,* Aug. 22, 1920.

9. Koessler, "1920 Gubernatorial Election," citing the *Butte (Mont.) Daily Bulletin,* Aug. 30, 1920.

10. Karlin, *Joseph M. Dixon,* 2:42–47.

11. Ibid., 2:46; *Billings (Mont.) Gazette,* Oct. 22, 1920.

12. *Hamilton (Mont.) Western News,* Sept. 10, 1920; *Big Timber (Mont.) Pioneer,* Sept. 30, 1920; *Lewistown (Mont.) Fergus County Argus,* Jan. 25, Oct. 29, 1918.

13. *Butte (Mont.) Miner,* Sept. 13, Oct. 2–Nov. 2, 1920; Burton K. Wheeler, *Yankee from the West: The Candid, Turbulent Life Story of the Yankee-Born U.S. Senator from Montana* (Garden City, N.Y: Doubleday, 1962), 174–75.

14. Koessler, "1920 Gubernatorial Election," 130, citing the *Havre (Mont.) Hill County Democrat,* Oct. 28, 1920; Wheeler, *Yankee from the West,* 180–81; Koessler, "1920 Gubernatorial Election," 91, citing the *Missoula (Mont.) Missoulian,* Sept. 10, 1920; *Missoula (Mont.) Missoulian,* Oct. 28, 1920.

15. Shirley Jean De Forth, "The Montana Press and Governor Joseph M. Dixon, 1920–1922" (master's thesis, Montana State University, 1959), 15, 33. For Scanlan's publicity efforts, see Karlin, *Joseph M. Dixon,* 2:59.

16. Waldron and Wilson, *Atlas of Montana Elections,* 82.

17. De Forth, "Montana Press," 45.

18. Koessler, "1920 Gubernatorial Election," 67.

19. *Butte (Mont.) Daily Bulletin,* Oct. 30, Nov. 5, 1920.

20. Karlin, *Joseph M. Dixon,* 2:61; De Forth, "Montana Press," 63, citing a *Hamilton (Mont.) Western News* editorial reprinted in the *Chinook (Mont.) Opinion,* Jan. 13, 1921.

21. Malone, Roeder, and Lang, *Montana,* 280–84.

22. Karlin, *Joseph M. Dixon,* 2:64–65.

23. See the Gazette Printing Company's annual reports for 1921 and 1923, on file at the Montana Secretary of State's Office, Helena.

24. For Dixon's comments on Dobell and Hutchens, see Joseph M. Dixon to Miles Romney, March 14, 1921, folder 3, box 32, Dixon Papers, Toole Archives, UM.

25. *Missoula (Mont.) Missoulian,* Feb. 12, March 3, 1919; Gutfeld, *Montana's Agony,* 120; Sheila MacDonald Stearns, "The Arthur Fisher Affair" (master's thesis, University of Montana, Missoula, 1969), 10; Karlin, *Joseph M. Dixon,* 2:69.

26. De Forth, "Montana Press," 59, 62, 66, 72–74, 78, citing the *Billings (Mont.) Gazette,* Jan. 6, 1921, *Anaconda (Mont.) Standard,* Jan. 5, 1921, *Missoula (Mont.) Missoulian,* Jan. 5, 1921, and *Butte (Mont.) Miner,* Feb. 14, 1921.

27. De Forth, "Montana Press," 97–99.

28. Karlin, *Joseph M. Dixon,* 2:87–88.

29. Ibid., 92–93; De Forth, "Montana Press," 107–8.

30. De Forth, "Montana Press," 92, citing the *Billings (Mont.) Gazette,* July 11, 1921, *Helena (Mont.) Independent,* July 9, 1921, and the *Butte (Mont.) Miner,* July 10, 1921. See also De Forth, "Montana Press," 111–12. For a reference to the "anvil chorus," see *Miles City (Mont.) Star,* July 11, 1921.

31. Karlin, *Joseph M. Dixon,* 2:111.

32. Ibid., 115.

33. Ibid., 116.

34. De Forth, "Montana Press," 148–49; Karlin, *Joseph M. Dixon,* 2:142.

35. De Forth, "Montana Press, 81, citing the *Billings (Mont.) Gazette,* April 17, 1921.

36. Dates for the establishment of an Associated Press bureau in Helena were

confirmed to the author by officials in New York, who said the move was part of a nationwide expansion. For complaints about Associated Press coverage, see Karlin, *Joseph M. Dixon,* 2:186.

37. Joseph Dixon to Sid Bennett, Feb. 23, 1922, folder 4, box 37, Dixon Papers, Toole Archives, UM.

38. De Forth, "Montana Press," 167–70; Karlin, *Joseph M. Dixon,* 2:118–19.

39. Karlin, *Joseph M. Dixon,* 2:130.

40. De Forth, "Montana Press," 224–25; Waldron and Wilson, *Atlas of Montana Elections,* 90–91.

41. Karlin, *Joseph M. Dixon,* 2:146.

42. Ibid., 2:173.

43. Ibid., 2:193.

44. Ibid., 2:179.

45. *Fort Benton (Mont.) River Press,* Oct. 29, 1924. For editorial stands by the *Whitefish News, Big Timber Pioneer,* and *Ryegate Reporter,* see the *Livingston (Mont.) Enterprise,* Oct. 4, 1924.

46. *Billings (Mont.) Gazette,* Oct. 8, 1924; *Missoula (Mont.) Missoulian,* Oct. 5, 1924; Karlin, *Joseph M. Dixon,* 2:197–98.

47. For an example of the "Copper Target" ads, see the *Fort Benton (Mont.) River Press,* Oct. 22, 1924. For reporting and editorials on the pamphlet, see the *Missoula (Mont.) Missoulian,* Oct. 3, 1924; and *Billings (Mont.) Gazette,* Oct. 4, 8, 1924.

48. Karlin, *Joseph M. Dixon,* 2:198, citing the *Red Lodge (Mont.) Carbon County Chronicle,* Oct. 29, 1924.

49. Karlin, *Joseph M. Dixon,* 2:181, 186. For a glowing portrait typical of the coverage Erickson received in the copper press, see French T. Ferguson's front-page profile, *Missoula (Mont.) Missoulian,* Nov. 2, 1924.

50. *Missoula (Mont.) Missoulian,* Nov. 2, 4, 1924.

51. For the cartoons, see *Missoula (Mont.) Missoulian,* Nov. 1, 1924; and *Billings (Mont.) Gazette,* Nov. 2, 1924. For the checks illustration, see *Missoula (Mont.) Missoulian,* Oct. 19, 1924; and *Billings (Mont.) Gazette,* Oct. 17, 1924.

52. Karlin, *Joseph M. Dixon,* 2:138–39; *Missoula (Mont.) Missoulian,* Oct. 13, 1924.

53. Waldron and Wilson, *Atlas of Montana Elections,* 98.

54. Joseph M. Dixon to Governor R. A. Nestos, Dec. 23, 1924, folder 1, box 49, Dixon Papers, Toole Archives, UM.

55. Fought, "John Hurst Durston," 120.

56. Ibid., 120–21.

57. Ibid., 117. Fought quotes an unpublished and unsigned carbon copy of a letter from Durston to Walsh, written July 22, 1912, and provided by Durston's daughter, Martha Bolles Palffy.

58. Wanamaker, "Eggleston of the Anaconda Standard," 254–55; *Butte (Mont.) Daily Post,* Jan. 1, 1913.

59. For details on Dickey's background and rise, see Jim Tracey's profile in the *Great Falls (Mont.) Tribune,* Feb. 17, 1986.

60. Fought, "John Hurst Durston," 122–23. See also Brier and Blumberg, *A Century of Montana Journalism,* 180–81.

61. Ibid.

CHAPTER 8

1. For the report of his death and extensive biographical detail, see the *Butte (Mont.) Miner,* March 3, 1925.

2. For Twain's assessment of Clark, see Mark Twain, "Banquet for a Senator," *Montana Journalism Review* 20 (1977): 35. The article, written in 1907, was republished from Bernard DeVoto's *Mark Twain in Eruption: Hitherto Unpublished Pages about Men and Events* (New York: Harper and Brothers, 1922). For background and characterizations of Clark, see Malone, *Battle for Butte,* 13–14, 82–83, 200.

3. For the reporting of Clark's second marriage, see *Anaconda (Mont.) Standard,* July 13, 1904; and *Butte (Mont.) Miner,* July 13, 1904. The incident is discussed at length in William Daniel Mangam, *The Clarks of Montana* (Washington, D.C., Service Printing Co., 1939), 84–97; and O. N. Malmquist, *The First 100 Years: A History of the Salt Lake Tribune, 1871–1971* (Salt Lake City: Utah State Historical Society, 1971), 173. Clark's example would also serve the political and journalistic ambitions of his business partner and fellow mining mogul, U.S. senator Thomas Kearns, who purchased the *Salt Lake Tribune* in 1901.

4. *Butte (Mont.) Miner,* March 3, 1925.

5. *Great Falls (Mont.) Tribune,* Oct. 23, 1903.

6. Barbara Jane Mittal, "The Montana Free Press Newspaper Chain, 1928–1929" (master's thesis, University of Montana, Missoula, 1971), 17–19; Karlin, *Joseph M. Dixon,* 2:202.

7. *Butte (Mont.) Miner,* July 30, 1926; *Missoula (Mont.) Missoulian,* Aug. 6, 1926.

8. For Hutchens's views on Ryan, see *Missoula (Mont.) Missoulian,* April 21, 1926.

9. *Missoula (Mont.) Missoulian,* Aug. 3, 20, 1917.

10. Toole, *Red Ribbons,* 113.

11. *Missoula (Mont.) Missoulian,* Sept. 24, 1926.

12. Karlin, *Joseph M. Dixon,* 2:210–11.

13. Ibid., 2:210–11; *Helena (Mont.) Independent,* March 31, 1926.

14. *Butte (Mont.) Miner,* July 1, 1927; Karlin, *Joseph M. Dixon,* 2:215–20.

15. *Butte (Mont.) Miner,* July 21, 1928.

16. Harris, "Dr. E. B. Craighead's *New Northwest,*" 133; Mittal, "Montana Free Press Newspaper Chain," 26, citing the *Missoula (Mont.) Daily Northwest,* May 19, 1927.

17. Mittal, "Montana Free Press Newspaper Chain," 31–36.

18. *Helena (Mont.) Independent,* May 24, 1928.

19. *Butte (Mont.) Miner,* July 28, 1928.

20. *Butte (Mont.) Daily Post,* Aug. 28, 1928.

21. Mittal, "Montana Free Press Newspaper Chain," 42.

22. Andrew C. Cogswell, "History of the *Montana Standard,*" manuscript in the author's possession, 2; *Butte (Mont.) Montana Free Press,* Sept. 17, 1928.

23. Mittal, "Montana Free Press Newspaper Chain," 67–68, citing the *Missoula (Mont.) Daily Northwest,* July 24, 1928; *Butte (Mont.) Miner,* July 11, 24, 1928; and Karlin, *Joseph M. Dixon,* 2:215.

24. For details on Rankin's involvement in the *Bulletin* and the Havre daily, see James J. Lopach and Jean A. Luckowski, *Jeannette Rankin: A Political Woman* (Boulder, University of Colorado Press, 2005), 34–35.

25. Karlin, *Joseph. M. Dixon*, 2:94, 101; Mittal, "Montana Free Press Newspaper Chain," 44, 70, 77.

26. *Missoula (Mont.) Daily Northwest*, July 24, 1928.

27. Mittal, "Montana Free Press Newspaper Chain," 67.

28. *Butte (Mont.) Miner*, as reprinted in the *Missoula (Mont.) Daily Northwest*, Aug. 21, 1928; Mittal, "Montana Free Press Newspaper Chain," 76.

29. Mittal, "Montana Free Press Newspaper Chain," 79–80, 72–75.

30. Ibid., 79–80; *Butte (Mont.) Montana Standard*, Nov. 5, 1928.

31. *Butte (Mont.) Montana Free Press*, Oct. 21, 1928.

32. Ibid., Nov. 2, 1928.

33. Waldron and Wilson, *Atlas of Montana Elections*, 113–18; Karlin, *Joseph. M. Dixon*, 2:233.

34. *Butte (Mont.) Montana Free Press*, Nov. 7, 1928.

35. Oswald Garrison Villard, "The Press Today: VIII. Montana and the 'Company'," *Nation*, July 9, 1930, 41.

36. *Butte (Mont.) Montana Free Press*, Jan. 13, 1929.

37. Mittal, "Montana Free Press Newspaper Chain," 64–65; Karlin, *Joseph M. Dixon*, 2:213.

38. Mittal, "Montana Free Press Newspaper Chain," 86.

39. *Butte (Mont.) Montana Free Press*, Dec. 8, 1928.

40. Ibid., Feb. 24, 1929.

41. Ibid.

42. Mittal, "Montana Free Press Newspaper Chain," 51.

43. Ibid., 52.

44. *Missoula (Mont.) Daily Northwest*, May 19, 1929; Mittal, "Montana Free Press Newspaper Chain," 92–93.

45. Mittal, "Montana Free Press Newspaper Chain," 93; Villard, "The Press Today," 41.

46. Mittal, "Montana Free Press Newspaper Chain," 47–49.

47. Ibid., 97, 99; *Great Falls (Mont.) Tribune*, May 21, 1929.

48. For its stance on bootleg joints and landlords, see *Butte (Mont.) Montana Free Press*, Feb. 24, 1929.

49. Mitall, "Montana Free Press Newspaper Chain," 97; *Missoula (Mont.) Missoulian*, May 21, 1929.

50. For a national perspective on the trend toward politically independent journalism, see Mott, *American Journalism*, 384–85.

51. Edwards resigned as the paper's managing director in 1924 due to illness and the failure of his Forsyth bank. He died on October 12, 1925, of cancer. For details of his career, see the *Billings (Mont.) Gazette*, Oct. 13, 1925. For the changes in the paper's ownership, see annual corporation reports for 1923 and 1929, on file at the Montana Secretary of State's Office, Helena.

52. Fairmont Investment Company articles of incorporation, on file at the Montana Secretary of State's Office, Helena.

53. Wanamaker, "Eggleston of the *Anaconda Standard*," 298; *Butte (Mont.) Montana Standard*, Nov. 6, 1929.

CHAPTER 9

1. Linda Lawson, *Truth in Publishing: Federal Regulation of the Press's Business Practices, 1880–1920* (Carbondale: Southern Illinois University Press, 1993), 16–18.

2. Ibid., 70, 100–103.

3. Ibid., 102.

4. Florence H. Sanden, "Consolidation of Montana Newspapers: Their Tendency Toward Standardization and Present Ownership" (master's thesis, Columbia University, 1930), 32.

5. Sanden, "Consolidation of Montana Newspapers," 32, 18–19.

6. Ibid., 16, 14.

7. Ibid., 28, 29–31.

8. Ibid., 32, 33.

9. William H. Lyon, *Those Old Yellow Dog Days: Frontier Journalism in Arizona, 1859–1912* (Tucson: Arizona Historical Society, 1994), 84–86; James W. Byrkit, *Forging the Copper Collar: Arizona's Labor Management War of 1901–1921* (Tucson: University of Arizona Press, 1982), 59–60, 82, 111, 156.

10. For a discussion of American press criticism in the early twentieth century, see David Mark Chalmers, *The Social and Political Ideas of the Muckrakers* (New York: Citadel, 1964), 40–44; Upton Sinclair, *The Brass Check: A Study of American Journalism* (Pasadena, Calif.: privately printed, 1920), 242.

11. Villard, "The Press Today," 39–41.

12. Ibid.

13. Ibid.

14. See minutes of Fairmont Investment Company board of directors meeting, Jan. 5, 1932, in the appendix of Catharine Louise Astle, "Opinions of Newsmen about their Employment by Anaconda Company Newspapers" (senior thesis, University of Montana School of Journalism, 1972).

15. *Anaconda (Mont.) Standard*, Feb. 17, 1904; Silver Bow County coroner's report on the death of William Kiley, Feb. 16, 1904, Silver Bow County Coroner's Register, 1904, p. 206, Butte-Silver Bow Public Archives, Butte, Montana (hereafter BSBPA, Butte).

16. Death figures were compiled from Silver Bow County Coroner's Register, 1918, BSBPA, Butte; *Butte (Mont.) Daily Post*, Nov. 23, 1918.

17. Silver Bow County Coroner's Register, 1941, pp. 12–15, BSBPA, Butte.

18. Cogswell, "History of the *Montana Standard*," 29.

19. Ibid., 30.

20. *Butte (Mont.) Montana Standard*, May 9–12, 16–17, 1934.

21. Ibid., May 11–12, Sept. 1, 14, 16, 20, 1934. For background and a discussion of the strike's implications, see Laurie Mercier, *Anaconda: Labor, Community, and Culture in Montana's Smelter City* (Urbana: University of Illinois Press, 2001), 51–56.

22. "Lee Enterprise's Purchase of the Anaconda Company's Newspapers: An Explanation," Erlandson chap., 2–3. The author obtained a copy of this unpublished manuscript detailing Lee's view of events surrounding the sale from former Lee CEO Lloyd Schermer. The work is broken into chapters by various authors.

23. Thomas Payne, "Politics under the Copper Dome," in *The Montana Past, An Anthology* (Missoula, Mont.: University of Montana Press, 1969), 310.

24. Toole, *Twentieth-Century Montana*, 273.

25. *Helena (Mont.) Montana Record-Herald*, Jan. 1, 9, 29, March 1, 13, 14, 1935; *Missoula (Mont.) Missoulian*, March 13, 14, 1935.

26. Waldron and Wilson, *Atlas of Montana Elections*, 141.

27. *House Journal of the Twenty-Fourth Legislative Assembly of the State of Montana, Jan. 7–March 7, 1935* (Helena, Mont.: State Publishing, 1935). From 1930 to 1939, the Standard Publishing Company reported nearly eighty thousand dollars in operating losses. Over the same period, the Post Publishing Company reported an operating profit of slightly more than thirty-eight thousand dollars. Standard Publishing Company Ledger, volumes 1129–31, Anaconda Company Records, MHS, Helena; Post Publishing Company Ledger, ibid.

28. For details on the investigation, see *House Journal*. See also the *Helena (Mont.) Western Progressive*, March 8, 1935.

29. *House Journal*, 917, 922; *Helena (Mont.) Western Progressive*, March 8, 1935.

30. *Billings Gazette*, March 5, 1935; *House Journal*, 918–22.

31. *House Journal*, 774–76, 918–20.

32. *House Journal*, 777.

33. For coverage of the investigation, see the *Billings (Mont.) Gazette*, March 5, 8, 9, 1935; the *Missoula (Mont.) Missoulian*, March 2, 1935; and the *Great Falls (Mont.) Tribune*, March 2, 3, 1935.

34. *House Journal*, 926.

35. *House Journal*, 947; *Helena (Mont.) Montana Record-Herald*, March 8, 1935.

36. *Helena (Mont.) Western Progressive*, March 8, 1935.

37. For Walsh's role in buying the *Independent* and his later frustrations with Campbell, see J. Leonard Bates, *Senator Thomas J. Walsh of Montana: Senator Thomas J. Walsh of Montana: Law and Public Affairs, from TR to FDR* (Urbana: University of Illinois Press, 1999), 84–85.

38. For Bruce's background, see Harry Billings, "The *People's Voice*: The Dream and the Reality," *Montana Journalism Review* 20 (1977): 2–3.

39. For an example, see the *Helena (Mont.) Western Progressive*, March 25, 11, 1932.

40. For samples of the paper's editorial stances, see ibid.

41. *Helena (Mont.) Western Progressive*, Sept. 6, 1935, as cited in Richard Ruetten, "Anaconda Journalism: The End of an Era," *Journalism Quarterly* 37 (Winter 1960): 10.

42. Ruetten, "Anaconda Journalism," 10, citing the *Helena (Mont.) Western Progressive*, Aug. 23, 1935. For an example of the editorial tributes to Campbell, see the *Miles City (Mont.) Star*, Dec. 19, 1938.

43. *Lewistown (Mont.) News-Democrat*, Aug. 16, 1935; *Helena (Mont.) Western Progressive*, Aug. 28, 1935.

44. For details on the *Bulletin*'s demise and William Dunne's move to New York, see Wetzel, "Making of an American Radical," 123.

45. For Polk's attacks on the *Producers News* and details of Taylor's career, see Vindex, "Radical Rule in Montana," 12, 15.

46. For details of the demise of the *Producers News,* see Vindex, "Radical Rule in Montana," 16; and McDonald, "'A Paper of, by, and for the People,'" 32–33.

47. For an assessment of the copper press's coverage of O'Connell's reelection bid, see William E. Larson, "News Management in the Company Press: The Anaconda Copper Mining Company's *Missoulian, Billings Gazette* and *Helena Independent, Independent Record,* 1938–1944" (master's thesis, University of Montana, 1971), 10, 23–32, 138; Malone, Roeder and Lang, *Montana,* 307; Harry Billings, "The *People's Voice,*" 3.

48. Harry Billings, "The *People's Voice,*" 3.

49. *Helena (Mont.) People's Voice,* Dec. 6, 1939, Nov. 13, 1940.

50. Ibid., Dec. 1, 13, 1939.

51. Ibid.

52. "Gretchen and Harry Billings," in *The Native Home of Hope: People and the Northern Rockies,* ed. Thomas N. Bethell, Deborah E. Tuck, and Michael S. Clark (Salt Lake City: Howe Brothers, 1986), 141. Circulation could climb as high as twelve thousand during election campaigns.

53. C. Howard McDonald, *Voices in the Big Sky! A Concise History of Radio and Television in Montana from the 1920s to the Present* (Bozeman, Mont.: BIG M Broadcast Services, 1992), 10, 13, 75–78; Ronald P. Richards, "Montana's Pioneer Radio Stations: A Hobby Becomes an Industry," in *A Century of Montana Journalism,* 78.

54. KGIR speech, Aug. 9, 1941, folder 4, box 578, James E. Murray Papers (hereafter Murray Papers), MSS 91, Toole Archives, UM.

55. Ibid.

56. Marcosson, *Anaconda,* 225–27.

57. Larson, "News Management," 135.

58. Ibid., 59.

59. Ibid., 88–89.

60. *Helena (Mont.) People's Voice,* Oct. 9, 1940.

61. Larson, "News Management," 63, 88; Joseph Kinsey Howard, "The Montana Twins in Trouble," *Harper's,* Sept. 1944, 334–42; Joseph Kinsey Howard, *Montana: High, Wide and Handsome* (1943; repr., Lincoln: University of Nebraska Press, 1959), 251–74; Larson, "News Management," 91–107.

62. John Gunther, *Inside U.S.A.* (New York: Harper and Brothers, 1947), 171.

CHAPTER 10

1. *Butte (Mont.) Inter Mountain,* Sept. 4, 1903; Sinclair, *Brass Check,* 242; Villard, "The Press Today," 39–41.

2. U.S. Congress, Senate Committee on Privileges and Elections, *Report of the Committee on Privileges and Elections,* 2274–75, 2456–59.

3. For a history of the Fairmont Corporation, see "Application of Consent to Transfer Control of Buttrey Broadcast, Inc., License of Station KFBB, Great Falls, Montana, from Fred Birch to the Fairmont Corporation and Supplementary Letters, Documents and Information," Federal Communications Commission file no. BTC-1068 (hereafter FCC file), U.S. Federal Communications Commission Records, 1950–52, microfilm 47, MHS, Helena.

4. For the early days of KFBB, see Richards, "Montana's Pioneer Radio Stations," 80–81. See also FCC file, MHS, Helena.

5. FCC file, MHS, Helena.

6. Ibid.

7. Fred Martin, "A Publisher's Statement: Anatomy of a Failing Newspaper," *Montana Journalism Review* 11 (1968): 16; *Great Falls (Mont.) Tribune*, March 13, 1951; Jyl Hoyt, "Montana Writer Joseph Kinsey Howard: Crusader for the Worker, Land, Indian and Community" (master's thesis, University of Montana, Missoula, 1988), 18, 25.

8. Martin, "A Publisher's Statement," 16; Senator James E. Murray to W. F. Flinn, May 11, 1943, folder 5, box 579, Murray Papers, Toole Archives, UM.

9. Terry Taylor Dwyer, *Looking Back in Black and White: 42 years as a Montana Newsman* (Fort Benton, Mont.: Coolbrook, 2003), 20–21.

10. For coverage of the Bonner affair, see the *Great Falls (Mont.) Tribune*, May 6, 9, 1950; *New York Times*, May 6, 1950; *New Orleans Times-Picayune*, May 6, 8, 1950; *Spokane (Wash.) Spokesman-Review*, May 6, 1950; and the *Billings (Mont.) Gazette*; *Missoula (Mont.) Missoulian*; *Butte (Mont.) Montana Standard*; and *Helena (Mont.) Independent Record*, May 7, 1950.

11. For background on federal regulation of broadcasting, see Michael Emery and Edwin Emery, *The Press in America: An Interpretative History of the Mass Media*, 7th ed. (Englewood Cliffs, N.J., 1992), 275.

12. Fairmont Corporation application to purchase KFBB, Jan. 21, 1951, FCC file, MHS, Helena.

13. Ibid.

14. John Evanko Jr. to FCC chairman, Feb. 2, 1951, FCC file, MHS, Helena.

15. Roy H. Glover to FCC Secretary T. J. Slowie, Feb. 18, 1951, ibid.

16. John Jarussi to FCC, Sept. 10, 1951, ibid.; Saims Myllymaki to Harry S. Truman, Dec. 8, 1951, ibid.

17. Raymond S. Graham to FCC, Oct. 4, 1951, ibid.; Jerry O'Connell to FCC, Sept. 17, 1951, ibid.; *Helena (Mont.) People's Voice*, Sept. 9, 1951.

18. FCC to Fairmont Corporation, Aug. 8, 1951, FCC file, MHS, Helena.

19. Gunther, *Inside U.S.A.*, 167.

20. *Helena (Mont.) People's Voice*, Sept. 21, 1951; Harry L. Billings to Senator James E. Murray, Oct. 2, 1951, FCC file, MHS, Helena; FCC to Jerry O'Connell, Sept. 26, 1951, ibid.

21. Fairmont Corporation to FCC, Jan. 22, 1952, FCC file, MHS, Helena.

22. Ibid.

23. Patrick Murphy Malin to FCC chairman Paul A. Walker, May 23, 1952, ibid.

24. FCC to Fairmont Corporation, May 28, 1952, ibid.

25. Fairmont Corporation to FCC, July 10, 1952, ibid.

26. "Monopoly vs. Public Power," *New Republic*, Dec. 3, 1951; "Anaconda's Big Steal," *Nation*, Jan. 5, 1952.

27. Joseph M. Schiltz, "Montana's Captive Press," *Montana Opinion* 1 (June 1956).

28. *Denver Post*, April 6, 13, 20, 27, May 4, 25, 1952.

29. Ibid., April 6, 1952.

30. Ibid.

31. Ibid.; Dwyer, *Looking Back in Black and White,* 20.

32. *Denver Post,* May 4, 1952.

33. Ibid.

34. Ibid, April 6, 1952.

35. Ibid.

36. Ibid., April 13, 1952.

37. Marcosson, *Anaconda,* 67–70, 308–10.

38. Ibid., 316–18, 259–61.

39. Astle, "Opinions of Newsmen," 27.

40. Schiltz, "Montana's Captive Press."

41. Ibid.

42. Ibid.

43. Ibid.

44. Ibid.

45. *Missoula County (Mont.) Times,* July 13, 1956, reprinted as "One Man's Opinion," *Montana Opinion* 1 (Oct. 1956): 29.

46. *Cut Bank (Mont.) Pioneer Press,* July 12, 1956, reprinted as "What Other Editors Say," *Montana Opinion* 1 (Feb. 1957): 12.

47. "Anaconda Country," *Economist,* Sept. 7, 1957, 765–66.

48. Robert Miller interview, in *Not in Precious Metals Alone,* 217.

49. Ruth James Towe, "The Lee Newspapers of Montana; The First Three Years, 1959–1962" (master's thesis, University of Montana, 1969), 120; John Thomas McNay, "Breaking the Copper Collar: The Sale of the Anaconda Newspapers and the Professionalization of Journalism in Montana" (master's thesis, University of Montana, 1991), 69–74.

50. Robert Miller interview, in *Not in Precious Metals Alone,* 217. See also Astle, "Opinions of Newsmen."

51. Gary Sorenson, interview by author, Missoula, Mont., Aug. 14, 2004.

52. Duane W. Bowler interview in *Not in Precious Metals Alone,* 218.

53. John Newhouse, unpublished manuscript history of Lee's Montana experience written in the mid-1970s (hereafter Newhouse manuscript), chap. 17. The author obtained a copy of the manuscript from former Lee chairman Lloyd Schermer.

54. *Denver Post,* April 6, 1952; Towe, "Lee Newspapers of Montana," 61.

55. Towe, "Lee Newspapers of Montana," 60–61.

56. Towe, "Lee Newspapers of Montana," 59–60. Richard T. Ruetten, "Anaconda Journalism: The End of an Era," *Journalism Quarterly* 37 (Winter 1960), 7.

57. Ibid., 59–60, 63. For examples of the *Missoulian's* letters-to-the-editor style, see *Missoula (Mont.) Missoulian,* Aug. 2, 27, 1917.

58. Albert Gaskill interview, in *Not by Precious Metals Alone,* 218.

59. Towe, "Lee Newspapers of Montana," 163–64.

60. According to Exhibit 5 of Fairmont's FCC application, Fairmont's net income from its newspapers totaled just $25,142.73 for 1949. Fairmont Corporation FCC application b, FCC file, MHS, Helena; Towe, "Lee Newspapers of Montana," 163–64.

61. *Columbia Falls (Mont.) Hungry Horse News,* June 5, 1959.

CHAPTER 11

1. Richard Morrison to Philip Adler, April 12, 1965, "History of Montana Newspapers," Donald W. Anderson Papers, 1941–1971 (hereafter Anderson Papers), MSS 157, Toole Archives, UM. Most references to the collection include box and folder information. However, some recent contributions have yet to be indexed and are referred to by folder name or alphabetical title.

2. "Lee Enterprises Purchase of the Anaconda Company's Montana Newspaper," Anderson chap., p. 16.

3. Towe, "Lee Newspapers of Montana," 44–45.

4. Morrison to Adler, April 12, 1965; Towe, "Lee Newspapers of Montana," 24. Weed made the announcement at the company's sixty-fourth annual stockholders meeting in Anaconda. *Livingston (Mont.) Park County News,* May 28, 1959.

5. "Lee Enterprises Purchase of the Anaconda Company's Montana Newspapers," Anderson chap., p. 1.

6. Ibid., Anderson chap., p. 2.

7. For Anderson's apprehensions about conditions on the sale, see "Lee Enterprises Purchase of the Anaconda Company's Montana Newspapers," Anderson chap., p. 17. See also Don Anderson to Ruth Towe, May 2, 1963, in Towe, "Lee Newspapers of Montana," 210; Gilluly, *Press Gang,* 144.

8. "Lee Enterprises Purchase of the Anaconda Company's Montana Newspapers," Anderson chap., pp. 8, 27.

9. Lee Enterprises, *The Lee Group: Mid-America to the Mountains, 1960* (Davenport, Iowa: Lee Enterprises, 1960), 4–5.

10. "Lee Enterprises Purchase of the Anaconda Company's Montana Newspapers," Anderson chap., pp 13–14.

11. Towe, "Lee Newspapers of Montana," 26; Fred Seaton to Don Anderson, June 22, 1959, folder 4, box 3, Anderson Papers, Toole Archives, UM. Other interested parties included Edd E. Roundtree, a former newsman from Palo Alto, California, who wanted to purchase the *Missoulian* only. A Helena man, G. D'Oench Jr., sought to buy the *Helena Independent Record.* Edd Roundtree to Lee Loomis, May 23, 1959, folder 4, box 8, ibid.; G. D'Oench to Phil Adler, May 26, 1959, ibid.

12. "Lee Enterprises Purchase of the Anaconda Company's Montana Newspapers," Anderson chap. 5. After a tour of Anaconda's papers in January 1959, the Ridder organization expressed interest in the Billings and Missoula dailies. John Cowles of the Cowles media group expressed special interest in the *Billings Gazette* before and after the sale to Lee. John Cowles to Lee Loomis, June 3, 1959, folder 4, box 8, Anderson Papers, Toole Archives, UM.

13. For biographical materials on Anderson, see the biographical notes in the guide to Anderson Papers, Toole Archives, UM. See also Gilluly, *Press Gang,* 143; *Madison (Wisc.) Wisconsin State Journal,* April 27, 1978.

14. Don Anderson to John H. Powell, June 5, 1959, folder 1, box 3, Anderson Papers, Toole Archives, UM.

15. Towe, "Lee Newspapers of Montana," 44.

16. Ibid., 51.

17. "Lee Enterprises Purchase of the Anaconda Company's Montana Newspapers," Anderson chap., p. 17.

18. Ibid., Anderson chap., p. 3.

19. Ibid., 16.

20. For details on how the story broke, see *Livingston (Mont.) Park County News*, June 4, 1959.

21. *Helena (Mont.) People's Voice*, May 29, 1959.

22. Gretchen Billings to Don Anderson, June 15, 1959, folder 10, box 8, Anderson Papers, Toole Archives, UM.

23. For the announcement and details of its play, see *Missoula (Mont.) Missoulian*, June 2, 1959; and *Billings (Mont.) Gazette*, June 2, 1959.

24. Ibid. For the radio announcer's comment, see a letter from "Steve" to Don Anderson, June 5, 1959, folder 1, box 3, Anderson Papers, Toole Archives, UM.

25. "Montana's Free Press," *Editor & Publisher*, June 13, 1959, 6.

26. *Salem (Oreg.) Oregon Statesman*, June 6, 1959; "Chain of Copper," *Time Magazine*, June 1, 1959, 68.

27. *Great Falls (Mont.) Tribune*, June 2, 1959; *Miles City (Mont.) Star*, June 2, 1959; *Kalispell (Mont.) Daily Inter Lake*, June 2, 1959.

28. *Lewistown (Mont.) Daily News*, June 3, 1959.

29. *Harlowton (Mont.) Times*, June 5, 1959.

30. *Hamilton (Mont.) Western News*, June 12, 1959.

31. *Columbia Falls (Mont.) Hungry Horse News*, June 5, 1959.

32. Don Anderson to Richard T. Ruetten, March 25, 1960, folder 8, box 8, Anderson Papers, Toole Archives, UM; Walter McLeod to Don Anderson, June 11, 1959, folder 5, box 4, ibid.

33. Merrill G. Burlingame to Don Anderson, June 30, 1959, folder 1, box 3, ibid.; John Cowles to Lee Loomis, June 3, 1959, folder 4, box 8, ibid.; Lee Loomis to John Cowles, June 4, 1959, ibid.

34. Fred Martin to C. Jay Parkinson, May 23, 1959, Fred Martin file, ibid.

35. Don Anderson to Jefferson Jones, June 5, 1959, Fred Martin file, Anderson Papers, Toole Archives, UM; Fred J. Martin to C. Jay Parkinson, May 27, 1959, ibid.; *Livingston (Mont.) Park County News*, May 28, 1959.

36. Ruetten, "Anaconda Journalism," 3–9; Don Anderson to Richard T. Ruetten, March 25, 1960, folder 8, box 8, Anderson Papers, Toole Archives, UM.

37. "Lee Enterprises Purchase of the Anaconda Company's Montana Newspapers," Anderson chap., p. 24.

38. Ibid., 25.

39. Don Anderson to John H. Powell, June 5, 1959, folder 1, box 3, Anderson Papers, Toole Archives, UM.

40. Towe, "Lee Newspapers of Montana," 136.

41. Ibid., 93.

42. Ibid., 94.

43. Ibid., 100.

44. Ibid., 133. For Schermer's account of the earthquake coverge, see Newhouse manuscript, chap. 2, p. 1.

45. Towe, "Lee Newspapers of Montana," 114–15; McNay, "Breaking the Copper Collar," 46–47; Don Anderson to Richard Morrison, Nov. 10, 1960, folder 10, box 4, Anderson Papers, Toole Archives, UM.

46. Don Anderson to Duane Bowler, Oct. 24, 1961, Duane Bowler file, Anderson Papers, Toole Archives, UM.

47. *Butte (Mont.) Montana Standard*, April 5, 6, 7, 9, 1961. See also McNay, "Breaking the Copper Collar," 71–74.

48. Don Anderson to Richard Morrison, April 13, 1961, folder 2, box 5, Anderson Papers, Toole Archives, UM.

49. Towe, "Lee Newspapers of Montana," 123, 139–40.

50. *Billings (Mont.) Gazette*, April 29, 1978.

51. Tom Mooney to Don Anderson, Feb. 15, 1960, Tom Mooney file, Anderson Papers, Toole Archives, UM; *Butte (Mont.) Montana Standard*, Feb. 11, 1960; Don Anderson to Phil Adler, Jan. 15, 1960, folder 1, box 1, Anderson Papers, Toole Archives, UM.

52. Ed Renouard to Phil Adler, Jan. 15, 1960, folder 1, box 1, Anderson Papers, Toole Archives, UM.

53. For commentary on citizens' reaction to the strike, see Don Anderson to C. Jay Parkinson, June 2, 1959, C. Jay Parkinson file, Anderson Papers, Toole Archives, UM. See also Don Anderson to C. Jay Parkinson, Feb. 1, 1960, ibid.

54. Don Anderson to Tom Mooney, Feb. 17, 1960, Tom Mooney file, ibid.

55. Newhouse manuscript, chap. 2, p. 2.

56. For the *Missoulian's* increasingly confrontational position on environmental issues, see "The Sands of Self" editorial, Sept. 4, 1970. For an overview of the *Billings Gazette's* concern with strip-mining, see Newhouse manuscript, chap. 15.

57. Newhouse manuscript, chap. 15.

58. C. Jay Parkinson to Phil Adler, Dec. 15, 1970, folder 5, box 2, Anderson Papers, Toole Archives, UM.

59. J. E. Corette to Don Anderson, July 8, 1964, folder C, ibid.

60. Don Anderson to J. E. Corette, n.d., ibid.

61. J. E. Corette to Don Anderson, Jan. 6, 1971, folder 5, box 2, ibid.

EPILOGUE

1. For an insider's view of Anaconda's demise, see Eugene C. Tidball, "What Ever Happened to the Anaconda Company?" *Montana The Magazine of Western History* 47 (Summer 1997): 60–64.

2. Don Anderson to Phil Adler, Jan. 11, 1971, folder 5, box 2, Anderson Papers, Toole Archives, UM; Malone, Roeder and Lang, *Montana*, 380.

3. For an assessment of Lee near the end of its second decade in Montana, see Nathaniel Blumberg, "The Media and Montana," *Montana Journalism Review* 21 (1978–79): 5-7.

4. For Lee's in-house debate over the issue of local autonomy in the late 1960s, see Newhouse manuscript, chap. 18.

5. For contemporary assessments of Lee's reputation in Montana and nationally, see Alicia C. Shepard's "Big Sky's Big Player," *American Journalism Review* 21 (Oct. 1999): 30–36; Lori Robertson's "Lee Who?" *American Journalism Review* 27 (June–July 2005: 42–46, 48–53).

BIBLIOGRAPHY

ARCHIVAL COLLECTIONS

Anaconda Copper Mining Company Records, 1876–1974. MC 169. Montana Historical Society Research Center, Helena.

Anderson, Don. Writings. SC 1211. Montana Historical Society Research Center, Helena.

Anderson, Don W. Papers. MSS 157. K. Ross Toole Archives, University of Montana, Missoula.

Billings, Harry L. and Gretchen. Papers, 1940–84. Collection 2095. Merrill G. Burlingame Special Collections, Montana State University Libraries, Bozeman.

Daly, Marcus. Papers, 1873–1900. SC 63. Montana Historical Society Research Center, Helena.

Dixon, Joseph M. Papers. MSS 55. K. Ross Toole Archives, University of Montana, Missoula.

Federal Communications Committee File No. BTC-1068. "Application of Consent to Transfer Control of Buttrey Broadcast, Inc., License of Station KFBB, Great Falls, Montana, from Fred Birch to the Fairmont Corporation and Supplementary Letters, Documents and Information." U.S. Federal Communications Commission Records, 1950–52. Microfilm 47. Montana Historical Society Research Center, Helena.

Montana Council of Defense Records, 1916–1921. RS 19. Montana Historical Society Research Center, Helena.

Montana Governors Papers. MC 35. Montana Historical Society Research Center, Helena.

Murray, James E. Collection. MSS 91. K. Ross Toole Archives, University of Montana, Missoula.

Neill Family Papers, 1886–1964. MC 248. Montana Historical Society Research Center, Helena.

Roeder, Richard B. Research and Personal Papers, 1949–95. Collection 2346. Merrill G. Burlingame Special Collections, Montana State University Libraries, Bozeman.

Shober, John H. Family. Papers, 1832–1952. MC 69. Montana Historical Society Research Center, Helena.

Silver Bow County Coroner's Registers, 1894–1973. Butte-Silver Bow Public Archives, Butte, Montana.

GOVERNMENT DOCUMENTS AND PUBLICATIONS

House Journal of the Twenty-Fourth Legislative Assembly of the State of Montana, January 7–March 7, 1935. Helena, Mont.: State Publishing, 1935.

Montana Secretary of State's Office, Helena, articles of incorporation and annual corporation reports on file: Enterprise Publishing Company (Livingston), Fairmont Investment Company (Delaware), Fruitgrowers Publishing Company (Missoula), Gazette Printing Company (Billings), the Independent Publishing Company (Helena), the Leader Company (Great Falls), Livingston Publishing Company, the Missoulian Publishing Company, Montana Record Publishing Company (Helena), News Publishing Company (Billings), the Sentinel Publishing Company (Missoula).

Montana Supreme Court. "In the Matter of the Receivership of the First Trust & Savings of Billings, Montana. Gazette Printing Co., et al. Respondents, v. McConnell, Appellant." Case No. 3075. Copy in State Law Library, Helena, Montana.

U.S. Congress. Senate. Committee on Privileges and Elections. *Report of the Committee on Privileges and Elections of the United States Senate Relative to the Right and Title of William A. Clark to a Seat as Senator from the State of Montana.* 56th Cong., 1st sess., 1900, S. Rept.1052. 3 vols.

BOOKS

Astle, John. *Only in Butte: Stories off the Hill.* Butte, Mont.: Holt Group, 2004.

Bates, J. Leonard. *Senator Thomas J. Walsh of Montana: Law and Public Affairs, from TR to FDR.* Urbana: University of Illinois Press, 1999.

Bethell, Thomas N., Deborah E. Tuck, and Michael S. Clark, eds. *The Native Home of Hope: People and the Northern Rockies.* Salt Lake City: Howe Brothers, 1986.

Boorstin, Daniel. *The Americans: The National Experience.* New York: Random House, 1966.

Braley, Berton. *Pegasus Pulls a Hack: Memoirs of a Modern Minstrel.* New York: Minton, Balch, 1934.

Brier, Warren J. and Blumberg, Nathan B., eds. *A Century of Montana Journalism.* Missoula, Mont.: Mountain Press, 1971.

Byrkit, James W. *Forging the Copper Collar: Arizona's Labor Management War of 1901–1921.* Tucson: University of Arizona Press, 1982.

Calvert, Jerry W. *The Gibraltar: Socialism and Labor in Butte, Montana, 1895–1920.* Helena: Montana Historical Society Press, 1988.

Chalmers, David Mark. *The Social and Political Ideas of the Muckrakers.* New York: Citadel, 1964.

Connolly, Christopher Powell. *The Devil Learns to Vote, the Story of Montana.* New York: Covici, Friede, 1938.

Dary, David. *Red Blood and Black Ink: Journalism in the Old West.* New York: Alfred A. Knopf, 1998.

DeVoto, Bernard. *Mark Twain in Eruption: Hitherto Unpublished Pages about Men and Events.* New York: Harper and Brothers, 1922.

Dwyer, Terry Taylor. *Looking Back in Black and White: 42 Years as a Montana Newsman.* Fort Benton, Mont.: Coolbrook, 2003.

Dyar, Ralph E. *News for an Empire: The Story of the Spokesman-Review of Spokane, Washington, and of the Field It Serves.* Caldwell, Idaho: Caxton, 1952.

Eggleston, Charles H. *Helena's Social Supremacy.* Pamphlet on file at the University of Montana School of Journalism.

Emery, Michael C., and Edwin Emery. *The Press in America: An Interpretive History of the Mass Media.* 7th ed. Englewood Cliffs, N.J.: Prentice-Hall, 1992.

Emmons, David M. *The Butte Irish: Class and Ethnicity in an American Mining Town, 1875–1925.* Urbana: University of Illinois Press, 1989.

Federal Writers' Program. *Copper Camp: Stories of the World's Greatest Mining Town, Butte, Montana.* New York: Hastings House, 1943.

Federal Writers' Project. *The WPA Guide to 1930s Montana.* 1939. Reprint, Tucson: University of Arizona Press, 1994.

Fritz, Harry W., Mary Murphy, and Robert R. Swartout Jr., eds. *Montana Legacy: Essays on History, People, and Place.* Helena: Montana Historical Society Press, 2002.

Gilluly, Sam. *The Press Gang: A Century of Montana Newspapers, 1885–1985.* Helena: Montana Press Association, 1985.

Glasscock, Carl B. *The War of the Copper Kings: Greed, Power and Politics, the Billion Dollar Battle for Butte, Montana, the Richest Hill on Earth.* 1935. Reprint, Helena, Mont.: Riverbend, 2002.

Gunther, John. *Inside U.S.A.* New York: Harper and Brothers, 1947.

Gutfeld, Arnon. *Montana's Agony: Years of War and Hysteria, 1917–1921.* Gainesville: University Presses of Florida, 1979.

Howard, Joseph Kinsey. *Montana: High, Wide and Handsome.* 1943. Reprint, Lincoln: University of Nebraska Press, 1959.

Hudson, Robert V. *The Writing Game: A Biography of Will Irwin.* Ames: Iowa State University Press, 1982.

Hutchens, John K. *One Man's Montana; An Informal Portrait of a State.* Philadelphia: J. B. Lippincott, 1964.

Irwin, Will. *The American Newspaper.* Edited by Clifford F. Weigle and David G. Clark. Ames: Iowa State University Press, 1969.

Karlin, Jules A. *Joseph M. Dixon of Montana.* 2 vols. Missoula: University of Montana, 1974.

Karolevitz, Robert F. *Newspapering in the Old West: A Pictorial History of Journalism and Printing on the Frontier.* Seattle: Superior Pub., 1965.

Lawson, Linda. *Truth in Publishing: Federal Regulation of the Press's Business Practices, 1880–1920.* Carbondale: Southern Illinois University Press, 1993.

Lawson, Thomas W. *Frenzied Finance: The Crime of Amalgamated.* New York: Ridgway-Thayer, 1906.

Lee, James Melvin. *History of American Journalism*. Garden City, N.Y.: Garden City Pub., 1923.

Lopach, James J. and Luckowski, Jean A. *Jeannette Rankin: A Political Woman*. Boulder: University Press of Colorado, 2005.

Lukas, J. Anthony. *Big Trouble: A Murder in a Small Western Town Sets Off a Struggle for the Soul of America*. New York: Simon and Schuster, 1997.

Lyon, William H. *Those Old Yellow Dog Days: Frontier Journalism in Arizona, 1859– 1912*. Tucson: Arizona Historical Society, 1994.

MacMillan, Donald. *Smoke Wars: Anaconda Copper, Montana Air Pollution, and the Courts, 1890–1924*. Helena: Montana Historical Society Press, 2000.

Malmquist, O. N. *The First 100 Years: A History of the Salt Lake Tribune, 1871– 1971*. Salt Lake City: Utah State Historical Society, 1971.

Malone, Michael P., *The Battle for Butte: Mining and Politics on the Northern Frontier, 1864–1906*. Seattle, University of Washington Press, 1981.

Malone, Michael P., and Richard B. Roeder, eds. *The Montana Past; An Anthology*. Missoula: University of Montana Press, 1969.

———. *Montana's Past: Selected Essays*. Missoula: University of Montana, 1973.

Malone, Michael P., Richard B. Roeder, and William L. Lang. *Montana: A History of Two Centuries*. Rev. ed. Seattle: University of Washington Press, 1991.

Mangam, William Daniel. *The Clarks of Montana*. Washington, D.C., Service Printing, 1939.

Marcosson, Isaac F. *Anaconda*. New York: Dodd, Mead, 1957.

McChesney, Robert W., and Jim Nichols. *It's the Media, Stupid*. New York: Seven Stories, 2000.

McDonald, C. Howard. *Voices in the Big Sky! A Concise History of Radio and Television in Montana from the 1920s to the Present*. Bozeman, Montana: BIG M Broadcast Services, 1992.

Mercier, Laurie. *Anaconda: Labor, Community, and Culture in Montana's Smelter City*. Urbana: University of Illinois Press, 2001.

Morris, Patrick F. *Anaconda, Montana: Copper Smelting Boom Town on the Western Frontier*. Bethesda, Md: Swann, 1997.

Mott, Frank Luther. *American Journalism; A History, 1690–1960*. 3d ed. New York: Macmillan, 1962.

Murphy, Jerre C. *The Comical History of Montana: A Serious Story for Free People* . . . . San Diego: E. L. Scofield, 1912.

Murphy, Mary. *Mining Cultures: Gender, Work, and Leisure in Butte, 1914–41*. Urbana: University of Illinois Press, 1997.

Nasaw, David. *The Chief: The Life of William Randolph Hearst*. Boston: Houghton Mifflin, 2001.

Not in Precious Metals Alone: A Manuscript History of Montana. Helena: Historical Society Press, 1976.

Progressive Men of the State of Montana. 2 vols. Chicago: A. W. Bowen, 1903.

Renshaw, Patrick. *The Wobblies: The Story of Syndicalism in the United States*. Garden City, N.Y.: Doubleday, 1967.

Seldes, George. *Lords of the Press.* New York: J. Messner, 1938.

——. *One Thousand Americans.* New York: Boni and Gaer, 1947.

Shoebotham, H. Minar. *Anaconda: Life of Marcus Daly, the Copper King.* Harrisburg, Pa.: Stackpole, 1956.

Sinclair, Upton. *The Brass Check: A Study of American Journalism.* Pasadena, Calif.: privately printed, 1920.

Stout, Tom. *Montana: Its History and Biography . . . .* 3 vols. Chicago: American Historical Society, 1921.

Swanberg, W. A. *Citizen Hearst: A Biography of William Randolph Hearst.* New York: Bantam, 1967.

Swartout, Robert R., Jr., and Harry W. Fritz, eds. *The Montana Heritage: An Anthology of Historical Essays.* Helena: Montana Historical Society Press, 1992.

Toole, John H. *Red Ribbons: A Story of Missoula and its Newspaper.* Davenport, Iowa: Lee Enterprises, 1989.

Toole, K. Ross. *Montana; An Uncommon Land.* Norman: University of Oklahoma Press, 1959.

——. *Twentieth-Century Montana; A State of Extremes.* Norman: University of Oklahoma Press, 1972.

——, Rex C. Myers, and Harry W. Fritz. *Montana and the West: Essays in Honor of K. Ross Toole.* Boulder, Colo.: Pruett, 1984.

Waldron, Ellis. *Montana Politics since 1864: An Atlas of Elections.* Missoula: Montana State University Press, 1958.

——, and Paul B. Wilson, *Atlas of Montana Elections, 1889–1976.* Missoula: University of Montana, 1978.

Wheeler, Burton K. *Yankee from the West: The Candid, Turbulent Life Story of the Yankee-Born U.S. Senator from Montana.* Garden City, N.Y.: Doubleday, 1962.

Whetstone, Daniel W. *Frontier Editor.* New York: Hastings House, 1956.

Work, Clemens P. *Darkest before Dawn: Sedition and Free Speech in the American West.* Albuquerque: University of New Mexico Press, 2005.

ARTICLES

Amick, Robert. M., Jr. "Vitriol, Wormwood and Gall: The Brazen Butte Bulletin." *Montana Journalism Review* 10 (1967): 30–33.

"Anaconda Country." *Economist,* September 7, 1957, 765–66.

"Anaconda's Big Steal," *Nation,* January 5, 1952.

Anderson, Don. "Lee's Purchase of the Anaconda Dailies." *Montana Journalism Review* 19 (1976): 20–22.

——. "A Lee Executive's Response: The Economics of Success." *Montana Journalism Review* 11 (1968): 21–25.

Billings, Gretchen. "The *People's Voice*: Comforting the Afflicted." *Montana Journalism Review* 20 (1977): 5–6.

Billings, Harry. "The *People's Voice*: The Dream and the Reality." *Montana Journalism Review* 20 (1977): 2–3.

Blumberg, Nathaniel. "The Media and Montana." *Montana Journalism Review* 21 (1978–79): 2–9.

Breitenstein, William G. "A Champion for 'Sons of Toil': The Rocky Mountain Husbandman." *Montana Journalism Review* 10 (1967): 28–29.

Brier, Warren J. "'Quartz Upon the Brain': A Newspaper for Montana Miners." *Montana Journalism Review* 13 (1970): 44–50.

"Chain of Copper." *Time Magazine,* June 1, 1959, 68.

Davison, Stanley R., and Dale Tash. "Confederate Backwash in Montana Territory." *Montana The Magazine of Western History* 17 (October 1967): 50–58.

Emmons, David M. "The Orange and the Green in Montana: A Reconsideration of the Clark-Daly Feud." *Arizona and the West* 28 (Autumn 1986): 225–45.

Fought, John P. "John Hurst Durston: Editor in the Montana Capital Fight." *Montana Journalism Review* 3 (1960): 20–26.

Goligoski, Robert J. "Thomas J. Dimsdale: Montana's Pioneer Editor." *Montana Journalism Review* 10 (1967): 7–9.

Halverson, Guy, and William E. Ames. "The Butte Bulletin: Beginnings of a Labor Daily." *Journalism Quarterly* 46 (1969): 260–66.

Hood, Charles E., Jr. "Time of Change: Lee's Decade in Montana." *Montana Journalism Review* 13 (1970): 25–28.

Housman, Robert L. "The Frontier Journalist in Montana." *Montana Journalism Review* 16 (1973): 56.

Howard, Joseph Kinsey. "The Montana Twins in Trouble." *Harper's,* September 1944, 334–42.

Irwin, Will. "The American Newspaper." 15 parts, *Collier's,* January 11–July 29, 1911.

Johnson, Charles S. "The Montana Council of Defense." *Montana Journalism Review* 16 (1973): 2–16.

Johnson, Dorothy M. "Montana's First Newspaper." *Montana Journalism Review* 1 (1958): 9–12.

———. "Three Hundred Grand!" *Montana The Magazine of Western History* 10 (January 1960): 40–50.

MacDonald, Suzanne Lagoni. "The People's Voice: The War with the Legion." *Montana Journalism Review* 20 (1977): 7–15.

Malone, Michael P. "Montana Politics and the New Deal." *Montana The Magazine of Western History* 21 (January 1971): 2–11.

Martin, Fred. "A Publisher's Statement: Anatomy of a Failing Newspaper." *Montana Journalism Review* 11 (1968): 16.

McDonald, Verlaine Stoner. "'A Paper of, by, and for the People': The *Producers News* and the Farmers' Movement in Northwestern Montana, 1918–1937." *Montana The Magazine of Western History* 48 (Winter 1998): 18–33.

"Monopoly vs. Public Power." *New Republic,* December 3, 1951.

Montana Fourth Estate, Montana State Press Association newsletter. Vol. 20 (December 1959).

"Montana Newspaper Hall of Fame: Capt. James Hamilton Mills," *Montana Journalism Review* 4 (1961): 34.

"Montana Newspaper Hall of Fame: W. K. Harber," *Montana Journalism Review* 14 (1971): 1.

"Montana's Free Press." *Editor & Publisher,* June 13, 1959, 6.

MSU Journalism Seniors. "Montana's Daily Press in the 1960 Campaign." *Montana Journalism Review* 4 (1961): 7–12.

Myers, Rex C. "Montana's Negro Newspapers, 1894–1911." *Montana Journalism Review* 16 (1973): 17–18.

"One Man's Opinion," *Montana Opinion* 1 (October 1956): 29.

Pratt, William C. "Rural Radicalism on the Northern Plains, 1912–1950." *Montana The Magazine of Western History* 42 (Winter 1992): 42–54.

Reinemer, Vic. "A Hard Look at Montana Journalism." *Montana Journalism Review* 4 (1961): 13–16.

Richards, Ronald P. "Montana's Pioneer Radio Stations: A Hobby Becomes an Industry." *Montana Journalism Review* 6 (1963): 26–28.

Robertson, Lori "Lee Who?" *American Journalism Review* 27 (June–July 2005): 42–46, 48–53.

Roeder, Richard B. "Montana Progressivism: Sound and Fury—and One Small Tax Reform." *Montana The Magazine of Western History* 20 (Autumn 1970): 18–26.

Ruetten, Richard T. "Anaconda Journalism: The End of an Era." *Journalism Quarterly* 37 (Winter 1960): 3–9, 10.

———. "Togetherness: A Look into Montana Journalism." *Call Number* 21 (Fall 1959): 4–12.

Schiltz, Joseph M. "Montana's Captive Press." *Montana Opinion* 1 (June 1956): 1–11.

Shepard, Alicia C. "Big Sky's Big Player." *American Journalism Review* 21 (October 1999): 30–36.

Smith, Steve L. "Ray Rocene: Profile of a Sportswriter." *Montana Journalism Review* 14 (1971): 40–44.

Swibold, Dennis L. "So Bad for So Long." *Montana Journalism Review* 29 (2000): 46–50.

———. "The Education of a Muckraker: The Journalism of Christopher Powell Connolly," *Montana The Magazine of Western History* 53 (Summer 2003): 2–19.

Tidball, Eugene C. "What Ever Happened to the Anaconda Company?" *Montana The Magazine of Western History* 47 (Summer 1997): 60–68.

Twain, Mark. "Banquet for a Senator." *Montana Journalism Review* 20 (1977): 35.

Villard, Oswald Garrison. "Montana and the Company." *Nation* (July 1930): 39–41.

Vindex, Charles. "Radical Rule in Montana: The Amazing Years." *Montana The Magazine of Western History* 18 (Winter 1968): 3–16.

Walter, Dave. "Weaving the Current: Montana's Watershed Events of Two Centuries, Part V: 1947–1972." *Montana Magazine*, September–October 2000, 37–39.

Wanamaker, Ralph. "When Bryan Came to Butte." *Montana Journalism Review* 16 (1973): 39–46.

"What Other Editors Say," *Montana Opinion* 1 (February 1957): 12.

NEWSPAPERS
Montana Newspapers
Anaconda Standard
Anaconda Weekly Review
Billings Evening Journal

Billings Gazette
Bozeman Chronicle
Bozeman Daily Chronicle
Butte Bulletin
Butte Daily Bulletin
Butte Daily Post
Butte Evening News
Butte Miner
Butte Socialist
Butte Times
Chinook Opinion
Colored Citizen (Helena)
Cut Bank Pioneer Press
Daily Inter Lake (Kalispell)
Daily Inter Mountain (Butte)
Daily Northwest (Missoula)
Daniels County Leader (Scobey)
Democrat-News (Lewistown)
Fergus County Argus (Lewistown)
Great Falls News
Great Falls Tribune
Harlowton News
Harlowton Times
Havre Promoter
Helena Herald
Helena Independent
Helena Independent Record
Helena Journal
Hill County Democrat (Havre)
Hungry Horse News (Columbia Falls)
Inter Mountain (Butte)
Lewistown Daily News
Lewistown Democrat
Libby News
Livingston Enterprise
Madisonian (Virginia City)
Meagher County Republican (White Sulphur Springs)
Medicine Lake Wave
Miles City Star
Missoula County Times (Missoula)
Missoula Democrat
Missoula Herald
Missoula Sentinel
Missoulian
Montana Daily Record (Helena)

Montana Free Press (Butte)
Montana Kaimin (Missoula)
Montana News (Helena)
Montana Post (Virginia City)
Montana Record-Herald (Helena)
Montana Socialist (Butte)
Montana Staats-Zeitung (Helena)
Montana Standard (Butte)
Mountaineer (Marysville)
New North-West (Deer Lodge)
New Northwest (Missoula)
Park County News (Livingston)
People's Voice (Helena)
Press (Helena)
Producers News (Plentywood)
Reveille (Butte)
River Press (Fort Benton)
Rocky Mountain Gazette (Helena)
Rocky Mountain Husbandman (White Sulphur Springs)
Scobey Sentinel
Townsend Star
Weekly Express (Big Timber)
Western News (Hamilton)
Western News (Libby)
Western Progressive (Helena)
Whitefish News
Yellowstone Journal (Miles City)

Other Newspapers
Denver Post
New Orleans Times-Picayune
New York Times
Oregon Statesman (Salem)
Spokesman-Review (Spokane)
Wisconsin State Journal (Madison)

UNPUBLISHED WORKS

Astle, Catharine Louise. "Opinions of Newsmen about their Employment by Anaconda Company Newspapers." Senior thesis, University of Montana School of Journalism, 1972.
Breitenstein, William G. "A History of Early Journalism in Montana, 1863–1890." Master's thesis, Montana State University, 1915.
Brod, Marian Holter. "The *Montana Staats-Zeitung* 1914–1917: A German Newspaper in America during World War I." Master's thesis, University of Montana, 1979.

Cates, David Allen. "The Senate Campaign and Affairs of W. A. Clark as Reported by the *Anaconda Standard* and the *Butte Miner*, Oct. 25, 1898 through Nov. 8, 1898." Senior thesis, University of Montana School of Journalism, 1979.

Cogswell, Andrew C. "History of the *Montana Standard*." Unpublished manuscript in the author's possession.

———. "The Sources, Transmission and Handling of World War News in Representative Montana Newspapers from 1914–1917." Master's thesis, University of Minnesota, 1943.

De Forth, Shirley Jean. "The Montana Press and Governor Joseph M. Dixon, 1920–1922." Master's thesis, Montana State University, 1959.

Foor, Forrest L. "The Senatorial Aspirations of William A. Clark, 1898–1901: A Study in Montana Politics." PhD diss., University of California, Berkeley, 1941.

Fought, John P. "John Hurst Durston, Editor: The *Anaconda Standard* in the Clark-Daly Feud." Master's thesis, Montana State University, 1959.

Fritz, Nancy Rice. "The Montana Council of Defense." Master's thesis, University of Montana, 1966.

Halverson, Guy Ole. "The *Butte Bulletin*; A Newspaper of Montana Progressivism." Master's thesis, University of Washington, 1966.

Harris, Lyle E. "Dr. E. B. Craighead's *New Northwest*: 1915–1920." Master's thesis, University of Montana, 1967.

Housman, Robert L. "Early Montana Journalism as a Reflection of the American Frontier in the New Northwest." PhD diss., University of Missouri, 1934.

Hoyt, Jyl. "Montana Writer Joseph Kinsey Howard: Crusader for the Worker, Land, Indian and Community." Master's thesis, University of Montana, 1988.

Johnson, Charles S. "An Editor and a War: Will A. Campbell and the *Helena Independent*, 1914–1921." Master's thesis, University of Montana, 1977.

Koessler, Mary Lou. "The 1920 Gubernatorial Election in Montana." Master's thesis, University of Montana, 1971.

LaGrande, Daniel J. "Voice of a Copper King: A Study of the (Butte) *Reveille*, 1903–1906. Master's thesis, University of Montana, 1971.

Larson, William E. "News Management in the Company Press: The Anaconda Copper Mining Company's *Missoulian*, *Billings Gazette* and *Helena Independent*, *Independent Record*, 1938–1944." Master's thesis, University of Montana, 1971.

"Lee Enterprises Purchase of the Anaconda Company's Montana Newspapers: An Explanation." 1974. MS. Montana Historical Society Research Center, Helena, and Donald W. Anderson Papers, K. Ross Toole Archives, University of Montana, Missoula.

McNay, John Thomas. "Breaking the Copper Collar: The Sale of the Anaconda Newspapers and the Professionalization of Journalism in Montana." Master's thesis, University of Montana, 1991.

Mittal, Barbara Jane. "The Montana Free Press Newspaper Chain, 1928–1929." Master's thesis, University of Montana, 1971.

"Montana Historical Newspaper Project: A Union List of Montana Newspapers in Montana Repositories." 1968. MS. Montana Historical Society Research Center, Helena.

Newhouse, John. Manuscript history of Lee's Montana experience. Copy in possession of author.

Paxson, John Mills. "The Candidate and the Company: The 1920 Gubernatorial Campaign of Burton K. Wheeler and its Treatment by the Montana Press." Senior thesis, University of Montana School of Journalism, 1972.

Roeder, Richard B. "Montana in the Early Years of the Progressive Period." PhD diss., University of Pennsylvania, 1971.

Sanden, Florence H. "Consolidation of Montana's Newspapers; Their Tendency toward Standardization and Present Ownership." Master's thesis, Columbia University, 1930.

Stearns, Sheila MacDonald. "The Arthur Fisher Affair." Master's thesis, University of Montana, 1969.

Thomson, Janet C. "The Role of Lee Mantle in Montana Politics, 1889–1900, An Interpretation." Master's thesis, Montana State University, 1956.

Toole, K. Ross. "Marcus Daly: A Study of Business in Politics." Master's thesis, Montana State University, 1948.

Towe, Ruth James. "The Lee Newspapers of Montana; The First Three Years, 1959– 1962." Master's thesis, University of Montana, 1969.

Wanamaker, Ralph H. "Eggleston of the *Anaconda Standard*." Master's thesis, University of Montana, 1978.

Wetzel, Kurt. "The Making of an American Radical: Bill Dunne in Butte." Master's thesis, University of Montana, 1970.

INDEX

All newspapers are listed under the name of their city.

ACLU. *See* American Civil Liberties Union
Adler, Philip, 320, 331, 336, 337, 343; Anderson and, 315, 316; Lee and, 317; photo of, 315; Renouard and, 335; strike coverage and, 334
advertising, 90, 98, 113, 138, 249, 250, 251, 254, 315, 333; Amalgamated, 87; Anaconda, 214; in *Anaconda Standard*, 33, 34, 50, 59–60; growth in, 329; Montana Power, 318 (illus.); political, 214, 223, 268, 270, 283; revenues from, 247
AFL-CIO, 267, 275
Aitken, Walter, 72, 320
Alderson, William W., 24
Allende, Salvador, 342
Alley, Roy S., 141, 156, 157
Amalgamated Copper Company: cartoon about, 97 (illus.), 108, 130 (illus.), 312 (illus.); consolidation by, 85, 95; criticism of, 111, 117, 120, 122–23; formation of, 75, 89; growth of, 134; money from, 79; Montana Power and, 141; political/journalistic influence of, 141; Progressive reforms and, 91; shutdown of, 93–96, 101, 103–4, 105; support of, 101–2, 122–23. *See*

also Anaconda Company/Anaconda Copper Mining Company
American Brass Company, 295
American Civil Liberties Union (ACLU), 295
American Federation of Labor, 274
American Newspaper Guild, 288
American Protective Association, 61
American Railway Union, 51
Anaconda (Marcosson), 301
Anaconda, Mont., 2; capital fight and, 38, 39, 48, 53, 54, 56–59
Anaconda Company/Anaconda Copper Mining Company: accountability for, 253; cartoon about, 205 (illus.), 312 (illus.); character/reputation of, 213, 290, 295; corporate culture of, 125, 302; coverage of, 263, 297, 334; criticism of, 56, 117, 126, 205, 236–37, 244, 246–47, 260, 287–88, 303, 323, 324, 325; global operations of, 280, 287, 342; influence of, 277, 302; legal record of, 281–82, 294; Montana Power and, 265–66; newspapers and, 126, 135–36, 180, 183–84, 192, 213–14, 291, 309; ownership issue and, 257, 259, 276, 282–83, 284, 286, 302, 309; press policy of, 261, 294; sale by, 250, 322–24, 325; secretiveness of, 135, 293; smelter of, 124 (photo); strike against, 170–73; support for, 153,

Anaconda Company/Anaconda Copper Mining Company *(cont.)* 158, 201; union negotiations and, 329; water system and, 234. *See also* Amalgamated Copper Company; "Montana Twins"

Anaconda *Evening Recorder*, 172

"Anaconda for Capital" clubs, 47, 56

Anaconda journalism, 329, 344, 345; criticism of, 301–2, 325; impact of, 341–42

Anaconda Mine, 2, 7, 8

Anaconda Sales Company, 295

Anaconda Standard: Amalgamated and, 76, 79, 84, 130, 131, 287; Anaconda Company and, 153, 181; anniversary of, 6, 8, 11, 14, 72–73; artists of, 73, 73 (photo), 83; Bisbee strike and, 169; Butte *Inter Mountain* and, 6–7, 35, 42; Butte *Miner* and, 66, 240–41; Butte *Reveille* and, 102; capital fight and, 40, 47, 48, 51–52, 55, 56, 57, 58, 59; cartoon from, 62 (illus.), 70 (illus.), 71 (illus.), 80–83, 81 (illus.), 82 (illus.), 130 (illus.), 135 (illus.); circulation of, 9, 37, 43, 50, 127; Clark and, 49, 80; competition from, 115; Copenharve and, 161; corporate power and, 112, 129; criticism of, 66; Daly and, 2, 4–5, 7, 27, 31, 37, 70, 301; Daly death and, 85, 86 (illus.); described, 4–5, 6–7; Dobell and, 172; Durston and, 29, 31, 35, 41, 128, 144, 224, 226, 254; editorials in, 129; Eggleston and, 144–45, 254; growth of, 49, 50; Heinze and, 106; illustrations from, 5, 6, 7, 52, 62, 108; inaugural issue of, 33–34; Kiley death and, 262; Kilroy and, 205; Little murder and, 174, 175; Neill and, 114; office of, 33, 36 (photo); pollution and, 43–44, 131, 133, 134; public-relations function of, 130–31; Rankin speech and, 177; Ryan and, 130; staff of, 42 (photo); Stone and, 180; success for, 8–9, 37; Walsh and, 138; Wheeler and, 201, 202, 203

Anaconda Typographical Union, 3

Anaconda Weekly Review, 28, 33, 34

Anderson, Don, 323, 336, 342; Adler and, 315, 316; encouragement from, 331, 334; Lee and, 317–18, 337; local coverage and, 332; Martin and, 327; McVey and, 328–29; newspaper business and, 319; on open debate, 333; ownership and, 328; Parkinson and, 316; photo of, 331; retirement of, 343; sale and, 320–21, 326, 329; strike coverage and, 334

Anderson, Forest, 306

antitrust issues, 100, 119, 294, 295, 296

Anti-Trust Party, 139

Aronson, J. Hugo, 327

Ashland Citizen (Ashland, N.C.), 78

Associated Press, 101, 141, 148, 154, 212, 213, 217, 238; *Anaconda Standard* and, 79; Bonner and, 289; bureau, 67, 364n36; copper press and, 298, 332; Dixon and, 219; Gazette Printing Company and, 249; Murray and, 279, 288; stories by, 269, 293, 306, 322, 326

Astle, Tom, 308

Ayers, Roy, 241

Bair, Charles M., 150, 151

Ball, J. P., Jr., 54

Barbour, Chauncey, 25

Bigelow, Albert S., 53

Big Timber *Pioneer*, 188, 202, 216

Big Timber *Weekly Express*, 72, 320

Billings, Gretchen, 322

Billings, Harry, 275; FCC application and, 292, 293; photo of, 275

Billings Evening Journal, 150, 153, 213

Billings Free Press, 249

Billings Gazette, 151, 169, 188, 213, 249, 253; Anaconda and, 149, 153, 209, 290; Anderson and, 334; capital fight and, 54; Carter and, 150; cartoon from, 222 (illus.); censorship and, 187; Clark and, 74, 79; Daly and, 79; Dixon and, 201, 203, 209, 210, 215,

Billings Gazette (cont.)
217, 219, 220, 223; editorials in, 308; Edwards and, 150, 153; end of, 330; Lee and, 316; Little murder and, 174, 175; local coverage by, 332; Marcosson book and, 301; metal mines tax and, 223; Murray and, 281; ownership of, 258; pollution and, 335; property tax reform and, 121; Rankin and, 178, 182, 281; Shaw and, 151, 152, 153; Stout and, 307, 319; Wheeler and, 203

Billings Herald, 149

Billings *Montana Nonpartisan,* 273

Billings Post, 149

Billings *Vociferator,* 149

Birch, Fred, 286

Bird, Frank, 248

Bisbee *Arizona Daily Star,* 259

Bisbee *Daily Review* (Bisbee, Ariz.), 169, 259

Bisbee strike, 169, 173

Blake, Henry N., 20

Blue Bird Mine, 33

Bole, William, 10, 63, 64, 65, 114; photo of, 64

Bonfils, Fred, 142

Bonner, John, 289

Boorstin, Daniel, 21

Boos, George, 54

boosterism, 17, 21, 88, 133

Boston and Montana Band, 2, 11, 14

Boston and Montana Company, 53; smelter, 93, 94 (photo), 95 (photo)

Boulder Age, 118

Bourquin, George M., 186–87

Bowler, Burley, 197, 274

Bowler, Duane "Doc," 304–5, 307

Bozeman *Avant Courier,* 24

Bozeman Chronicle, 17, 64; capital fight and, 53; Daly and, 71; Dobell letters to, 171–72

Bozeman Courier, 21

Bozeman Daily Chronicle, 324; Anderson and, 315; Lee and, 326; licensing law and, 190

Bradley, Omar, 192

Braley, Berton, 110, 139

Brantly, Theodore, 15, 16, 72

Brass Check, The (Sinclair), 259–60

Brooks, Harry, 117, 246, 261

Browne, C. H., 214

Bruce, H. S. "Cap," 271, 275; Anaconda and, 276, 277; resignation of, 272

Bryan, William Jennings, 10, 61

Buffalo *Courier Express* (Buffalo, N.Y.), 258

Burke, Emmett: photo of, 278

Burlingame, Merrill G., 326

Butte, Anaconda and Pacific Railway, 2–3, 296

Butte, Mont.: capital fight and, 53, 56, 57, 58; celebration in, 94; photo of, xx, 44; pollution in, 43–46

Butte Bulletin, 186, 190; Anaconda and, 214; Campbell and, 189; cartoon from, ii (illus.); Dunne and, 216, 273; end of, 271; organization of, 184; publication of, 191–92; Rankin and, 243

Butte Daily Bulletin: Anaconda Standard and, 205; cartoon from, 205 (illus.), 228 (illus.); copper press and, 192; defiance by, 191; Dobell and, 231; "Red scare" and, 204–5; Sinclair and, 260; Taylor and, 197; Wheeler and, 201, 203

Butte Daily Post, 187, 209, 230, 276, 310; Anaconda and, 181, 290; censorship and, 148; Clark, Jr., and, 239; Dickey and, 226, 276; Durston and, 143–44, 224, 225, 226, 227, 253; end of, 330; Little murder and, 173–74; Martin and, 227, 327; McDougal and, 262; *Montana Standard* and, 330; "newsboys club" of, 256 (photo); ownership of, 285; Rankin speech and, 177; Severson and, 298–99; Speculator Fire and, 262; strike and, 264; Wheeler and, 203; Woolston and, 250

Butte Daily Post Building, 253

Butte Evening News, 111, 241; Braley and, 110; end of, 115; Heinze and, 97, 109, 115; Kilroy and, 109, 115, 138, 139; reputation of, 110

Butte Hill, 44; photo from, 287

Butte *Inter Mountain,* 1, 7–8, 15, 24, 109, 153, 330; Amalgamated and, 79, 98, 101–2, 105, 138; *Anaconda Standard* and, 6–7, 35, 42; Braley and, 110; Butte *Reveille* and, 102; capital fight and, 55; cartoon from, 77 (illus.); Clark, Jr., and, 239; Clark and, 28, 49; competition with, 11, 28, 115; criticism of, 43; Daly and, 16, 37, 72; on Durston, 10, 35, 37, 225; independence of, 98; Mantle and, 26, 42–43; Mills and, 10; office of, 31 (photo); ownership of, 285; pollution and, 46, 131, 134; "progress" edition of, 41–42; reincarnation of, 144, 225; Ryan and, 130; struggle for, 17

Butte *Labor World,* 103

Butte Miner, 24, 72, 87, 109, 113, 114, 139; Amalgamated and, 100; Anaconda and, 152, 214, 236–37, 242; *Anaconda Standard* and, 66, 240–41; Butte *Reveille* and, 102; Campbell and, 143; capital fight and, 47, 53, 55, 56, 58, 59; cartoon about, 228 (illus.); cartoon from, 83, 83 (illus.), 92 (illus.); censorship and, 148; Clark, Jr., and, 238, 239, 240; Clark and, 11, 25, 26, 34, 35, 49, 78–79, 99, 108, 145, 181, 231; competition from, 28, 115; Conley and, 211; Daly and, 27, 28; Dixon and, 202, 211, 215; Dobell and, 171, 228, 230, 231, 232, 247; Durston and, 35; elections and, 61; Erickson and, 216; Heinze and, 77, 106; Hutchens and, 247; Keith and, 98; Little murder and, 173–74, 175; Marcosson and, 301; office of, 31 (photo); pollution and, 45; Rankin speech and, 177–78; strike coverage by, 172;

Walsh and, 138; Wheeler and, 202, 203; Whiteside and, 67, 68–69

Butte Miners Union, 168

Butte Miners Union Hall: bombing of, 146, 147 (photo)

Butte *Montana Bulletin,* 68

Butte *Montana Free Press:* Anaconda and, 246–47; cartoon from, 240 (illus.); Clark, Jr., and, 240, 241, 251; copper press and, 248–49; Dixon and, 242; Erickson and, 244–45; Hutchens and, 233, 247; Rankin and, 242–43, 244; Woolston and, 250

Butte *Montana Socialist,* 145, 146, 148

Butte *Montana Standard,* 244, 264, 268, 321; Anaconda and, 265, 290, 334; Anderson and, 329; *Butte Daily Post* and, 330; changes for, 328–29, 333–35; and *Courier Express* compared, 258; Dickey and, 276; first issue of, 240–41; Gaskill and, 308–9; Lee and, 329; mining accidents and, 263; ownership of, 285; pollution and, 336, 350n11; sale and, 329; scandal and, 305; strike coverage by, 263–64, 334, 335; subscriptions to, 241, 329

Butte Post Publishing Company, 268

Butte Reduction Works, 66

Butte *Reveille,* 99, 184; Amalgamated and, 100, 101, 106, 108, 111; *Anaconda Standard* and, 102; cartoon from, 83, 97 (illus.), 107 (illus.), 108–109, 109 (illus.), 312 (illus.); Clark and, 102; criticism of, 105, 109; decline of, 110, 111, 115; extra by, 105 (illus.); "Fusion" campaign and, 100; Heinze and, 77, 97, 101, 102, 104, 106, 107, 273; Keith and, 101; Kilroy and, 139; O'Farrell and, 100; Socialist reforms and, 103

Butte *Socialist,* 145, 148

Butte *Sun,* 98

Butte *Times,* 66

Butte Typographical Union, 184, 189

Buttrey, F. A., 286

Campbell, A. J., 72
Campbell, William A., 192, 210, 231, 234, 244, 267, 269, 285; Anaconda and, 252–53; anti-German paranoia and, 165–66; career of, 142–43; cartoon about, 198 (illus.); Clark, Jr., and, 238; Conley and, 211, 212; copper dailies and, 271; criticism of, 197, 272; Democratic conservatives and, 143; Dickey and, 268; Dixon and, 208–9, 220; German-American press and, 166, 167; Harlowton incident and, 170; IWW and, 146; Lanstrum and, 213; Little murder and, 175; Montana Loyalty League and, 188; Nelson and, 273; patron for, 209; photo of, 185; Progressive Democrats and, 271; Rankin charges and, 181, 182; "Red scare" and, 189; Stewart and, 185; Wheeler and, 202; Wobblies/Socialists and, 148
Canadian Pacific Railroad, 99, 100
capital fight, 39, 40, 47–48, 51–59, 63, 114; Anaconda Company and, 58
Carnegie, Andrew, 56
Carter, Thomas, 27, 28, 83, 115; Amalgamated smelter and, 132; cartoon about, 312 (illus.); corporate merger bill and, 89; Daly and, 79; Dixon and, 137; Shaw and, 152
cartoons, 70, 73, 80–83, 83, 108–9; examples of, ii, 62, 70, 71, 77, 81, 82, 83, 92, 97, 107, 109, 135, 194, 196, 198, 205, 218, 221, 222, 228, 240, 312
Cascade County Trades and Labor Assembly, 291
censorship, 164, 187, 189, 190, 279, 289; *Anaconda Standard* and, 148; selective, 252; self-, 306, 331
Chicago, Milwaukee, St. Paul and Pacific Railroad (Milwaukee Road), 156, 157
Chicago Chronicle, 142
Chicago *Inter Ocean,* 271
Chicago Journal, 156
Childs, Marquis, 330

Chinook Opinion, 117, 246, 261; Dixon and, 204, 216
Clancy, William, 103
Clark, Archie, 239
Clark, Charles, 231, 232
Clark, Walter Van Tilburg, 301
Clark, William A., 10, 27, 31, 34, 145, 148, 149; Amalgamated and, 97, 98, 99, 114; Anaconda and, 172, 234; banquet and, 15; capital fight and, 39, 40, 47, 53, 54, 56, 59; cartoon about, 62 (illus.), 70 (illus.), 71 (illus.), 77 (illus.), 81, 81 (illus.), 82 (illus.), 83; corruption of, 74, 112, 118, 229; criticism of, 28, 65, 66, 67, 80, 102, 111, 112, 234; Daly and, 17, 28, 42, 48–49, 61, 65, 72, 74, 108, 302; death of, 229, 231; decorated carriage of, 41 (photo); election of, 16, 90, 92, 96; "Fusion" campaign of, 76–77, 80, 98, 100; Heinze and, 75–76, 77, 108; Kearns and, 13, 366n3; newspaper business and, 25, 26, 34, 230; ownership issue and, 259; photo of, 63, 126; political ambitions of, 49, 52, 65–66, 85, 229–30; railroad of, 17; Romney and, 119; support for, 85, 106; youth of, 11
Clark, William A., Jr., 172–73; Anaconda and, 239, 240, 260; assault by, 236–37; career of, 231–32; newspaper business and, 231, 250–51, 260
Clark Fork River, 333; pollution in, 335, 336
Clemens, Samuel Langhorne, 27, 229
Cleveland, Grover, 48
Cogswell, Andrew, 262, 263
Cohen, Charles, 148
Cold War, 304, 317, 330
Collier's, 110
Collingswood, Charles, 286
Collins, Jerre, 24
Columbia and Western Railway, 100
Columbia Gardens (Butte, Mont.), 161, 177, 290

Columbia Falls *Hungry Horse News,* 310,
325–26
Columbus News: newsmen from, 116
(photo)
Comical History of Montana, The
(Murphy), 259
Communications Act of 1934, 289
Communist Party, 273, 274
Comstock Lode, 2, 27
Conley, Frank, 211–13, 232, 243
Connolly, Christopher Powell, 15, 72
Conrad, William G., 69, 114
Cooney, Edward H., 69, 128, 188,
352n7
Copenharve, Charles, 143, 148, 161,
162
Copper Commando, 281
copper editors, 261; limits on, 263, 265,
302–3, 306, 307, 308
copper kings, 17, 49, 63, 64, 183; capital fight and, 57; "free silver" and,
61; Lee newspapers and, 343; war of
the, xx, 17, 37
copper press: Anaconda and, 299,
341; Associated Press and, 298, 332;
cartoon about, ii (illus.), 107 (illus.), 312 (illus.); criticism of, 120,
248–49, 273, 279–80, 301–4, 320,
322, 325; defensiveness of, 265, 267;
Dixon and, 203, 207, 215, 219, 220,
222; editorial targets of, 308; elections and, 259, 281; end of, 297, 321,
324; legacy of, 344–45; limits on,
299, 304, 306, 309; negligence by,
297–98; ownership issue and, 248,
258, 259–60, 282–83; problems for,
280, 310, 327; selling, 313–14; staffing of, 310; transformation of, 227,
252
"Copper Target" (advertisement), 218
Copper Target (pamphlet), 217
Copper Trust Gang: cartoon about, 97
(illus.)
copper wars, 14, 59, 99, 149, 180, 208,
252, 253, 285, 309; Clark and, 230;

corruption of, 259; Durston and,
225; end of, 109, 115–16, 127; news-
papers and, 65
Corette, John E., 337
corporate merger bill, 89–90
corruption, 74, 112, 118, 229, 259; political, 52–53, 55, 56, 59, 61, 59, 74, 113,
115; press, 59, 61, 62
Corrupt Practices Act, 120, 268, 270
Coughlin, Father Charles, 272
Cowan, Lyle, 189
Cowles, John, 318, 326–27, 373n12
Cowles Media, 326, 345
Craighead, Barclay, 155, 156, 203, 237
Craighead, Edwin B., 155, 203; death
of, 237; NPL and, 199
Craney, Edmund, 278, 279; photo of,
278
criminal syndicalism law, 185–86
Cummins, James, 226
Cut Bank Pioneer Press, 245, 246, 261,
303; criticism of, 195; Dixon and,
204, 216; Little murder and, 176

Daily Worker (Communist Party newspaper), 273
Daly, Marcus, 14, 114, 125, 143, 149;
Amalgamated and, 16; banquet
and, 16; Bryan and, 10; capital fight
and, 40, 41, 47, 48, 53, 54, 56, 57, 59,
63; Clark and, 17, 28, 42, 48–49, 61,
65, 72, 74, 108, 302; corruption of,
74; criticism of, 11, 83; death of, 85,
86, 90, 92, 128; Durston and, 8–9,
10, 28–31, 34, 36, 37, 85, 223, 254;
economic empire of, 75; editorial
policy and, 71–72; election and, 84;
Heinze and, 76; influence of, 59,
119; journalism and, 26–27, 350n5;
Kelley and, 300; newspaper business and, 25–26, 70–71; ownership
question and, 283; patronage of, 37;
photo of, 2, 9; Romney and, 119;
unions and, 50, 56; vote spending
by, 52; youth of, 2

Daly, Margaret, 11, 144
Daly Bank and Trust Company, 98
Dana, Charles, 178, 232
Davis, Warren B., 234, 244
Davitt, Michael, 99
Debs, Eugene, 51, 108
Deer Lodge *Independent,* 21
Deer Lodge *New North-West,* 10, 21, 25; Durston and, 19; Mills and, 23, 24; offices of, 20 (photo)
Deer Lodge *Powell County Call,* 133
Democratic Party: Anaconda and, 216; Clark and, 11; Daly and, 9, 84; Dobell and, 231, 247; financial panic/depression and, 60; "free silver" and, 61; "Fusion" campaign and, 84; NPL and, 203
Dempsey, Tom, 309
Denton Recorder, 246, 261
Denver Post, 300; Anaconda journalism and, 301; reputation of, 142; Severson and, 297, 307
Denver *Rocky Mountain News,* 11
"de. Q." (artist), 108
Des Moines Register, 318
Dickey, James H., Jr., 226, 253, 269–70, 290, 307, 314, 315; annual reports and, 285; investments by, 268; oversight by, 276
Dimsdale, Thomas J., 20
direct primary law, 118, 121
Dixon, Joseph M., 122, 150, 151, 152, 158; Amalgamated and, 132, 137, 141, 357n19, 24; Anaconda and, 133, 157, 207, 215, 217, 219, 227, 260; career of, 136; cartoon about, 218 (illus.), 221 (illus.), 222 (illus.); Clark, Jr., and, 232; Clark and, 243, 245; Conley and, 212; criticism of, 155, 201, 202, 207, 210, 213–14, 215, 216–17, 220; defeat of, 222–23; Erickson and, 219; Heinze/shutdown and, 96; Hutchens and, 236; independence of, 136–37; Kelley and, 141; Kilroy and, 140; legislative agenda of, 206–7, 208, 209,

211, 213, 215; Murphy and, 157; photo of, 136; politics and, 137–38, 216; publishing and, 154; radio and, 278; Rankin and, 178, 243; Stone and, 140; support for, 201, 203, 204, 209, 212, 215–16, 241, 242; Townley and, 202; Walsh and, 138; Wheeler and, 202, 203, 206
Dobell, J. Larry, 210, 235, 252, 253, 271, 272; career of, 171–72; cartoon about, 228 (illus.); censorship and, 148; Clark, Jr., and, 228, 247; Clark and, 99, 181, 209, 230, 231; criticism of, 172, 231; Erickson and, 216, 248; Hutchens and, 209, 247; IWW and, 148, 173; licensing law and, 190; lobbyists and, 248; politics of, 172; Rankin and, 244; resignation of, 228, 232; retirement of, 236; Socialists and, 145–46, 148
Doherty, Charles, 303
drought, 206, 207; photo of, 207
Duncan, Lewis, 145, 148
Dunne, Finley Peter, 127
Dunne, William F., 184, 189, 191, 192, 199; Farmer-Labor Party and, 216; on Kilroy, 205; Montana Council of Defense and, 190; photo of, 190; "Red scare" and, 204–5; Taylor and, 197
Durston, John (father), 30
Durston, John Hurst, 79, 107, 209, 252; Anaconda and, 133, 225; capital fight and, 40, 47, 48, 55–59; career of, 8–9, 19, 42, 223–25; censorship and, 148; Clark and, 67, 80, 84–85; convention and, 10; Daly and, 8–9, 10, 28–31, 34, 36, 37, 85, 223, 254; death of, 253–54; Democratic Party and, 34; Dickey and, 226; editorials by, 37, 43, 47, 70, 128, 144; Eggleston and, 29; Heinze and, 76, 84–85; legacy of, 254; Mantle and, 43; Mills and, 19, 26; national issues and, 127; newspaper business and, 49, 50; photo of, 9, 225; pollution and, 43–44, 46, 131; Rankin and, 244; Republican politics and, 30–31;

Durston, John Hurst *(cont.)*
resignation of, 143; respect for, 225–26;
Ryan and, 130; Senate hearings and,
74; Socialist Party and, 106; toasts by,
16; Walsh and, 144, 224; youth of, 30
Durston, Mary Harwood, 30
Durston, Sarah Hurst, 30
Dutton, Alfred M., 108
Dwyer, Terry, 288–89
Dye, E. A. "Shorty," 306, 307

East Helena Record, 18 (photo)
economic issues, 51, 53, 116, 209, 215
Economist, 304
Editor & Publisher, 323
Edwards, Frank J., 356n45
Edwards, Jonathan E., 150, 151–52, 222;
Anaconda and, 153; death of, 253,
367n51; Dixon and, 137, 138, 201,
209, 210, 215; investment by, 359n51;
Shaw and, 152
Eggleston, Charles H., 31, 60, 128, 188,
254, 309; Anaconda and, 56, 225; capital fight and, 47, 48; censorship and,
164; Clark and, 49, 80; Copenharve/
Stevens firing and, 162; Daly and, 37;
Durston and, 29; editorial page and,
35, 37; Election Day and, 85; Helena
and, 55–56; poetic parody by, 134;
Senate hearings and, 74; Wheeler
and, 200; writing of, 144–45
Eggleston, William Greene, 78, 91, 112,
117; capital fight and, 59; Clark and,
111; direct primary law and, 118;
Gordon and, 113; Heinze and, 113;
political reforms and, 111
Elm Orlu Mine, 145, 217, 237; Clarks
and, 172–73, 230; photo of, 172
environmental issues, 131, 335–37, 342,
343, 375n56
Erickson, John E., 241, 243; cartoon
about, 240 (illus.); criticism of, 242,
244–45, 248; Dixon and, 219; Dobell
and, 247; election of, 222, 245–46; radio and, 278; support for, 216

Erickson, Leif, 281, 298
Erlandson, Edwin, 264, 265
Espionage Act, 169–70
Evanko, John, Jr., 291
Evans, L. O., 134, 188
"Everett Massacre," 168

Fairmont Investment Corporation,
253, 276; Anaconda and, 286, 292,
303; daily newspapers of, 261; FCC
and, 290–91, 293, 295, 296; KFBB
and, 286, 290, 294; newspaper stock
and, 285–86; press policy of, 330;
sale and, 313, 314, 315
Farmer-Labor Party, 216
farmers: cartoon about, 194 (illus.);
homesteading by, 125; political re-
form and, 117
Farmers Union, 267, 272, 274, 275, 332
Federal Communications Commission
(FCC): Anaconda and, 292, 293,
296; Fairmont and, 290–91, 293,
295, 296; ownership question and,
284; public interest and, 289
Federal Power Commission, 263
Federated Newspapers, 319
Ferguson, French, 154
Fiedler, Leslie, 301
First National Bank of New York: cor-
porate merger bill and, 89
First Trust and Savings Bank (Billings,
Mont.), 150
Fisher, Arthur, 210
Fisk, Robert E., 22, 24, 30
Fisk brothers, 78, 114, 158
Flathead River, 296; dam on, 263
Flynn, Elizabeth Gurley, 168
Foor, Forrest L., 69
Ford, Sam C., 197, 201, 281
Forsyth Times, 87
Fort Benton *River Press,* 17, 24, 102, 104
121–22; advertising in, 138; Dixon
and, 138, 216; property tax reform
and, 121
Fort Peck Dam, 266

Fought, John, 144
Fowler, C. W., 270–71
"free silver," 60–61, 65, 66
free speech, 170, 187, 303
Frenzied Finance (Lawson), 113
"Fusion" campaign, 76–77, 80, 84, 98, 100, 139; cartoon about, 77 (illus.)

Gannett, 345
Garnet Mining News, 87
Gaskill, Bert, 308–9
Gazette Printing Company, 150, 153; Associated Press and, 249; Edwards and, 151, 253
German-language press: end of, 165–68
Gibbons, Tommy, 309
Gilluly, J. A., 176, 188, 190
Glasgow Courier, 157, 204
Glasgow *Valley County News,* 121, 273
Glendive *Dawson County Review,* 121, 204
Glover, Roy H., 290, 294, 300; copper press and, 291; editorials by, 308; Fairmont and, 291; KFBB and, 286
Gold Flint Mine, 31
Goodwin, C. C., 11, 13, 15, 58
Gordon, Sam, 112–13, 183; photo of, 24
Gould, Jay, 25, 257
Graybill, Leo, 298
Great Depression: Anaconda and, 262, 265, 280, 300; newspaper business and, 252, 262
Great Falls, Mont.: capital fight and, 58; celebration in, 93
Great Falls Leader, 114, 188, 288; Amalgamated and, 79; Butte *Reveille* and, 102; capital fight and, 53; Cooney and, 128; Howard and, 282
Great Falls Mill and Smeltermen's Union No. 16: FCC and, 292
Great Falls *Montana Nonpartisan,* 273; cartoon from, 198 (illus.)
Great Falls Tribune, 10, 153, 156, 246, 289, 345; Bole and, 64; Butte *Reveille* and, 102; capital fight and, 53, 58,

63; celebration and, 93; censorship and, 187; Clark, Jr., and, 231, 251; Clark and, 17, 63, 64, 78, 90, 98, 114; competition for, 343; Conrad and, 114; copper wars and, 65; Daly and, 63; Diamond Jubilee of, 65; FCC and, 293; Harber and, 123; Immel and, 270; Little murder and, 176; Martin and, 327; Murray and, 288; ownership of, 258; purchase of, 63, 64; Rankin and, 243; sale and, 324, 325; Severson and, 298; shutdown and, 96; Warden and, 64, 244, 313, 314; Wheeler and, 202; Whiteside and, 67
Great Northern Railway, 33, 60, 142
Greeley, Horace, 24
Greene Cananea Copper Company, 295
Greenfield, Charles D., 67, 188
Grubisch, Henry, 167
Gunther, John, 282–83

Hamilton *Ravalli County Democrat,* 71, 85
Hamilton *Western News,* 11, 17, 165, 199, 290, 337; Anaconda and, 202; Clark and, 85; Dixon and, 206, 209; Little murder and, 176; Romney and, 87, 117, 118–19; shutdown and, 104
Hammaker, Kenneth, 248
Hammond, Andrew B., 54
Hamner, Ed, 224
"Handcar Limited," 51; illustration of, 52
Harber, William K., 17, 113, 117; Amalgamated and, 122–23; career of, 121–22; on newspapers, 102; photo of, 122; Progressive reforms and, 122; on shutdown, 104
Harlowton, Mont.: incident at, 170
Harlowton Times, 216, 324–25
Harper's, 282
Harrison, Benjamin, 33, 48
Hauser, Samuel T., 25, 65
Havre Daily News-Promoter, 243

Havre *Herald,* 121
Havre *Hill County Democrat,* 202
Havre *Plaindealer,* 121
Havre Promoter, 169–70, 203
Haywood, William "Big Bill," 110, 146, 168, 169
Hearst, George, 7, 26
Hearst, Phoebe, 8
Hearst, William Randolph, 7, 164, 178, 232, 247, 274; on *Anaconda Standard,* 8; illustration of, 8
Heinze, F. Augustus, 90, 97, 101, 104, 150, 182, 184; Amalgamated and, 95, 96, 103, 105, 106, 109, 115; Anti-Trust Party of, 139; cartoon about, 77 (illus.), 92 (illus.), 107 (illus.); Clancy and, 103; Clark and, 75–76, 77, 96, 98, 108; copper wars and, 99; corruption of, 118; Daly and, 76; Eggleston and, 113; "Fusion" campaign of, 76–77, 80, 84, 98, 100, 139; influence of, 110, 131; Kilroy and, 138; lawsuits by, 75–76, 100; O'Farrell and, 99, 100; patronage of, 78; photo of, 76; political demise of, 125, 127, 141; shutdown and, 96; Socialists and, 103; Standard Oil and, 106; working-class support for, 106
Helena, Mont.: capital fight and, 1, 38, 39, 41, 48, 53–59; celebration in, 39–41
Helena Capital Committee, 41
Helena *Colored Citizen,* 54
Helena Herald: Anaconda and, 158; capital fight and, 57; Clark and, 63, 78, 79; Fisk brothers and, 22, 114; independence of, 158; *Montana Daily Record* and, 114; office of, 22 (photo); printing contracts and, 24; Whiteside and, 67
Helena Independent, 72, 156, 198, 202, 267, 282; Amalgamated and, 84, 143; Anaconda and, 214, 252–53; *Anaconda Standard* and, 66; anti-German paranoia of, 165; Butte *Reveille* and, 102;

Campbell and, 142–43, 185, 234, 268; capital fight and, 54, 57, 58, 59; Clark, Jr., and, 238; Clark and, 65, 66, 68, 78, 114; Conley and, 211, 212; criticism of, 272; Daly and, 88; debt listing by, 271; Dickey and, 269–70, 276; directors/stockholders of, 142; Dixon and, 215, 217; Dunne/Smith and, 191; Eggleston and, 78, 91; Harlowton incident and, 170; Hutchens and, 178; independence of, 88; Little murder and, 175; *Montana Record-Herald* and, 213, 235, 304–5; Murray and, 281; Neill and, 66, 78, 79, 88, 90, 98; offices of, 340 (photo); printing contracts and, 90; Progressive Democrats and, 271; railroad regulation and, 120; Rankin and, 181, 281; sale of, 142; sedition and, 188; success for, 23; suits against, 89; war volunteers from, 164; Weiss and, 166; Whiteside and, 67
Helena Independent Record, 282, 307, 328; Anaconda and, 290; Dwyer and, 288; influence of, 305; sale and, 322; Severson and, 298; Sorenson and, 306; struggles of, 316; workplace diseases and, 297
Helena Journal: capital fight and, 48; improvements for, 50; makeup/presswork of, 33
Helena *Montana Daily Record,* 115, 137, 138, 142, 150, 152, 188; Associated Press and, 79; direct primary law and, 118; *Helena Herald* and, 114; Neill and, 90, 114
Helena *Montana News,* 107–8
Helena *Montana Record-Herald,* 152, 158; Anaconda and, 213, 252; Bisbee strike and, 169; Bourquin and, 186–87; Bowler and, 304–5, 306; Campbell and, 235; Conley and, 211, 212; coverage by, 266; Dickey and, 276; Dixon and, 203, 212, 216, 220, 221–22; *Helena Independent* and, 213, 235, 304–5; independence of, 153; Rankin

Helena *Montana Record-Herald (cont.)*
speech and, 178; sale of, 234; sedition
law and, 190
Helena *Montana Staats-Zeitung*, 164;
Campbell and, 166, 167; end of,
165–66, 167
Helena *Montana Stockman and Farmer*,
67, 71
Helena *Northwestern Stockman and
Farmer*, 121
Helena *People's Voice*, 282, 286, 297,
300, 337, 341; Anderson and, 322;
Bruce and, 275, 277; defective com-
munications wire and, 281; Dickey
and, 276; FCC application and, 292;
Lee and, 322; Murray and, 267
Helena *Press*, 91, 111, 112; end of, 117;
independence of, 113
Helena *Rocky Mountain Gazette*, 21,
22, 23
Helena's Social Supremacy (Eggleston),
55–56
Helena *Western Progressive*, 269, 286;
Bruce and, 271; copper press and,
276; Dobell and, 272; end of, 274, 275;
Fowler and, 270; Pearson and, 272
Hennessy, Dan, 103
Hennessy Building (Butte, Mont.), 226,
244, 253, 276
Hill, James J., 33, 257
Hill, Joe, 168
Hilleboe, Strand, 332, 343
Hobbins, Jim, 317
Hocking, T. J., 157, 204
Holmes, W. W., 183
homestead boom, 116, 125, 207
Hoover, William, 286
Housman, Robert L., 243
Howard, Joseph Kinsey, 282, 288
Hungry Horse Dam, 296
Hutchens, Martin J., 156, 157, 158, 231,
243, 250, 252, 253; Anaconda and,
233, 234; Bourquin and, 186; career
of, 178–79; Clark, Jr., and, 233, 237;
community controversies and, 234;

death of, 247; dismissal of, 232, 234;
Dixon and, 210, 236; Dobell and,
209, 232; Erickson and, 242, 244–
45; Little speech and, 174; metal
mines tax and, 223; photo of, 233;
Rankin and, 178, 179–80, 184, 244;
Wheeler and, 245

Immel, Ernest J., 238, 270
Industrial Workers of the World (IWW),
108, 110, 136, 162, 189, 191, 197, 232;
Anaconda Standard and, 170–71,
173; attack on, 149, 169, 170–71, 175,
176, 180, 185–86; in Butte, 173, 202;
Campbell and, 143; criticism of, 146,
147, 171, 173; Hutchens and, 233; repu-
tation of, 168, 170; Socialists and, 146;
strike by, 171, 173, 192; vigilantes and,
168; wildfires and, 233
inheritance tax, 207, 211
Inter Mountain Publishing Company,
98
International News Service, 249
Interstate Lumber Company, 290
Inverness *News*, 273
*Irish World and American Industrial
Liberator*, 27
IWW. *See* Industrial Workers of the
World

Jarussi, John, 291
Jerome News (Jerome, Ariz.), 259
Johns, T. J., 78
Jones, Lester J., 156, 157
Joseph (Nez Perce), 24
journalism: consequences of, 341; cor-
ruption in, 59, 61, 62; democracy
and, 341; frontier, 17, 19; new era
of, 337; yellow, 73, 302. *See also*
Anaconda journalism
Journalism Quarterly, 327–28
Judith Basin County Farmers Union,
291
Judith Gap Journal, 190
Junod, O. H., 214

Kalispell *Daily Inter Lake,* 203, 324
Kalispell *Times,* 182
Karlin, Jules, 141
KDYS (Great Falls), 277–78
Kearns, Thomas, 13, 366n3
Keith, Adelphus B., 11, 98, 101, 239
Kelley, Cornelius Frances "Con," 181, 226, 280; Anaconda and, 125; death of, 314; Dixon and, 141; KFBB and, 286; leadership of, 134, 300; photo of, 126
Kelly, Dan M., 217, 218, 248, 268
Kennedy, Will, 118
"Kept Press": cartoon about, 196 (illus.)
Kerosene Gang: attacking, 101
Kerr, Frank, 266
KFBB (Havre), 286, 290, 296, 297; ACLU and, 295; Anaconda and, 284; FCC and, 292, 293–94
KGIR (Butte), 279
Kiley, William, 262
Kilroy, Richard, 109, 110, 115, 209, 231, 252, 253; Anaconda and, 140, 201; career of, 138–39; criticism of, 205; departure of, 141; Dixon and, 140; "Red scare" and, 204; Rogers and, 104; Socialists and, 103; Wheeler and, 200, 202–3
Kipling, Rudyard, 127
Knight, H. L., 182
Knight-Ridder, 318
Kremer, J. Bruce, 188; photo of, 126

Labor Day, 2, 6; illustration of, 5
Labor League, 200
labor reforms, 313
labor unions, 50, 118, 269, 298, 310; capital fight and, 51, 55; copper press and, 163; revival of, 265; Socialist Party and, 129; tolerance for, 56
LaFollete, Robert M., 151
Lambert *Richland County Leader,* 273
Lanstrum, Oscar "Doc," 115, 138, 142, 150, 153, 358n24; Anaconda and, 158;

Campbell and, 209, 213; Dixon and, 137, 203, 212, 216; sale by, 234, 235; sedition law and, 190; Shaw and, 152
Lawson, Thomas, 113
Lee, Alfred W., 317
Lee Enterprises: Anaconda and, 316, 317, 321, 322, 334–35, 336; bid by, 318, 320; changes by, 322–23, 330, 332, 334, 336; copper press and, 322–23, 343; criticism of, 328, 331; Federated Newspapers and, 319; history of, 315, 317; independence and, 334; Montana Power and, 317; *Montana Standard* and, 329; ownership by, 327–28; sale and, 324, 326, 327
Lee newspapers, 342–45; map of, 337 (illus.)
Lee State Bureau, 332, 342
Leipheimer, E. G., 110, 139, 239, 244, 264
Levine, Louis, 210, 233
Lewistown Daily News, 324
Lewistown Democrat, 104
Lewistown *Democrat-News,* 154, 235; Associated Press and, 213; censorship and, 187; Dixon and, 215; office of, 235 (photo); Rankin charges and, 183
Lewistown Eagle, 78
Lewistown *Fergus County Argus,* 176, 187, 188, 190, 202; office of, 187 (photo)
Lewistown *Judith Basin News,* 107–8
Libby News, 69, 78
Libby *Western News,* 290
licensing law, 189–90
Little, Frank, 168; anti-war speeches by, 173–74; murder of, 162, 174–77, 233
Livingston Enterprise, 253, 290, 305, 337, 345; Daly and, 71; Dickey and, 276; Dixon and, 216; Lee and, 317; Martin and, 327
Livingston *Park County News,* 327
Livingston Post, 172

lobbying, 268, 270, 302, 304
Long, Huey, 272
Looking Back in Black and White (Dwyer), 289
Look, 318
Loomis, Lee, 317, 326
Los Angeles Philharmonic Orchestra, 232, 251
Lusitania: sinking of, 164

MacKinnon, Eugene, 269
Madison *Wisconsin State Journal*, 317, 319
Maginnis, Martin, 23
Malin, Patrick Murphy, 295
Malta *Enterprise*, 121
Mammoth Hot Springs: newspapers for, 51
Mansfield, Mike, 277, 292
Mantle, Lee, 24, 26, 79, 98, 144, 350n5; appointment of, 49; attack on, 42–43; banquet and, 15; Daly and, 49, 72; "free silver" and, 61; photo of, 43
Marcosson, Isaac F., 301
Margelin, John C., 212
Markham, Joseph, 268
Marlow, Thomas, 150, 235, 244
Martin, Fred, 226, 288, 327
Marysville *Mountaineer*, 59, 78, 112, 117
McCarthy, Charlie, 286
McClure's, 75, 104
McConnell, Odell W., 150, 151
McDougal, Donald, 262
McGill, T. O., 108
McGlynn, Mickey, 197
McKinley, William, 61
McLeod, Walter H., 326
McQuad, Hugh, 23
McVey, George, 328–29
Meagher, Thomas Francis, 99
metal mines tax, 220, 223; cartoon about, 218 (illus.), 221 (illus.), 222 (illus.)
Metal Mine Workers Union, 171, 173

Metcalf, Lee, 275, 277, 336; copper press and, 299–300; Lee newspapers and, 337
Midland Empire office building (Billings, Mont.), 249
Miles City Star, 150, 188, 235; Associated Press and, 213; Dixon and, 212, 216; independence of, 260; Rankin charges and, 182; sale and, 324
Miles City *Yellowstone Journal*, 24, 112, 150; Rankin charges and, 183
Miller, Robert, 305
Mills, James Hamilton, 25, 30, 31; convention and, 10; Durston and, 19, 26; editorials by, 21; partisanship and, 24; photo of, 20; printing contracts and, 24
Milltown Dam: pollution at, 335
Milwaukee Road. *See* Chicago, Milwaukee, St. Paul and Pacific Railroad
mining accidents: coverage of, 262–63, 288, 289, 334
mining industry: cartoon about, 218 (illus.), 221 (illus.), 222 (illus.)
Minneapolis Star, 318
Minnie Healy Mine, 103
Missoula, Mont.: capital fight and, 54
Missoula *Daily Northwest*, 241, 247, 249; Clark, Jr., and, 239; end of, 251; impact of, 237–38; Rankin and, 244
Missoula Democrat, 357n19
Missoula *Farmer-Labor Advocate*, 216
Missoula *Missoula County Times*, 303
Missoula *Montana Kaimin*, 322
Missoula *New Northwest*, 155, 199, 237, 273; Dixon and, 201; Fisher and, 210; Little murder and, 176; Wheeler and, 203
Missoula Sentinel, 153, 156, 200, 234, 251; Anaconda and, 290; Dixon and, 139, 140, 358n24; end of, 330; Hutchens and, 210; Kilroy and, 141; revival of, 154; Walsh and, 138
Missoula Times, 357n19

Missoulian, 24, 25, 96, 152, 174, 186, 231, 237; Amalgamated and, 79; Anaconda and, 149, 265, 290; Butte *Reveille* and, 102; capital fight and, 54, 59; cartoon from, 221 (illus.); Conley and, 211; Craighead and, 155; Dixon and, 136, 138, 141, 154, 203, 215, 217, 220, 221; Dobell and, 232; earthquake coverage by, 331–32; editorials in, 308, 330–31; environmental issues and, 335–36, 375n56; front page from, 219 (illus.); Hutchens and, 158, 179–80, 209–10, 233, 234, 236; independence of, 153, 158, 209–10; IWW/wildfires and, 233; Kilroy and, 140; Lee and, 316; letters to, 330–31; Levine firing and, 210; Little murder and, 176; metal mines tax and, 223; Mooney and, 308; Murray and, 281; political coverage by, 332; Rankin and, 178, 281; revival of, 154; Rocene and, 309; and *Spokesman-Review* compared, 326; Stone and, 128, 136, 140, 180

Missoulian Publishing Company, 157, 234, 290

Missouri River, 63; hydroelectric dams on, 287–88; Montana Power claims to, 298; public power development on, 266

Montana: High, Wide and Handsome (Howard), 282

Montana Central Railroad, 93

Montana Council for Progressive Action, 267, 275

Montana Council of Defense, 165, 186, 188–89; *Butte Daily Bulletin* and, 191; Campbell and, 188; criticism of, 190; Ford and, 201; licensing law and, 190; photo of, 185; vigilantism by, 197–98

Montana Development Association, 121, 154, 204

Montana Fish and Game: fishery biologists from, 336 (photo)

Montana Hotel (Anaconda, Mont.), 29, 128; banquet at, 14–15; described, 3, 4; photo of, 3, 4

Montana Loyalty League, 188, 197

Montana National Guard: bombing and, 148

Montana Opinion, 301, 303

Montana Power Company, 124, 150, 157, 201, 235, 282, 290, 291, 296; advertisement for, 214, 318 (illus.); Amalgamated and, 141; Anaconda and, 265–66; Clark/water system and, 234; copper press and, 268; coverage of, 263, 297; criticism of, 244, 248; Dixon and, 215; hydroelectric dams and, 287–88; Lee and, 317; Missouri River flows and, 298; O'Connell election and, 267; pollution and, 335, 336, 337; property taxes and, 154; river grab by, 303; Ryan and, 125; workers' compensation and, 216. *See also* "Montana Twins"

"Montana's Captive Press" (Schiltz), 301

Montana State Fair: photo of, 132

Montana State Press Association, xx, 3, 189; convention of, 1, 12, 72; Daly and, 16, 72

"Montana Twins," 265–66, 269, 271, 342; Corrupt Practices Act and, 268; influence of, 270; New Deal and, 266; prosecution of, 270; suits against, 288. *See also* Anaconda Company/Anaconda Copper Mining Company; Montana Power Company

Montana Union Railroad, 51

Mooney, Guy, 308

Mooney, Tom, 335

Morgan, J. P., 257

Morony, John G., 141

Morrison, Richard, 314

Moss, Preston B., 150, 151, 153

"Mr. Dooley" (Dunne), 127

"Mr. Dooley's Bartender" (Eggleston), 128

Murphy, Jerre C., 115, 136, 259, 356n45
Murphy, William L., 157, 290, 359n63
Murray, James A., 184
Murray, James E., 184, 266, 277, 288; Anaconda and, 279; FCC and, 292, 293; Missouri Valley Authority and, 298; photo of, 267; radio and, 279–80; Rankin and, 281; support for, 272
Murrow, Edward R., 286
Musselshell *Advocate,* 183
Myers, Henry L., 122, 176, 204
Myllymaki, Saims, 291

Naegele, Fred, 166–67
Nast, Thomas, 108
Nation, 246, 260, 296
National Bank Building (Helena, Mont.), 276
National Recovery Act, 266
NBC, 279
Neill, John S. M., 65, 111, 114, 117, 181; Amalgamated and, 91; Clark and, 68, 78, 88, 89–90, 91, 98–99; corporate merger bill and, 90; death of, 142; editorial independence and, 88; photo of, 66; on railroad rate regulation, 120
Nelson, John W., 272, 273
New Deal, 265, 271, 279; opposition to, 272; political challenges of, 266
New Orleans Times-Picayune, 289
New Republic, 296
"newsboys club": photo of, 256
newsmen: illustration of, 12–13
newspaper ownership, 248, 256, 302, 309, 327–28; anachronism of, 301; change in, 329–30; corporate, 258, 259–60; group, 328; questions of, 257, 258, 276, 282–83, 284, 285; statements of, 257
News Publishing Company, 276, 286
New York Herald, 5, 22, 67, 73
New York Journal, 7, 178–79, 247
New York *Journal of Commerce,* 318
New York Sun, 178, 247

New York Times, 75, 289
New York Tribune, 24
New York World, 178, 247
"Night Owl, The" program, 278 (photo)
Nolan, C. B., 15, 71–72, 142
Nonpartisan League (NPL), 194, 201, 273; Democratic Party and, 203; Dixon and, 208; office of, 208 (photo); politics and, 198–99, 200, 204; Taylor and, 195; Wheeler and, 199, 202
Northern Montana Roundup Association, 119
Northern Pacific Railroad, 51, 55, 89
NPL. *See* Nonpartisan League

O'Connell, Jerry J., 266, 272, 275, 292; defeat of, 274; election of, 267; KFBB case and, 293
O'Farrell, Patrick A., 77, 104; Amalgamated and, 99, 100, 101; Clark and, 101; departure of, 110; Heinze and, 99; Kilroy and, 139; photo of, 100; Socialists and, 103
Omaha Bee, 142
open-air roasting, 45, 46, 131
open pit mining: photo of, 287

Palmer, A. Mitchell, 204
Parkinson, C. Jay, 314, 315, 318, 320, 321, 337; Anderson and, 316; Martin and, 327
Parnell, Charles, 99
Parrot Smelter, 46
partisanship, 17, 24, 65, 252, 272
"Patriots Chorus": cartoon about, 198 (illus.)
Paul, W. J., 241
Payne, Thomas, 265
Pearson, Drew, 272, 330
Pegler, Westbrook, 330
Penwell, Lewis, 142, 271
People's Power League, 120
Pershing, John "Black Jack," 271
Phelps Dodge Company, 169, 259

Phoenix Gazette, 259
Placer Hotel (Helena, Mont.), 157, 248,
    267, 332, 342; lobbyists at, 268
Plains *Sanders County Signal,* 182
Plentywood Herald, 274
Plentywood *Producers News,* 216, 245,
    246, 261; cartoon from, 194 (illus.),
    196 (illus.); controversy for, 197; end
    of, 274; Taylor and, 195, 200, 274;
    Wheeler and, 203
political reform, 116, 128, 313, 342;
    Anaconda and, 125, 199, 200, 265,
    280; copper press and, 313; corpo-
    rate interference in, 104; corruption
    in, 52–53, 55, 56, 59, 61, 59, 74, 113,
    115; farmers and, 117; politics and,
    21, 49, 116, 252
Polk, Harry, 274
pollution, 336–37, 350n11; air, 44 (pho-
    to), 45, 46, 336; crusade against,
    43–45; smoke, 130–31, 133, 134; wa-
    ter, 45, 335, 336
Poole, Lewis, 305, 333
Poplar *Roosevelt County Independent,*
    273
Populists, 10, 48, 66; election of, 61;
    financial panic/depression and,
    60; "Fusion" campaign and, 84;
    railroads and, 119–20; "Silver
    Republicans" and, 65
Portland *Oregonian,* 49
"Post Office Department": licensing law
    and, 190
Post Publishing Company, 226, 369n27
pressmen's union, 357n5, 358n28
Progressive reforms, 91, 122, 126
Progressives, 115–16, 117–18, 128, 136,
    137, 271, 341; Amalgamated and,
    134; Anaconda and, 192; primary
    system and, 200; railroads and,
    119–20
Public Service Commission, 267
Puck, 110
Pulitzer, Joseph, 178, 232, 247
Pullman, George, 56

Pullman Palace Car Company: strike
    against, 10, 51

Quill magazine, 332
Quinn, John M., 40, 55, 56, 57, 58

radicals, 300; Amalgamated and, 134;
    copper press and, 163, 168
radio, 284, 295; development of, 277–
    80, 286
Rae, Will, 248
Railroad and Public Service Commis-
    sion, 266, 272
railroads: regulation of, 90, 119–20,
    195, 272
Rankin, Jeannette, 233, 243; charges
    by, 180, 181, 183; Copenharve and,
    161; criticism of, 182, 183; Little mur-
    der and, 162, 176, 177; NPL and, 199;
    ownership issue and, 259; speech
    by, 160 (photo), 161–62, 177–80;
    Stevens and, 161; support for, 182
Rankin, Wellington, 212; Clark and,
    243, 244, 245; Dixon and, 243;
    Murray and, 281; photo of, 242; ra-
    dio and, 278; sister's pacifism and,
    245; support for, 242–43
Read, John B., 11, 24
red-baiting, 277, 281, 290
Red Cross, 167, 188
Red Lodge *Carbon County Chronicle,*
    218; cartoon from, 218 (illus.)
Red Lodge *Carbon County Democrat,*
    71
Red Lodge Picket, 121
"Red scare," 189, 204–5, 281
Reed, John, 184
Reifenrath, Charles, 190
Renouard, Ed, 335
Republican Party: Amalgamated and,
    87; financial panic/depression and,
    60; "free silver" and, 61
"Reverend Jerry Rounder" (Walsworth),
    45
Rhone, Alex, 182

Rice, George C., 156, 157
Rickards, John E., 49
Ridder Corporation, 318, 373n12
Risken, Law, 299
Rocene, Ray, 309
Rockefeller, John D., 75, 83, 257; cartoon about, 97 (illus.), 108–9, 109 (illus.); portrayal of, 101
Rogers, Henry H., 75, 105, 229; criticism of, 104; newspaper campaign and, 79
Rogers, J. H., 21
Rome Sentinel (Rome, N.Y.), 178
Romney, Miles, Jr., 266, 325
Romney, Miles, Sr., 17, 113, 117; Amalgamated and, 87, 119, 120; career of, 118–19; Clark and, 85, 87; convention and, 10–11; Daly and, 119; Dixon and, 133, 206, 209; New Deal and, 266; NPL and, 199; photo of, 117, 206; reform measure by, 120–21; shutdown and, 104; "Taxation Talks" and, 214; Western News and, 87; World War I and, 164–65
Roosevelt, Franklin D.: court-packing plan and, 274; National Recovery Act and, 266; New Deal and, 265; radio and, 279
Roosevelt, Theodore, 31, 102, 133, 150; Amalgamated smelter and, 132; Dixon and, 137; trust-busting and, 119
Roote, Jesse B., 148, 231, 358n43
Rossland Miner (Rossland, B.C.), 99, 100
Ruder, Mel, 310, 325–26
Ruetten, Richard, 327–28
Rustler, 149
Ryan, John D., 129–30, 156, 181; Anaconda and, 125; criticism of, 177; death of, 280; Hutchens and, 233; leadership of, 134; name change and, 300; newspaper business and, 313; ownership question and, 283; photo of, 126
Ryegate Reporter, 216

Ryman, J. H. T., 155

Sage, James A., 234, 237
Salem Oregon Statesman, 323–24
Salt Lake Herald, 230
Salt Lake Tribune, 11, 13, 58, 366n3
Sanden, Florence: ownership issue and, 257, 258–59
Sanders, Wilbur Fisk, 14, 15, 16, 72
San Francisco Examiner, 8, 26
San Jose Mercury News (San Jose, Calif.), 318
San Pedro, Los Angeles, and Salt Lake Railroad, 17
Saturday Evening Post, 110
Scallon, William, 76, 103, 105, 109
Scanlan, Joseph D., 188, 260; Dixon and, 212, 219; Montana Record-Herald sale and, 235; Rankin charges and, 182
Schermer, Betty Adler: photo of, 331
Schermer, Lloyd, 343, 368n22; earthquake coverage and, 331–32; environmental issues and, 335–37; photo of, 331
Schiltz, John M., 304; Anaconda journalism and, 301–2; on copper editors, 302–3
Schneider, A. C.: photo of, 20
Scobey Daniels County Leader, 274; arson at, 197
Scobey Sentinel, 203
Scott, George, 248
Scripps-Howard, 318
Scripps League, 318
Scripps News Service, 109
Seaton, Fred, 319
Seattle Post-Intelligencer, 274
Securities and Exchange Commission, 293
sedition, 185, 187, 188, 190, 192
Sevareid, Eric, 286
Severson, Thor, 297, 298–99, 307
Shaw, Leon, 188, 201, 253; Anaconda and, 153, 209; censorship and, 187; Dixon

Shaw, Leon (cont.)
and, 219; Edwards and, 151–52; flight of,
269; metal mines tax and, 223; photo of,
152; Rankin charges and, 182
Shay, Walter, 248
Shearer, Charles, 148
Shearman Newspaper Corporation,
318
Shelby Promoter: hawking, 344 (photo)
silicosis, 208, 297
silver. See "free silver"
Silver Bank (Philipsburg, Mont.), 33
"Silver Republicans," 61, 65, 66
Sinclair, Upton, 205, 259–60, 261
Sioux City Tribune (Sioux City, S. Dak.),
142
Skelton, Red, 286
Smith, Addison, 23
Smith, R. Bruce, 184, 189, 190, 192
Smith, Robert B., 15, 72, 74
"smoke farmers," 300; cartoon about, 135
(illus.); suit by, 130–31, 132, 133–34
Socialist Party, 106, 136, 146; Anaconda
municipal government and, 102–3;
challenge by, 107; treatment of, 129
Socialists, 232, 300; Anaconda Standard
and, 129, 145; Butte government and,
145; campaign by, 146; Campbell
and, 143; copper press and, 163, 168;
criticism of, 145, 149; press, 145–46
Sokolsky, George, 330
Sorenson, Gary, 306
Speculator Mine, 162, 169, 173, 262
Spokane Spokesman-Review, 49, 289;
and Missoulian compared, 326;
shutdown and, 95, 96
Spriggs, A. E., 74
"Standard Oil Bogie," 81; cartoon
about, 82 (illus.)
Standard Oil Company, 75, 103, 112, 229;
Amalgamated and, 82; Clark-Heinze
press and, 83; corporate merger bill
and, 89; criticism of, 101, 104, 106;
Daly and, 16; reputation of, 76
Standard Oil Copper Trust, 102, 105

Standard Publishing Company, 163,
369n27
State Capitol Commission, 88
Stearns, Harold, 324–25
Steffens, Lincoln, 113
Stevens, Charles L., 161, 162
Stewart, Samuel V., 146, 148, 185, 188,
189; Campbell and, 143; tableware
and, 220
Stewart, W. R. C., 142
Stone, Arthur L., 60, 128, 154, 189, 224,
243, 309; career of, 136; Dixon and,
140; editorials by, 140; newswriting
policy and, 180; photo of, 137; toast
by, 16
Stout, Tom, 117, 235, 246, 272, 307, 319;
copper press and, 273; Dixon and,
215; Missoulian and, 154; photo of,
235; Rankin charges and, 183; topical boundaries and, 308
strikes, 10, 50, 51, 169, 170–73, 176, 184,
192, 357n5; coverage of, 172, 263–64,
288, 303, 334, 335
St. Paul Pioneer Press, 318
Sutherlin, Robert, 24
Sutherlin, William, 24
Swindlehurst, T. M., 142
Syracuse Standard (Syracuse, N.Y.), 8,
29, 30, 31, 35, 144

Taft, William Howard, 137, 150
Tammen, Harold, 142
Tarbell, Ida B., 75, 104, 113, 119
"Taxation Talks" (advertisement), 214
Taylor, Charles "Red Flag," 194, 199,
200, 245, 274; Farmer-Labor Party
and, 216; Pioneer Press and, 195; poli-
tics and, 195, 197; Wheeler and, 203
Teagarden, Sam, 246, 261
Teapot Dome Scandal, 246
"Ten Magic Words" (Poole), 333
Terry Tribune, 204
Thayer, Louis M.: photo of, 340
Thorkelson, Jacob, 275
Thurlby, Tom, 108

Tilton, D. W., 19
Time Magazine: copper press and, 296–97; sale and, 322, 323–24
Toole, John R.: cartoon about, 312 (illus.)
Toole, Joseph K., 106, 113, 121
Toole, K. Ross, 265, 301
Toomey, Edmond G., 269
Towe, Ruth, 329, 330, 332
Townley, Arthur C., 198–99, 200, 202
Townsend Star, 74
Trepp, David: photo of, 235
Trowbridge, J. W., 5, 6, 73
Truman, Harry S., 292
Twain, Mark, 27, 229

Union Pacific Railroad, 51
unions. *See* labor unions
United Farmers League, 274
United Press, 238, 241, 249, 251
University of Montana School of Journalism, 237, 304, 306; Stone and, 16, 189
U.S. Forest Service, 169
U.S. Justice Department, 299
U.S. Senate Committee on Privileges and Elections, 73–74
U.S. War Department, 281
Utah and Northern Railway, 25

vigilantes, 20; IWW and, 168; Little murder and, 174, 175; prosecuting, 197–98; Sanders and, 14; strike-breaking by, 169
Villard, Henry, 257
Villard, Oswald Garrison, 246, 260, 261
Virginia City *Madisonian*, 21, 71
Virginia City *Montana Post*, 10, 144; Mills and, 19, 20, 21; Sanders and, 14
Virginia City *Territorial Enterprise*, 27
Virginia City Times, 214

W. A. Clark estate: Clark, Jr., and, 239
Walker, Paul, 291

Walsh, J. H., 107–8
Walsh, Thomas J., 246, 319, 358n24; Bruce and, 271; death of, 272; Dixon and, 137, 138; Dobell and, 236; Durston and, 144, 224; journalism and, 369n37; Little murder and, 176, 177; Penwell and, 142; photo of, 242; Z Bar Network and, 278–79
Walsworth, Warren W. "Wally," 35, 128; censorship and, 148; convention and, 11; Heinze and, 76; pollution and, 45
Warden, Alex, 313, 314, 345; photo of, 314
Warden, Oliver S., 17, 63, 65, 114, 153, 244, 288, 313; Clark and, 78; convention and, 10; photo of, 64
War Industries Board, 191
Washington Times, 180
Washoe works: reopening of, 130, 131
Weed, Clyde E., 300, 314, 315, 321
Weir, T. B., 297
Weiss, Karl, 164, 166
Wellcome, John, 72
Wheeler, Burton K., 142, 161, 184, 199, 244, 272; Anaconda and, 290; court-packing plan and, 274; criticism of, 200, 202, 245; defeat of, 237, 245–46; Dixon and, 202, 203, 206; election of, 215; Kilroy and, 202–3; Little murder and, 174, 175, 176, 177; NPL and, 202; photo of, 199; portrayal of, 245–46; primary campaign of, 201; support for, 203, 204, 241, 272; Z Bar Network and, 278–79
Wheeler-Rayburn Bill, 266
Whetstone, Dan, 261, 304; copper press and, 303; Dixon and, 204; photo of, 246; Wheeler and, 245–46
Whitefish News, 216–17
Whiteside, Fred: photo of, 68; scandal involving, 67, 68–69, 72, 88, 89
White Sulphur Springs *Meagher County Republican*, 118

White Sulphur Springs *Rocky Mountain Husbandman,* 24
Wilkinson, Al, 248, 269
Willard, John, 307
William Andrews Clark Memorial Library (Los Angeles, Calif.), 232
Williams, Jerome, 188
Wilmarth, A. F., 108
Wilson, Harry, 201
Wilson, Woodrow, 143, 155, 163, 164
wire services, 79, 259
Wisconsin Power and Light, 317
Wobblies. *See* Industrial Workers of the World
Woody, Frank, 24
Woolston, Bryan, 250

workers' compensation, 120, 208, 216, 298
workplace diseases, 297, 298
World War I, 149, 319; volunteers for, 164–65

yellow journalism, 73, 302
Yellowstone National Park, 10, 33, 308; earthquake near, 331–32; newspapers for, 51
Yerkes, A. K., 53
Young, Lynn, 305

Zadick, Bill, 289
Z Bar Network, 278–79

Dennis Swibold is a professor at the University of Montana's School of Journalism. A former editor and reporter for newspapers in Montana and Arizona, he lives with his wife, Julie, and son, Colton, in Missoula.